Wonderland

STORY & ART BY
Yugo Ishikawa

4

WHAT THE...? ALICE, CAN YOU REALLY...

Alice and Iosif, a boy and girl who possess unearthly powers. What is the truth behind their existence?

Story

Yukko, along her with now-murdered parents and the rest of her neighborhood, found herself caught in a paranormal phenomenon that caused her to shrink to the size of a doll.

All signs point to one culprit: a strange girl called Alice, who can shrink and unshrink people at will.

The Self-Defense Force, looking to find Alice after she escaped custody, sent another mysterious child to find her: Iosif, a boy who can hop through the minds of small animals and human babies, take control, and use their eyes to find his prey.

With the existence of Alice and Iosif no longer a secret, the deep and complicated truth of what the Self-Defense Force—no, the entire nation of Japan—has been pursuing is now exposed, and it threatens to devour the country whole.

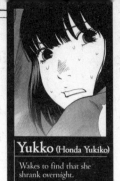

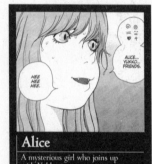

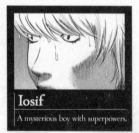

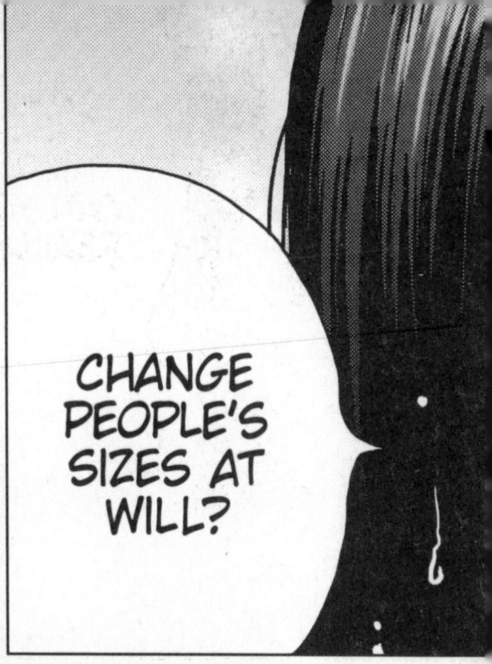
CHANGE PEOPLE'S SIZES AT WILL?

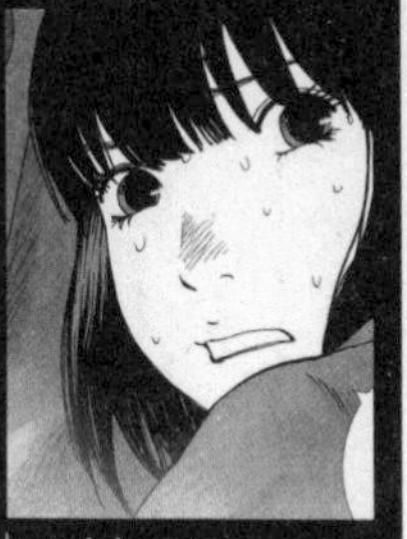

Yukko (Honda Yukiko)

Wakes to find that she shrank overnight.

Characters

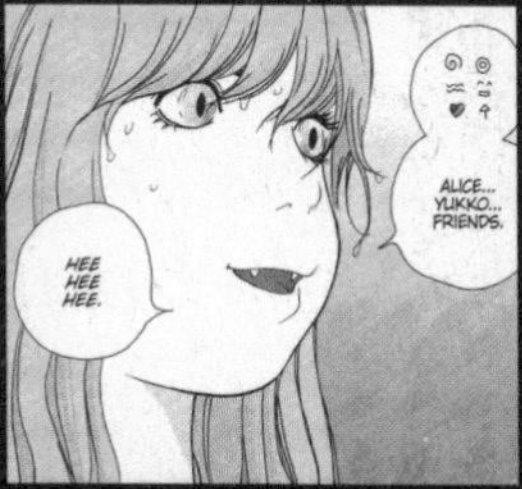
ALICE... YUKKO... FRIENDS.
HEE HEE HEE.

Alice

A mysterious girl who joins up with Yukko.

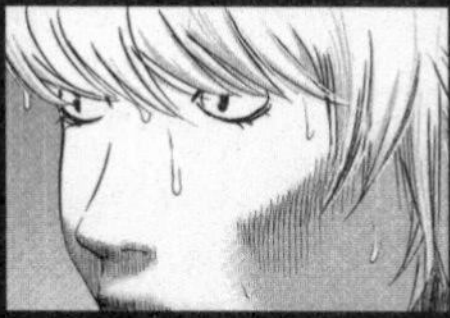

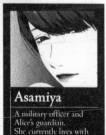

Iosif

A mysterious boy with superpowers.

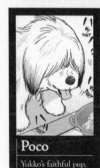

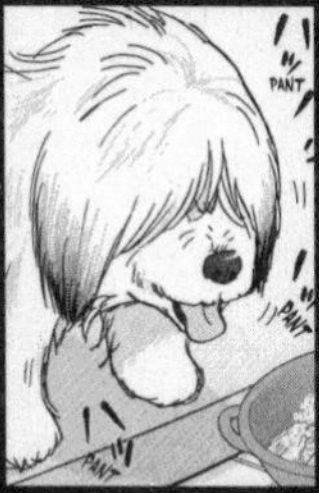
PANT
PANT
PANT

Poco

Yukko's faithful pup.

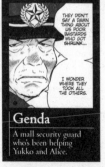

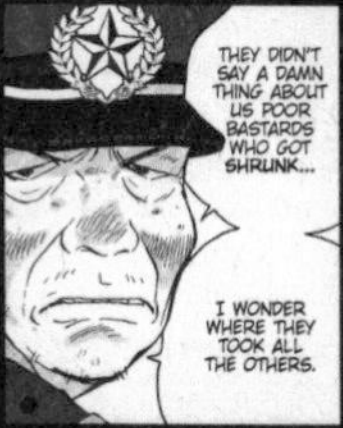
THEY DIDN'T SAY A DAMN THING ABOUT US POOR BASTARDS WHO GOT SHRUNK...
I WONDER WHERE THEY TOOK ALL THE OTHERS.

Genda

A mall security guard who's been helping Yukko and Alice.

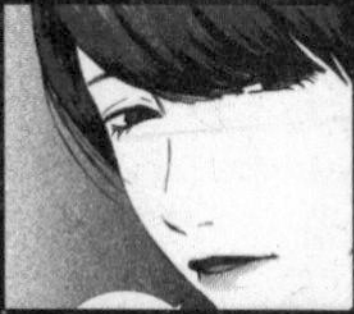

Asamiya

A military officer and Alice's guardian. She currently lives with Yukko.

Contents

Chapter 28: Secret

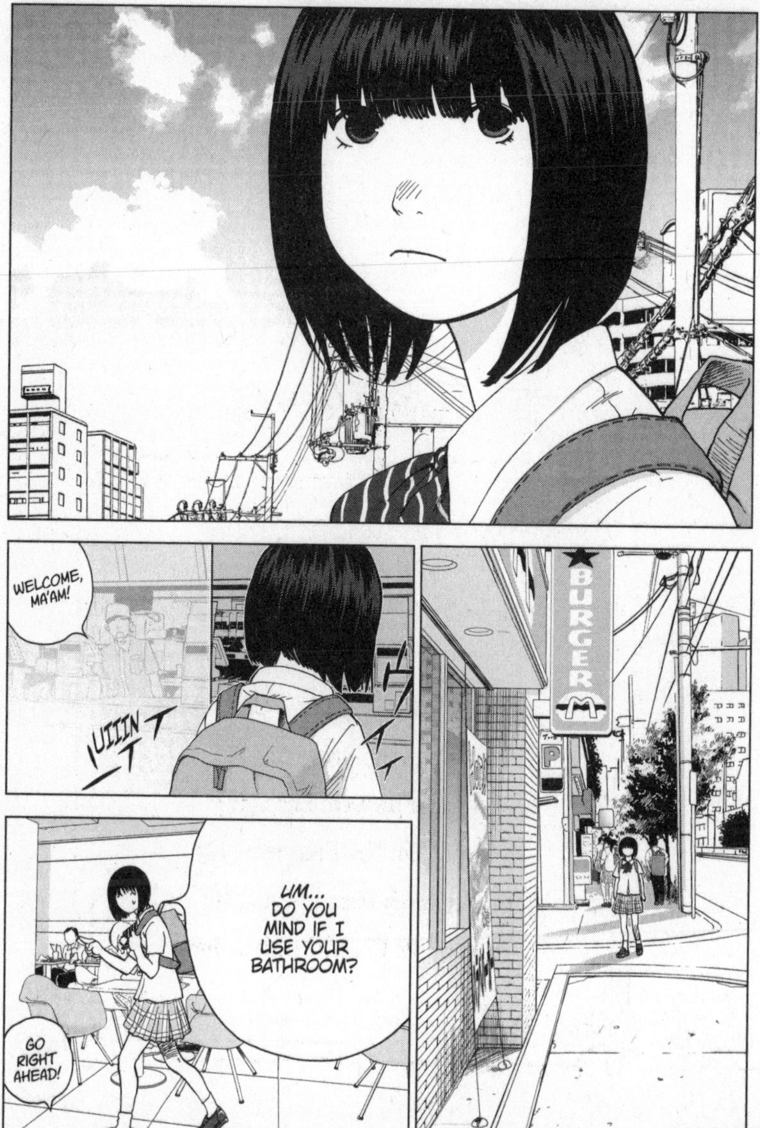
BURGER
WELCOME, MA'AM!
UIIIN
UM... DO YOU MIND IF I USE YOUR BATHROOM?
GO RIGHT AHEAD!

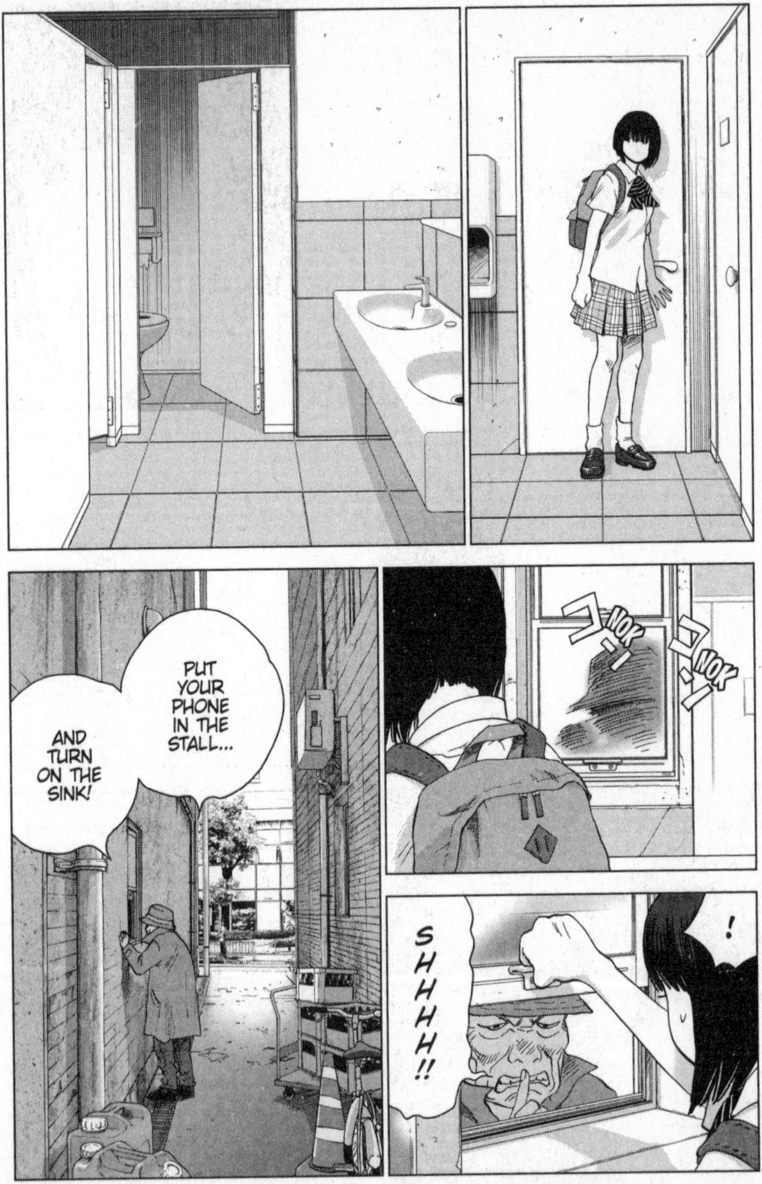
NOK
NOK
!
SHHHH!!
PUT YOUR PHONE IN THE STALL...
AND TURN ON THE SINK!

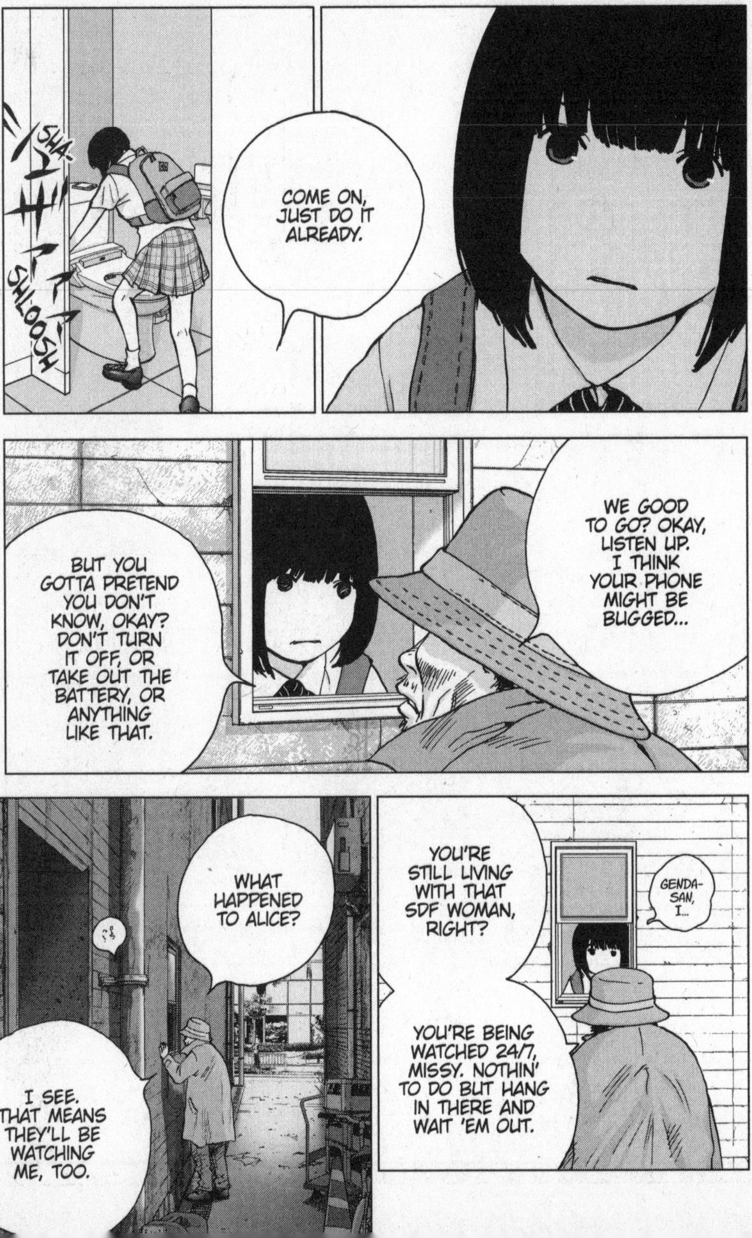
COME ON, JUST DO IT ALREADY.
SHA-
SHLOOSH
WE GOOD TO GO? OKAY, LISTEN UP. I THINK YOUR PHONE MIGHT BE BUGGED...
BUT YOU GOTTA PRETEND YOU DON'T KNOW, OKAY? DON'T TURN IT OFF, OR TAKE OUT THE BATTERY, OR ANYTHING LIKE THAT.
GENDA-SAN, I...
YOU'RE STILL LIVING WITH THAT SDF WOMAN, RIGHT?
YOU'RE BEING WATCHED 24/7, MISSY. NOTHIN' TO DO BUT HANG IN THERE AND WAIT 'EM OUT.
WHAT HAPPENED TO ALICE?
I SEE. THAT MEANS THEY'LL BE WATCHING ME, TOO.

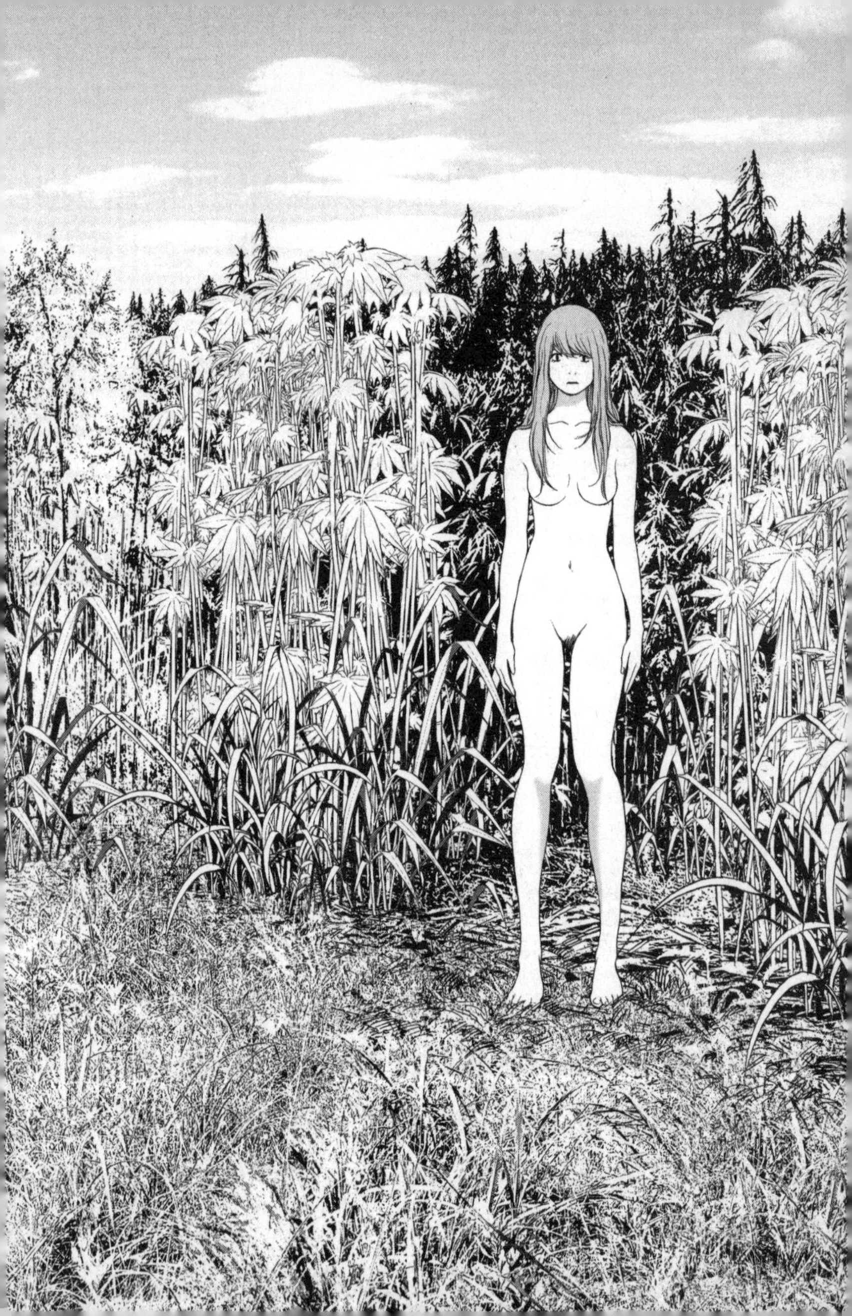

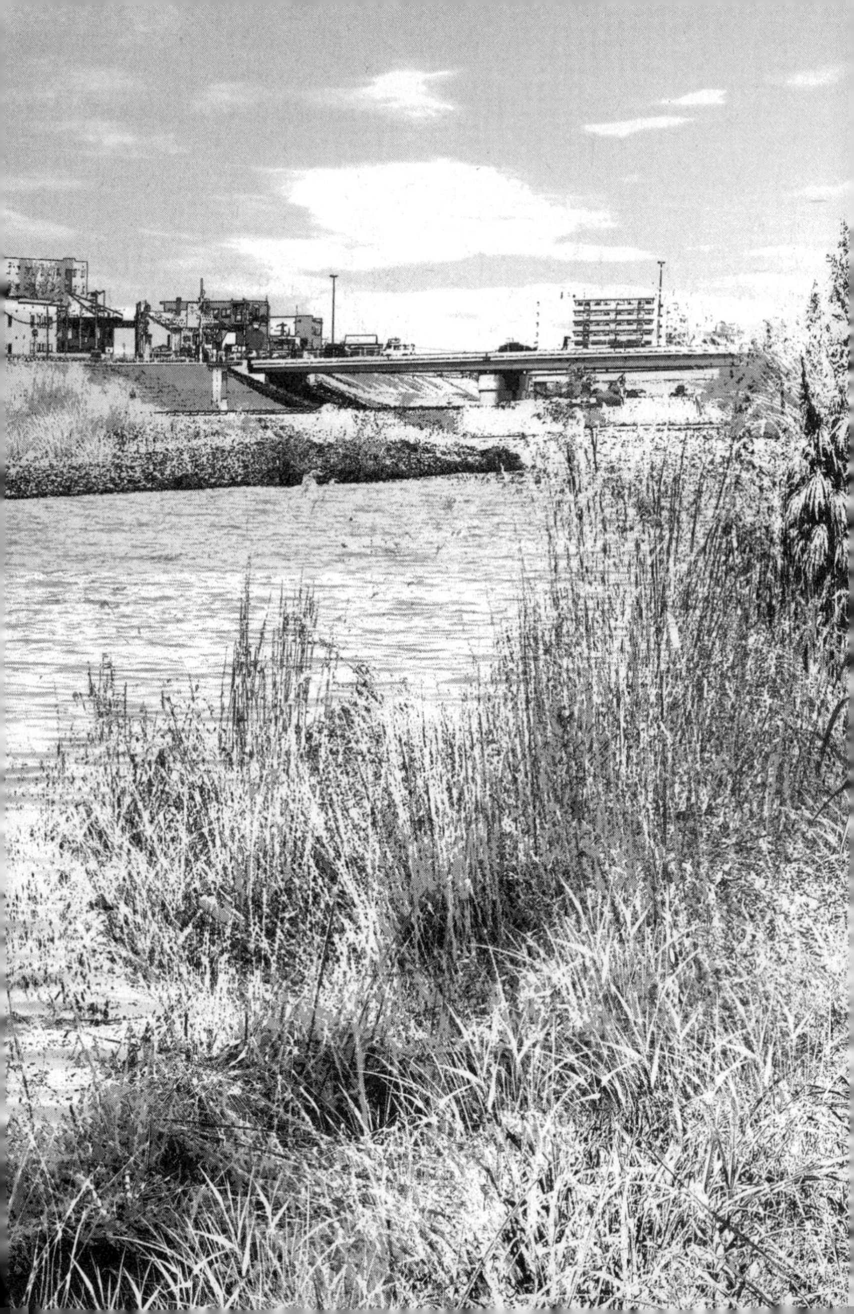

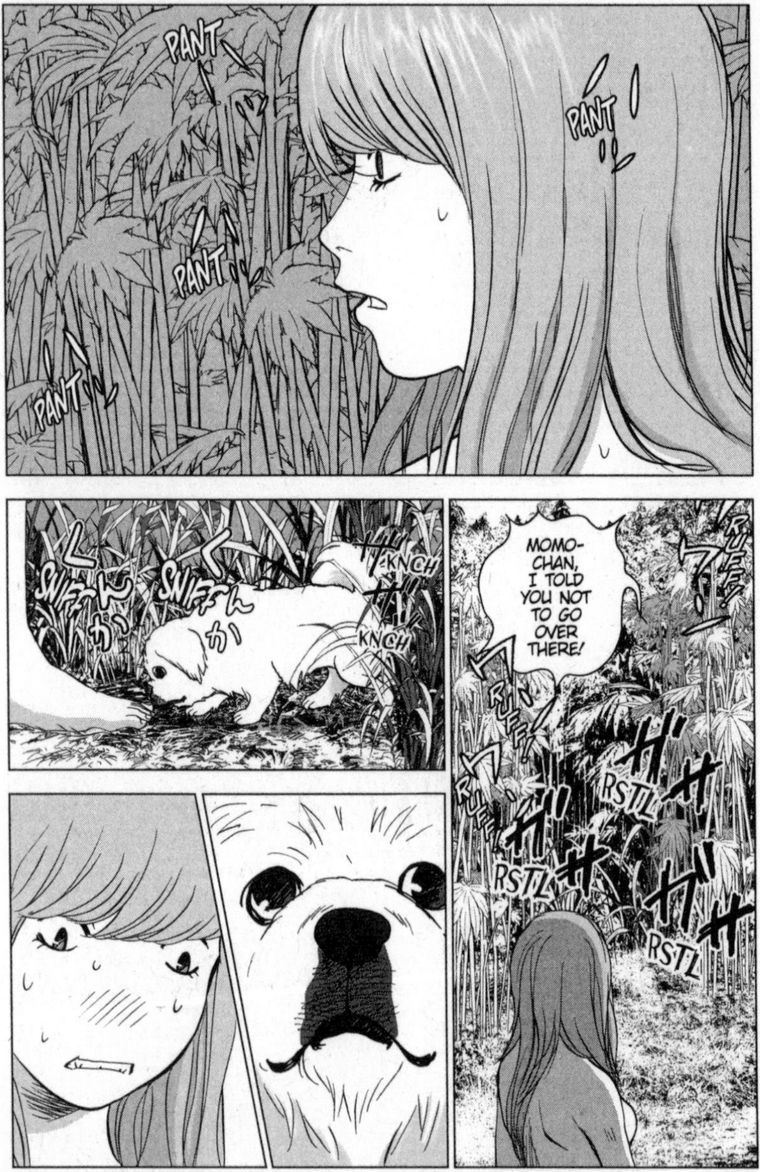
PANT
PANT
PANT
PANT
MOMO-CHAN, I TOLD YOU NOT TO GO OVER THERE!
RUFF!
RUFF!
RUFF!
RSTL
RSTL
RSTL
KNCH
KNCH
SNIFF
SNIFF

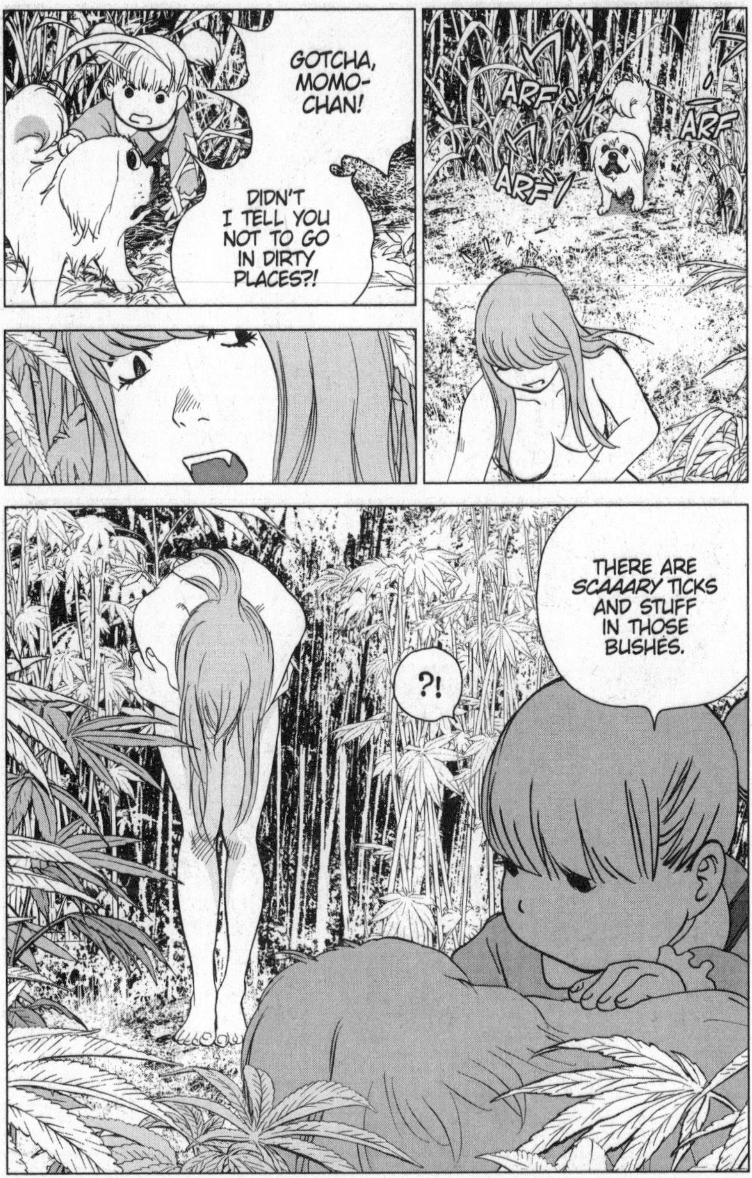
ARF
ARF
ARF
GOTCHA, MOMO-CHAN!
DIDN'T I TELL YOU NOT TO GO IN DIRTY PLACES?!
THERE ARE *SCAAARY* TICKS AND STUFF IN THOSE BUSHES.
?!

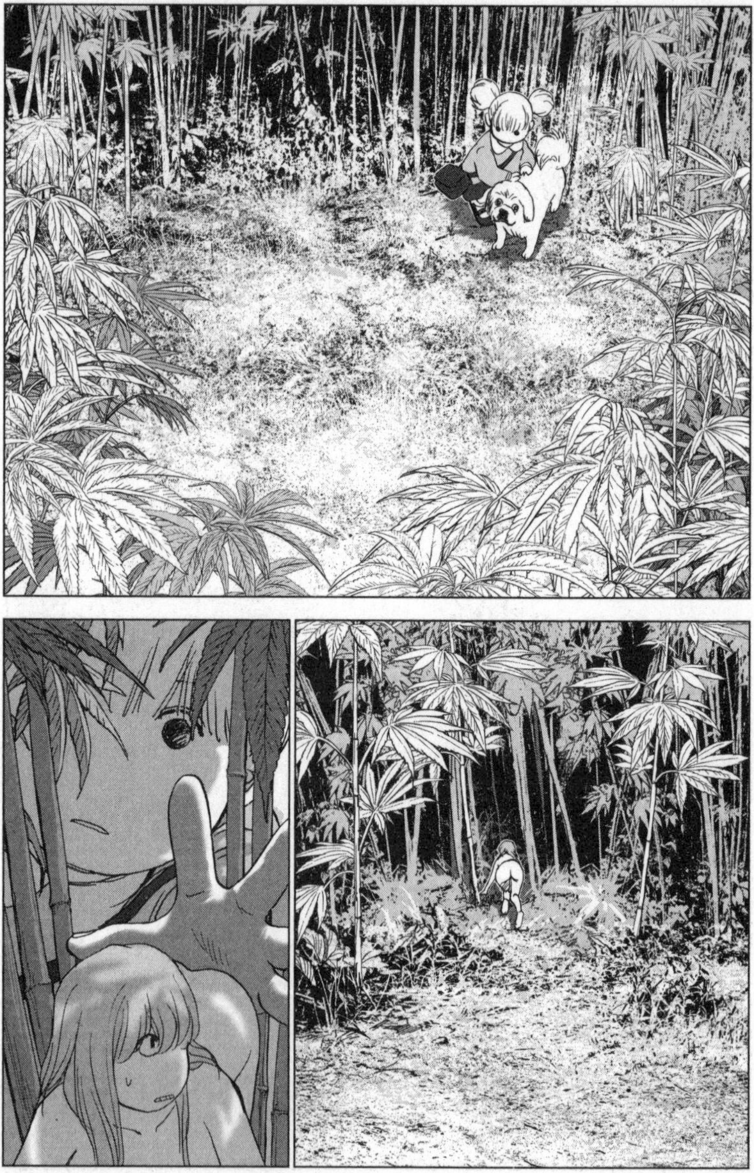

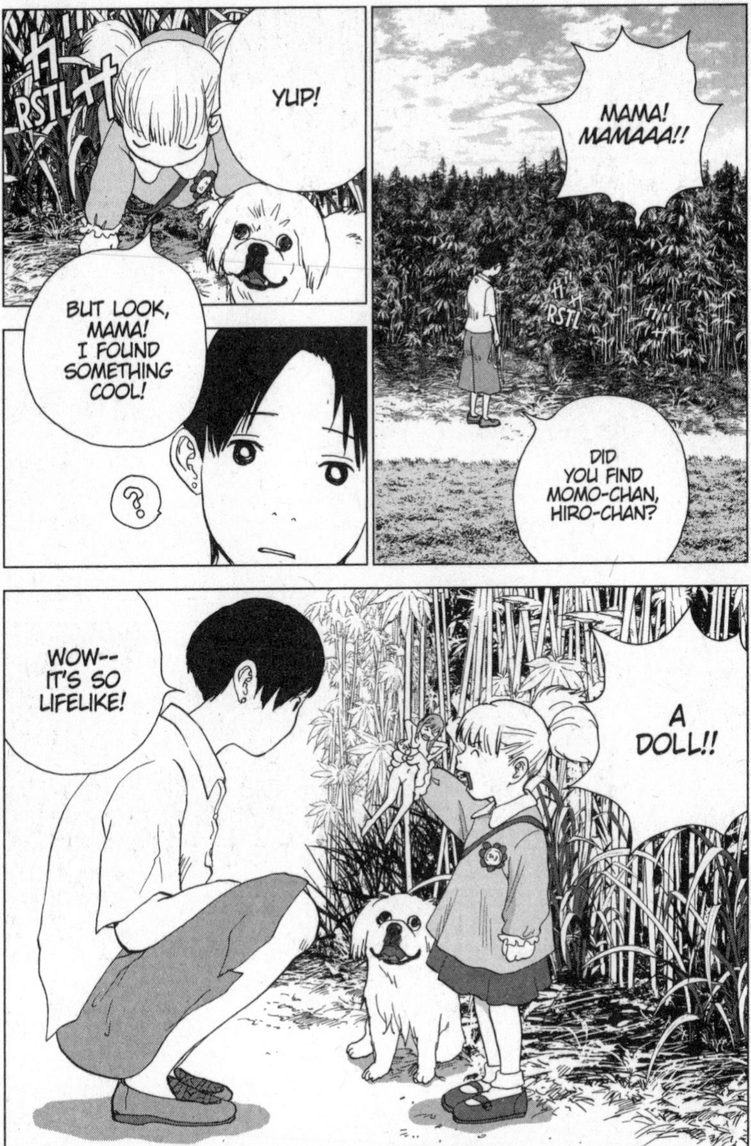
MAMA! MAMAAA!!
RSTL
DID YOU FIND MOMO-CHAN, HIRO-CHAN?
RSTL
YUP!
BUT LOOK, MAMA! I FOUND SOMETHING COOL!
?
A DOLL!!
WOW-- IT'S SO LIFELIKE!

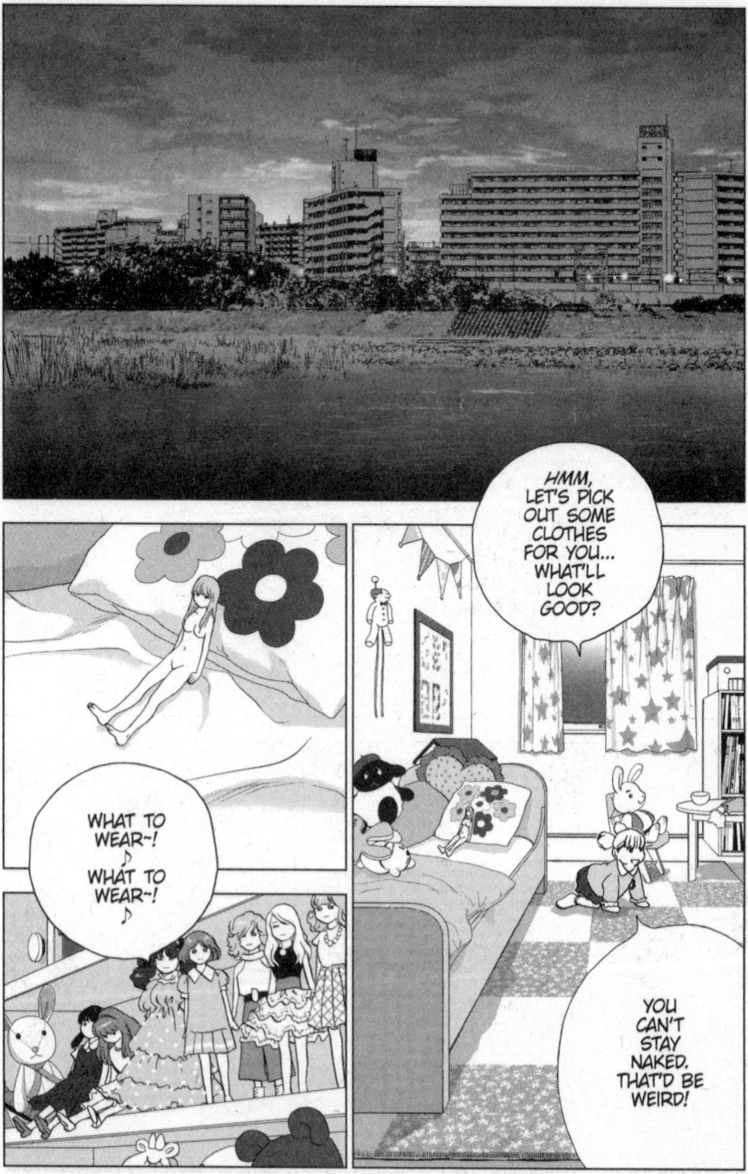
HMM, LET'S PICK OUT SOME CLOTHES FOR YOU... WHAT'LL LOOK GOOD?
YOU CAN'T STAY NAKED. THAT'D BE WEIRD!
WHAT TO WEAR~! ♪ WHAT TO WEAR~! ♪

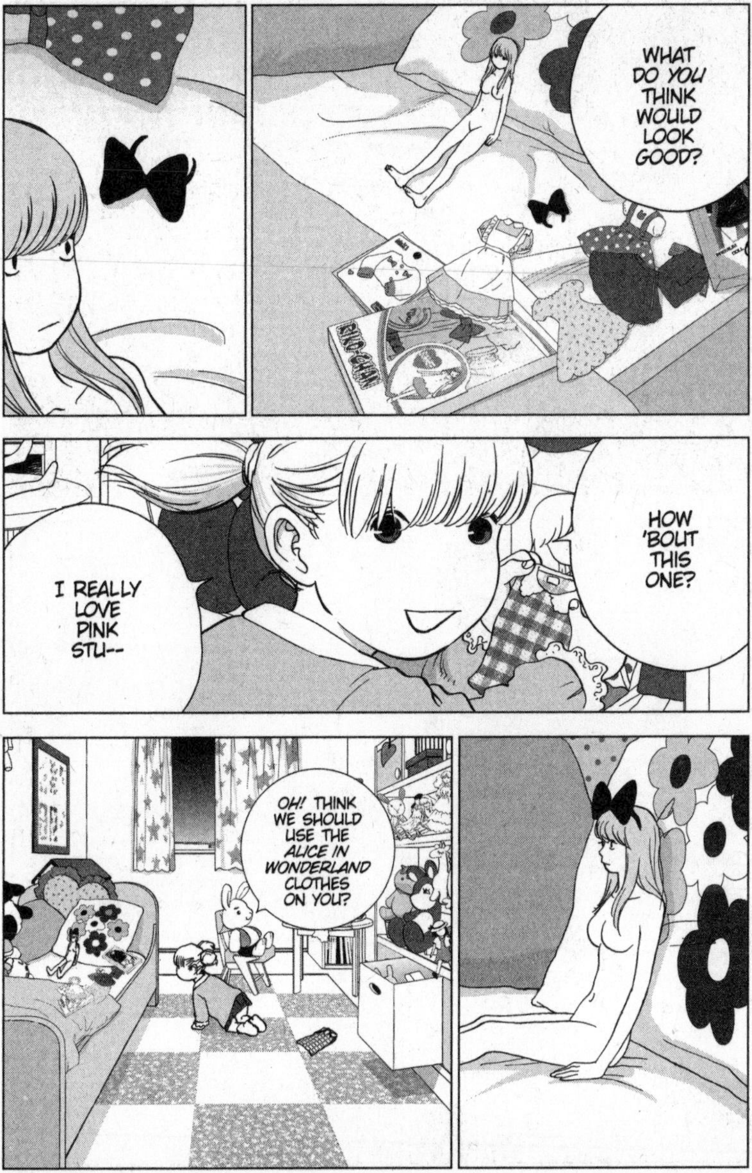
WHAT DO *YOU* THINK WOULD LOOK GOOD?
HOW 'BOUT THIS ONE?
I REALLY LOVE PINK STU--
OH! THINK WE SHOULD USE THE *ALICE IN WONDERLAND* CLOTHES ON YOU?

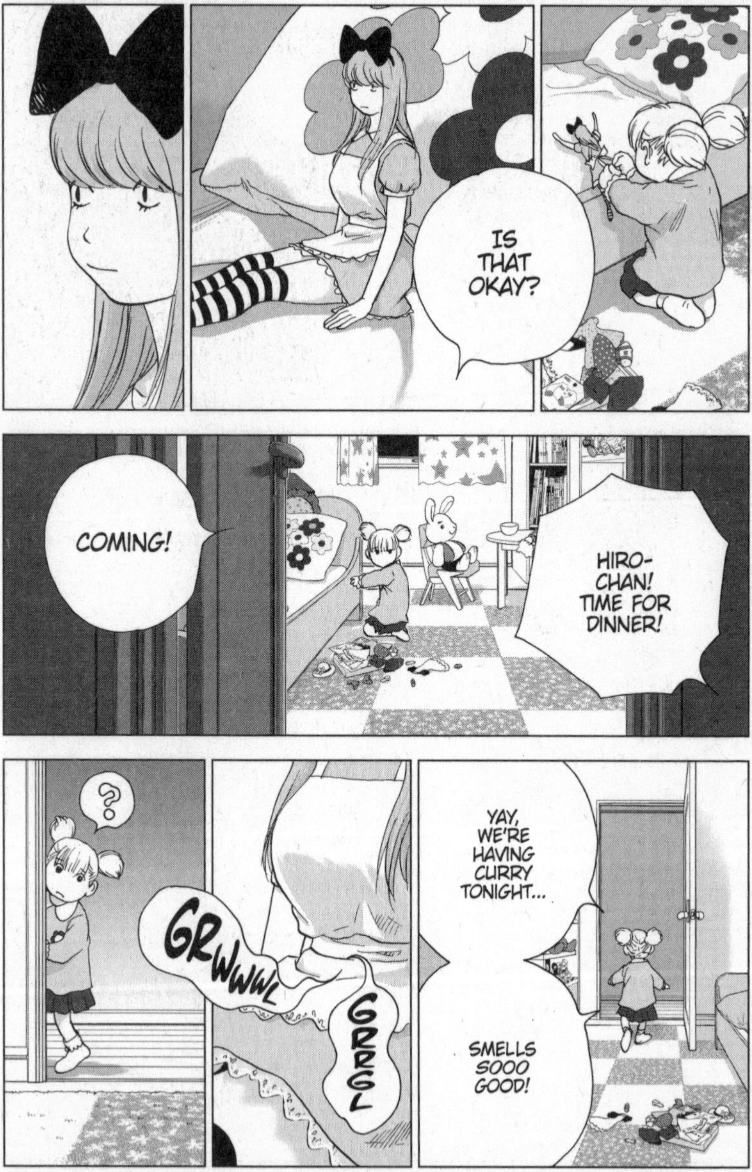
IS THAT OKAY?
HIRO-CHAN! TIME FOR DINNER!
COMING!
YAY, WE'RE HAVING CURRY TONIGHT...
SMELLS SOOO GOOD!
GRWWWL
GRRGL
?

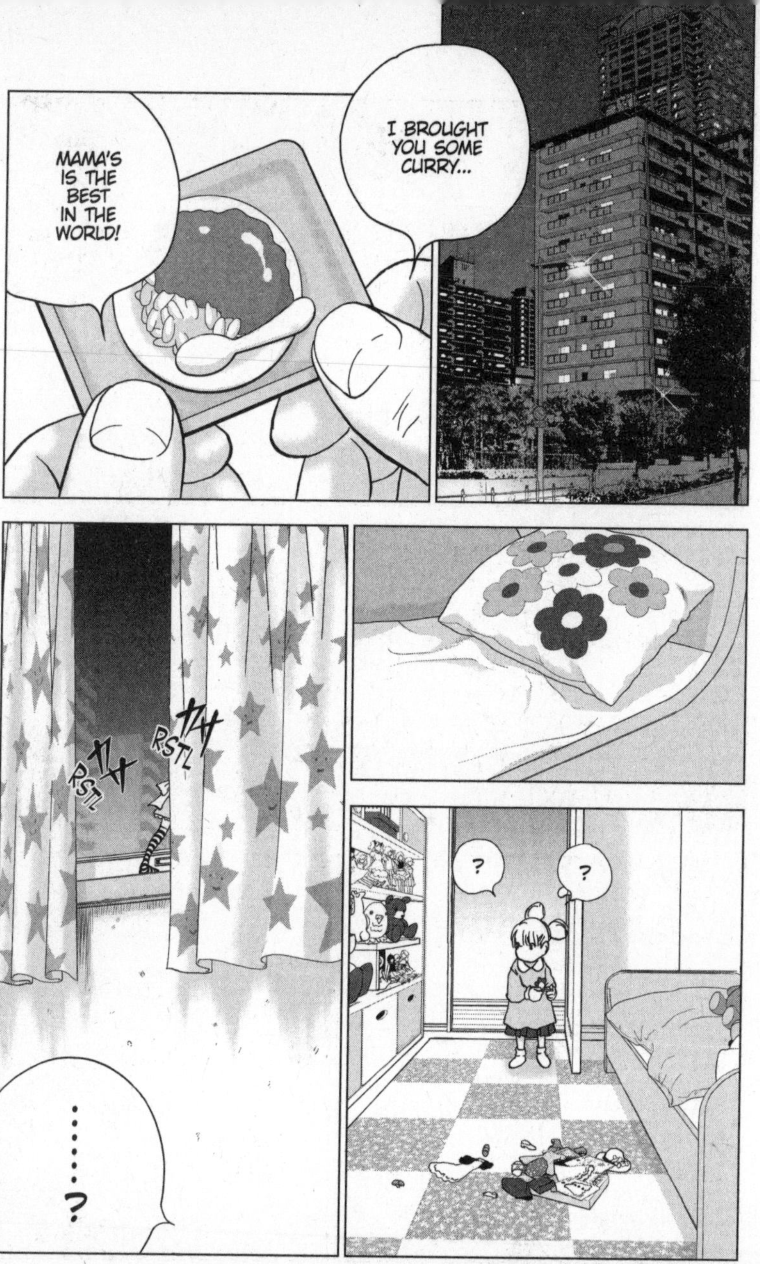
I BROUGHT YOU SOME CURRY...
MAMA'S IS THE BEST IN THE WORLD!
?
?
RSTL
RSTL
......?

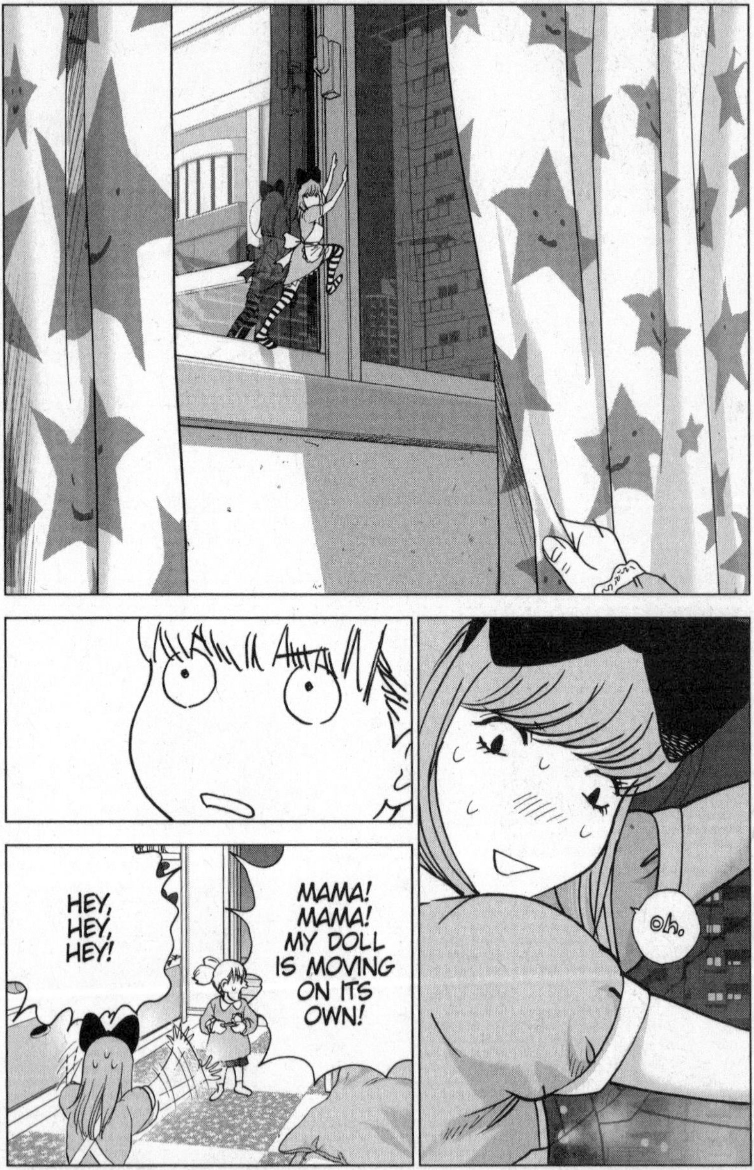
Oh.
MAMA! MAMA! MY DOLL IS MOVING ON ITS OWN!
HEY, HEY, HEY!

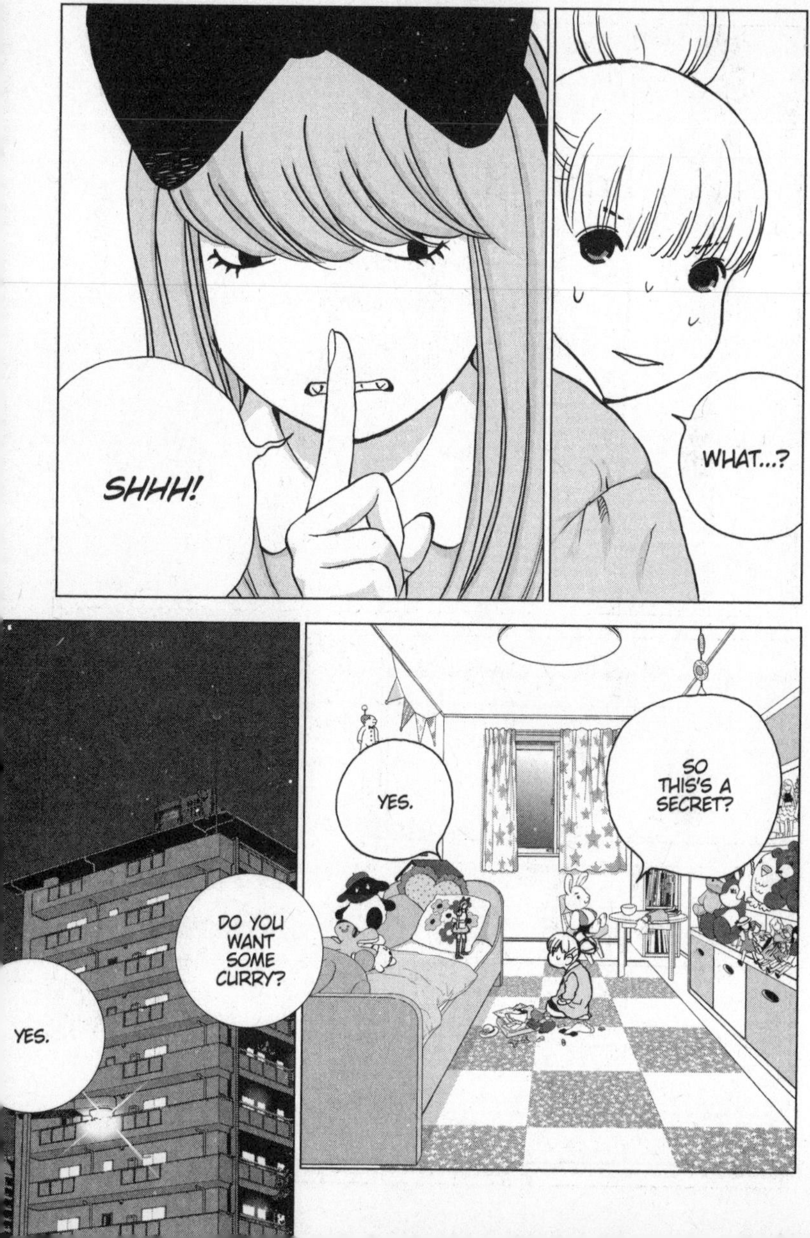
WHAT...?
SHHH!
SO THIS'S A SECRET?
YES.
DO YOU WANT SOME CURRY?
YES.

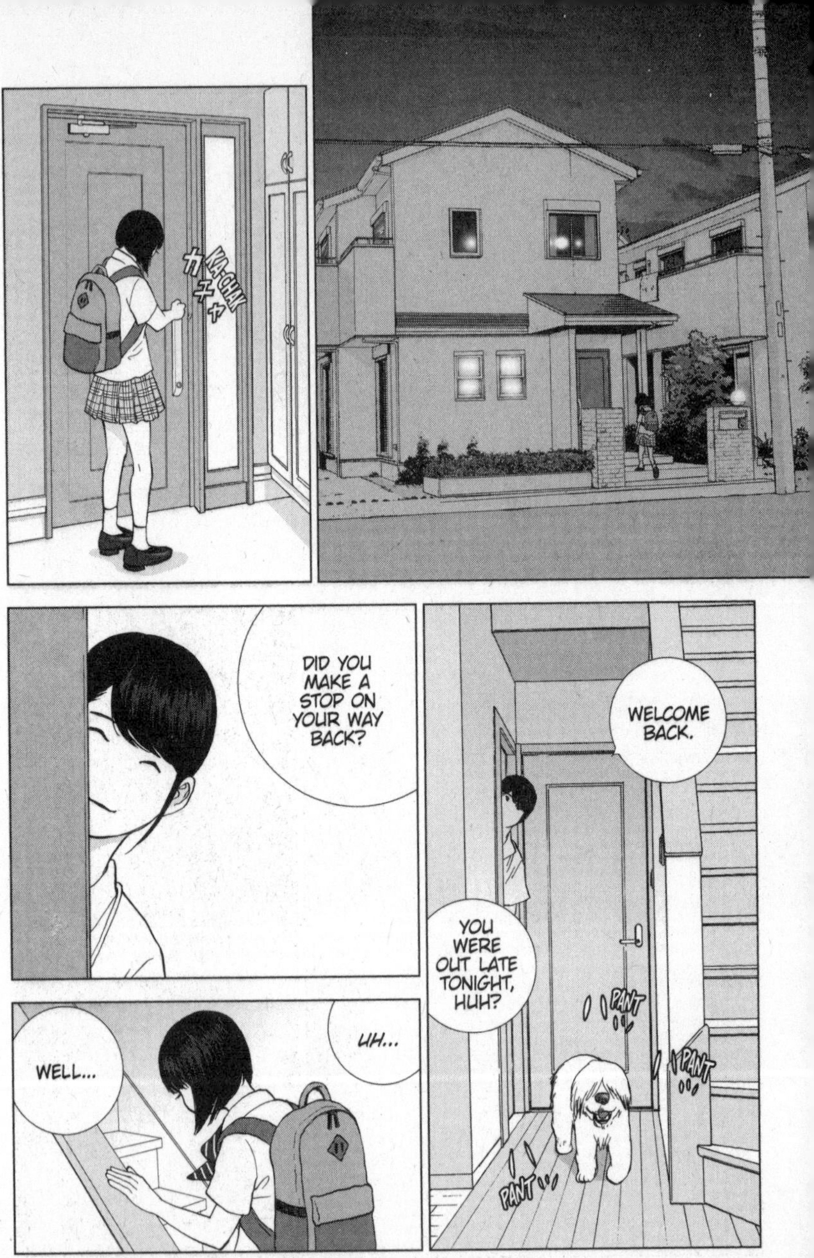
KA-CHAK
カチャ
WELCOME BACK.
YOU WERE OUT LATE TONIGHT, HUH?
PANT
PANT
PANT
DID YOU MAKE A STOP ON YOUR WAY BACK?
UH...
WELL...

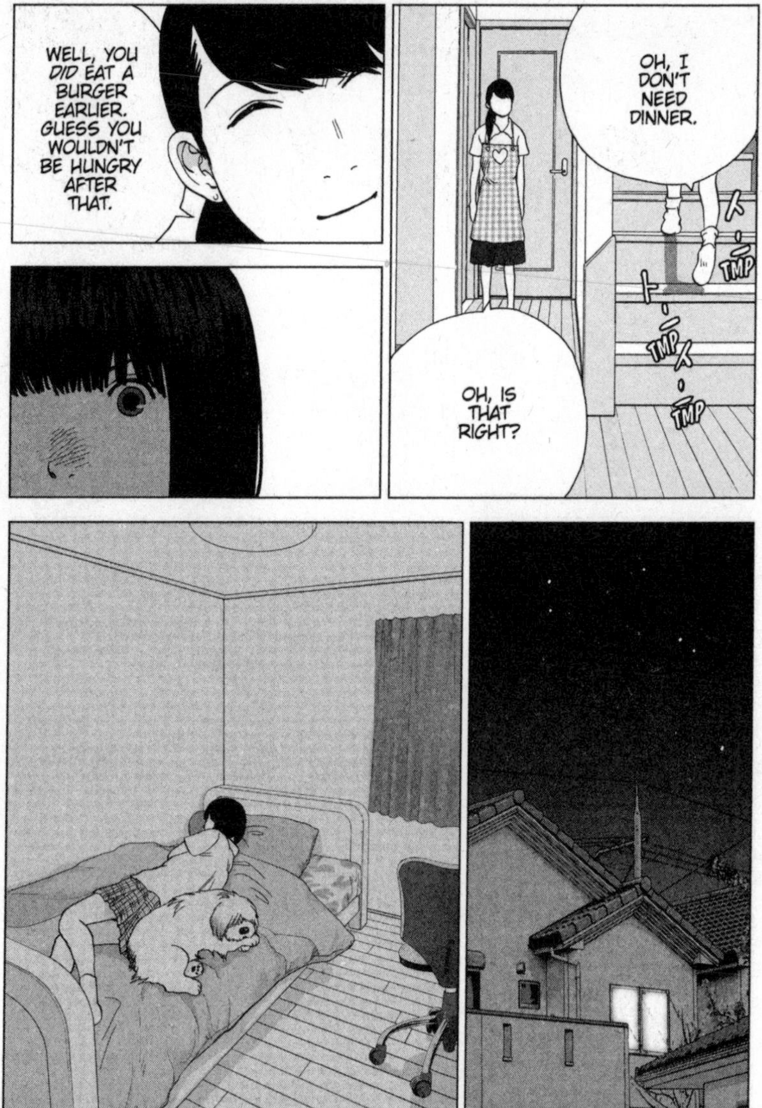

OH, I DON'T NEED DINNER.
TMP
TMP
TMP
OH, IS THAT RIGHT?
WELL, YOU *DID* EAT A BURGER EARLIER. GUESS YOU WOULDN'T BE HUNGRY AFTER THAT.

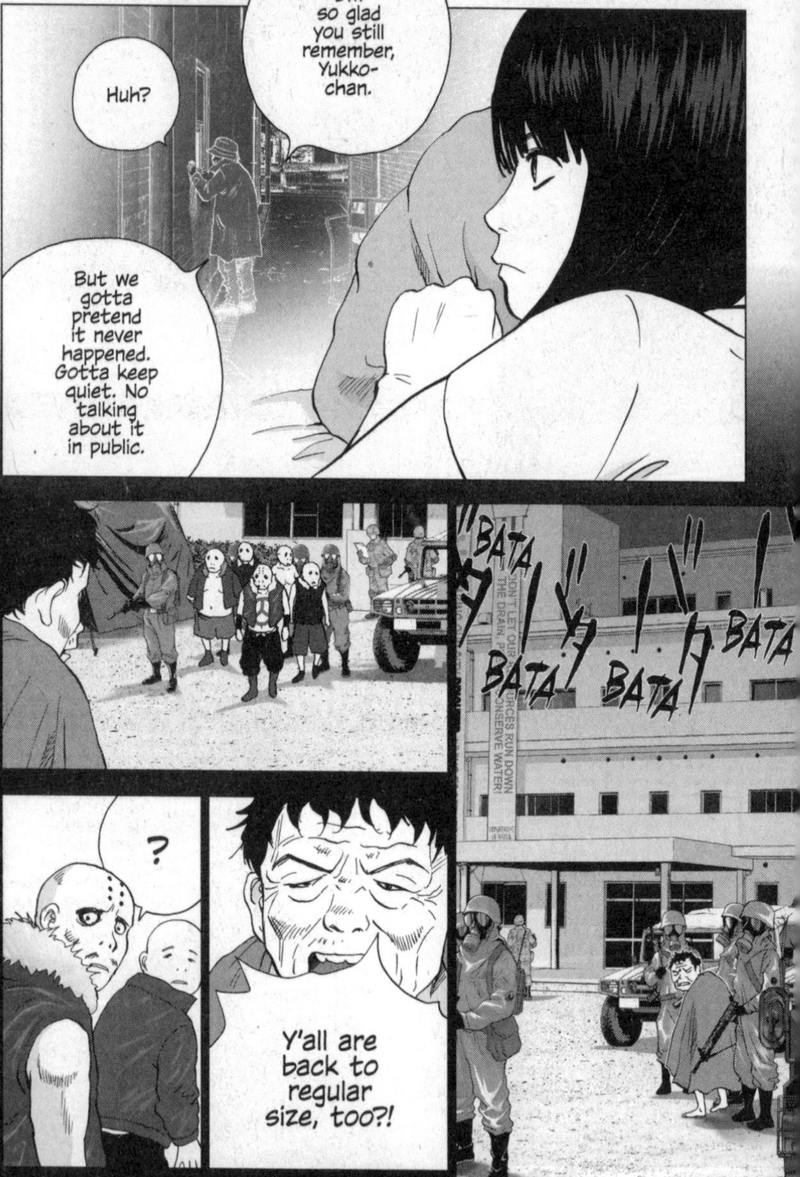
I'm so glad you still remember, Yukko-chan.
Huh?
But we gotta pretend it never happened. Gotta keep quiet. No talking about it in public.
BATA BATA BATA BATA BATA
Y'all are back to regular size, too?!
?

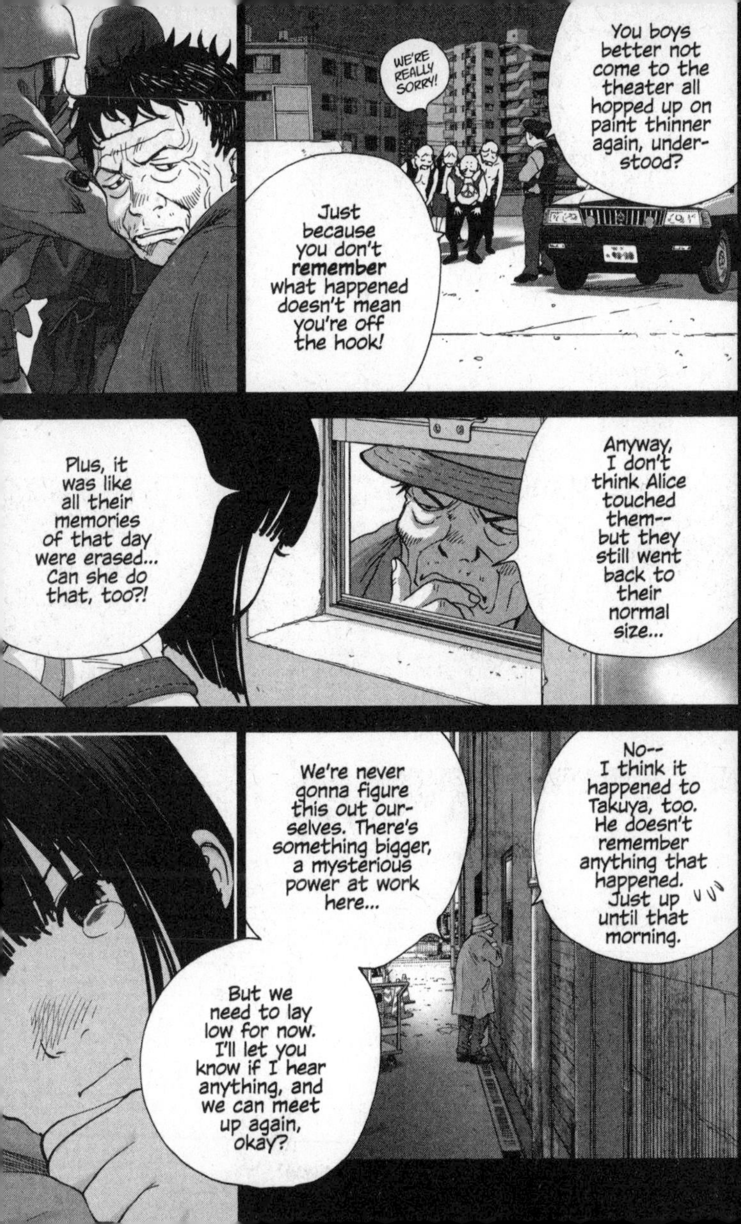
You boys better not come to the theater all hopped up on paint thinner again, understood?
WE'RE REALLY SORRY!
Just because you don't **remember** what happened doesn't mean you're off the hook!
Anyway, I don't think Alice touched them--but they still went back to their normal size...
Plus, it was like all their memories of that day were erased... Can she do that, too?!
No-- I think it happened to Takuya, too. He doesn't remember anything that happened. Just up until that morning.
We're never gonna figure this out ourselves. There's something bigger, a mysterious power at work here...
But we need to lay low for now. I'll let you know if I hear anything, and we can meet up again, okay?

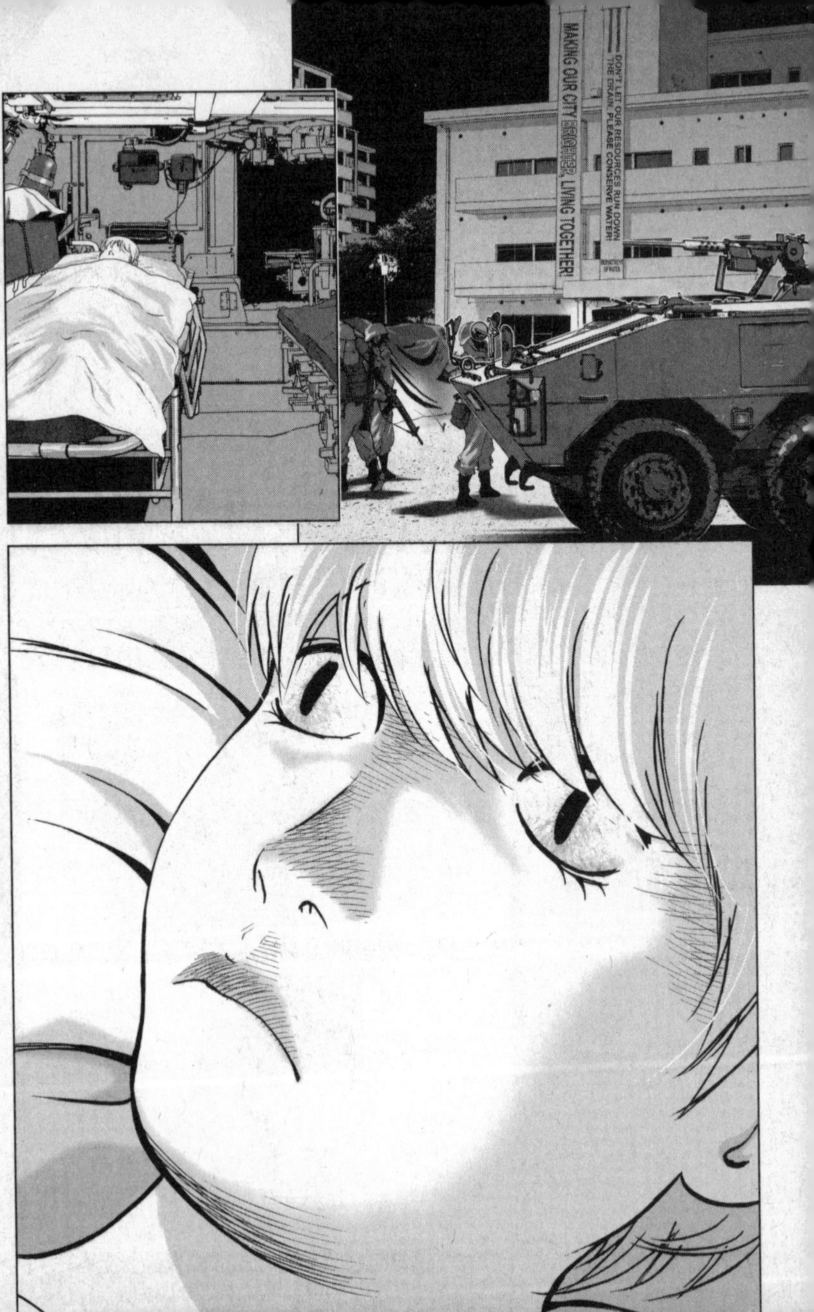
MAKING OUR CITY BRIGHTER, LIVING TOGETHER!
DON'T LET OUR RESOURCES RUN DOWN THE DRAIN. PLEASE CONSERVE WATER!
DEPARTMENT OF WATER

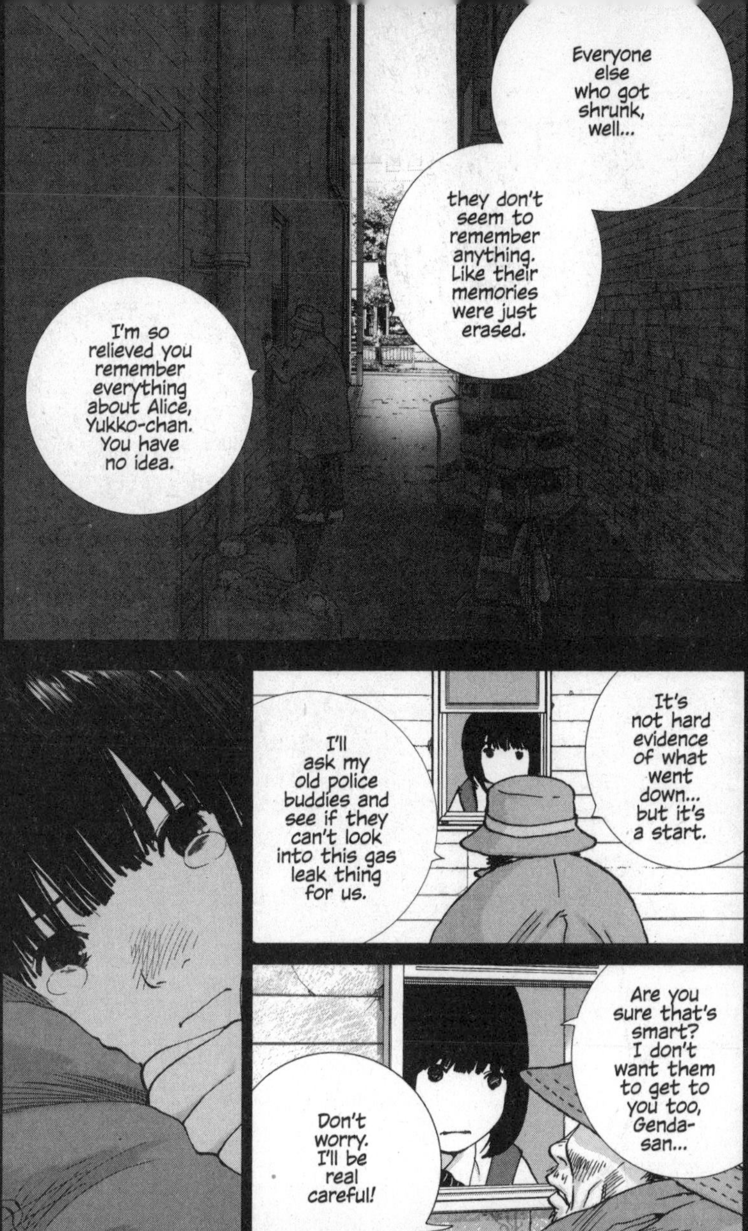
Everyone else who got shrunk, well...
they don't seem to remember anything. Like their memories were just erased.
I'm so relieved you remember everything about Alice, Yukko-chan. You have no idea.
It's not hard evidence of what went down... but it's a start.
I'll ask my old police buddies and see if they can't look into this gas leak thing for us.
Are you sure that's smart? I don't want them to get to you too, Genda-san...
Don't worry. I'll be real careful!

Chapter 29: Two People in the Past

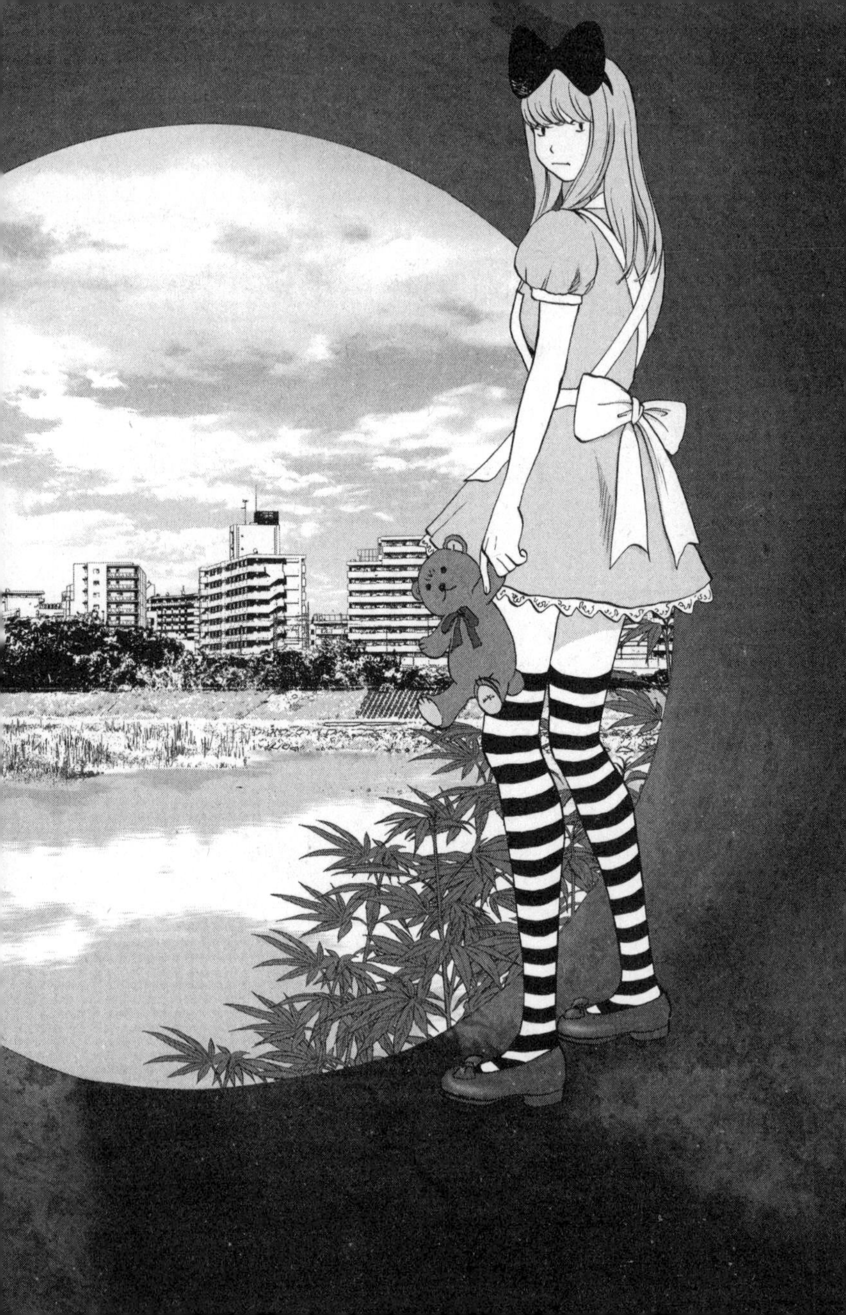

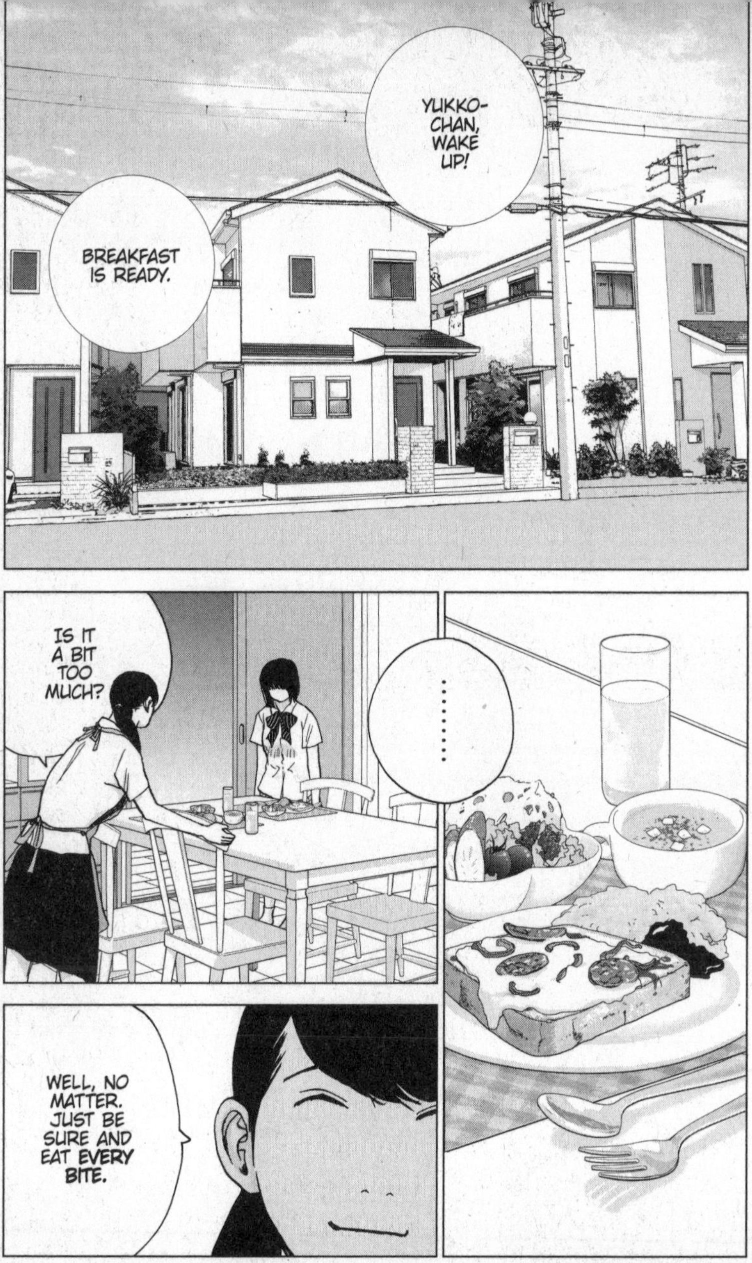
YUKKO-CHAN, WAKE UP!
BREAKFAST IS READY.
......
IS IT A BIT TOO MUCH?
WELL, NO MATTER. JUST BE SURE AND EAT EVERY BITE.

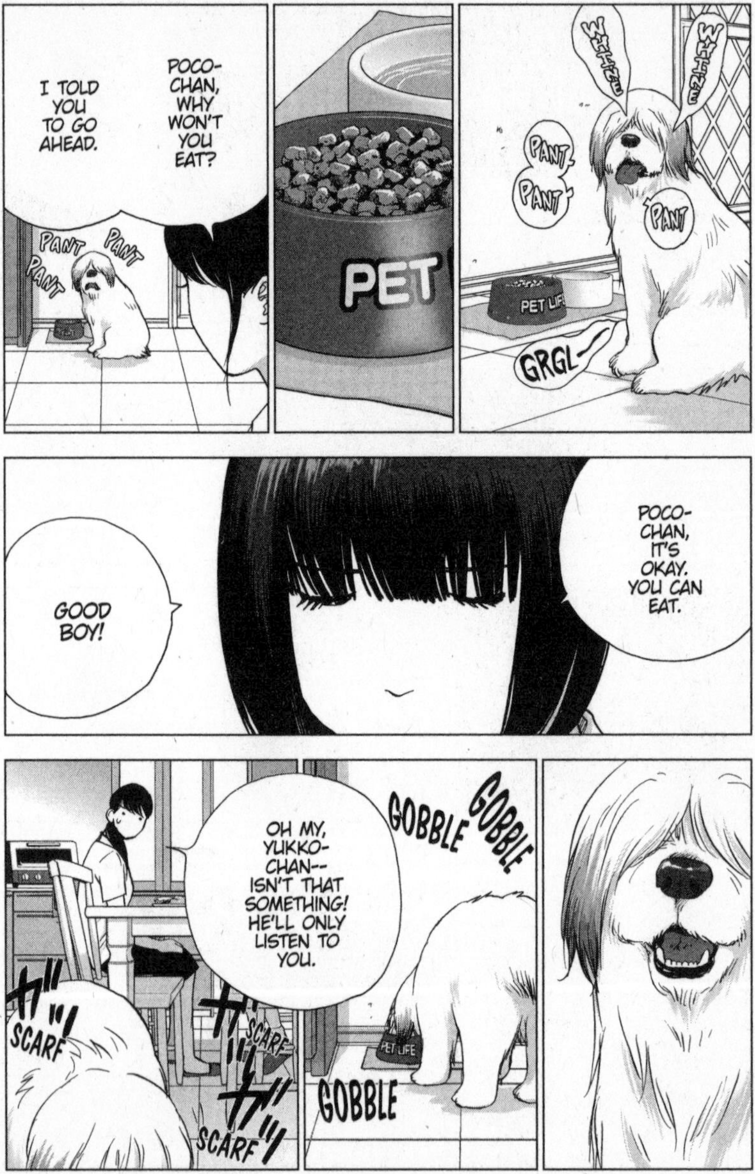
WHIIINE
WHIIINE
PANT
PANT
PANT
GRGL--
PET
PET LIFE
POCO-CHAN, WHY WON'T YOU EAT?
I TOLD YOU TO GO AHEAD.
PANT
PANT
PANT
POCO-CHAN, IT'S OKAY. YOU CAN EAT.
GOOD BOY!
GOBBLE
GOBBLE
PET LIFE
GOBBLE
OH MY, YUKKO-CHAN-- ISN'T THAT SOMETHING! HE'LL ONLY LISTEN TO YOU.
SCARF
SCARF
SCARF

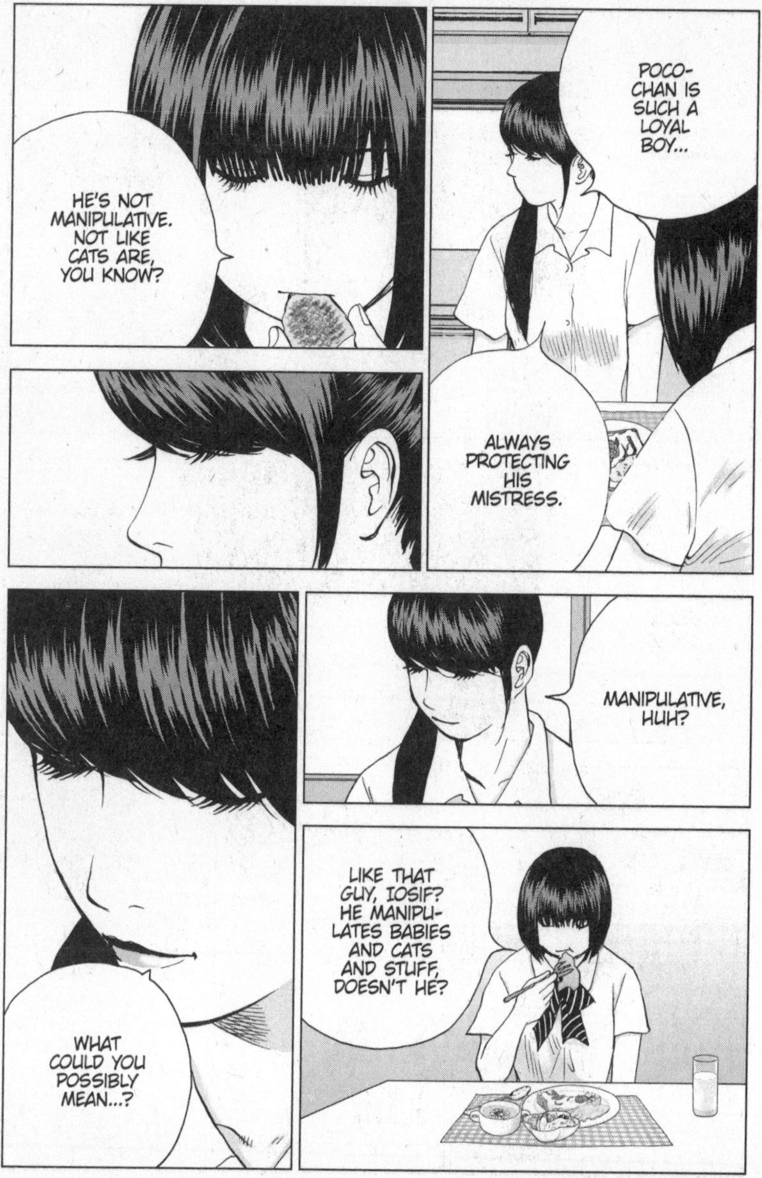
POCO-CHAN IS SUCH A LOYAL BOY...
ALWAYS PROTECTING HIS MISTRESS.
HE'S NOT MANIPULATIVE. NOT LIKE CATS ARE, YOU KNOW?
MANIPULATIVE, HUH?
LIKE THAT GUY, IOSIF? HE MANIPULATES BABIES AND CATS AND STUFF, DOESN'T HE?
WHAT COULD YOU POSSIBLY MEAN...?

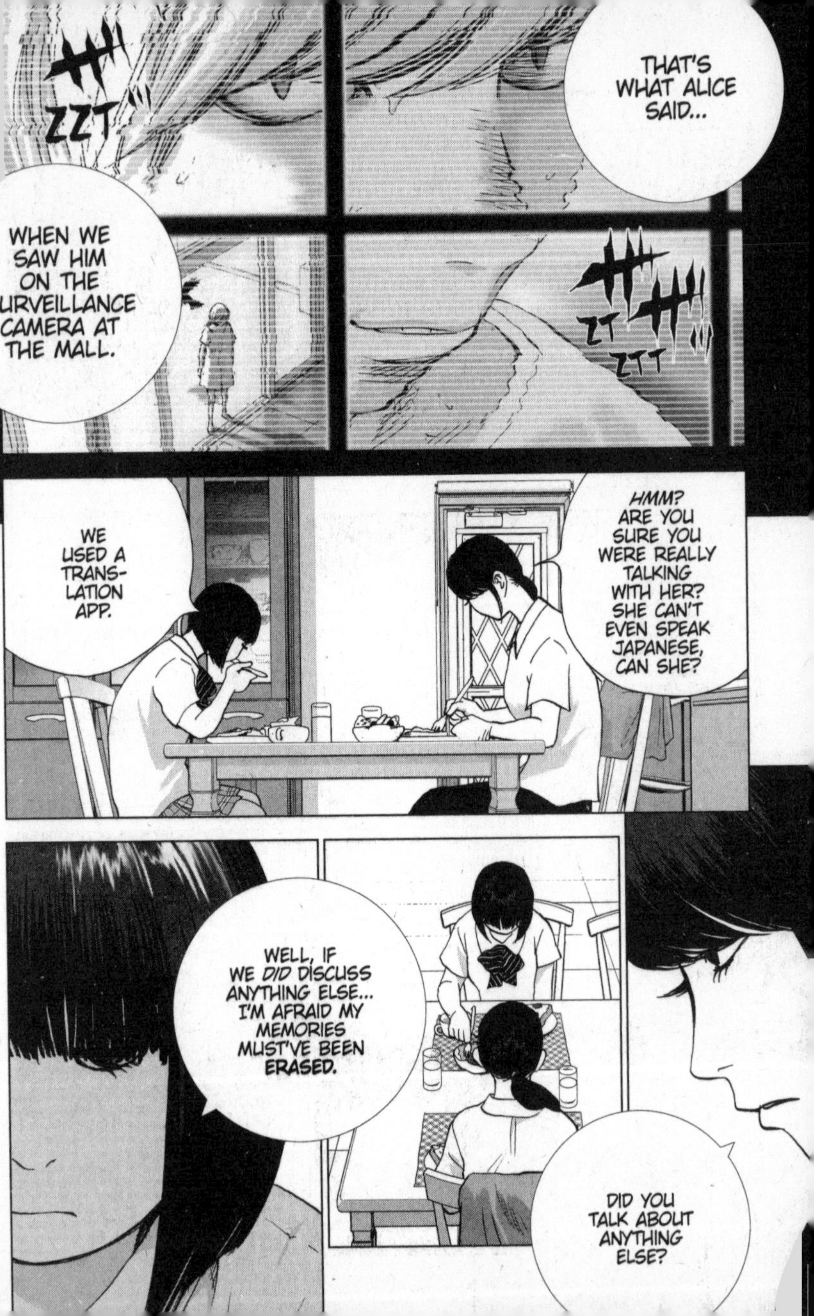
THAT'S WHAT ALICE SAID...
ZT
ZTT
ZZT
WHEN WE SAW HIM ON THE SURVEILLANCE CAMERA AT THE MALL.
HMM? ARE YOU SURE YOU WERE REALLY TALKING WITH HER? SHE CAN'T EVEN SPEAK JAPANESE, CAN SHE?
WE USED A TRANS-LATION APP.
DID YOU TALK ABOUT ANYTHING ELSE?
WELL, IF WE *DID* DISCUSS ANYTHING ELSE... I'M AFRAID MY MEMORIES MUST'VE BEEN ERASED.

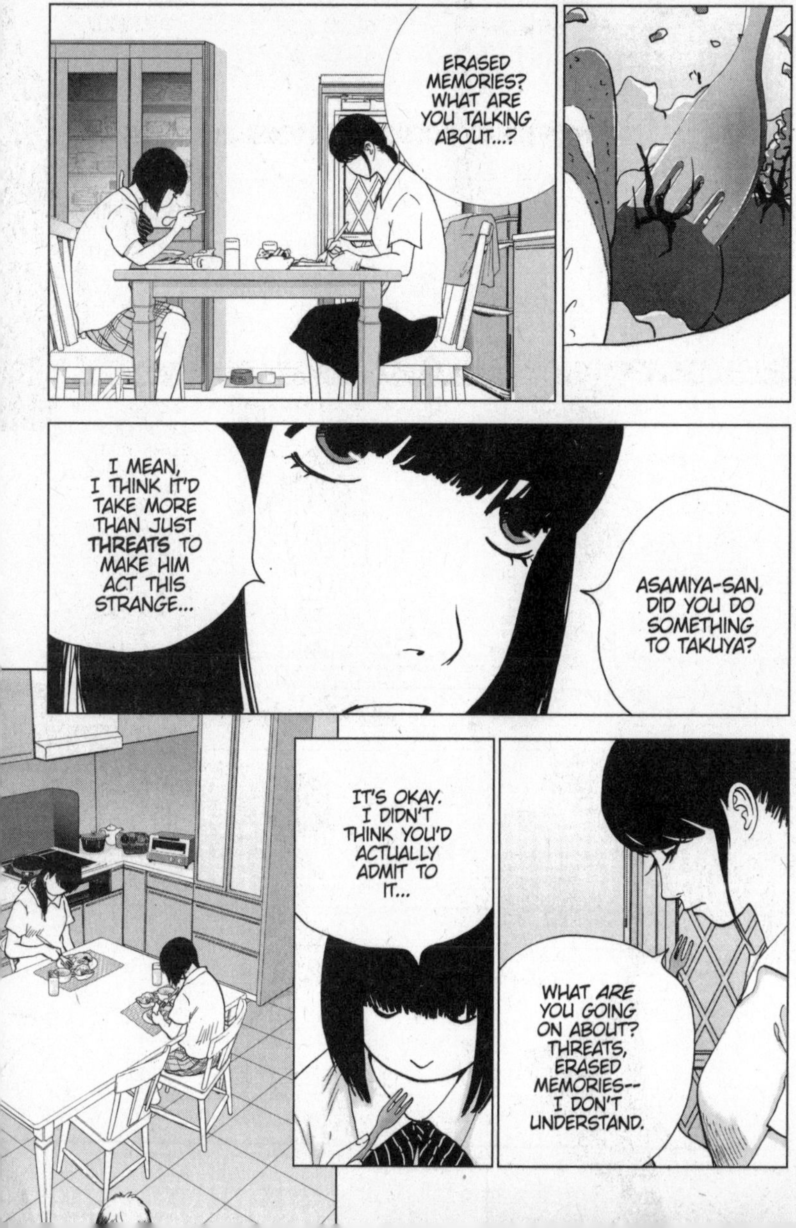
ERASED MEMORIES? WHAT ARE YOU TALKING ABOUT...?
ASAMIYA-SAN, DID YOU DO SOMETHING TO TAKUYA?
I MEAN, I THINK IT'D TAKE MORE THAN JUST THREATS TO MAKE HIM ACT THIS STRANGE...
WHAT *ARE* YOU GOING ON ABOUT? THREATS, ERASED MEMORIES-- I DON'T UNDERSTAND.
IT'S OKAY. I DIDN'T THINK YOU'D ACTUALLY ADMIT TO IT...

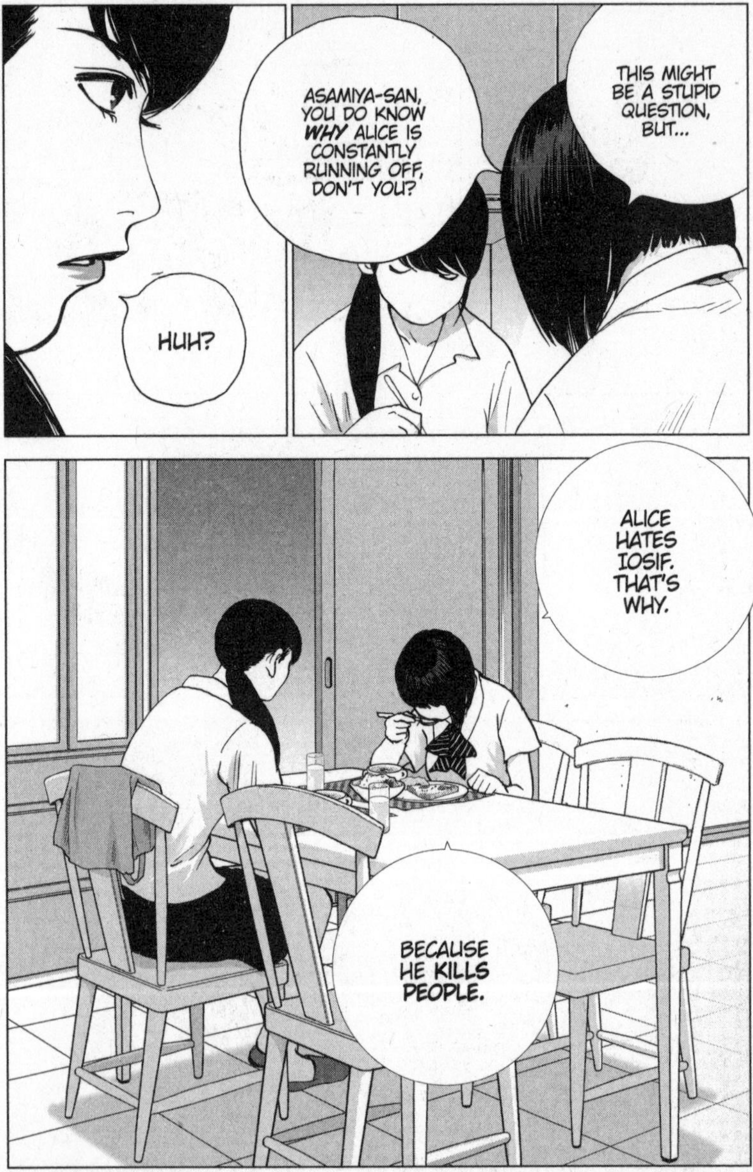
THIS MIGHT BE A STUPID QUESTION, BUT...
ASAMIYA-SAN, YOU DO KNOW *WHY* ALICE IS CONSTANTLY RUNNING OFF, DON'T YOU?
HUH?
ALICE HATES IOSIF. THAT'S WHY.
BECAUSE HE KILLS PEOPLE.

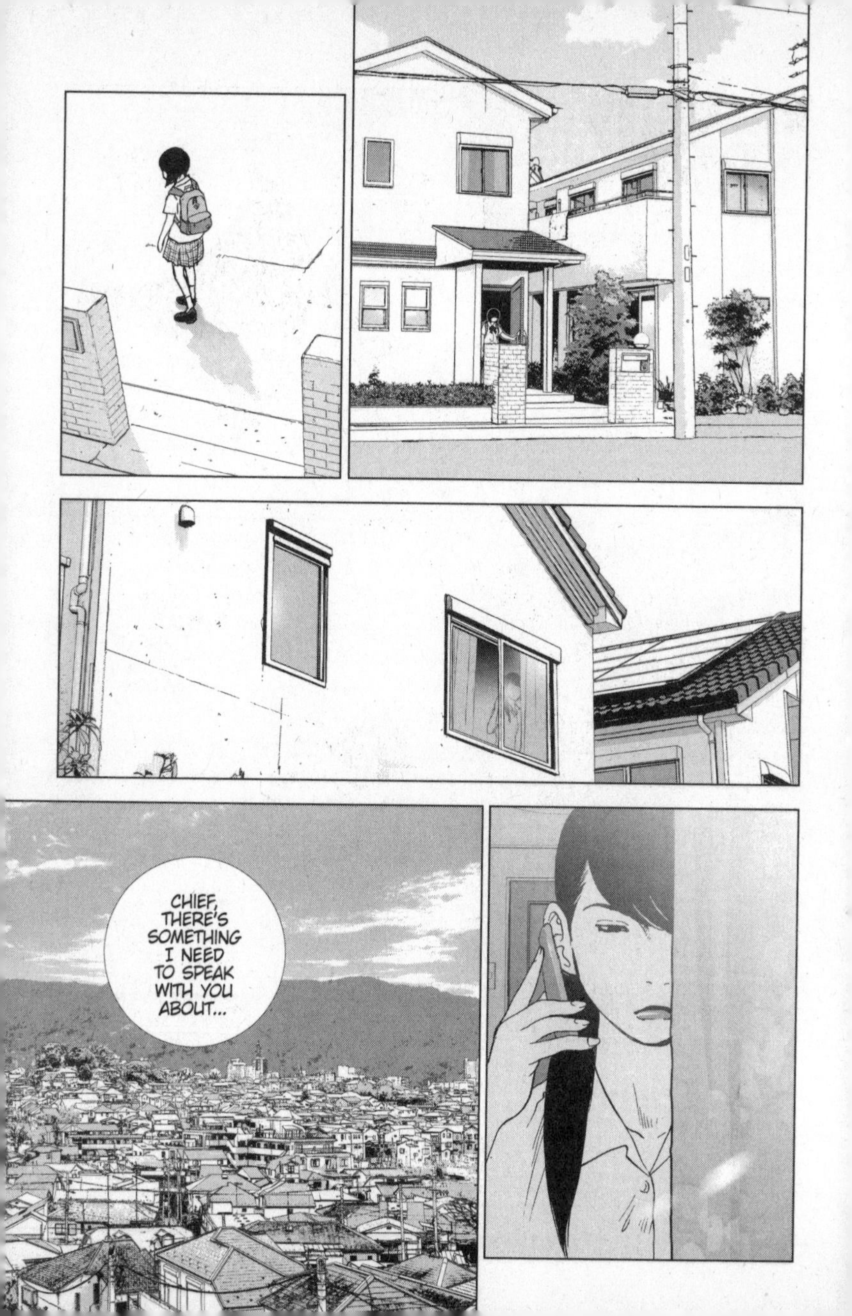
CHIEF, THERE'S SOMETHING I NEED TO SPEAK WITH YOU ABOUT...

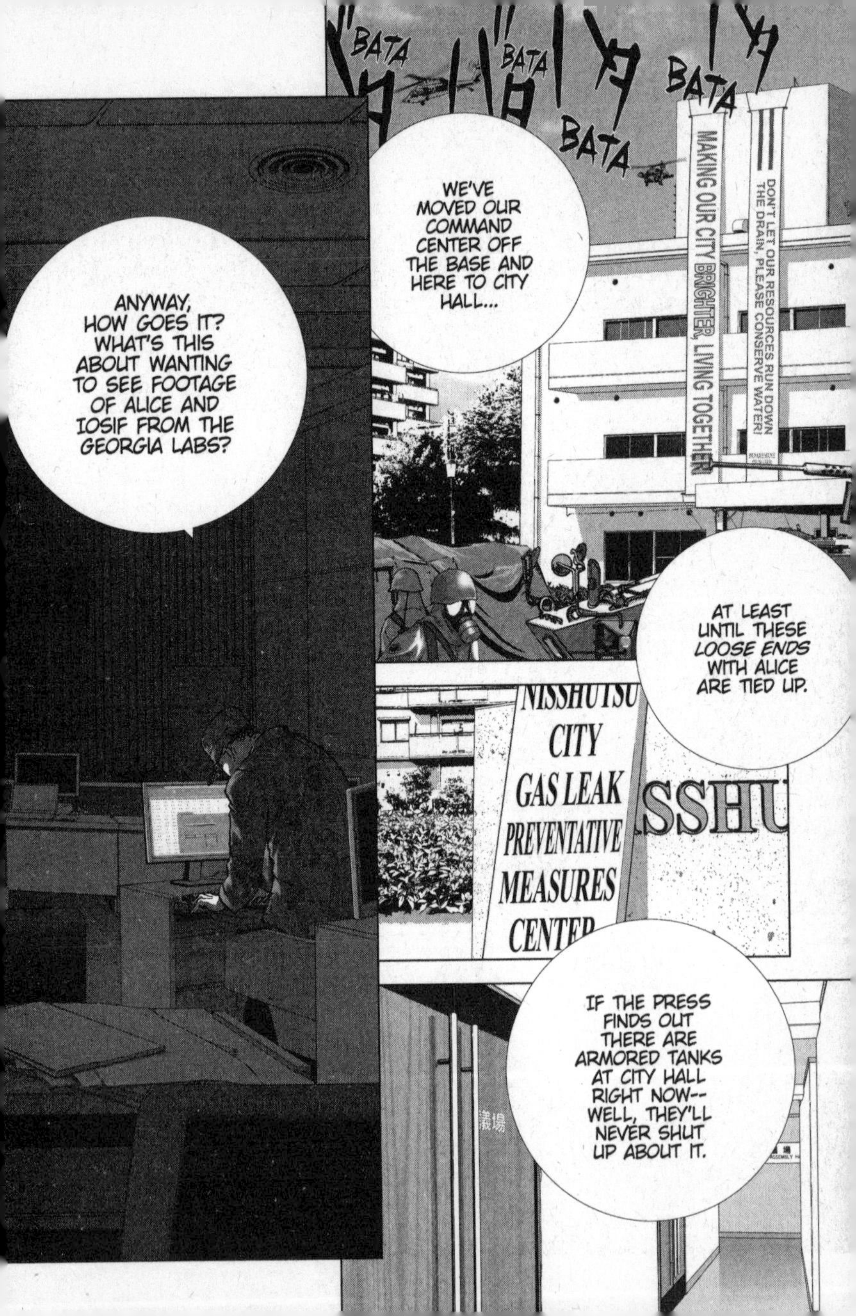
BATA BATA BATA BATA
WE'VE MOVED OUR COMMAND CENTER OFF THE BASE AND HERE TO CITY HALL...
MAKING OUR CITY BRIGHTER, LIVING TOGETHER
DON'T LET OUR RESOURCES RUN DOWN THE DRAIN, PLEASE CONSERVE WATER!
AT LEAST UNTIL THESE *LOOSE ENDS* WITH ALICE ARE TIED UP.
NISSHUTSU CITY GAS LEAK PREVENTATIVE MEASURES CENTER
IF THE PRESS FINDS OUT THERE ARE ARMORED TANKS AT CITY HALL RIGHT NOW-- WELL, THEY'LL NEVER SHUT UP ABOUT IT.
ANYWAY, HOW GOES IT? WHAT'S THIS ABOUT WANTING TO SEE FOOTAGE OF ALICE AND IOSIF FROM THE GEORGIA LABS?

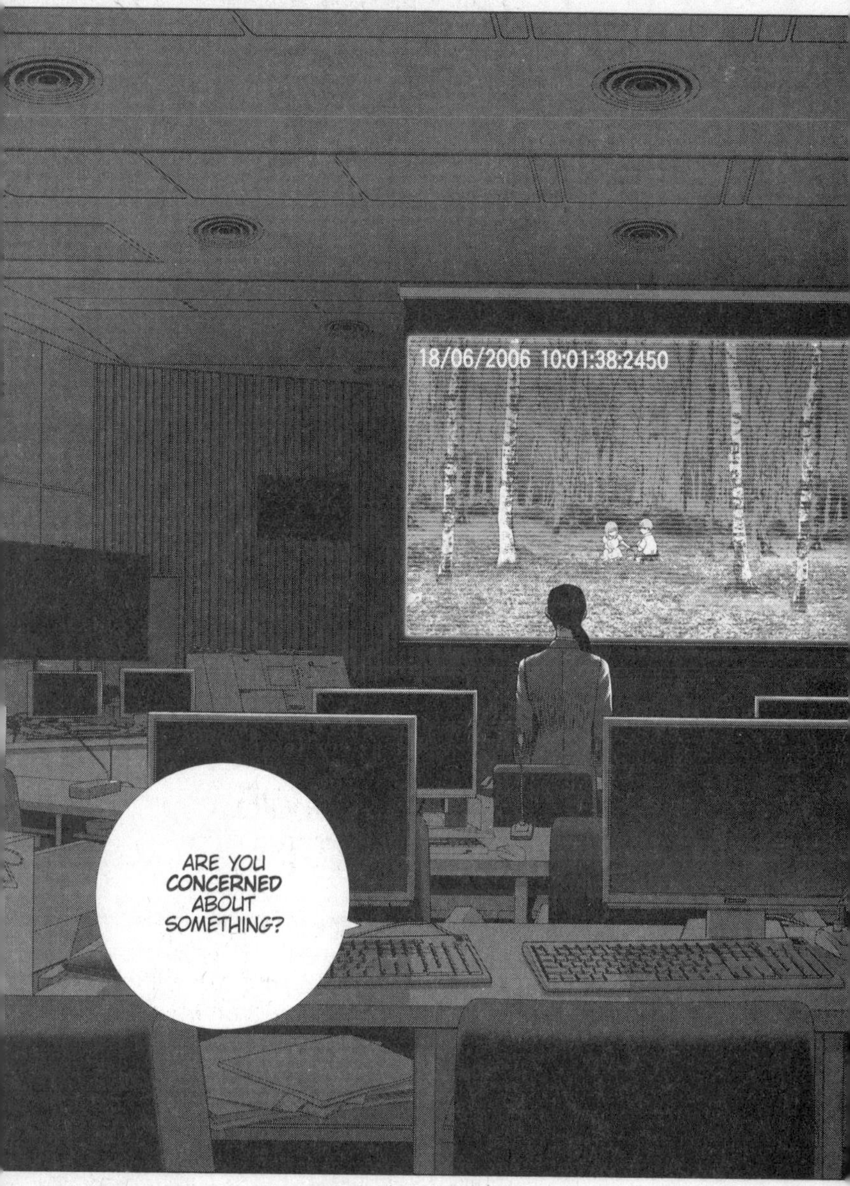
18/06/2006 10:01:38:2450
ARE YOU CONCERNED ABOUT SOMETHING?

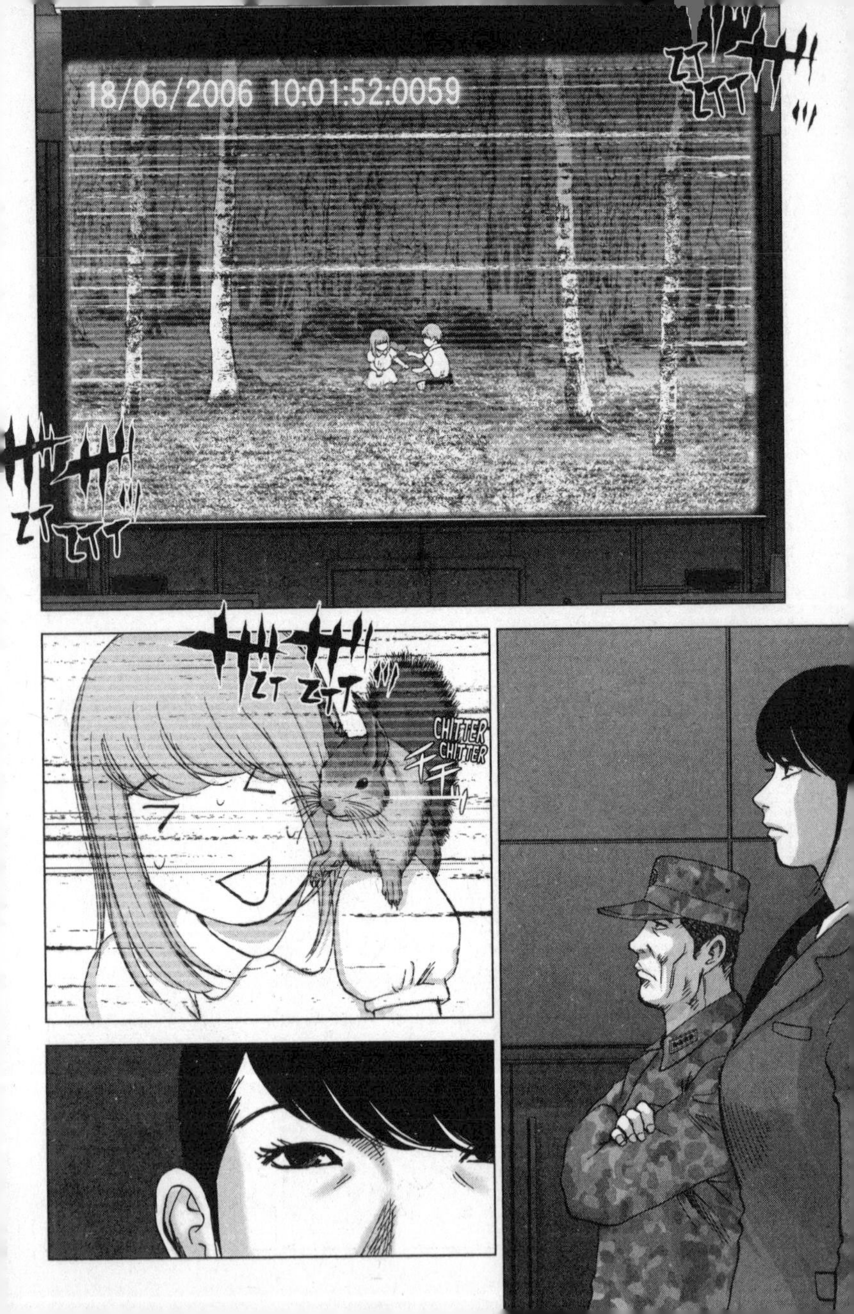
18/06/2006 10:01:52:0059
CHITTER CHITTER

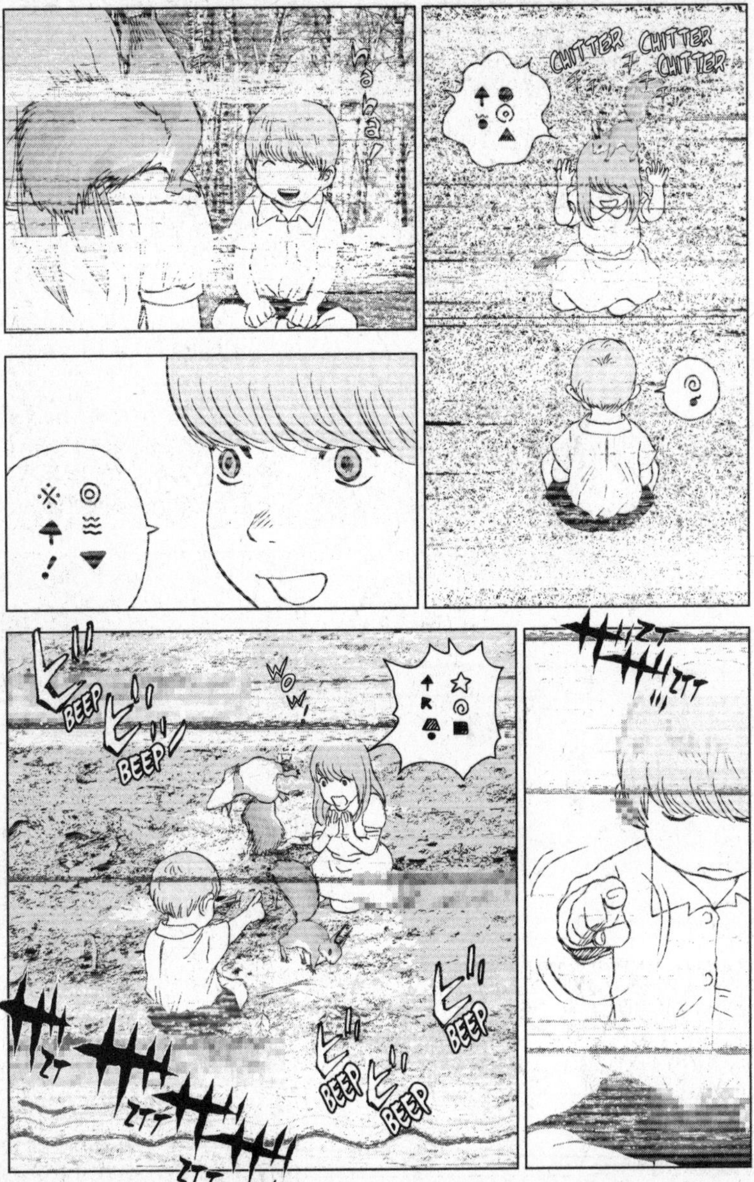
CHITTER CHITTER CHITTER
haha!
WOW!
BEEP BEEP
BEEP BEEP BEEP
ZT ZTT ZTT ZT
ZZT ZTT

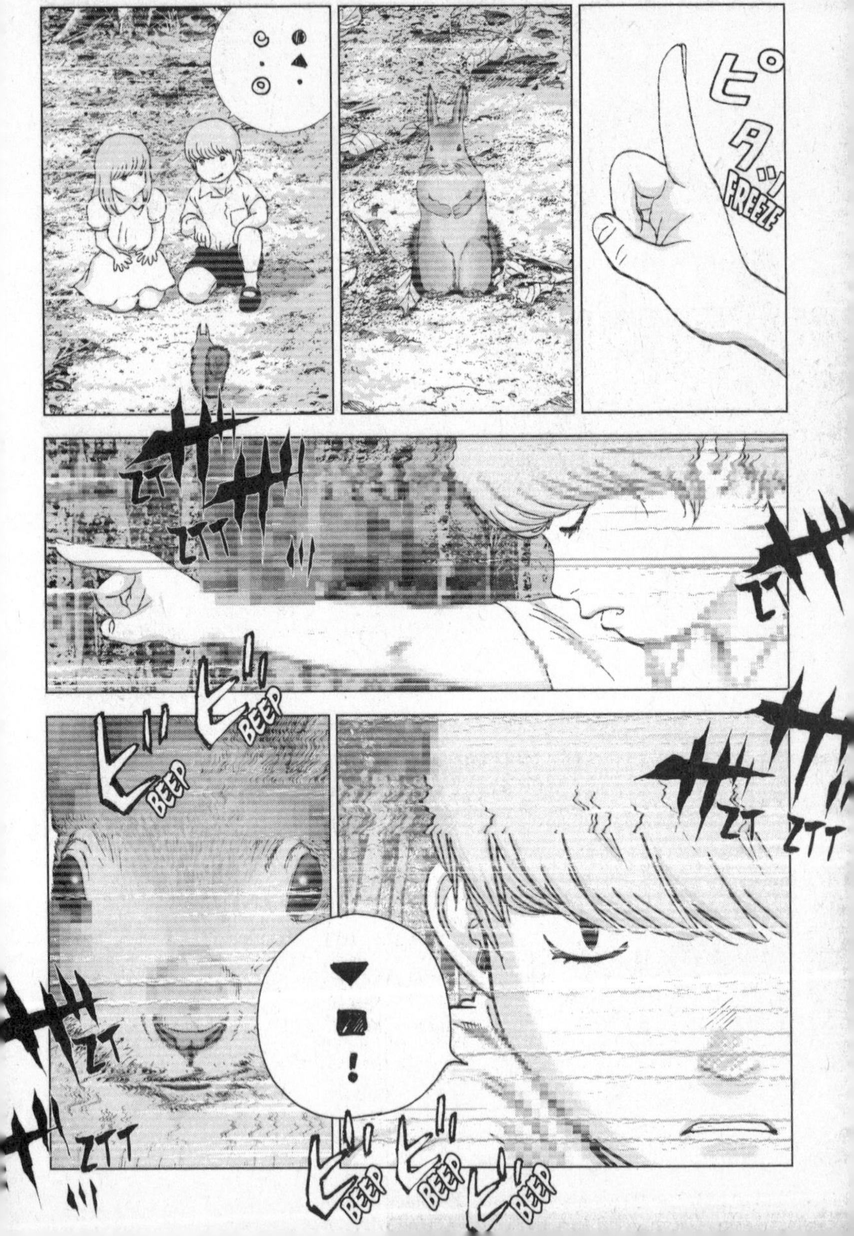
ピタッ
FREEZE
ZT
ZTT
ZT
ZTT
ビー
BEEP
ビー
BEEP
ZT
ZTT
!
ビー
BEEP
ビー
BEEP
ビー
BEEP

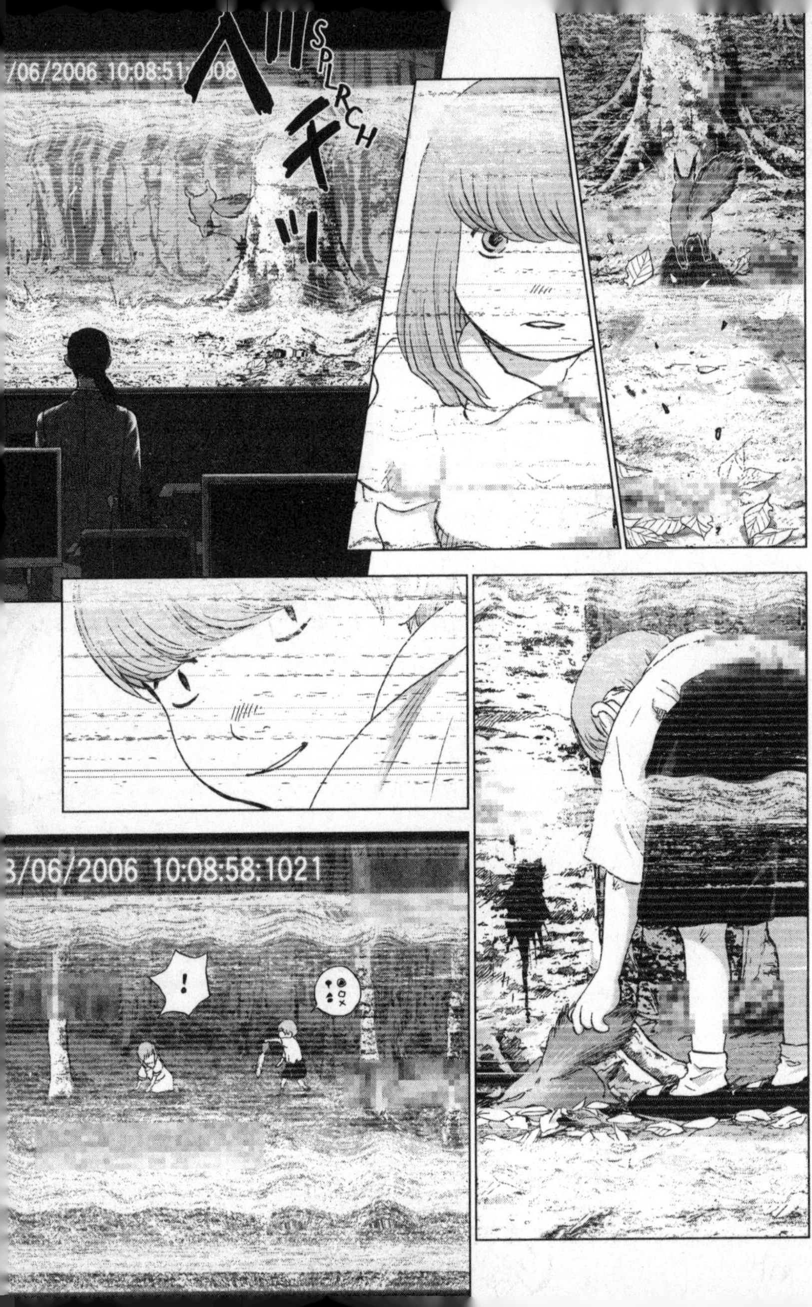
/06/2006 10:08:51
SPLRCH
3/06/2006 10:08:58:1021
!

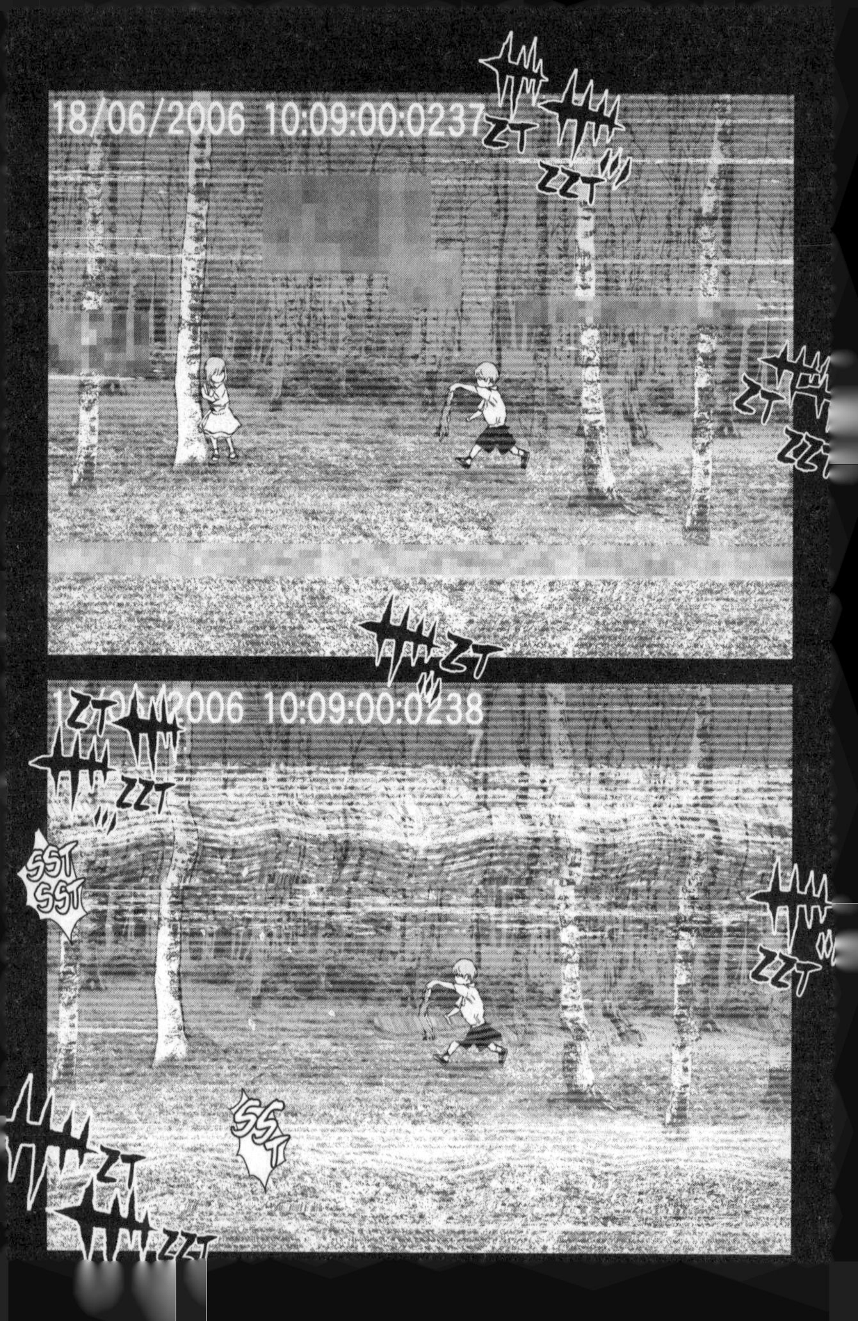

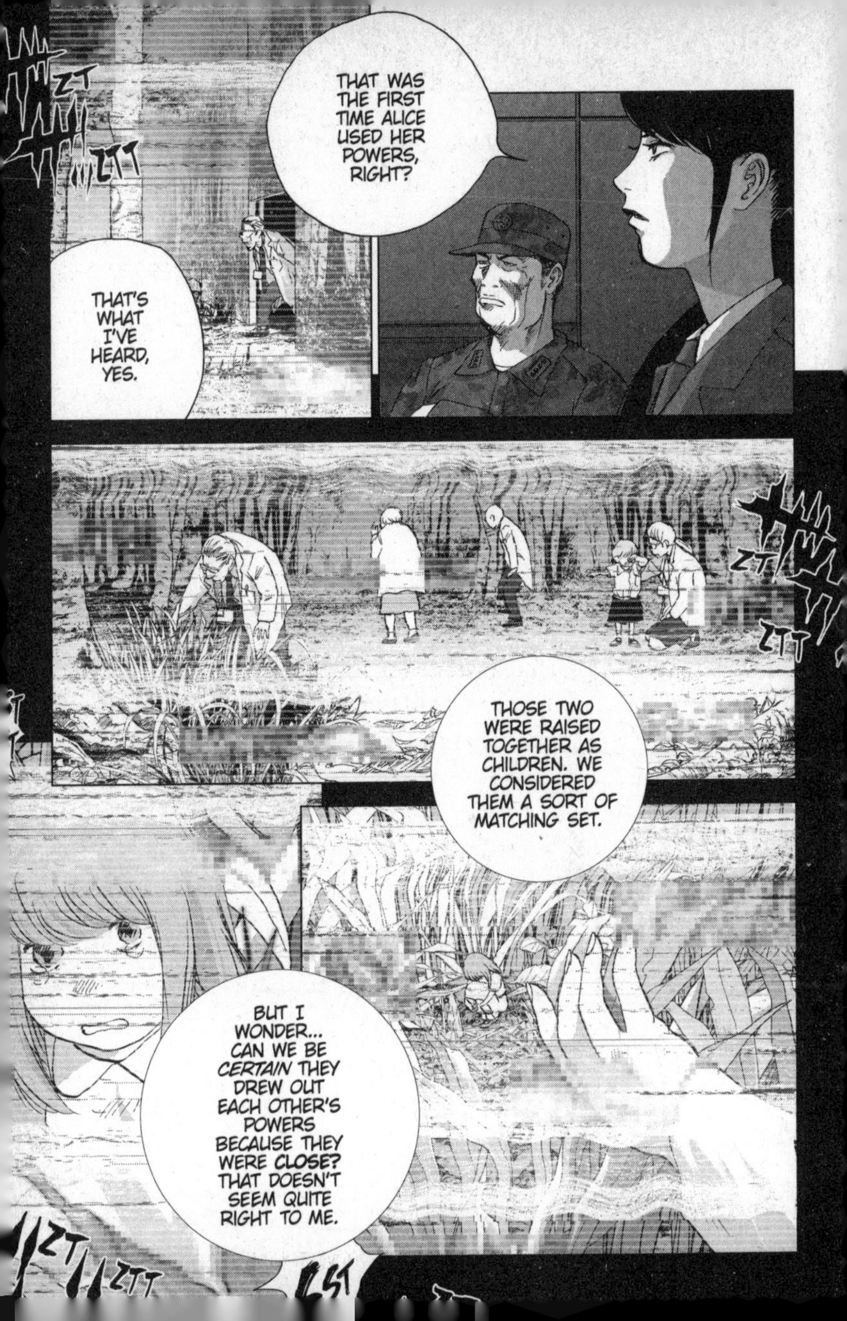
THAT WAS THE FIRST TIME ALICE USED HER POWERS, RIGHT?
THAT'S WHAT I'VE HEARD, YES.
ZT
ZTT
ZT
ZTT
THOSE TWO WERE RAISED TOGETHER AS CHILDREN. WE CONSIDERED THEM A SORT OF MATCHING SET.
BUT I WONDER... CAN WE BE *CERTAIN* THEY DREW OUT EACH OTHER'S POWERS BECAUSE THEY WERE *CLOSE*? THAT DOESN'T SEEM QUITE RIGHT TO ME.
ZT
ZTT

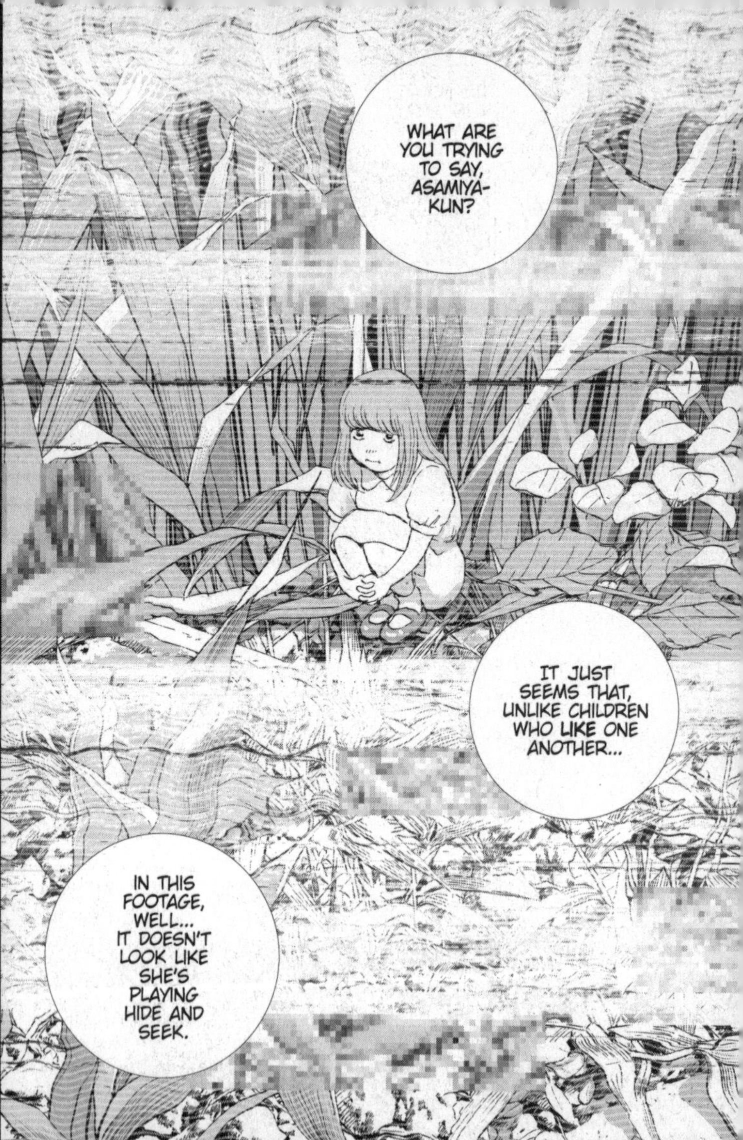
WHAT ARE YOU TRYING TO SAY, ASAMIYA-KUN?
IT JUST SEEMS THAT, UNLIKE CHILDREN WHO LIKE ONE ANOTHER...
IN THIS FOOTAGE, WELL... IT DOESN'T LOOK LIKE SHE'S PLAYING HIDE AND SEEK.

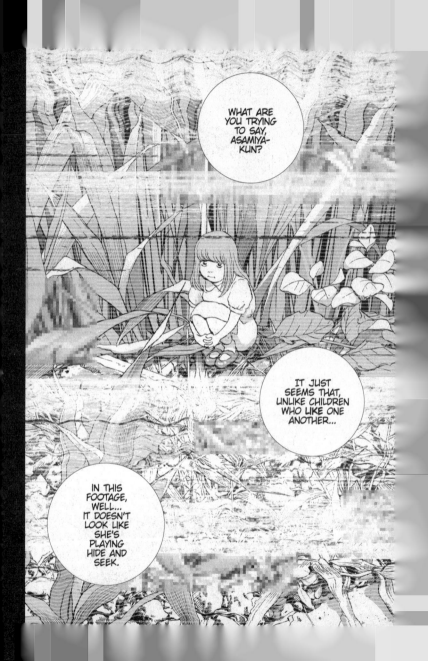

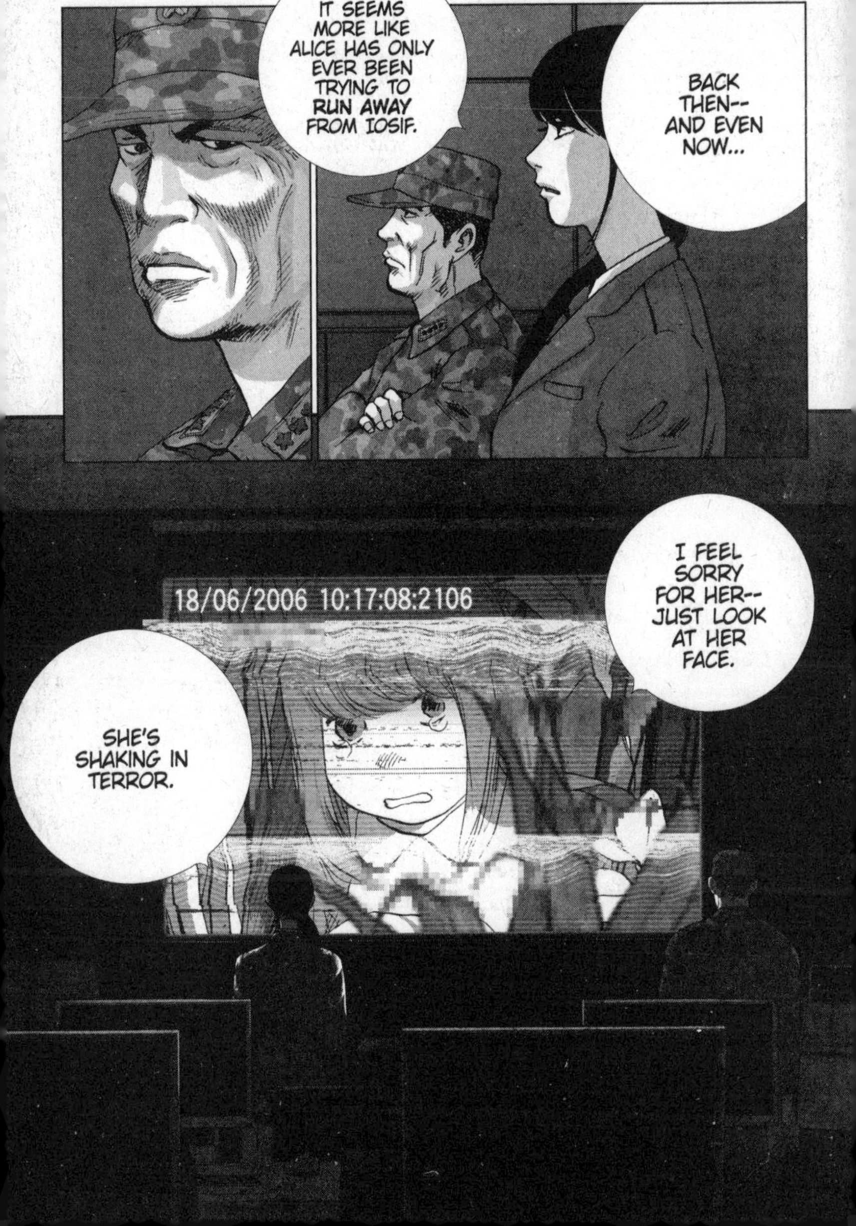
BACK THEN-- AND EVEN NOW...
IT SEEMS MORE LIKE ALICE HAS ONLY EVER BEEN TRYING TO RUN AWAY FROM IOSIF.
18/06/2006 10:17:08:2106
I FEEL SORRY FOR HER-- JUST LOOK AT HER FACE.
SHE'S SHAKING IN TERROR.

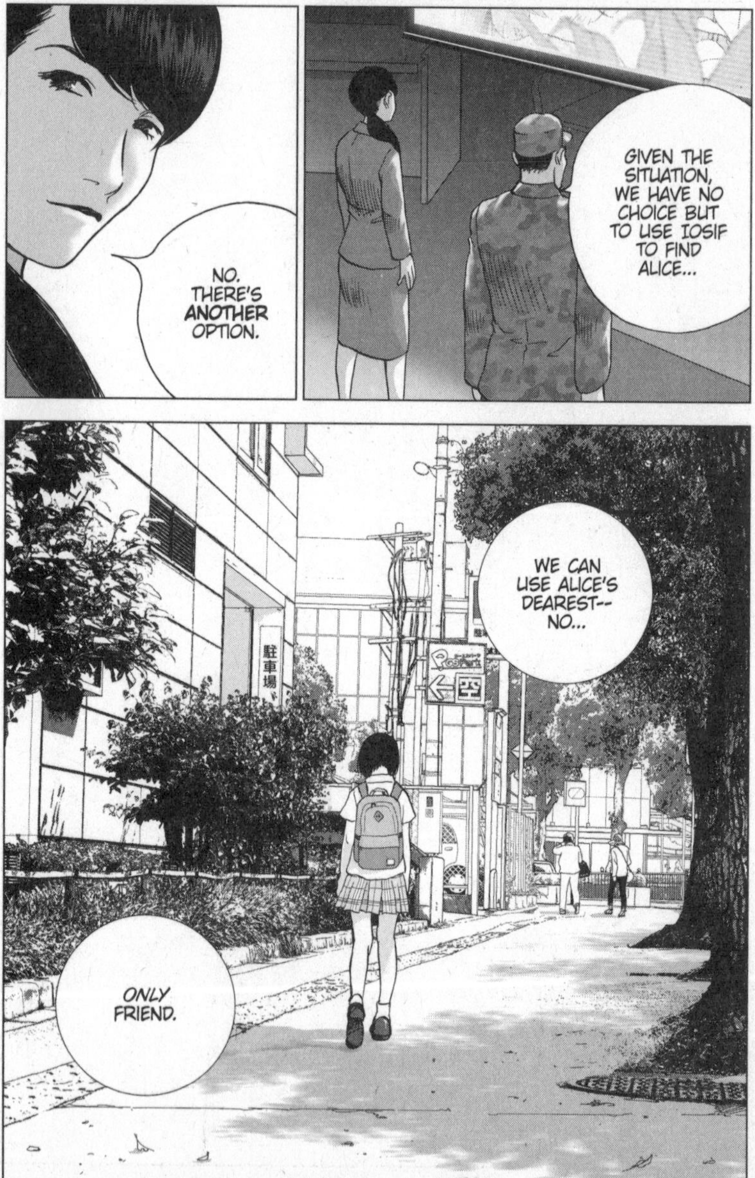
GIVEN THE SITUATION, WE HAVE NO CHOICE BUT TO USE IOSIF TO FIND ALICE...
NO. THERE'S **ANOTHER** OPTION.
駐車場
空
WE CAN USE ALICE'S DEAREST-- NO...
ONLY FRIEND.

Chapter 30: Mass

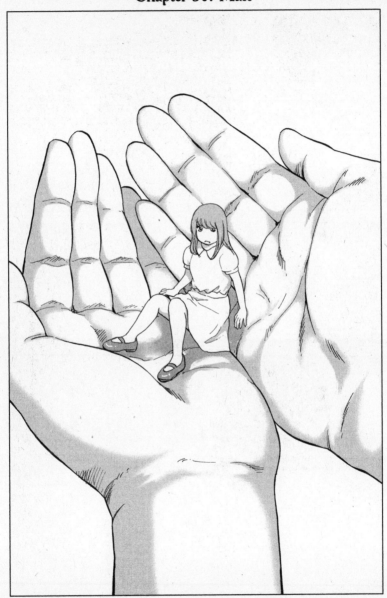

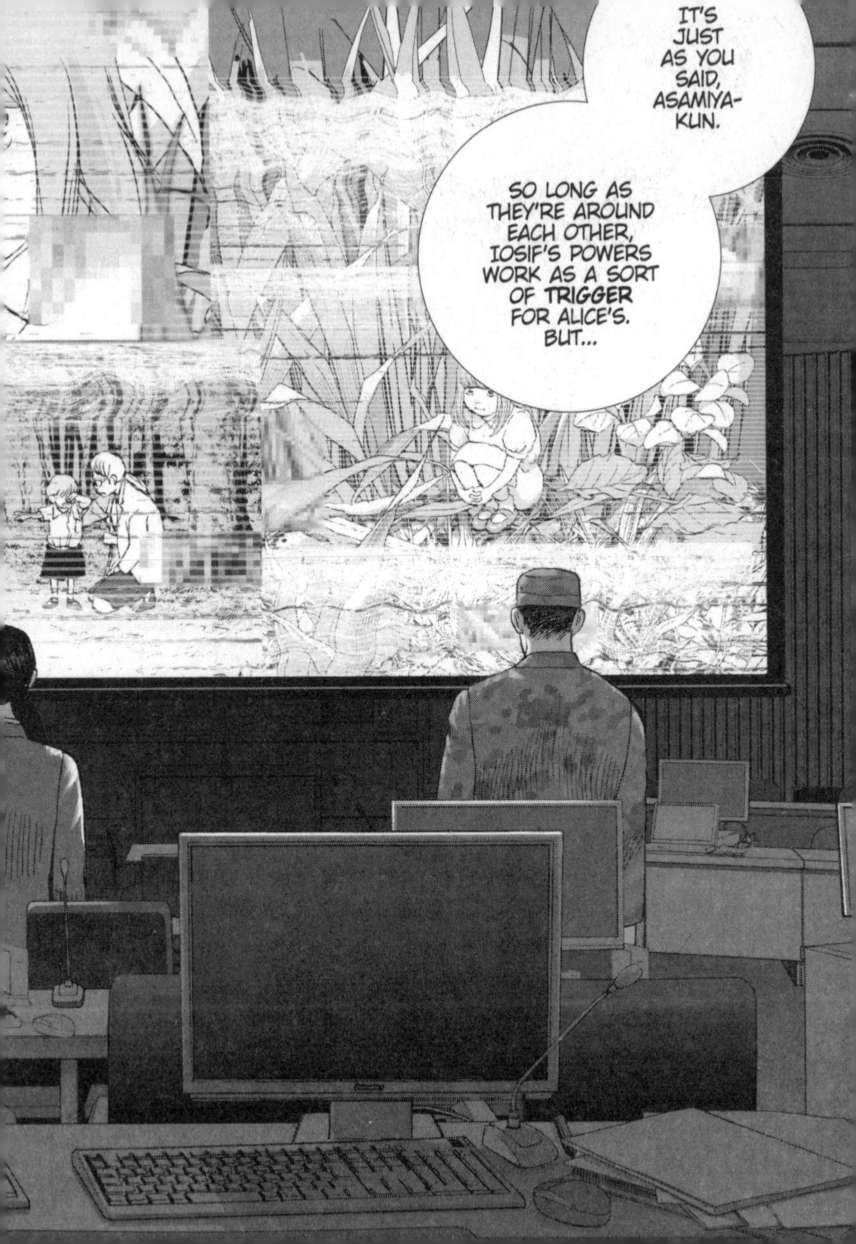
IT'S JUST AS YOU SAID, ASAMIYA-KUN.
SO LONG AS THEY'RE AROUND EACH OTHER, IOSIF'S POWERS WORK AS A SORT OF **TRIGGER** FOR ALICE'S. BUT...

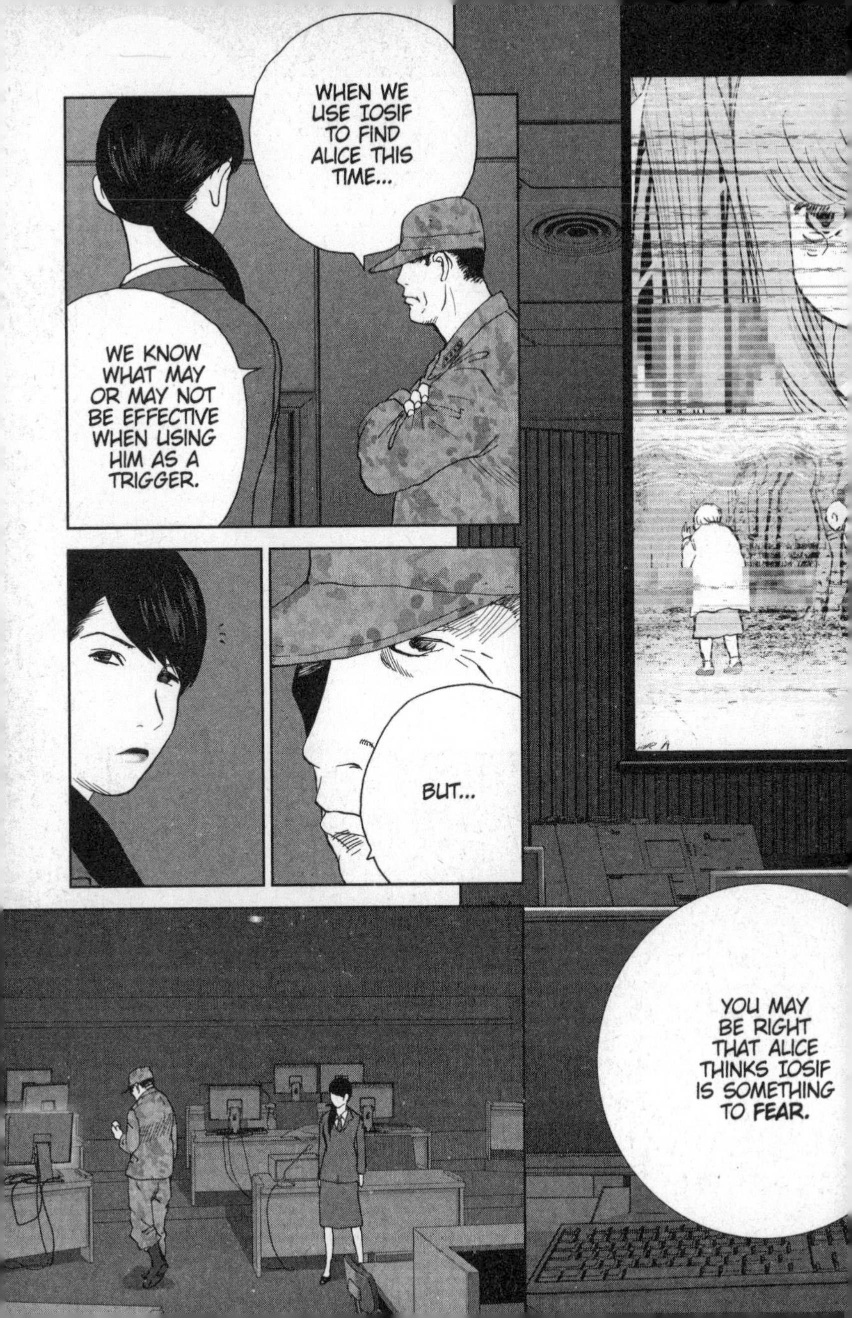
WHEN WE USE IOSIF TO FIND ALICE THIS TIME...
WE KNOW WHAT MAY OR MAY NOT BE EFFECTIVE WHEN USING HIM AS A TRIGGER.
BUT...
YOU MAY BE RIGHT THAT ALICE THINKS IOSIF IS SOMETHING TO FEAR.

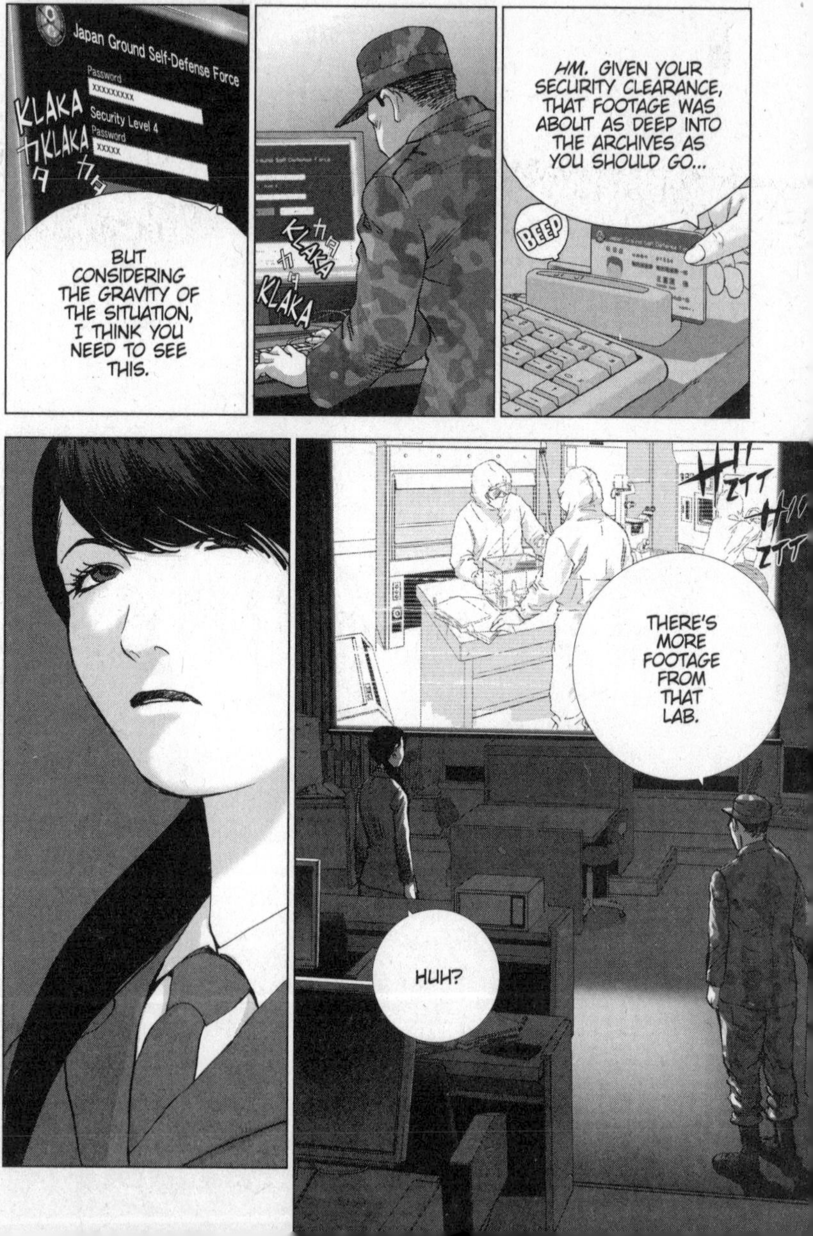
HM. GIVEN YOUR SECURITY CLEARANCE, THAT FOOTAGE WAS ABOUT AS DEEP INTO THE ARCHIVES AS YOU SHOULD GO...
BEEP
KLAKA KLAKA
Japan Ground Self-Defense Force
Password
Security Level 4
Password
KLAKA KLAKA
BUT CONSIDERING THE GRAVITY OF THE SITUATION, I THINK YOU NEED TO SEE THIS.
THERE'S MORE FOOTAGE FROM THAT LAB.
HUH?

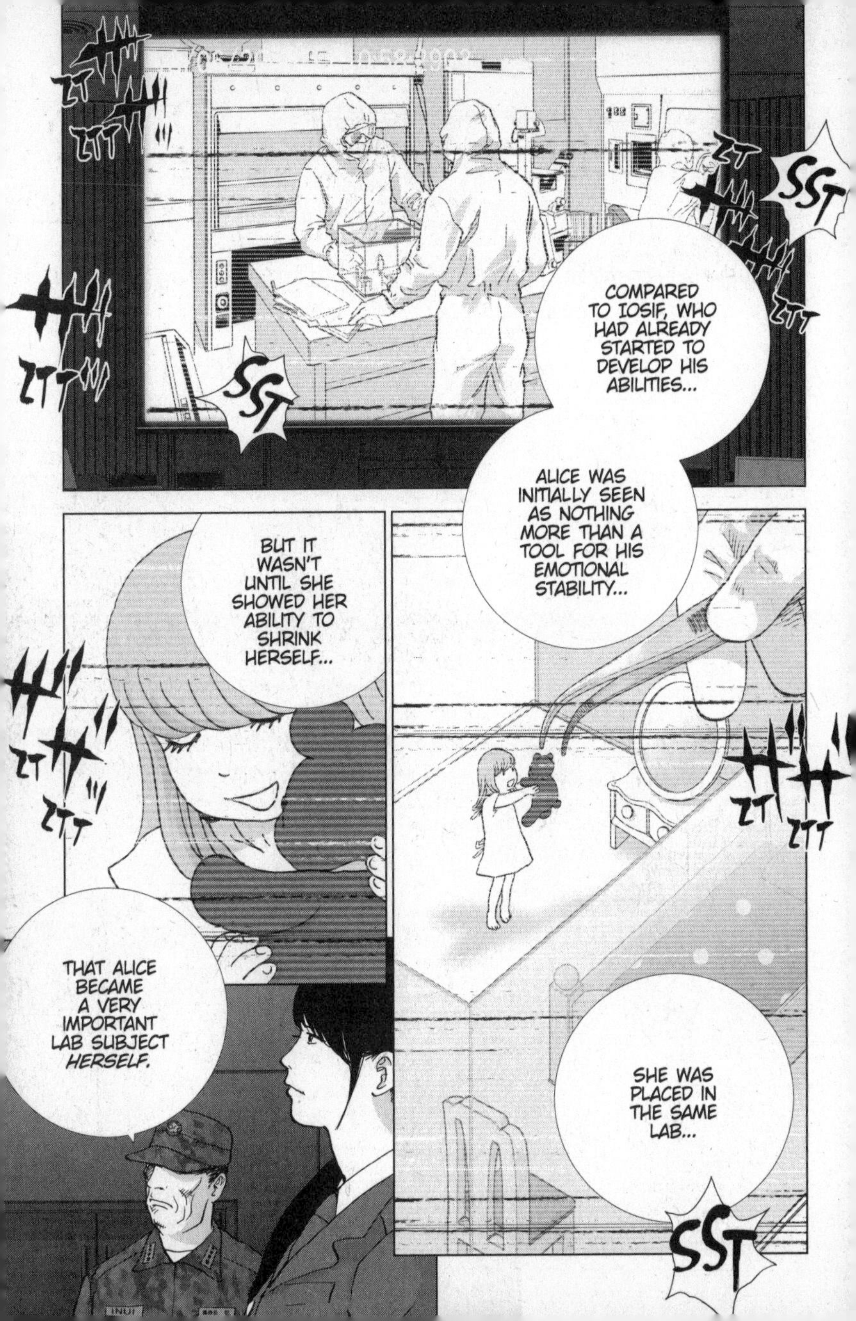
ZT
SST
ZTT
ZT
ZTT
ZTT
SST
COMPARED TO IOSIF, WHO HAD ALREADY STARTED TO DEVELOP HIS ABILITIES...
ALICE WAS INITIALLY SEEN AS NOTHING MORE THAN A TOOL FOR HIS EMOTIONAL STABILITY...
ZT
ZTT
SHE WAS PLACED IN THE SAME LAB...
SST
BUT IT WASN'T UNTIL SHE SHOWED HER ABILITY TO SHRINK HERSELF...
ZT
ZTT
THAT ALICE BECAME A VERY IMPORTANT LAB SUBJECT *HERSELF.*

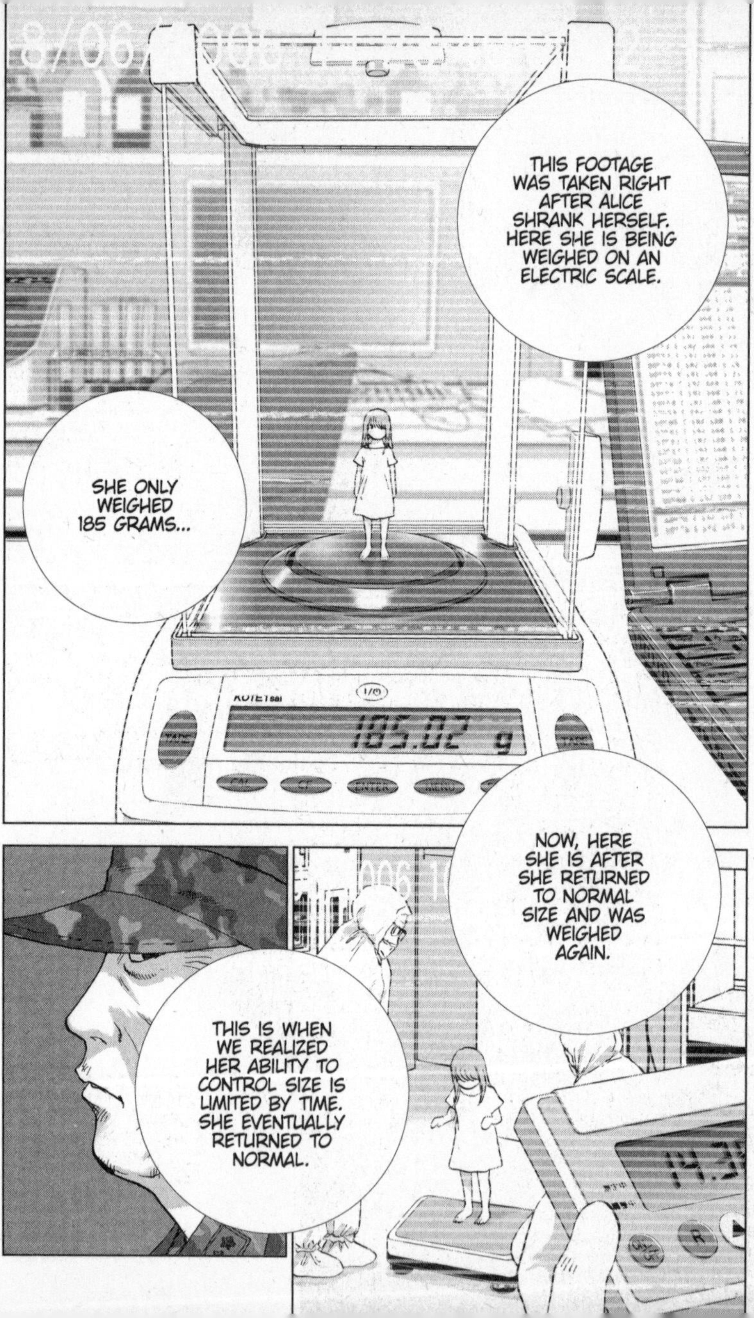
THIS FOOTAGE WAS TAKEN RIGHT AFTER ALICE SHRANK HERSELF. HERE SHE IS BEING WEIGHED ON AN ELECTRIC SCALE.
SHE ONLY WEIGHED 185 GRAMS...
185.02 g
NOW, HERE SHE IS AFTER SHE RETURNED TO NORMAL SIZE AND WAS WEIGHED AGAIN.
THIS IS WHEN WE REALIZED HER ABILITY TO CONTROL SIZE IS LIMITED BY TIME. SHE EVENTUALLY RETURNED TO NORMAL.

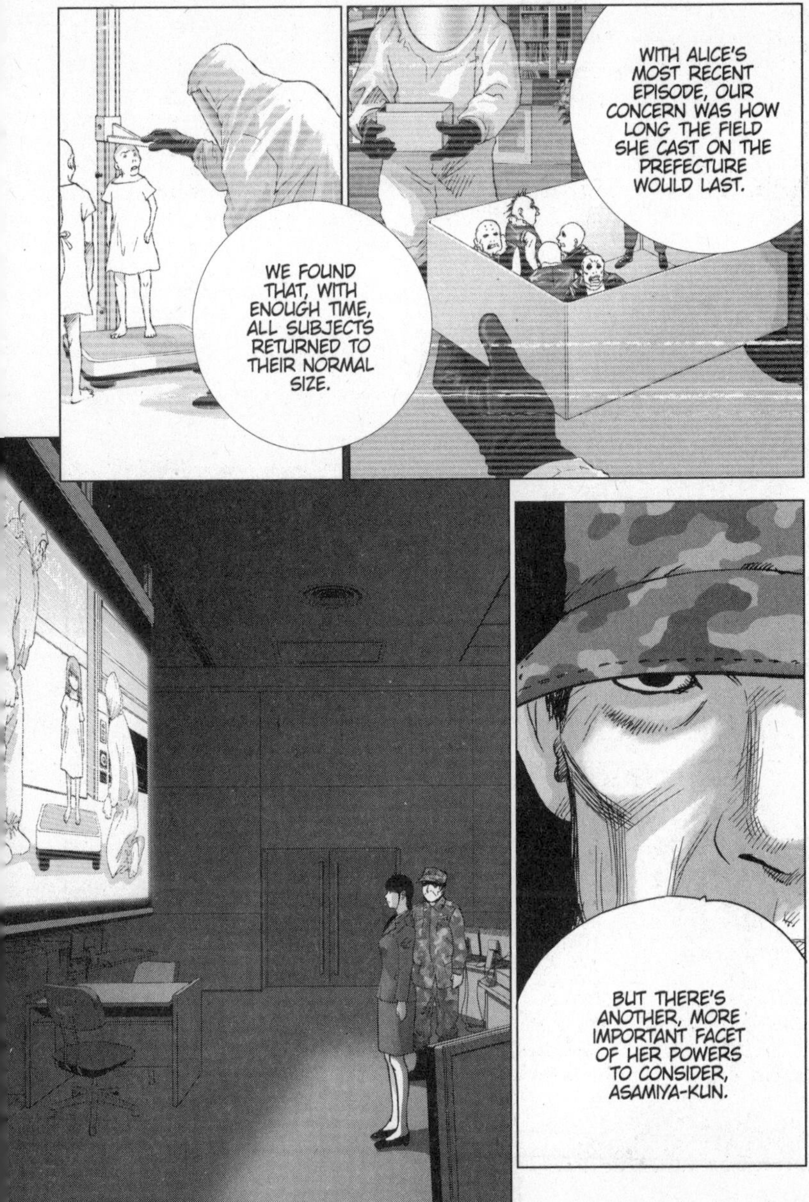
WITH ALICE'S MOST RECENT EPISODE, OUR CONCERN WAS HOW LONG THE FIELD SHE CAST ON THE PREFECTURE WOULD LAST.
WE FOUND THAT, WITH ENOUGH TIME, ALL SUBJECTS RETURNED TO THEIR NORMAL SIZE.
BUT THERE'S ANOTHER, MORE IMPORTANT FACET OF HER POWERS TO CONSIDER, ASAMIYA-KUN.

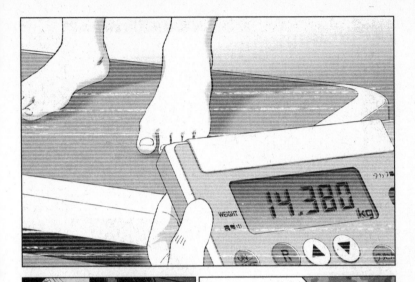

DO YOU
UNDERSTAND
THE LAW OF
CONSERVATION
OF MASS?

YES...

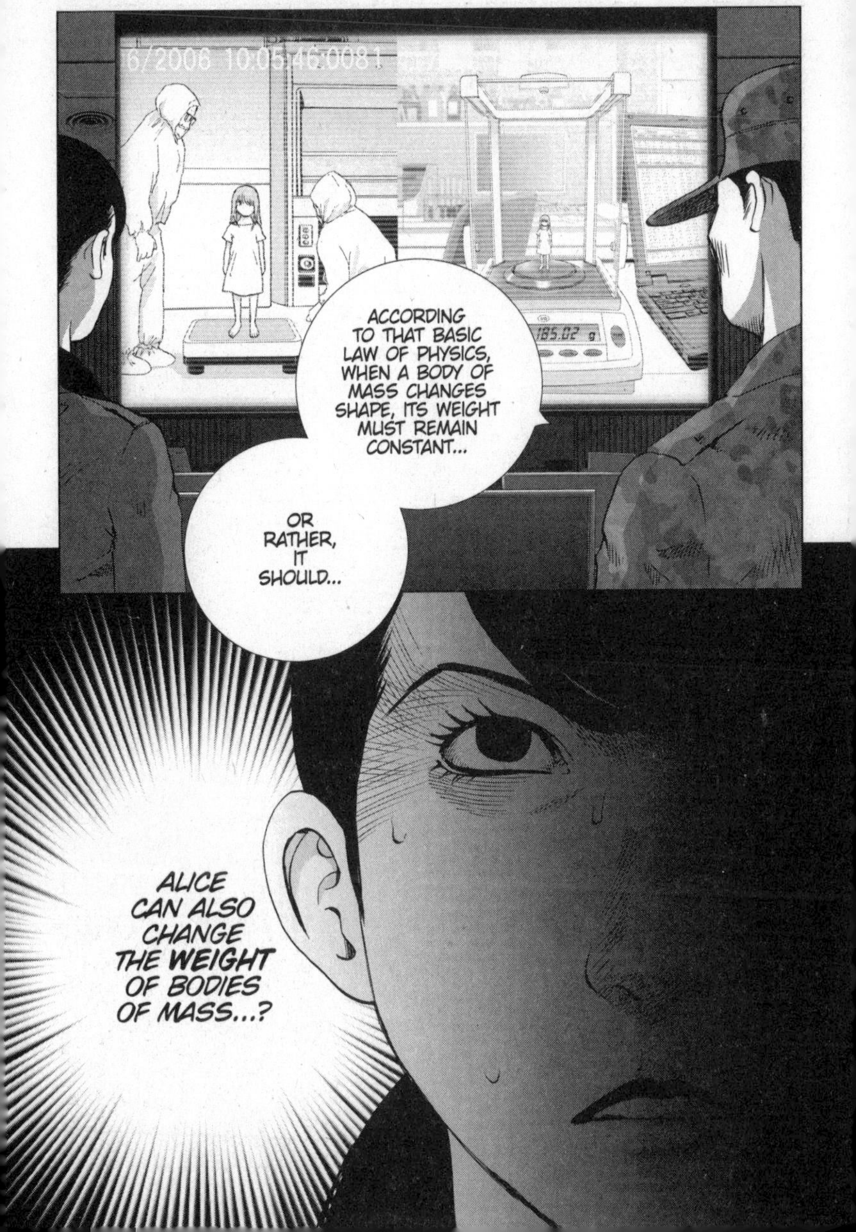
6/2006 10:05:46:0081
185.02 g
ACCORDING TO THAT BASIC LAW OF PHYSICS, WHEN A BODY OF MASS CHANGES SHAPE, ITS WEIGHT MUST REMAIN CONSTANT...
OR RATHER, IT SHOULD...
ALICE CAN ALSO CHANGE THE WEIGHT OF BODIES OF MASS...?

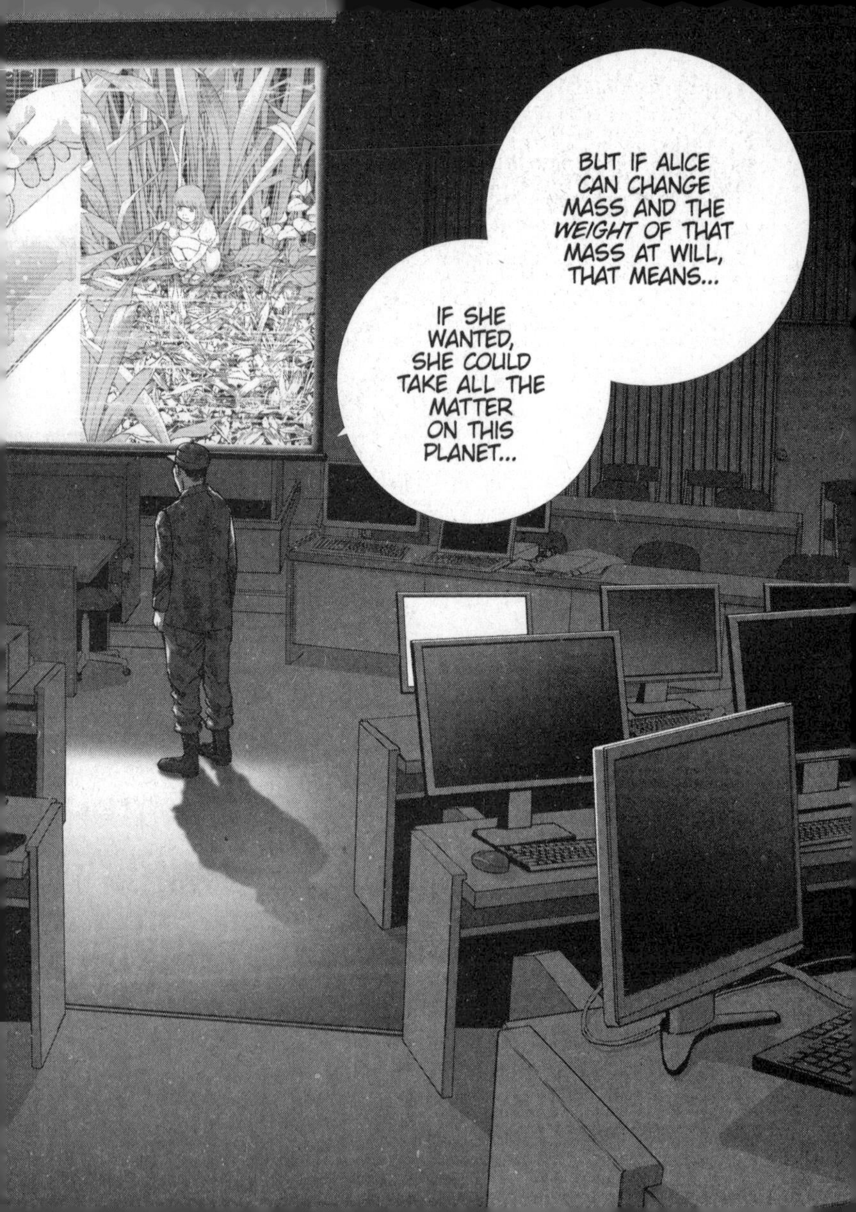
BUT IF ALICE CAN CHANGE MASS AND THE *WEIGHT* OF THAT MASS AT WILL, THAT MEANS...
IF SHE WANTED, SHE COULD TAKE ALL THE MATTER ON THIS PLANET...

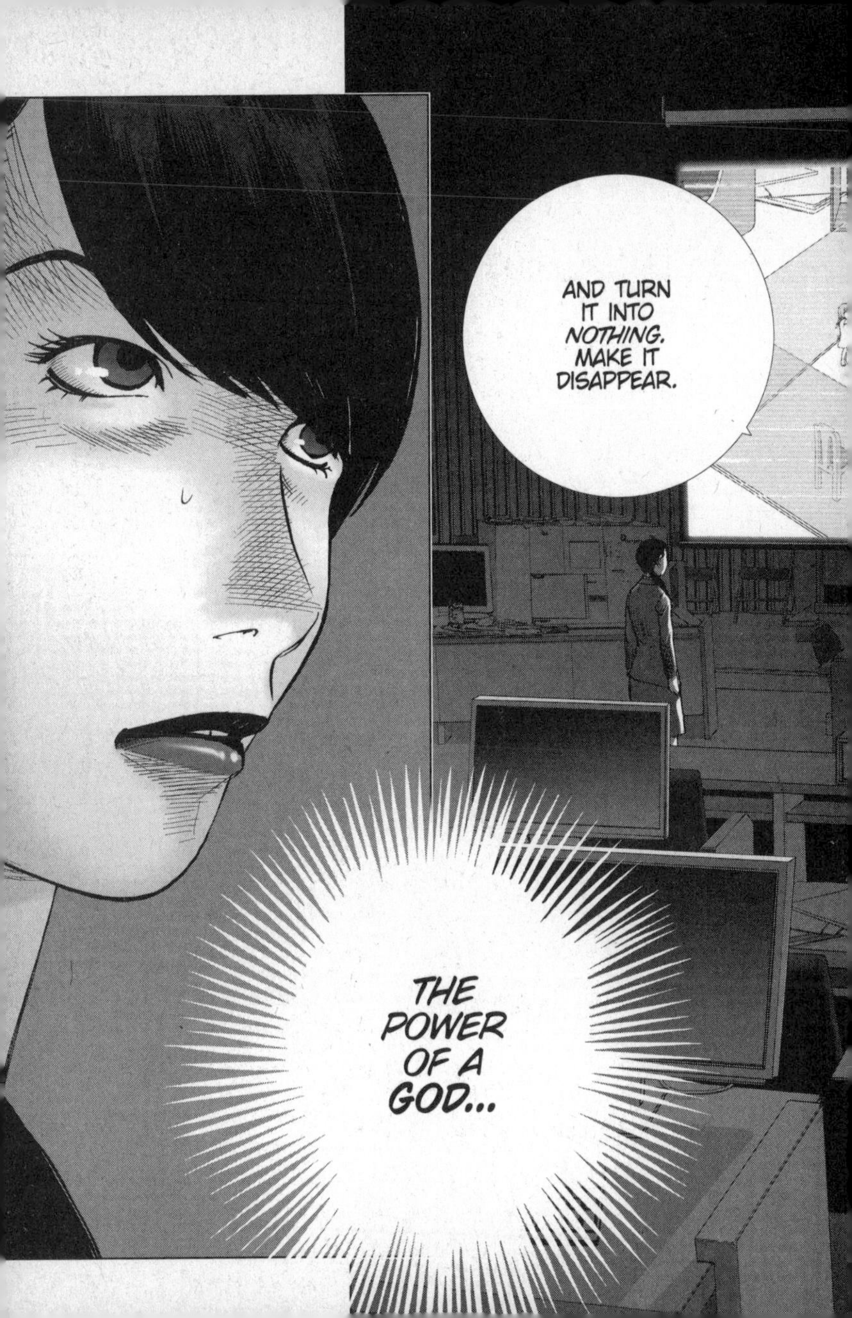
AND TURN IT INTO *NOTHING.* MAKE IT DISAPPEAR.
THE POWER OF A GOD...

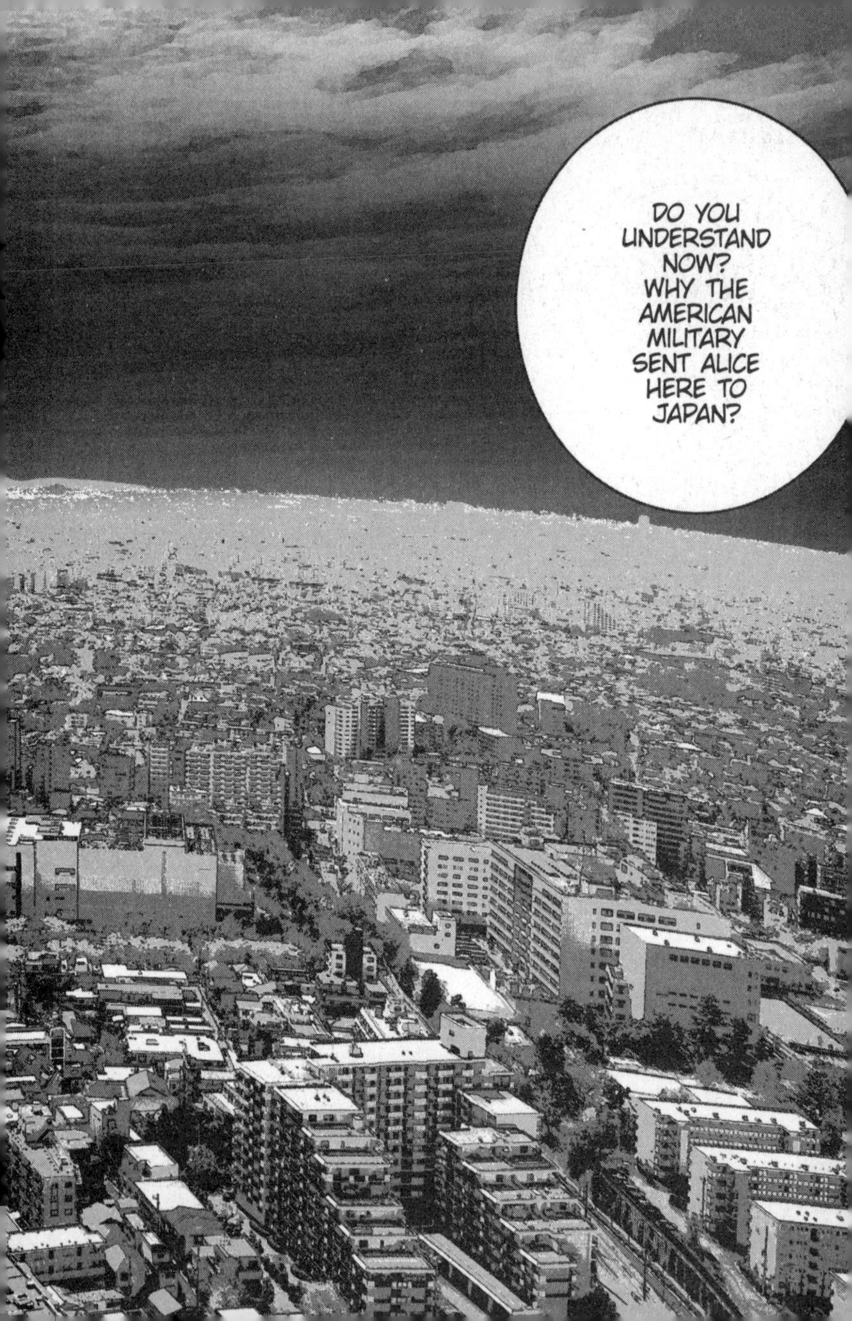
DO YOU UNDERSTAND NOW? WHY THE AMERICAN MILITARY SENT ALICE HERE TO JAPAN?

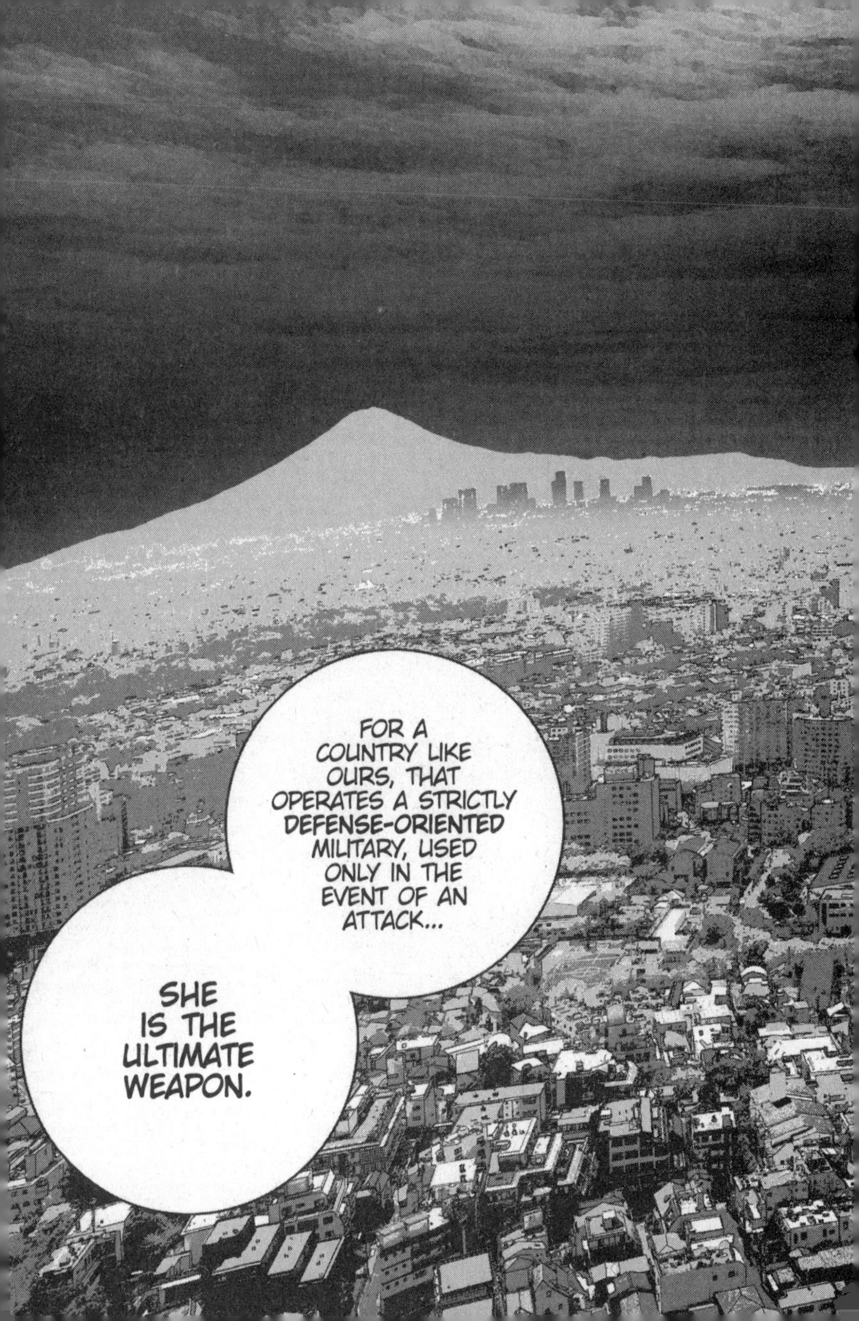
FOR A COUNTRY LIKE OURS, THAT OPERATES A STRICTLY DEFENSE-ORIENTED MILITARY, USED ONLY IN THE EVENT OF AN ATTACK...
SHE IS THE ULTIMATE WEAPON.

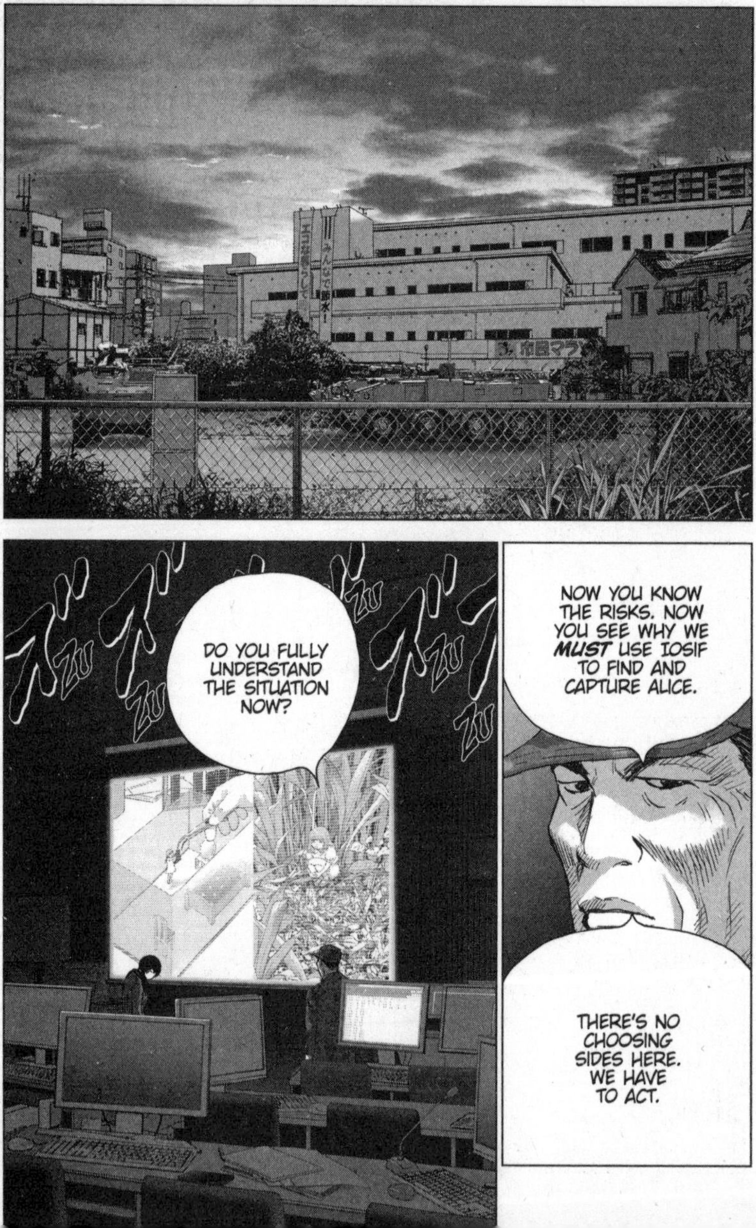
ZU ZU ZU ZU ZU
DO YOU FULLY UNDERSTAND THE SITUATION NOW?
NOW YOU KNOW THE RISKS. NOW YOU SEE WHY WE MUST USE IOSIF TO FIND AND CAPTURE ALICE.
THERE'S NO CHOOSING SIDES HERE. WE HAVE TO ACT.

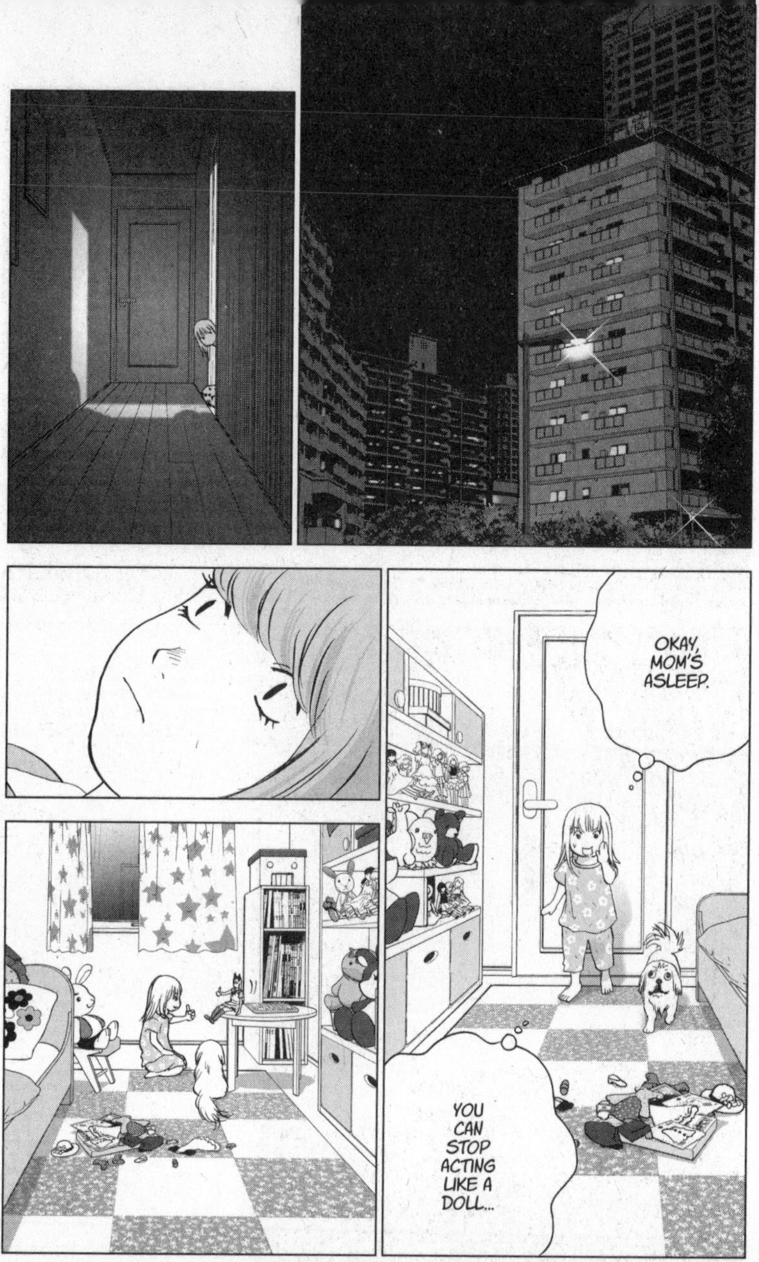
OKAY, MOM'S ASLEEP.
YOU CAN STOP ACTING LIKE A DOLL...

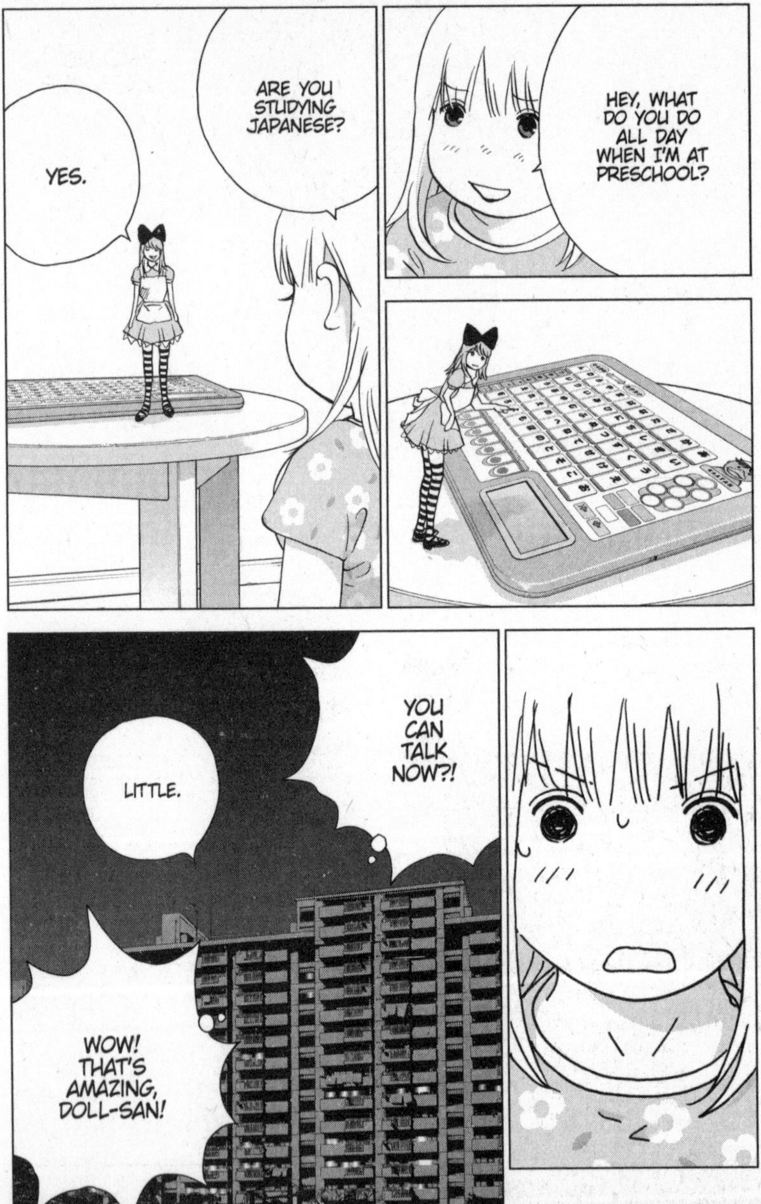
HEY, WHAT DO YOU DO ALL DAY WHEN I'M AT PRESCHOOL?
ARE YOU STUDYING JAPANESE?
YES.
YOU CAN TALK NOW?!
LITTLE.
WOW! THAT'S AMAZING, DOLL-SAN!

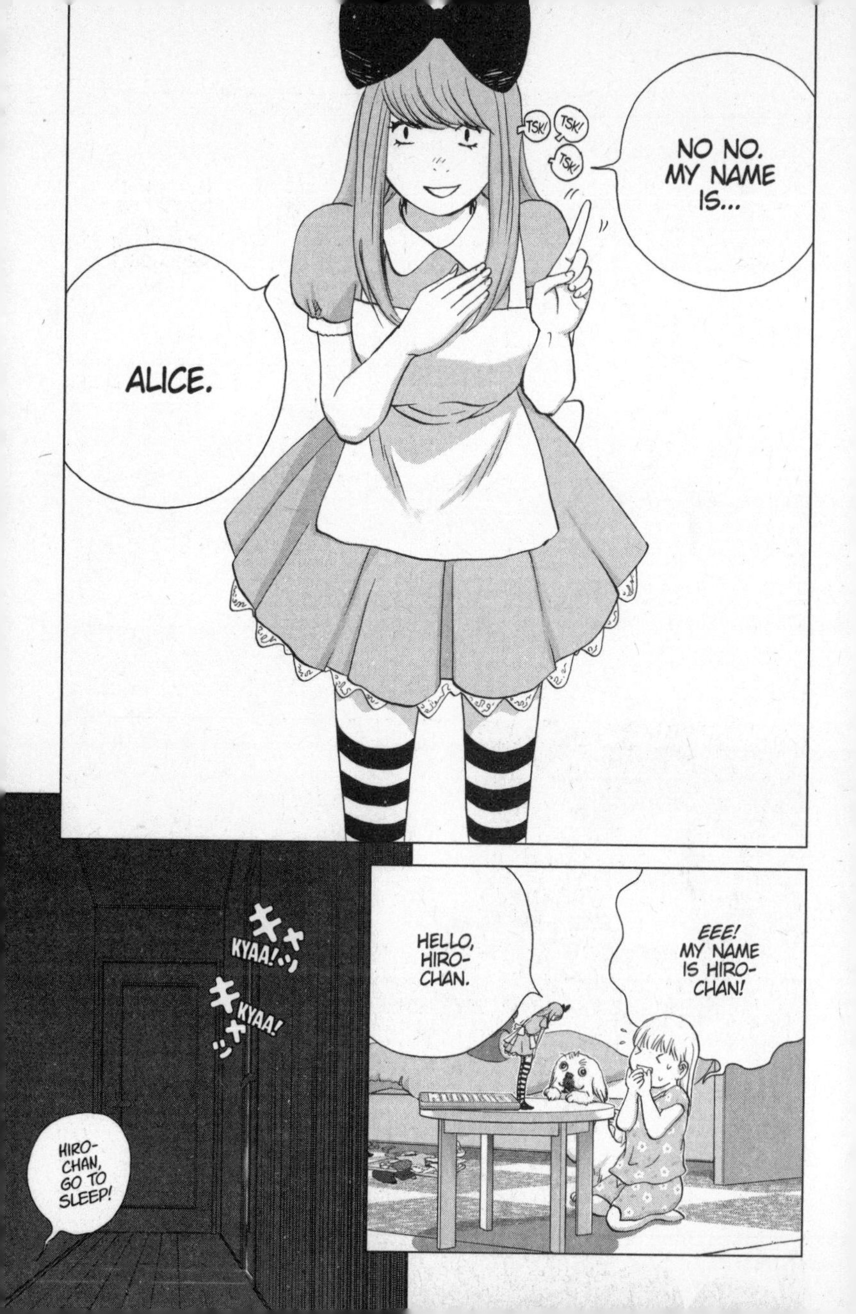
TSK!
TSK!
TSK!
NO NO. MY NAME IS...
ALICE.
EEE! MY NAME IS HIRO-CHAN!
HELLO, HIRO-CHAN.
キャッ KYAA!
キャッ KYAA!
HIRO-CHAN, GO TO SLEEP!

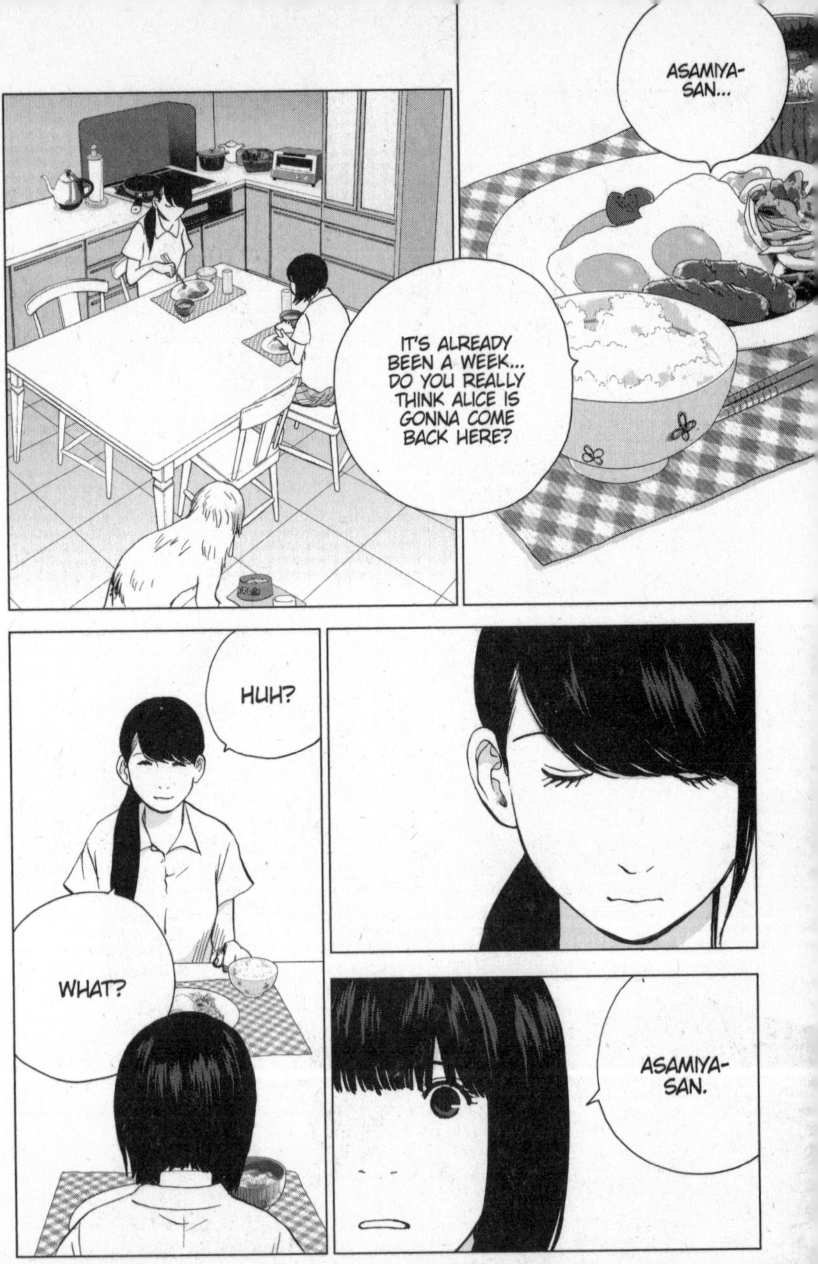
ASAMIYA-SAN...
IT'S ALREADY BEEN A WEEK... DO YOU REALLY THINK ALICE IS GONNA COME BACK HERE?
ASAMIYA-SAN.
HUH?
WHAT?

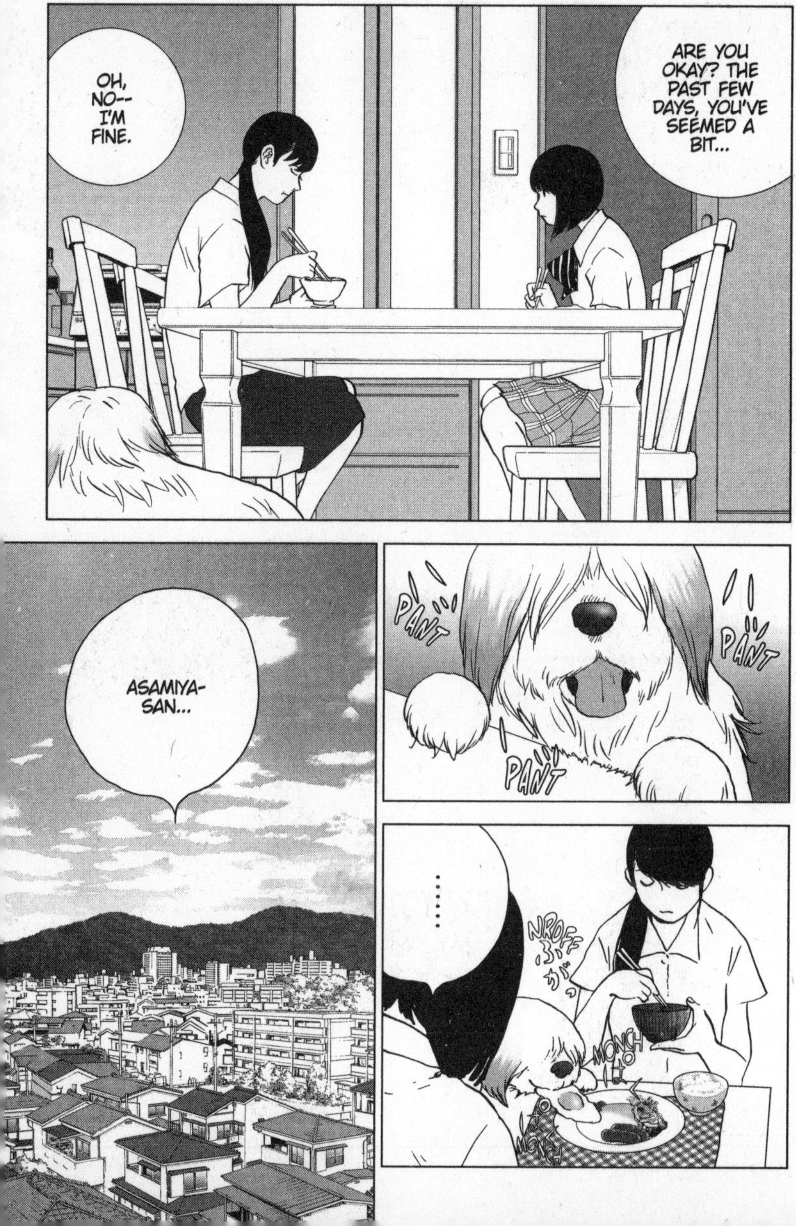
ARE YOU OKAY? THE PAST FEW DAYS, YOU'VE SEEMED A BIT...
OH, NO-- I'M FINE.
PANT
PANT
PANT
......
NROFF
MONCH
MONCH
ASAMIYA-SAN...

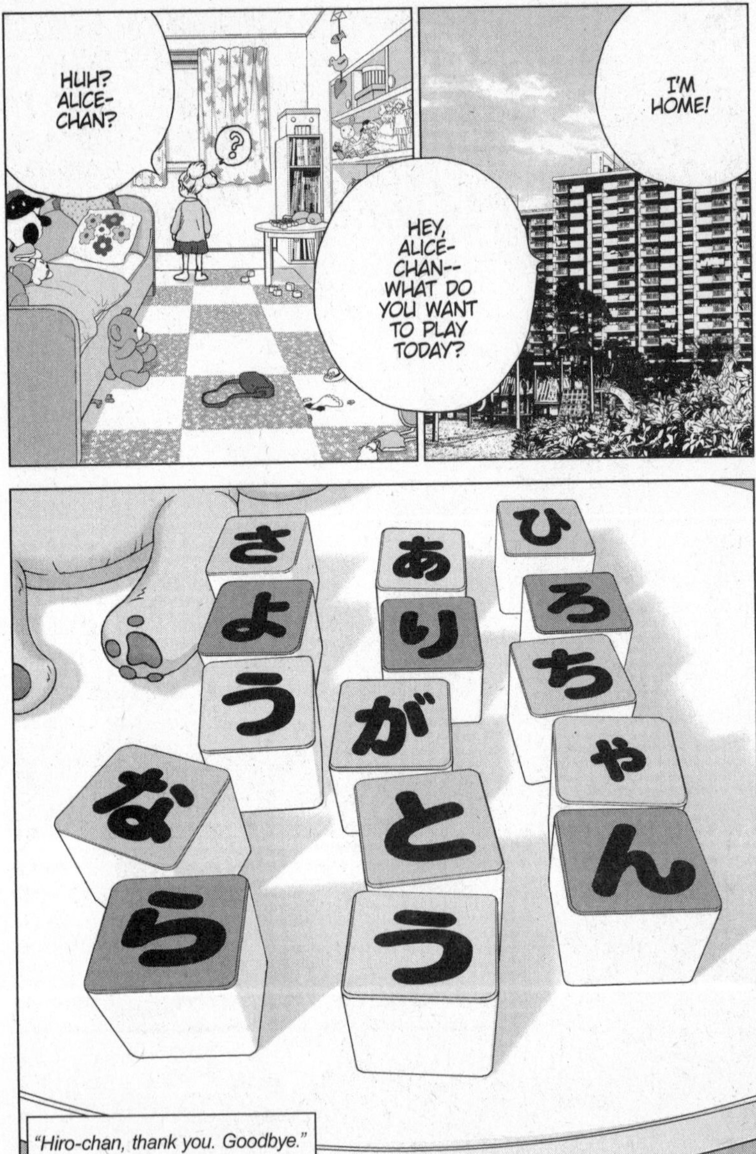
I'M HOME!
HEY, ALICE-CHAN-- WHAT DO YOU WANT TO PLAY TODAY?
HUH? ALICE-CHAN?
ひろちゃん
ありがとう
さようなら
"Hiro-chan, thank you. Goodbye."

Chapter 31: The Tiny Gifted Ones

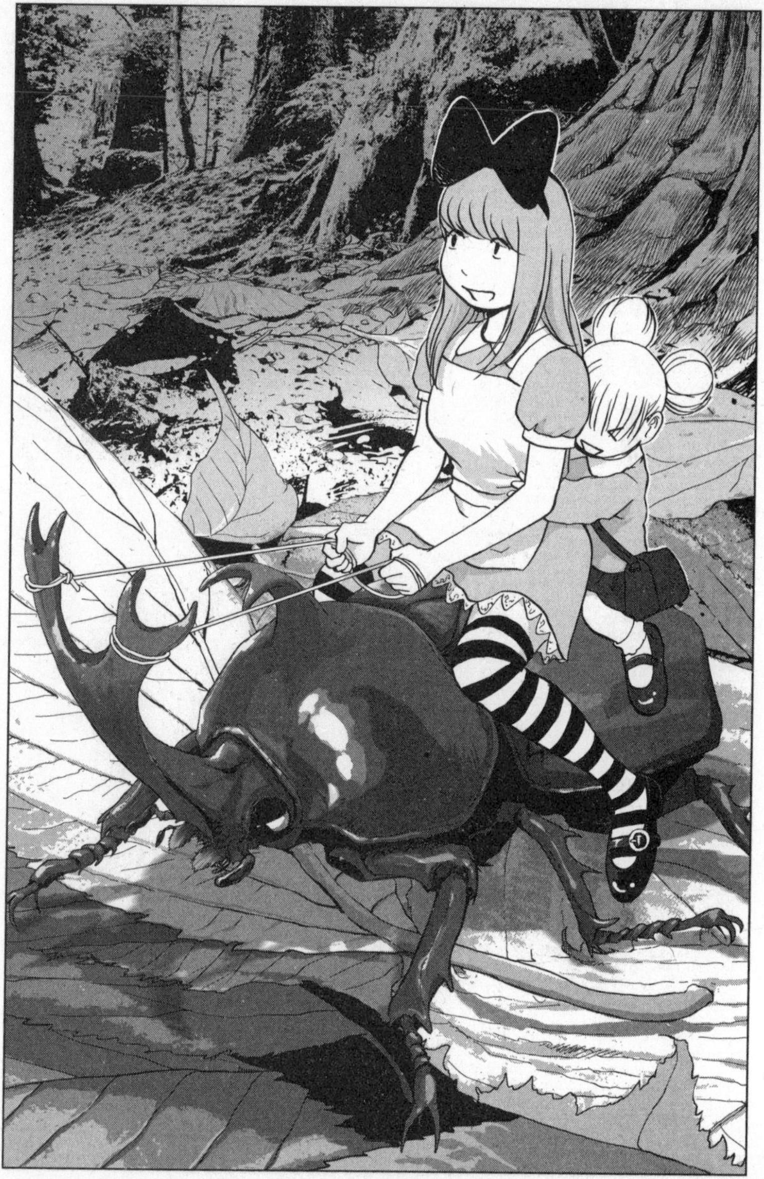

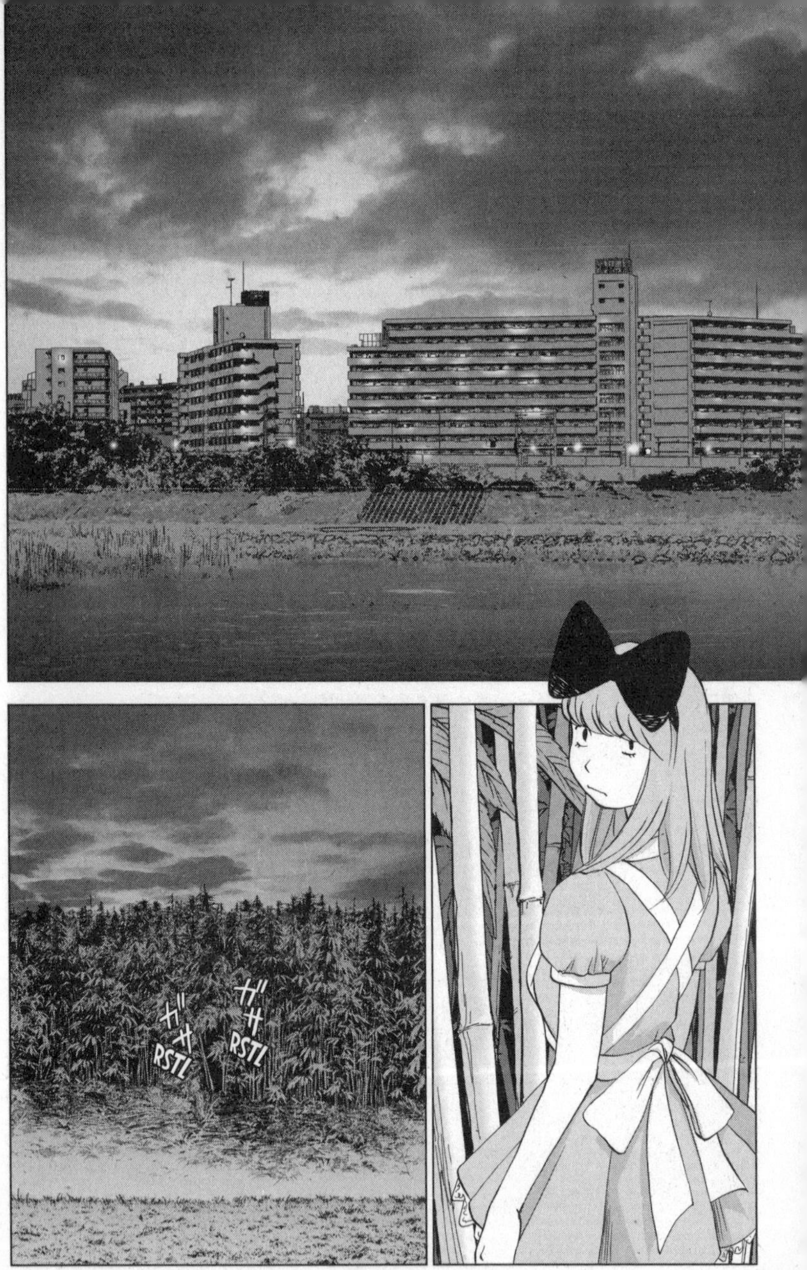
ガサ
RSTL
ガサ
RSTL

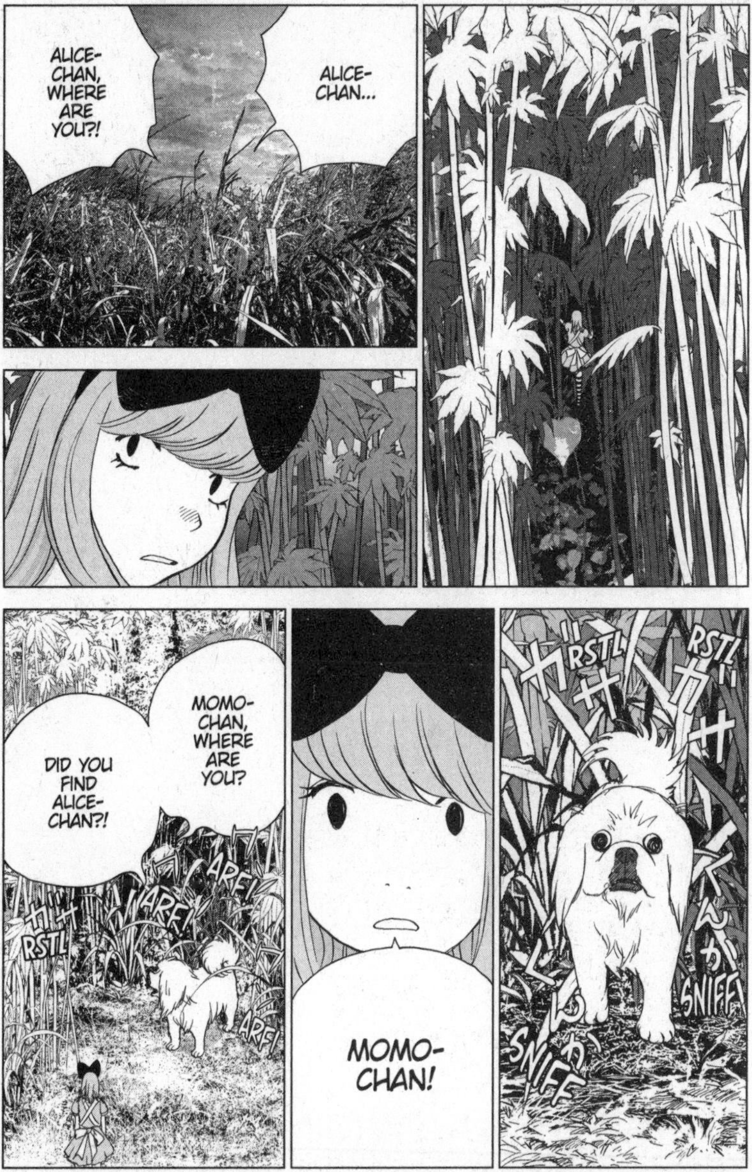
ALICE-CHAN...
ALICE-CHAN, WHERE ARE YOU?!
RSTL
RSTL
SNIFF
SNIFF
MOMO-CHAN!
MOMO-CHAN, WHERE ARE YOU?
DID YOU FIND ALICE-CHAN?!
ARF!
ARF!
ARF!
RSTL

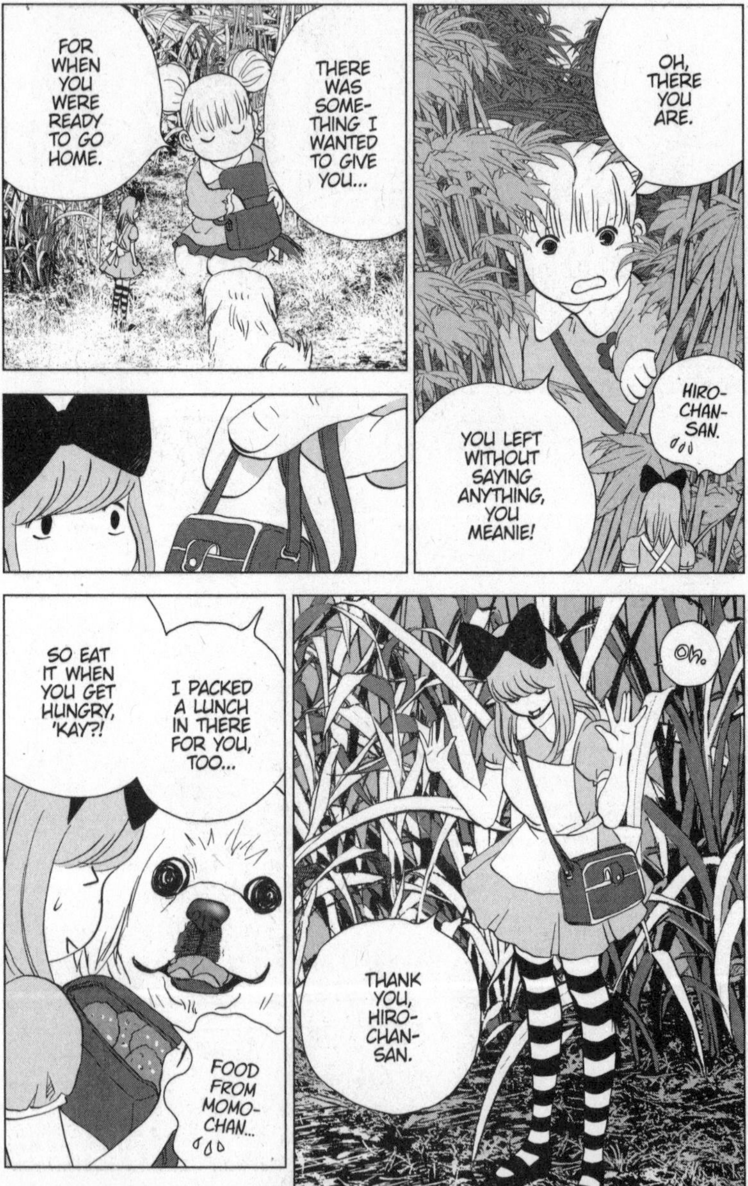
OH, THERE YOU ARE.
HIRO-CHAN-SAN.
YOU LEFT WITHOUT SAYING ANYTHING, YOU MEANIE!
THERE WAS SOME-THING I WANTED TO GIVE YOU...
FOR WHEN YOU WERE READY TO GO HOME.
Oh.
THANK YOU, HIRO-CHAN-SAN.
I PACKED A LUNCH IN THERE FOR YOU, TOO...
SO EAT IT WHEN YOU GET HUNGRY, 'KAY?!
FOOD FROM MOMO-CHAN...

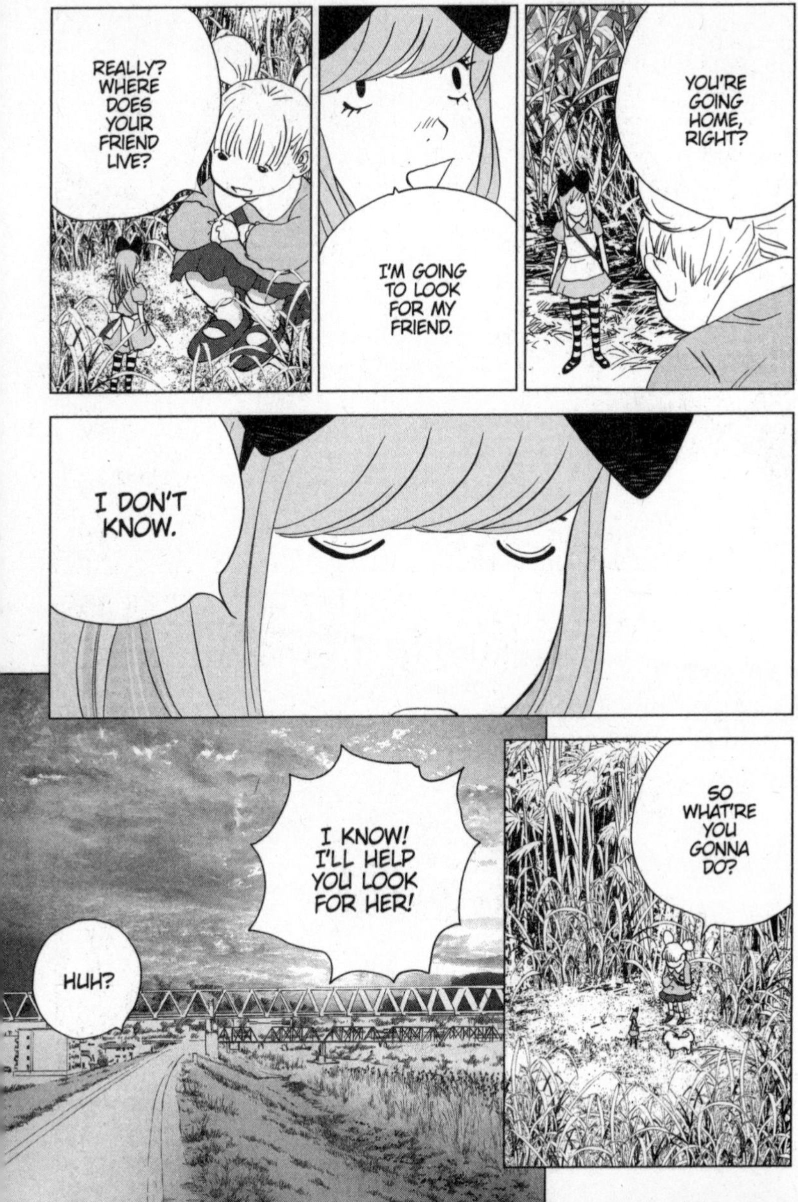
YOU'RE GOING HOME, RIGHT?
I'M GOING TO LOOK FOR MY FRIEND.
REALLY? WHERE DOES YOUR FRIEND LIVE?
I DON'T KNOW.
SO WHAT'RE YOU GONNA DO?
I KNOW! I'LL HELP YOU LOOK FOR HER!
HUH?

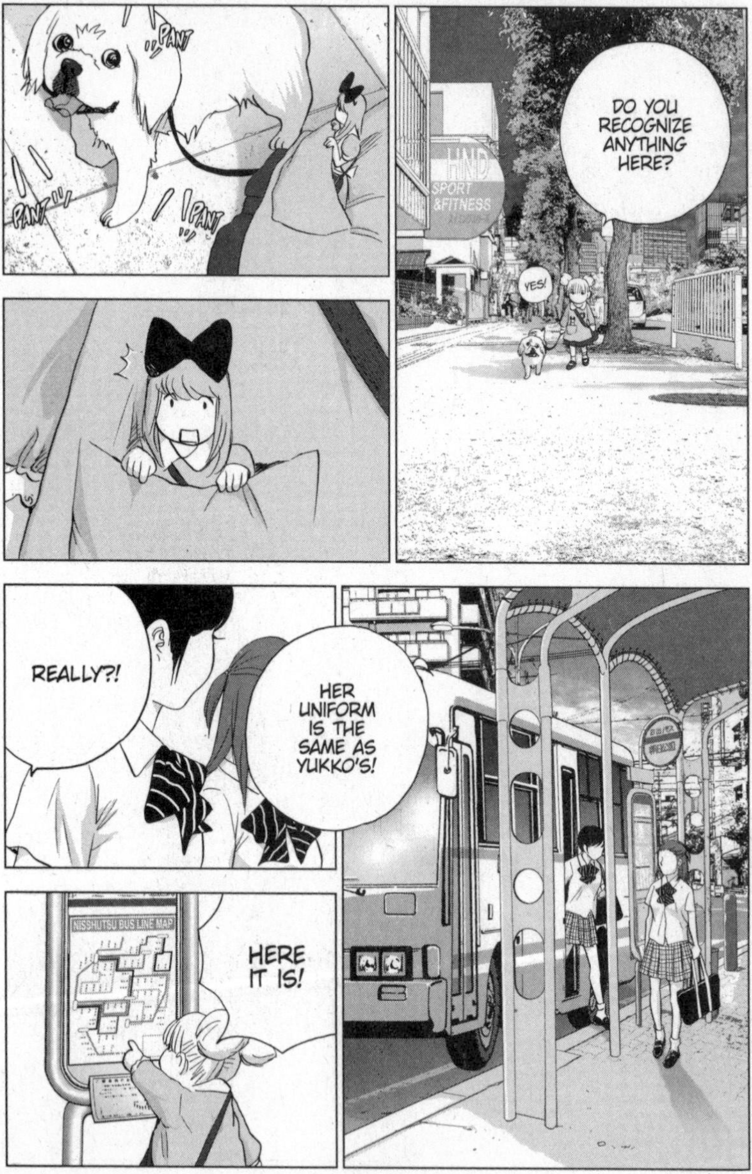
DO YOU RECOGNIZE ANYTHING HERE?
YES!
HND
SPORT &FITNESS
PANT
PANT
PANT
PANT
HER UNIFORM IS THE SAME AS YUKKO'S!
REALLY?!
NISSHUTSU BUS LINE MAP
HERE IT IS!

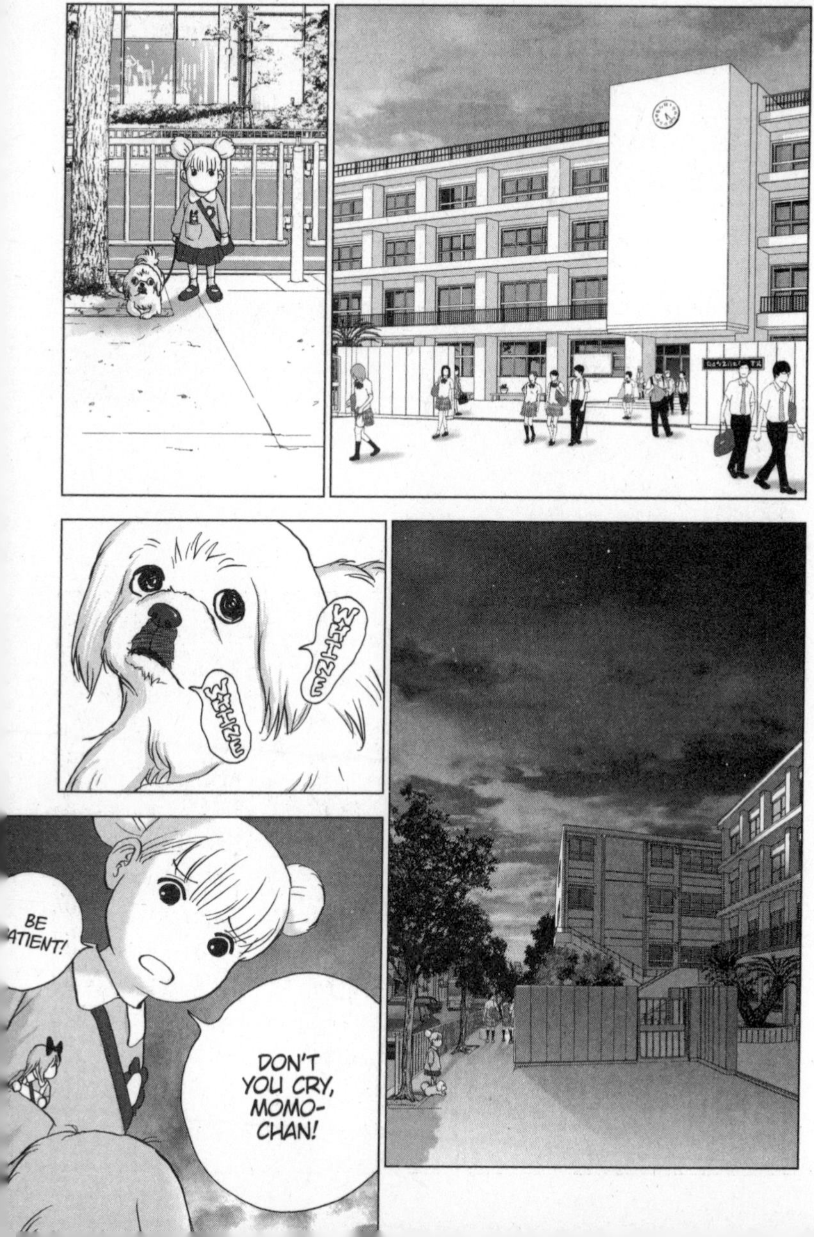
WHINE
WHINE
DON'T YOU CRY, MOMO-CHAN!
BE ATIENT!

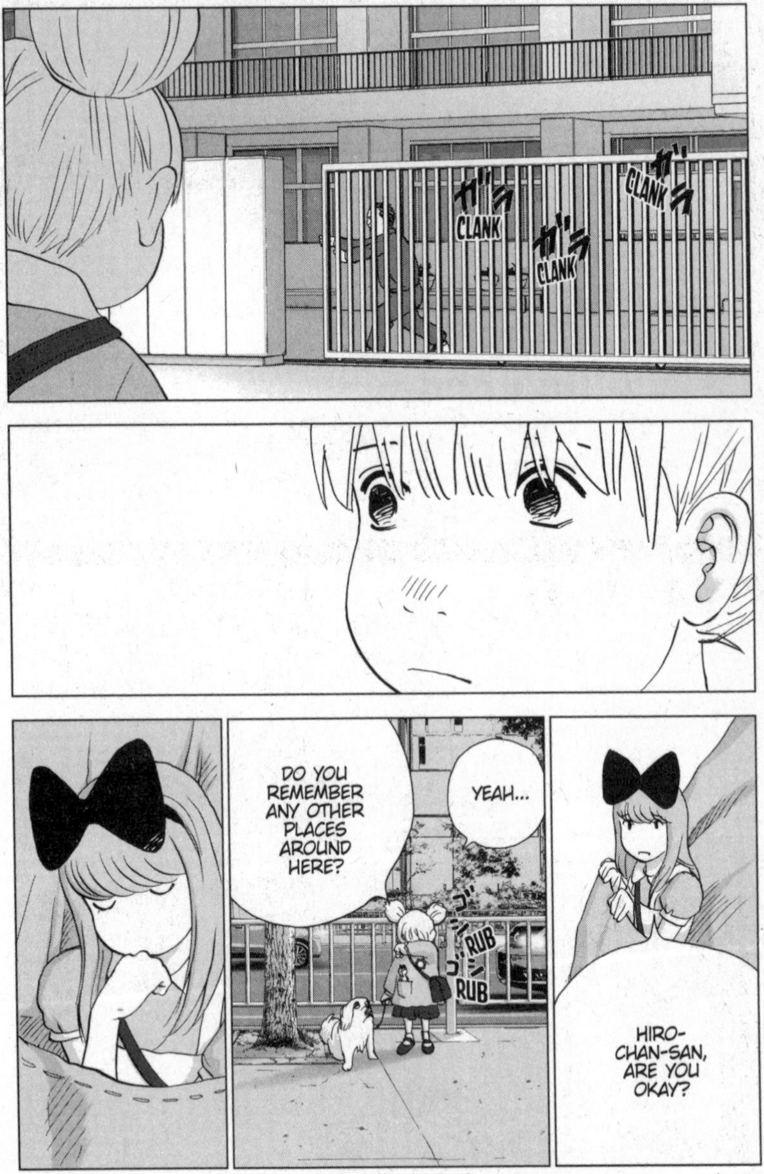
CLANK
CLANK
CLANK
HIRO-CHAN-SAN, ARE YOU OKAY?
YEAH...
DO YOU REMEMBER ANY OTHER PLACES AROUND HERE?
RUB
RUB

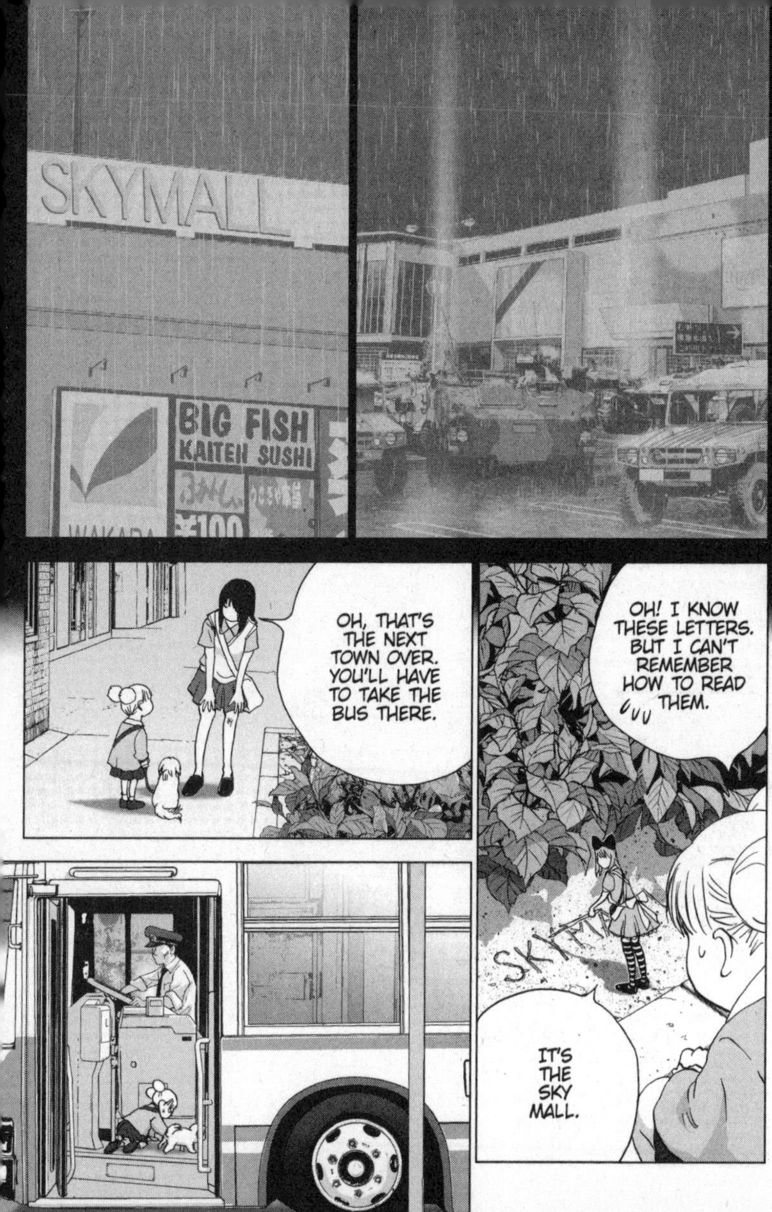

SKYMALL
BIG FISH
KAITEN SUSHI
¥100
OH! I KNOW THESE LETTERS. BUT I CAN'T REMEMBER HOW TO READ THEM.
UUU
IT'S THE SKY MALL.
OH, THAT'S THE NEXT TOWN OVER. YOU'LL HAVE TO TAKE THE BUS THERE.

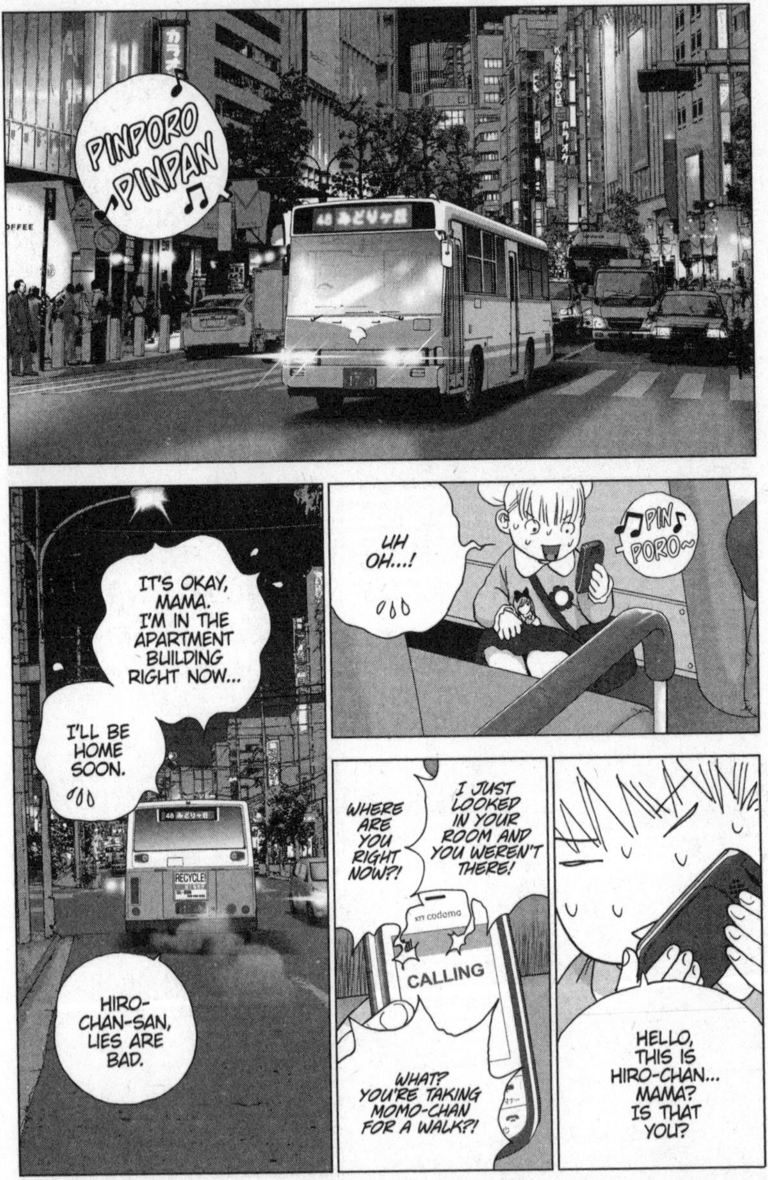
PINPORO PINPAN
UH OH...!
PIN PORO~
HELLO, THIS IS HIRO-CHAN... MAMA? IS THAT YOU?
I JUST LOOKED IN YOUR ROOM AND YOU WEREN'T THERE!
WHERE ARE YOU RIGHT NOW?!
CALLING
WHAT? YOU'RE TAKING MOMO-CHAN FOR A WALK?!
IT'S OKAY, MAMA. I'M IN THE APARTMENT BUILDING RIGHT NOW...
I'LL BE HOME SOON.
RECYCLE!
HIRO-CHAN-SAN, LIES ARE BAD.

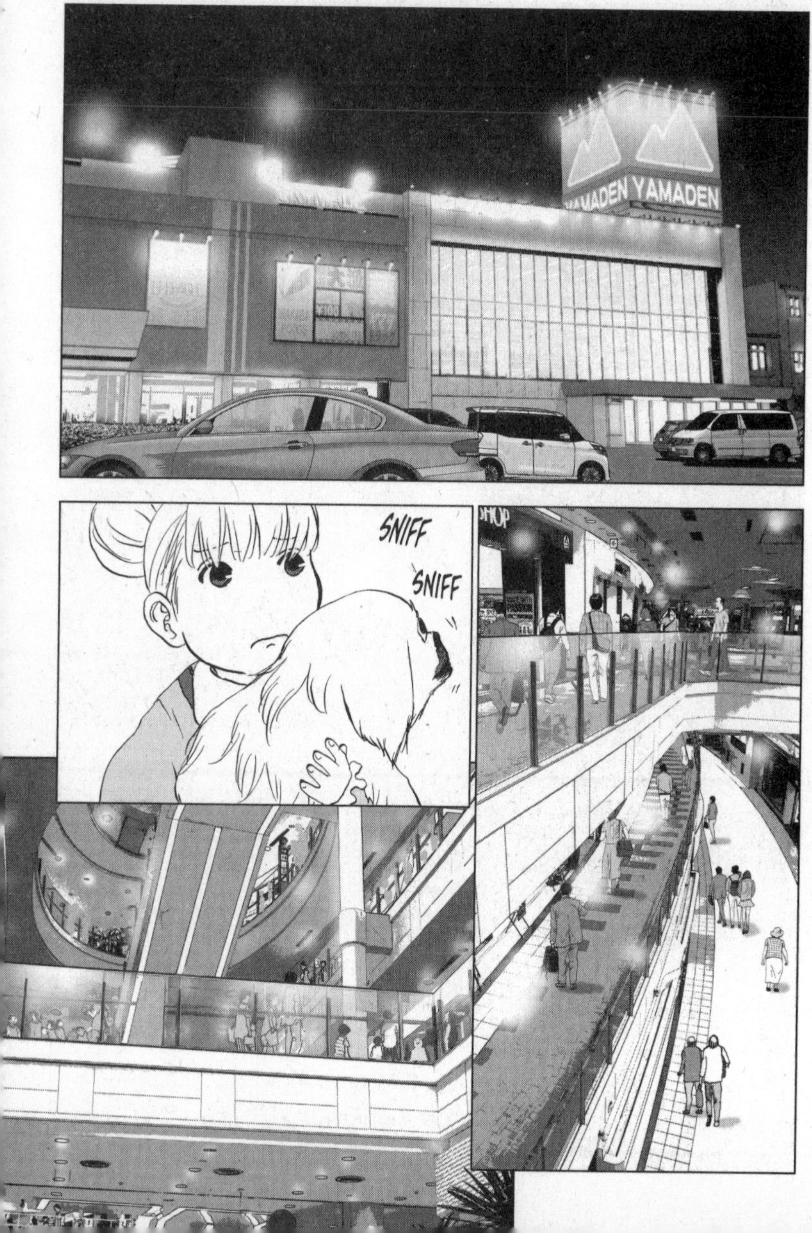
YAMADEN YAMADEN
SHOP
SNIFF
SNIFF

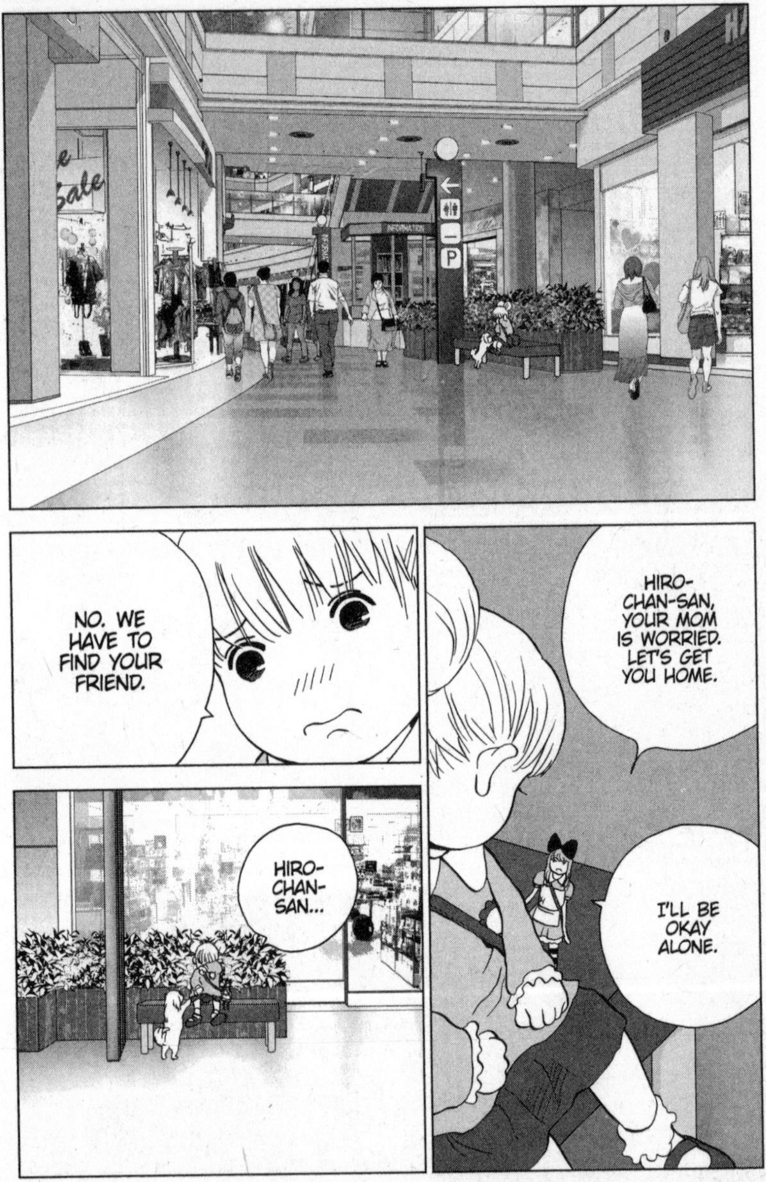
HIRO-CHAN-SAN, YOUR MOM IS WORRIED. LET'S GET YOU HOME.
I'LL BE OKAY ALONE.
NO. WE HAVE TO FIND YOUR FRIEND.
HIRO-CHAN-SAN...

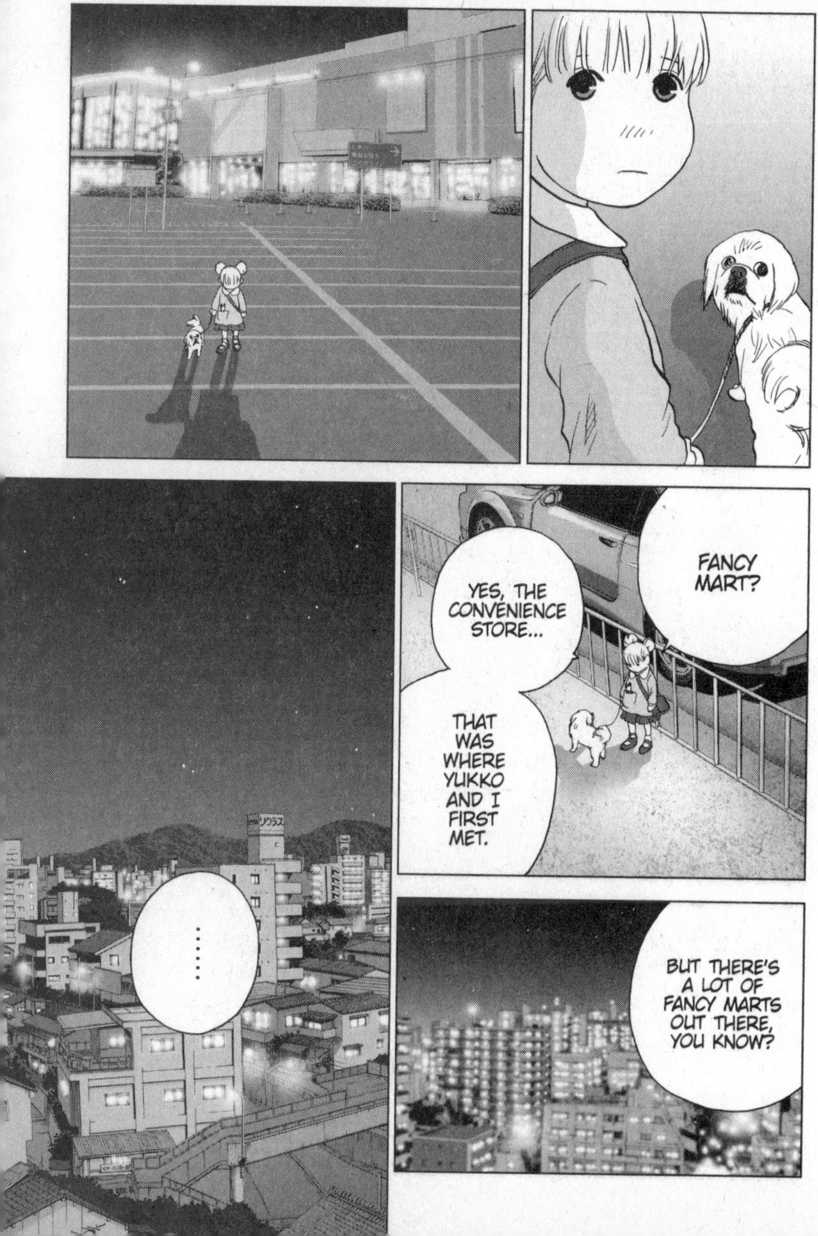
FANCY MART?
YES, THE CONVENIENCE STORE...
THAT WAS WHERE YUKKO AND I FIRST MET.
BUT THERE'S A LOT OF FANCY MARTS OUT THERE, YOU KNOW?
......

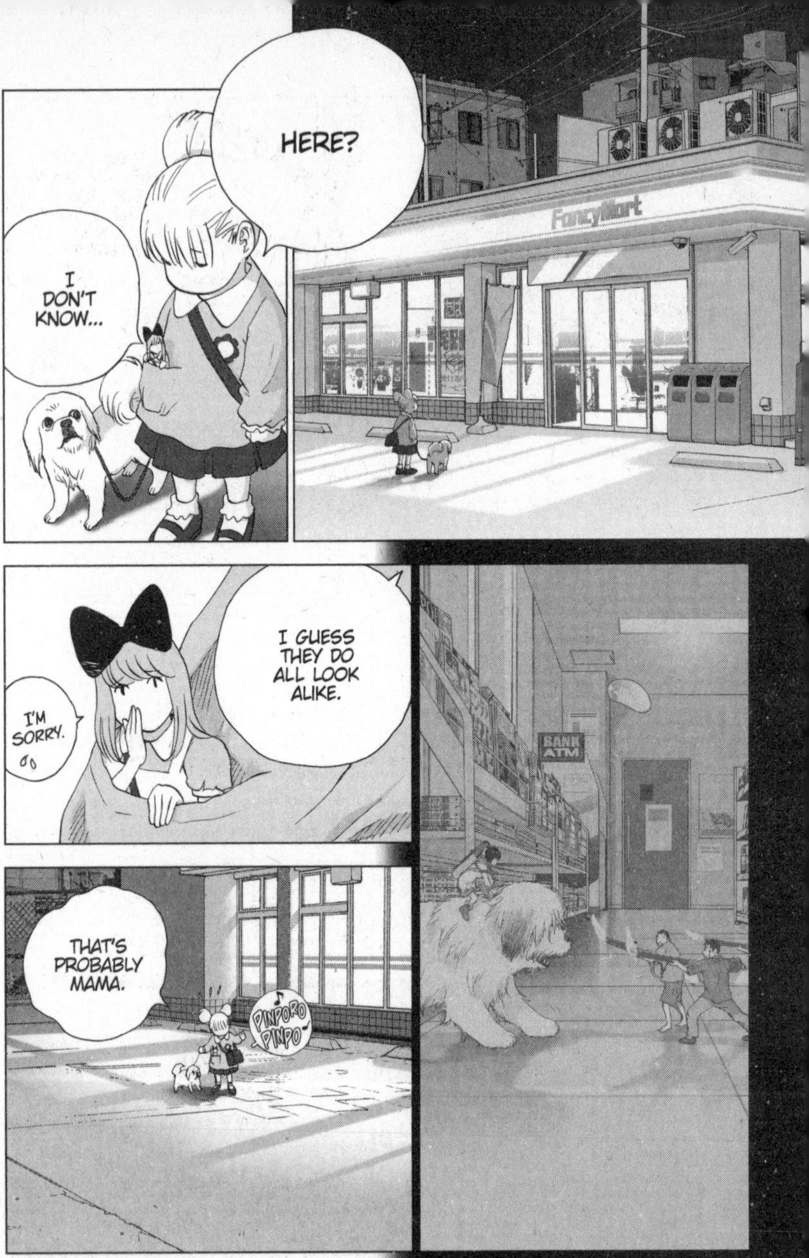
FancyMart
HERE?
I DON'T KNOW...
BANK ATM
I GUESS THEY DO ALL LOOK ALIKE.
I'M SORRY.
PINPORO PINPO
THAT'S PROBABLY MAMA.

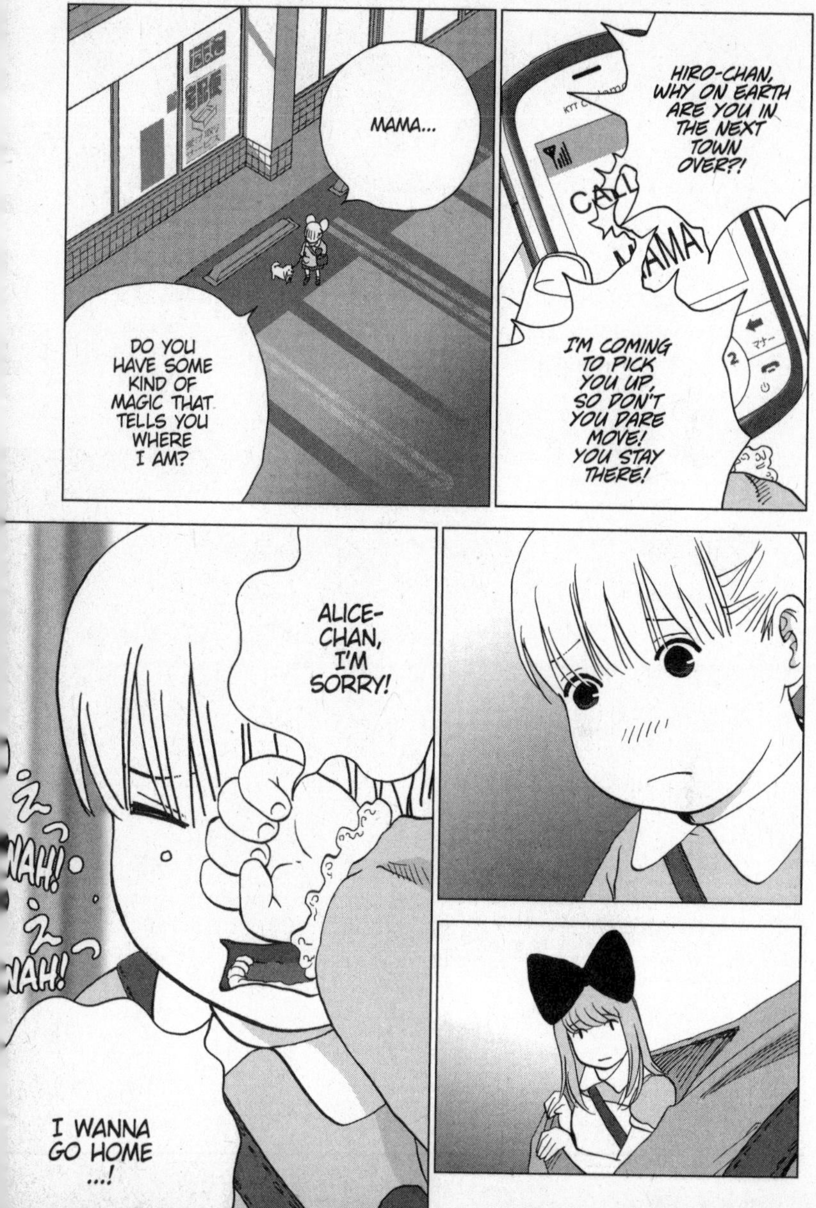
CALL
MAMA
HIRO-CHAN, WHY ON EARTH ARE YOU IN THE NEXT TOWN OVER?!
I'M COMING TO PICK YOU UP, SO DON'T YOU DARE MOVE! YOU STAY THERE!
MAMA...
DO YOU HAVE SOME KIND OF MAGIC THAT TELLS YOU WHERE I AM?
ALICE-CHAN, I'M SORRY!
えっ
えっ
I WANNA GO HOME ...!

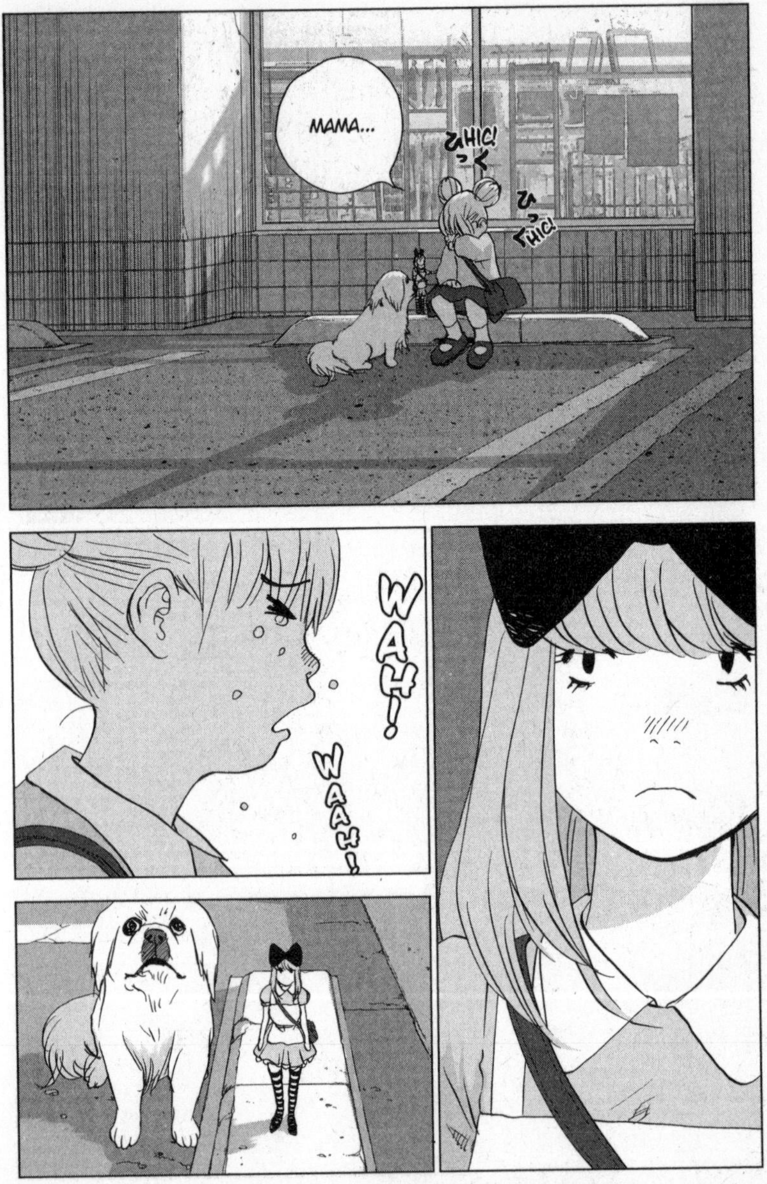

MAMA...
ひっく HIC!
ひっく HIC!
WAH!
WAAH!

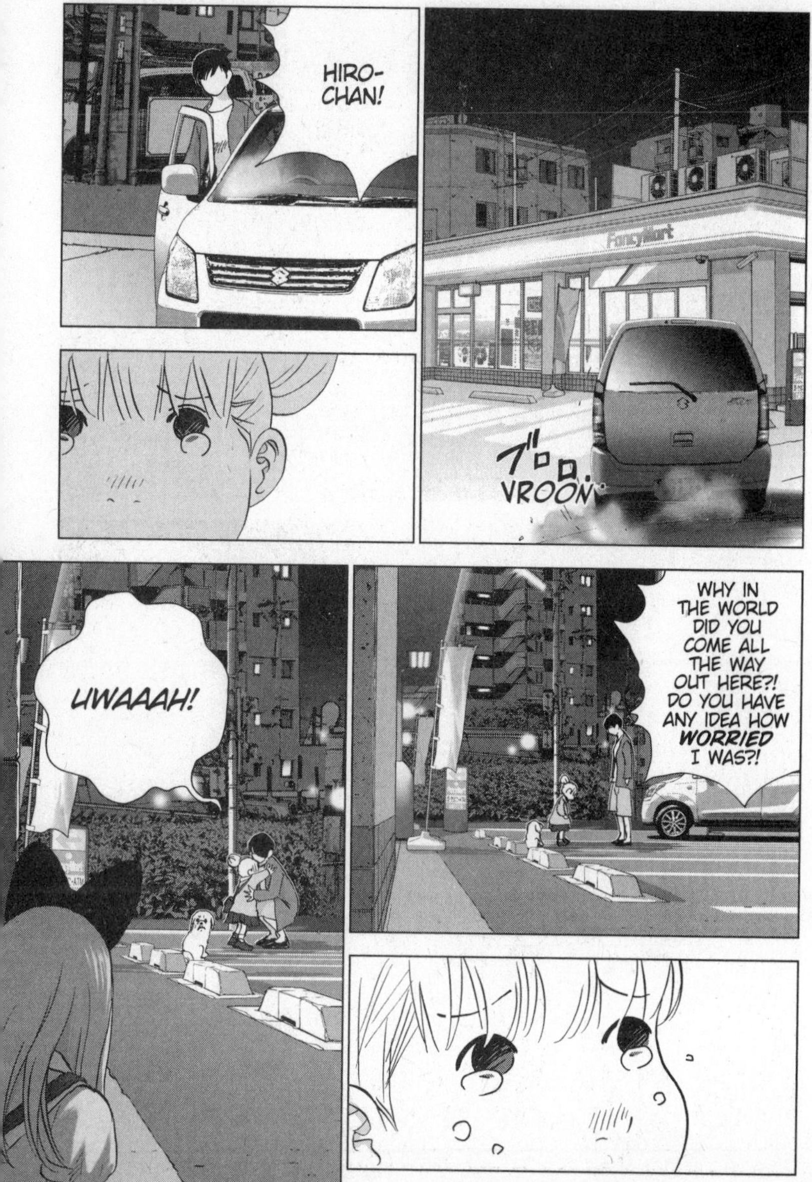
ブロロ
VROOM
HIRO-CHAN!
WHY IN THE WORLD DID YOU COME ALL THE WAY OUT HERE?! DO YOU HAVE ANY IDEA HOW **WORRIED** I WAS?!
UWAAAH!

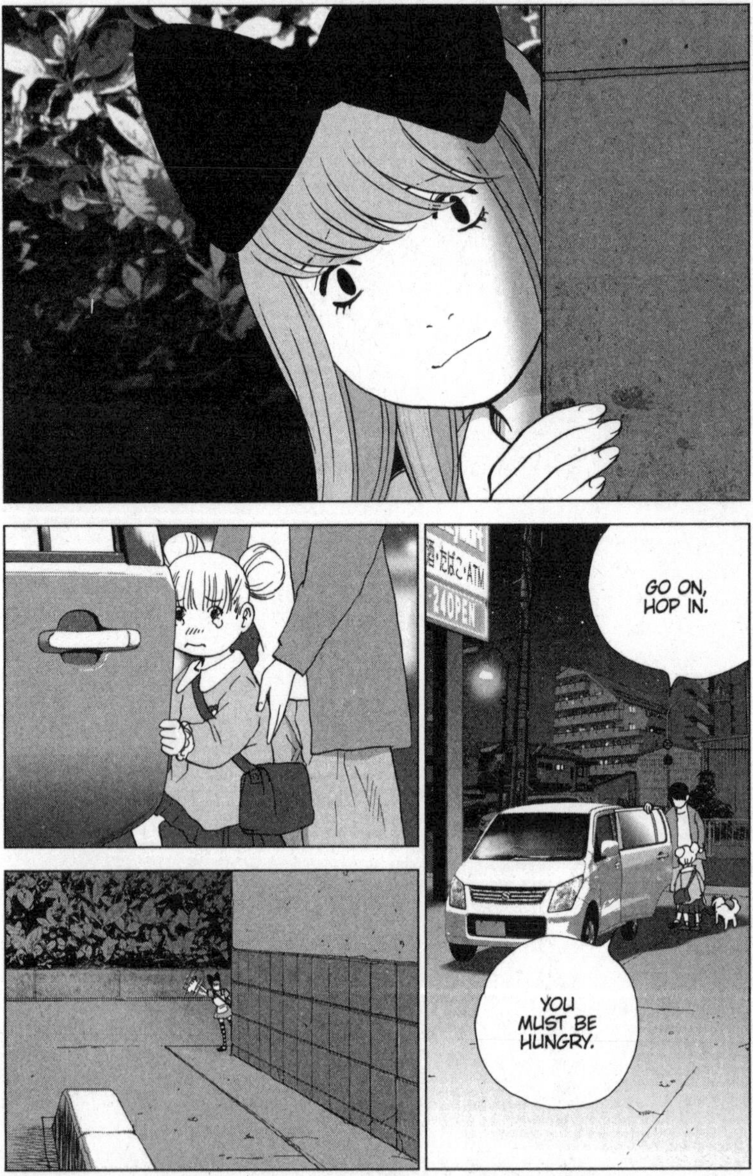
酒・たばこ・ATM
24OPEN
GO ON, HOP IN.
YOU MUST BE HUNGRY.

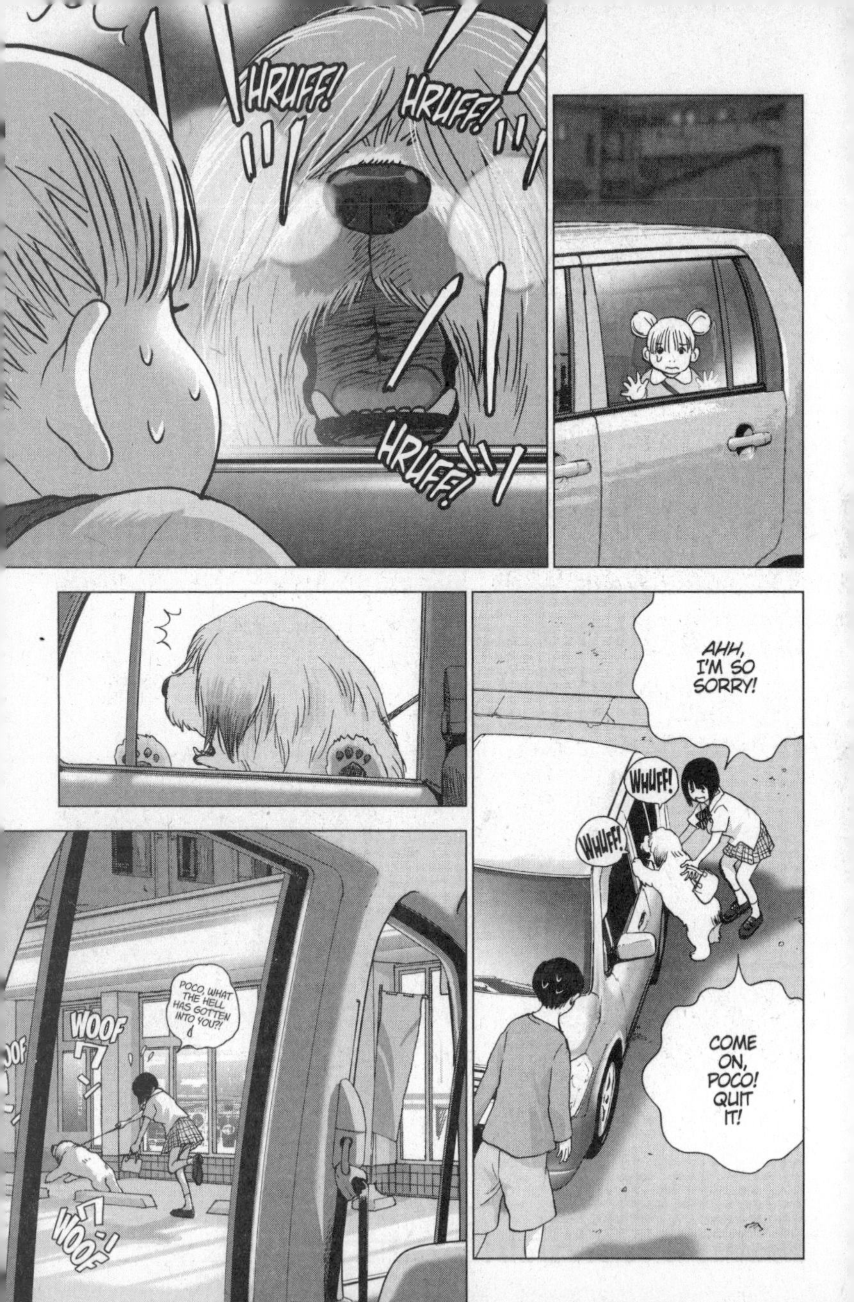
HRUFF!
HRUFF!
HRUFF!
AHH, I'M SO SORRY!
WHUFF!
WHUFF!
COME ON, POCO! QUIT IT!
POCO, WHAT THE HELL HAS GOTTEN INTO YOU?!
WOOF
WOOF

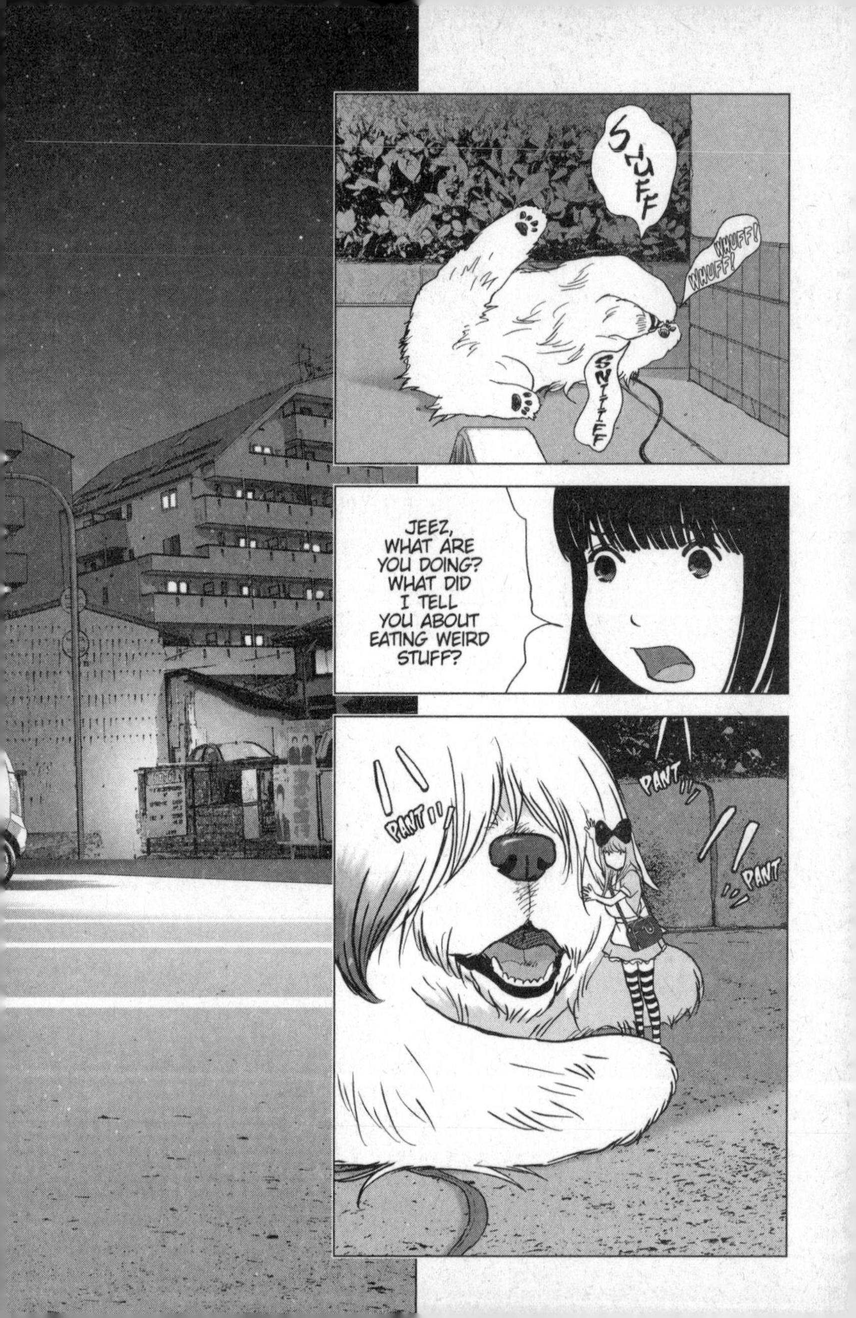
SNUFF
WHUFF! WHUFF!
SNIIIFF
JEEZ, WHAT ARE YOU DOING? WHAT DID I TELL YOU ABOUT EATING WEIRD STUFF?
PANT
PANT
PANT

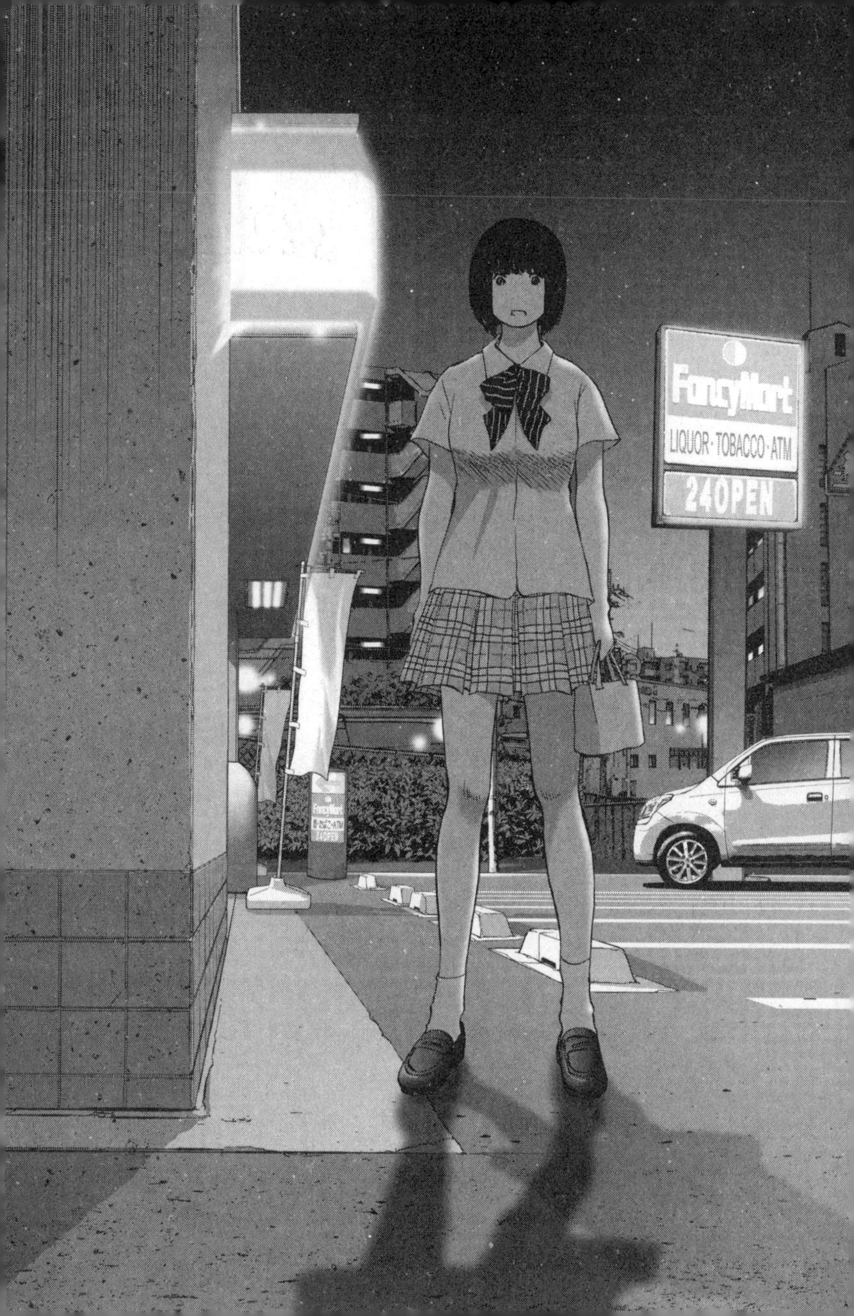
FancyMart
LIQUOR・TOBACCO・ATM
24OPEN

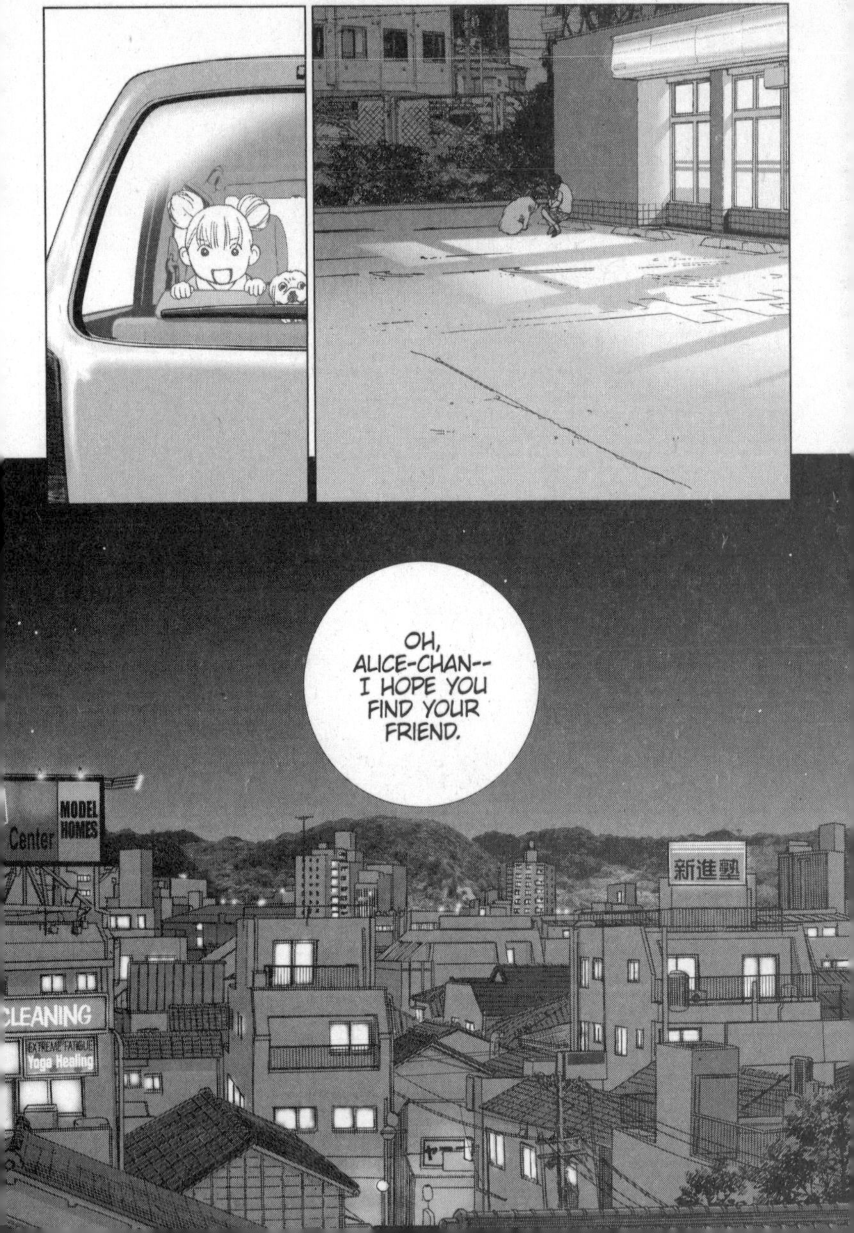
OH, ALICE-CHAN-- I HOPE YOU FIND YOUR FRIEND.
MODEL HOMES
Center
新進塾
CLEANING
EXTREME FATIGUE
Yoga Healing

Chapter 32: Dragnet

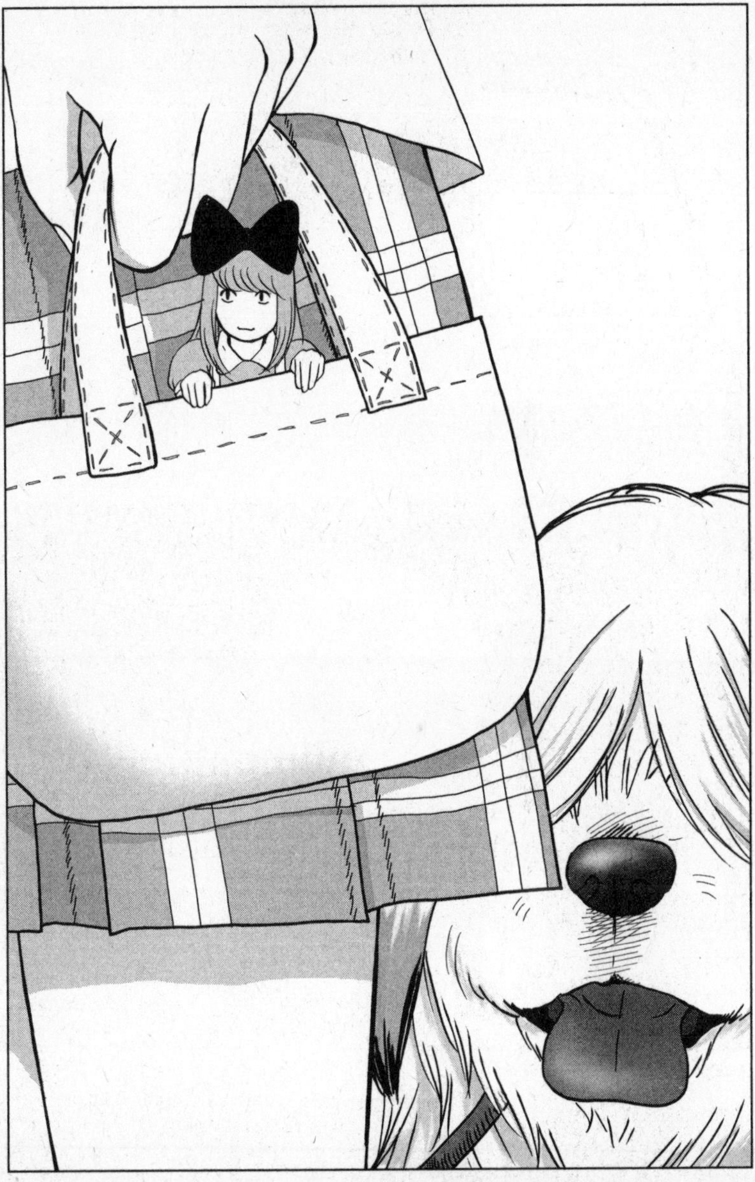

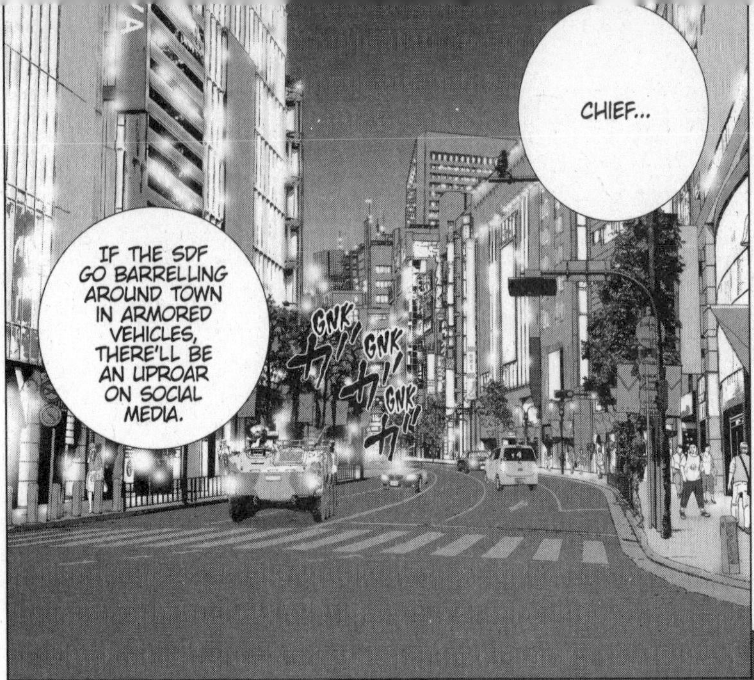
CHIEF...
IF THE SDF GO BARRELLING AROUND TOWN IN ARMORED VEHICLES, THERE'LL BE AN UPROAR ON SOCIAL MEDIA.
GNK
GNK
GNK
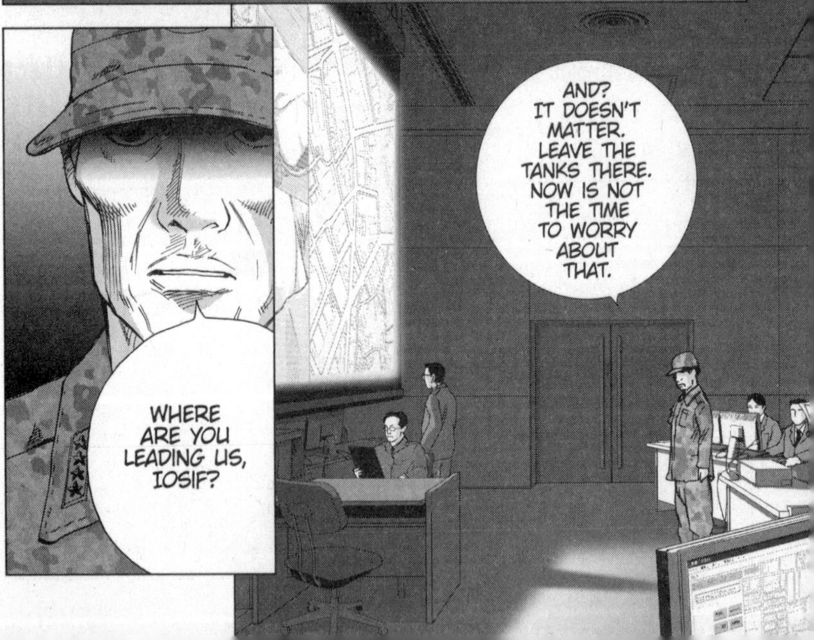
AND? IT DOESN'T MATTER. LEAVE THE TANKS THERE. NOW IS NOT THE TIME TO WORRY ABOUT THAT.
WHERE ARE YOU LEADING US, IOSIF?

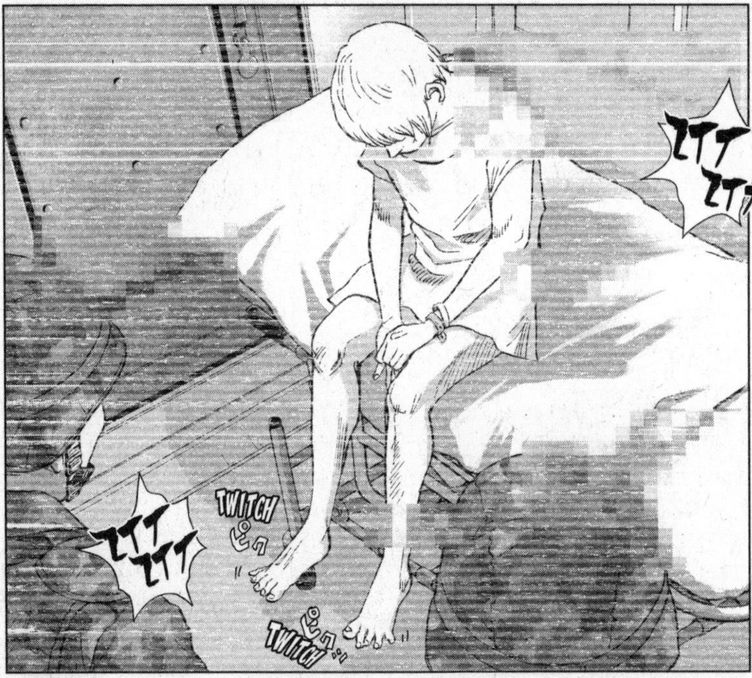
ZTT ZTT
TWITCH
ぴク
ZTT ZTT
ぴク
TWITCH
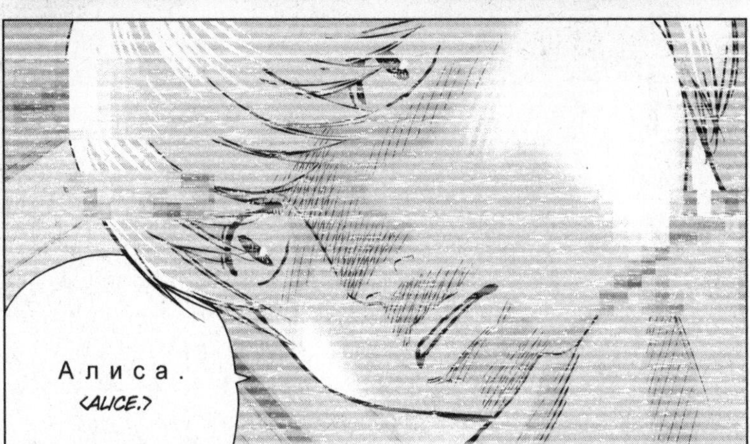
Алиса.
<ALICE.>

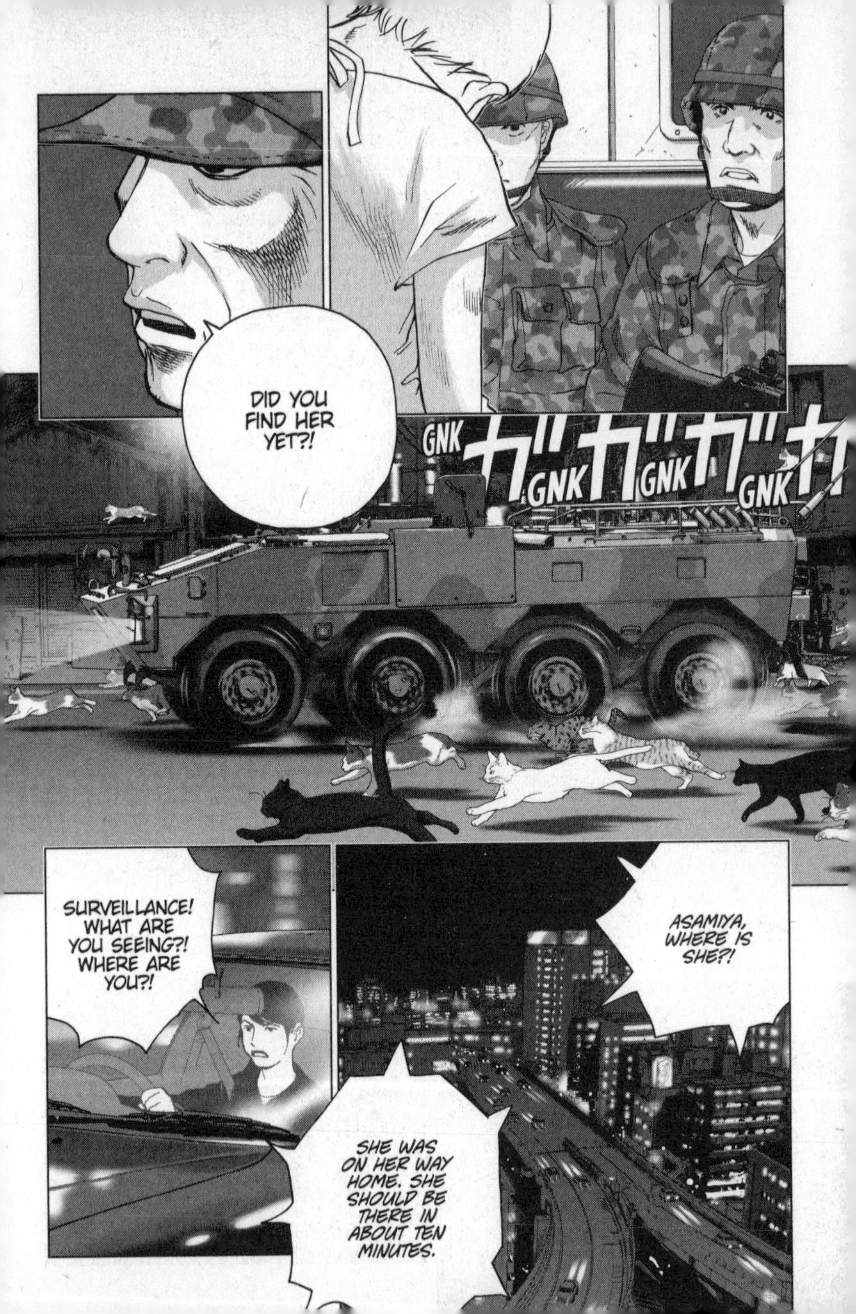
DID YOU FIND HER YET?!
GNK
ガ
GNK
ガ
GNK
ガ
GNK
ASAMIYA, WHERE IS SHE?!
SHE WAS ON HER WAY HOME. SHE SHOULD BE THERE IN ABOUT TEN MINUTES.
SURVEILLANCE! WHAT ARE YOU SEEING?! WHERE ARE YOU?!

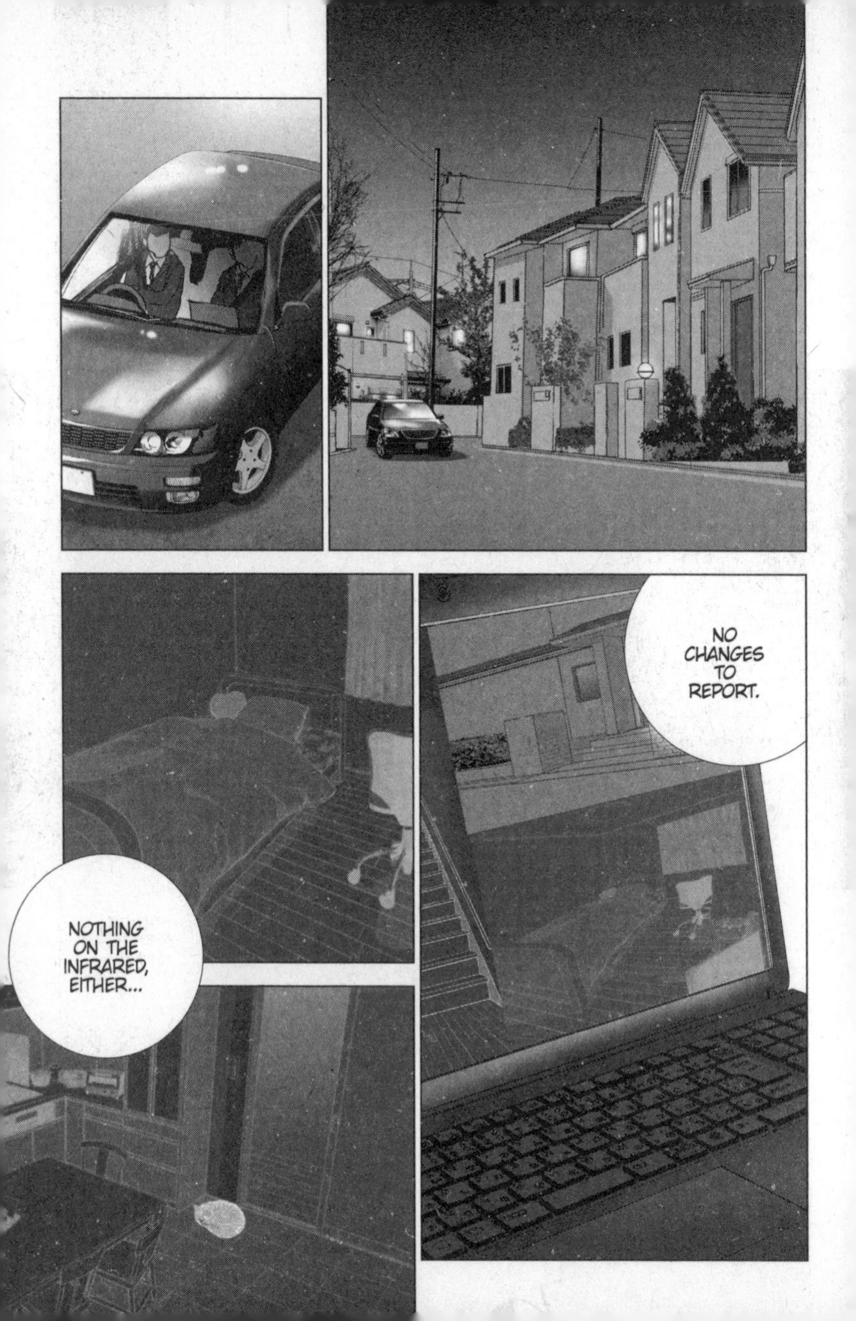
NO CHANGES TO REPORT.
NOTHING ON THE INFRARED, EITHER...

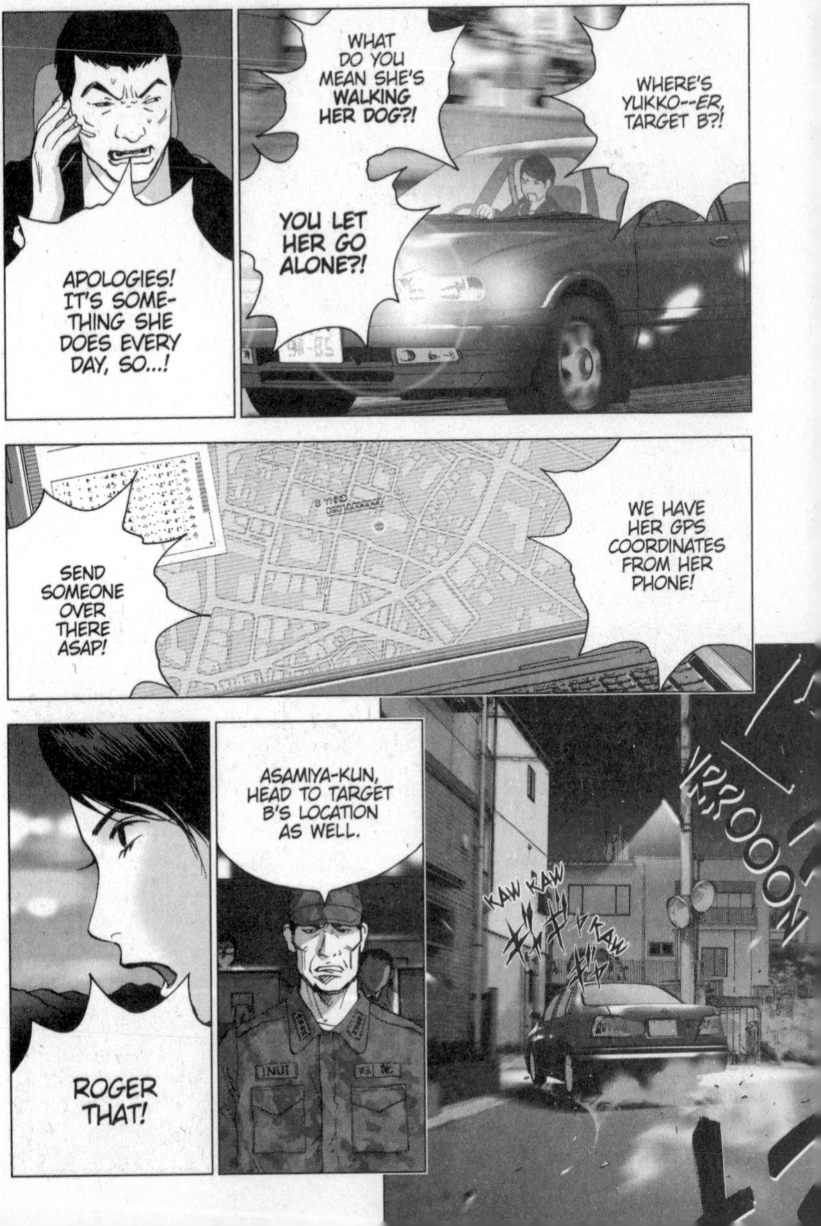
WHERE'S YUKKO--ER, TARGET B?!
WHAT DO YOU MEAN SHE'S WALKING HER DOG?!
YOU LET HER GO ALONE?!
APOLOGIES! IT'S SOME-THING SHE DOES EVERY DAY, SO...!
WE HAVE HER GPS COORDINATES FROM HER PHONE!
SEND SOMEONE OVER THERE ASAP!
VRROOOON
KAW KAW
KAW
ASAMIYA-KUN, HEAD TO TARGET B'S LOCATION AS WELL.
ROGER THAT!

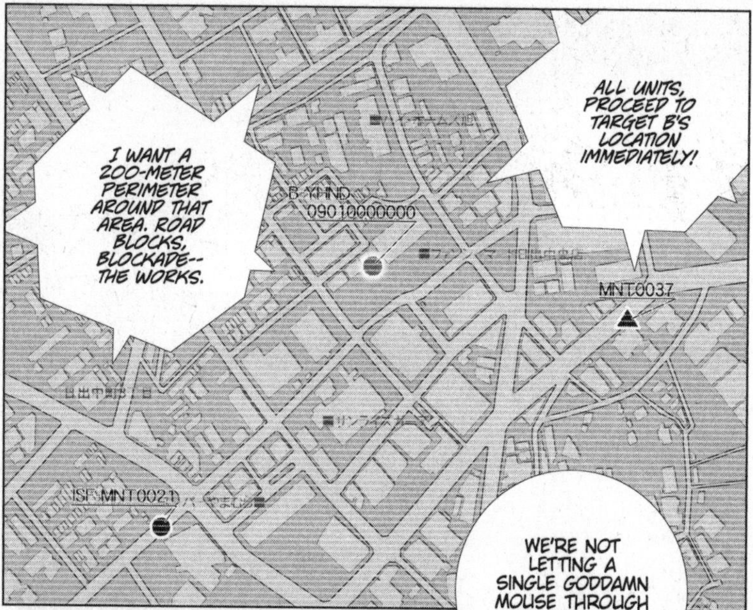
ALL UNITS, PROCEED TO TARGET B'S LOCATION IMMEDIATELY!
I WANT A 200-METER PERIMETER AROUND THAT AREA. ROAD BLOCKS, BLOCKADE--THE WORKS.
MNT.0037
WE'RE NOT LETTING A SINGLE GODDAMN MOUSE THROUGH THAT PERIMETER, YOU HEAR ME?
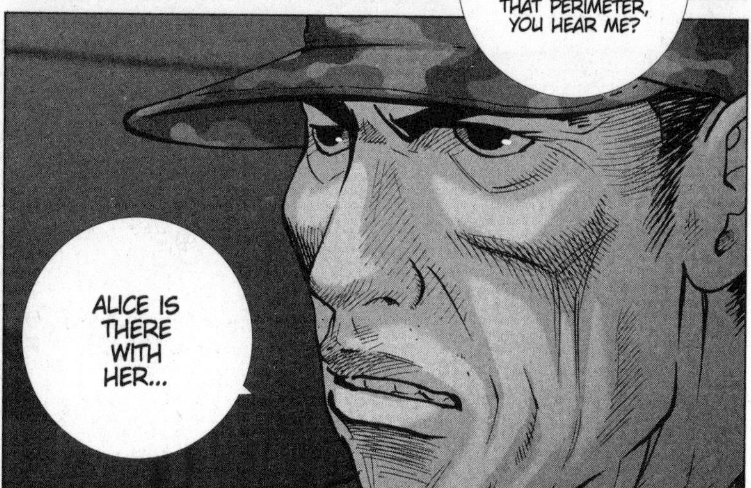
ALICE IS THERE WITH HER...

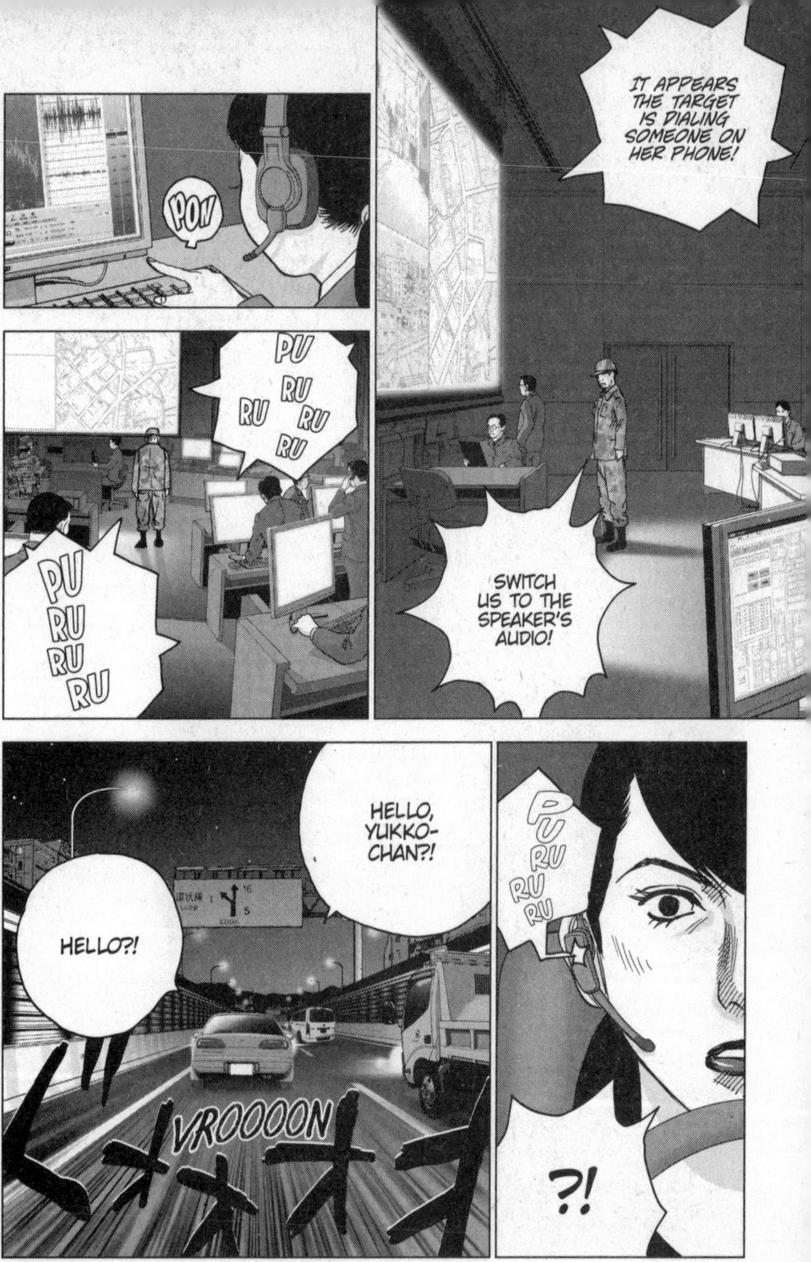
IT APPEARS THE TARGET IS DIALING SOMEONE ON HER PHONE!
SWITCH US TO THE SPEAKER'S AUDIO!
PON
PU RU RU RU RU
PU RU RU RU
PU RU RU RU
?!
HELLO, YUKKO-CHAN?!
HELLO?!
VROOOON

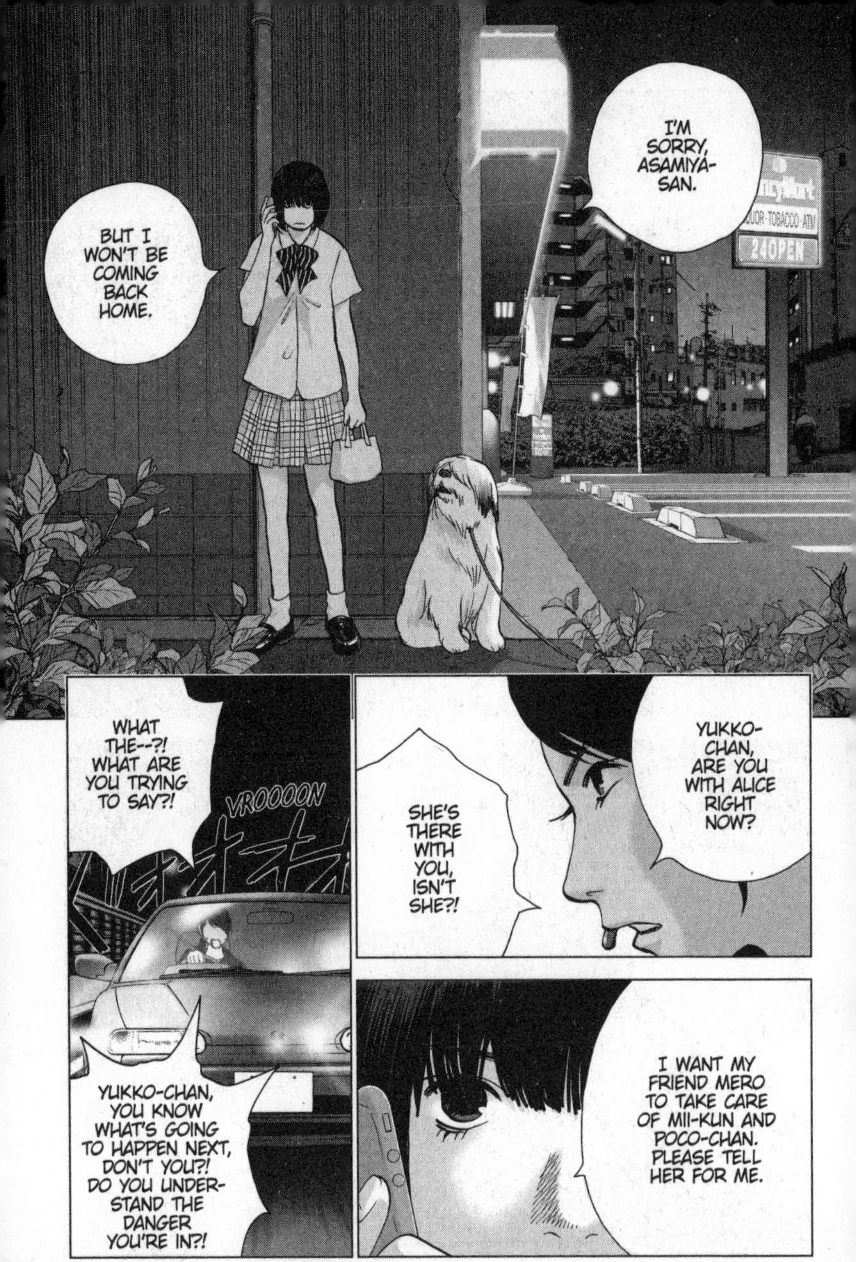
I'M SORRY, ASAMIYA-SAN.
BUT I WON'T BE COMING BACK HOME.
24OPEN
YUKKO-CHAN, ARE YOU WITH ALICE RIGHT NOW?
SHE'S THERE WITH YOU, ISN'T SHE?!
I WANT MY FRIEND MERO TO TAKE CARE OF MII-KUN AND POCO-CHAN. PLEASE TELL HER FOR ME.
WHAT THE--?! WHAT ARE YOU TRYING TO SAY?!
VROOOON
YUKKO-CHAN, YOU KNOW WHAT'S GOING TO HAPPEN NEXT, DON'T YOU?! DO YOU UNDER-STAND THE DANGER YOU'RE IN?!

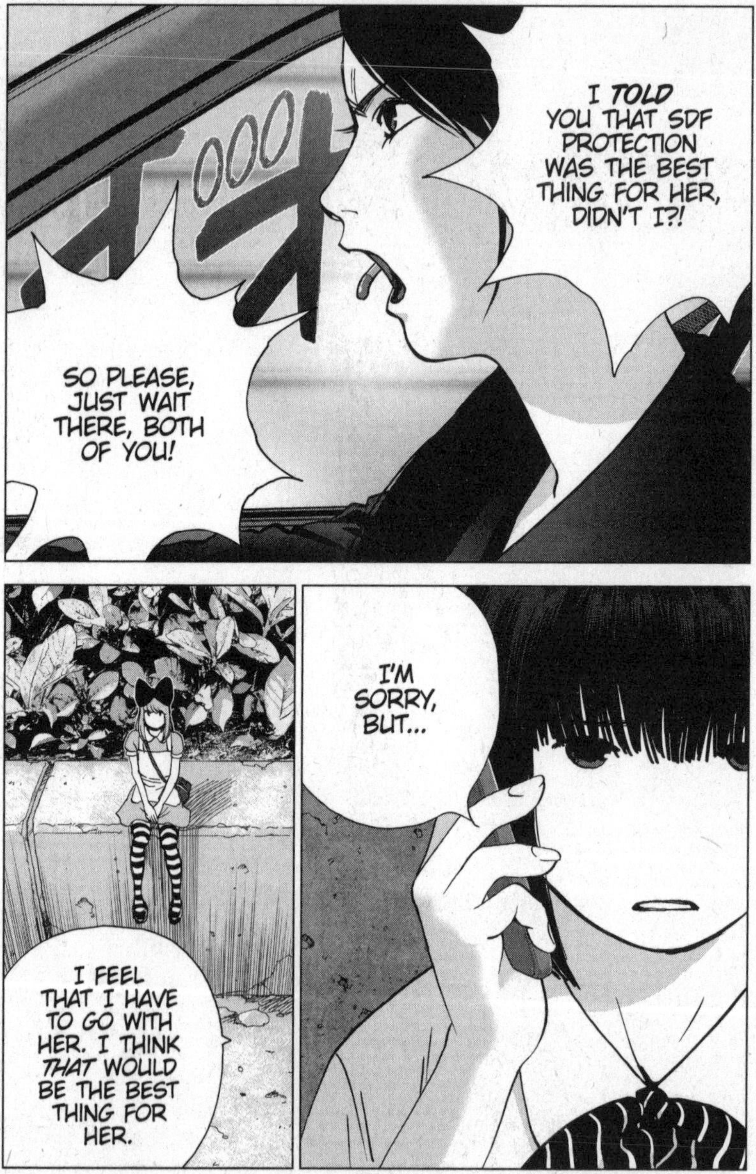
I *TOLD* YOU THAT SDF PROTECTION WAS THE BEST THING FOR HER, DIDN'T I?!
SO PLEASE, JUST WAIT THERE, BOTH OF YOU!
I'M SORRY, BUT...
I FEEL THAT I HAVE TO GO WITH HER. I THINK *THAT* WOULD BE THE BEST THING FOR HER.

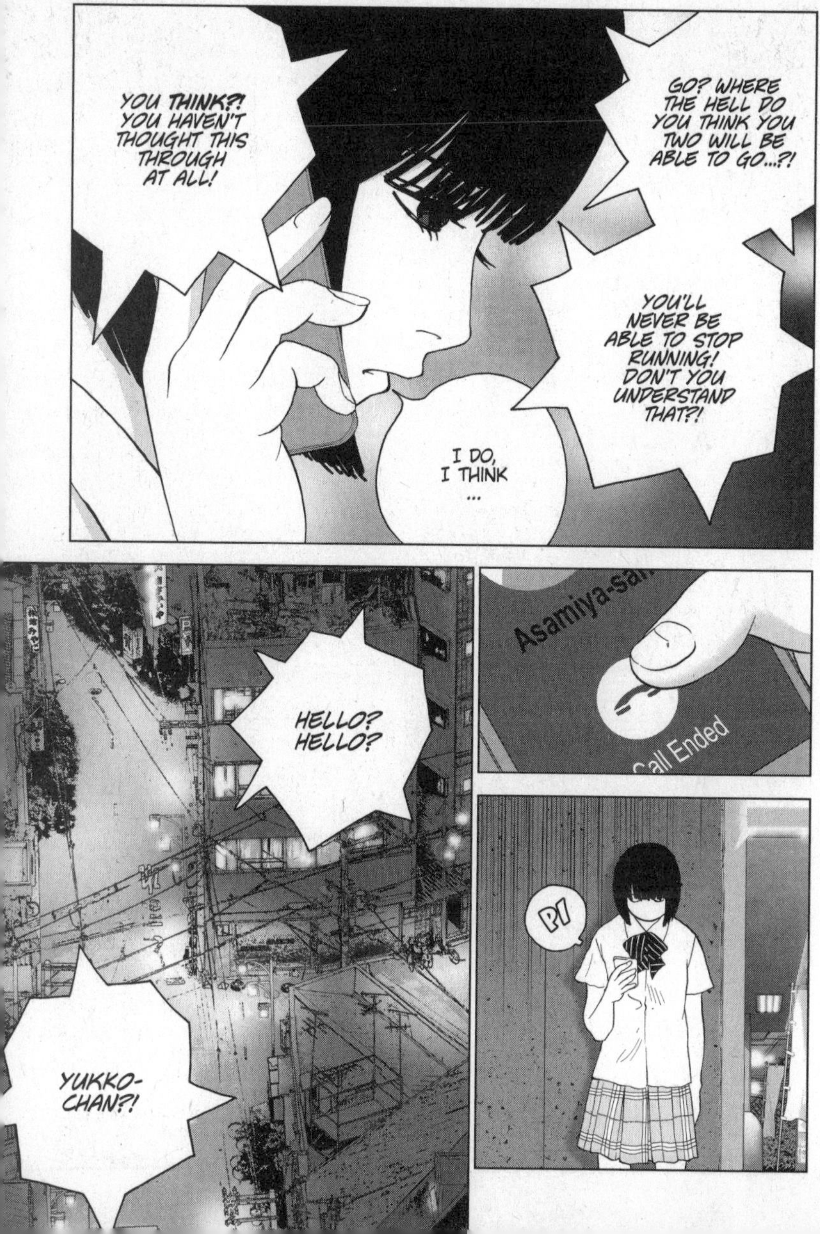
GO? WHERE THE HELL DO YOU THINK YOU TWO WILL BE ABLE TO GO...?!
YOU'LL NEVER BE ABLE TO STOP RUNNING! DON'T YOU UNDERSTAND THAT?!
I DO, I THINK ...
YOU THINK?! YOU HAVEN'T THOUGHT THIS THROUGH AT ALL!
Asamiya-sa
Call Ended
PI
HELLO? HELLO?
YUKKO-CHAN?!

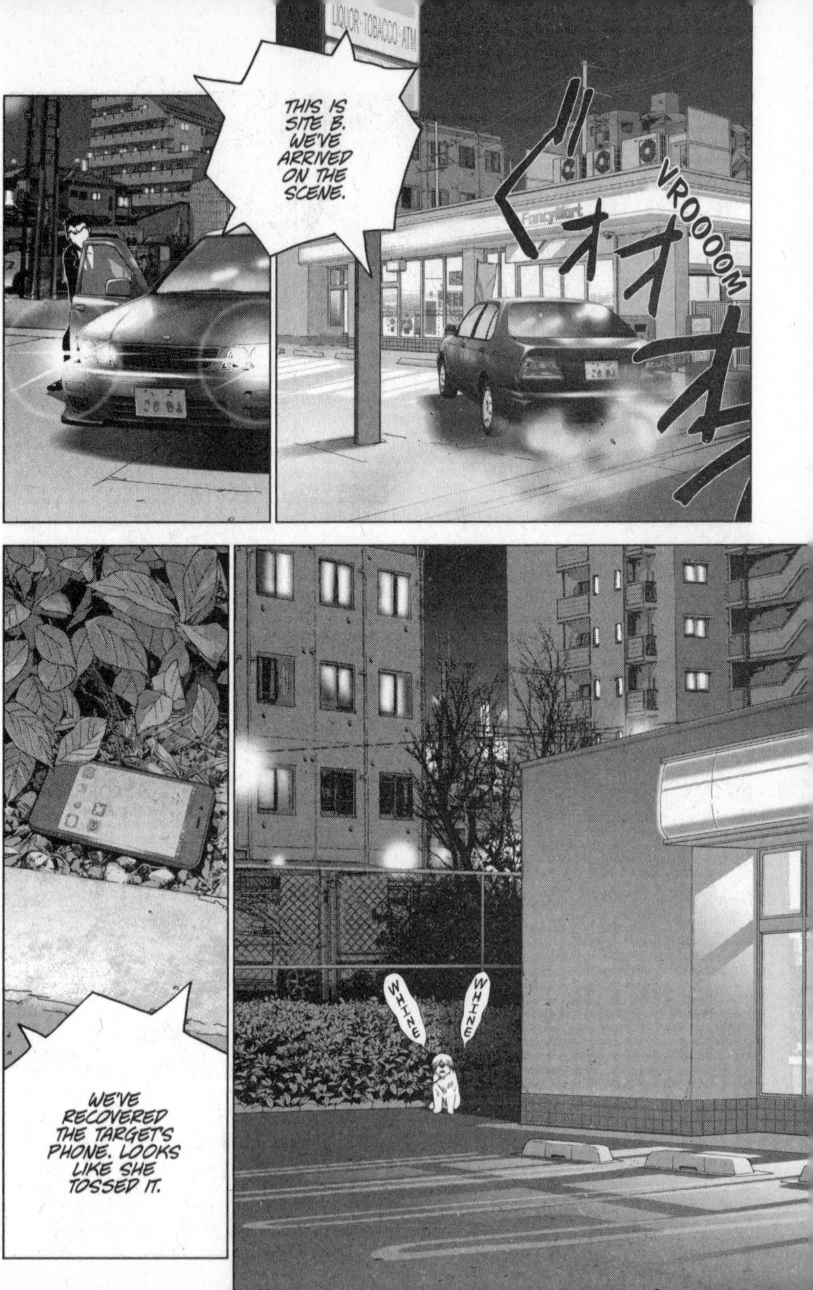
LIQUOR·TOBACCO·ATM
VROOOOM
THIS IS SITE B. WE'VE ARRIVED ON THE SCENE.
WHINE
WHINE
WE'VE RECOVERED THE TARGET'S PHONE. LOOKS LIKE SHE TOSSED IT.

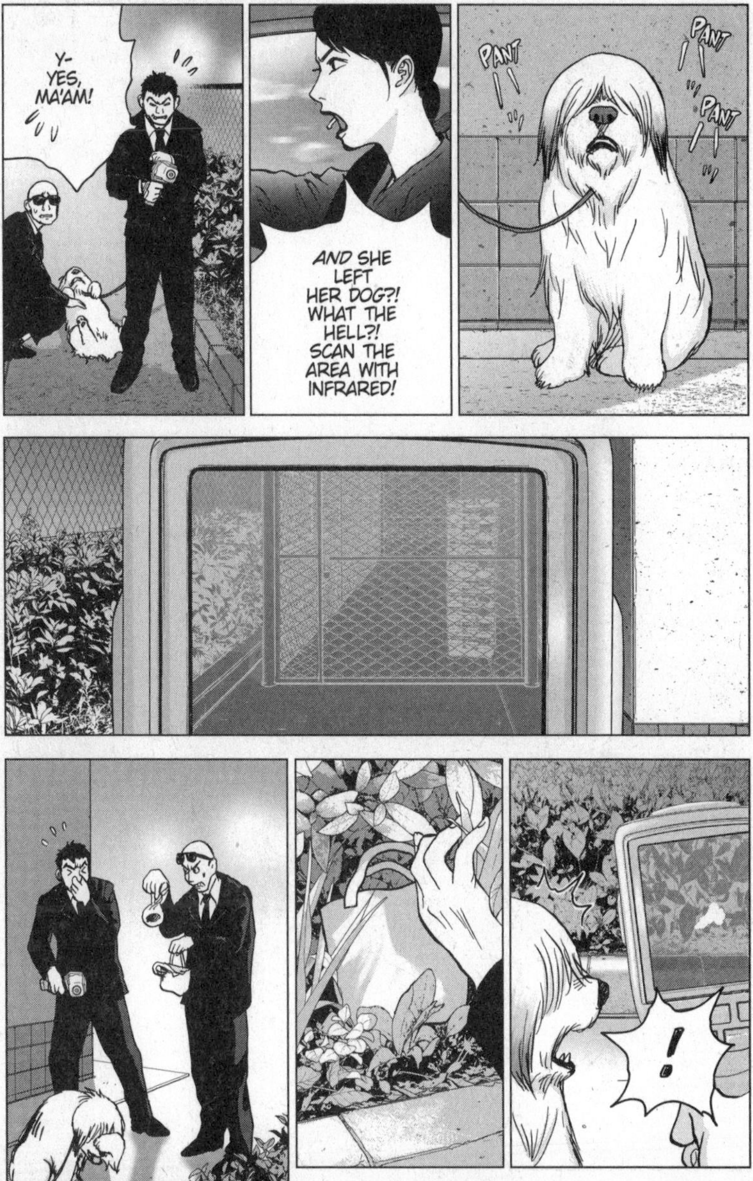
PANT
PANT
PANT
AND SHE LEFT HER DOG?! WHAT THE HELL?! SCAN THE AREA WITH INFRARED!
Y- YES, MA'AM!
!

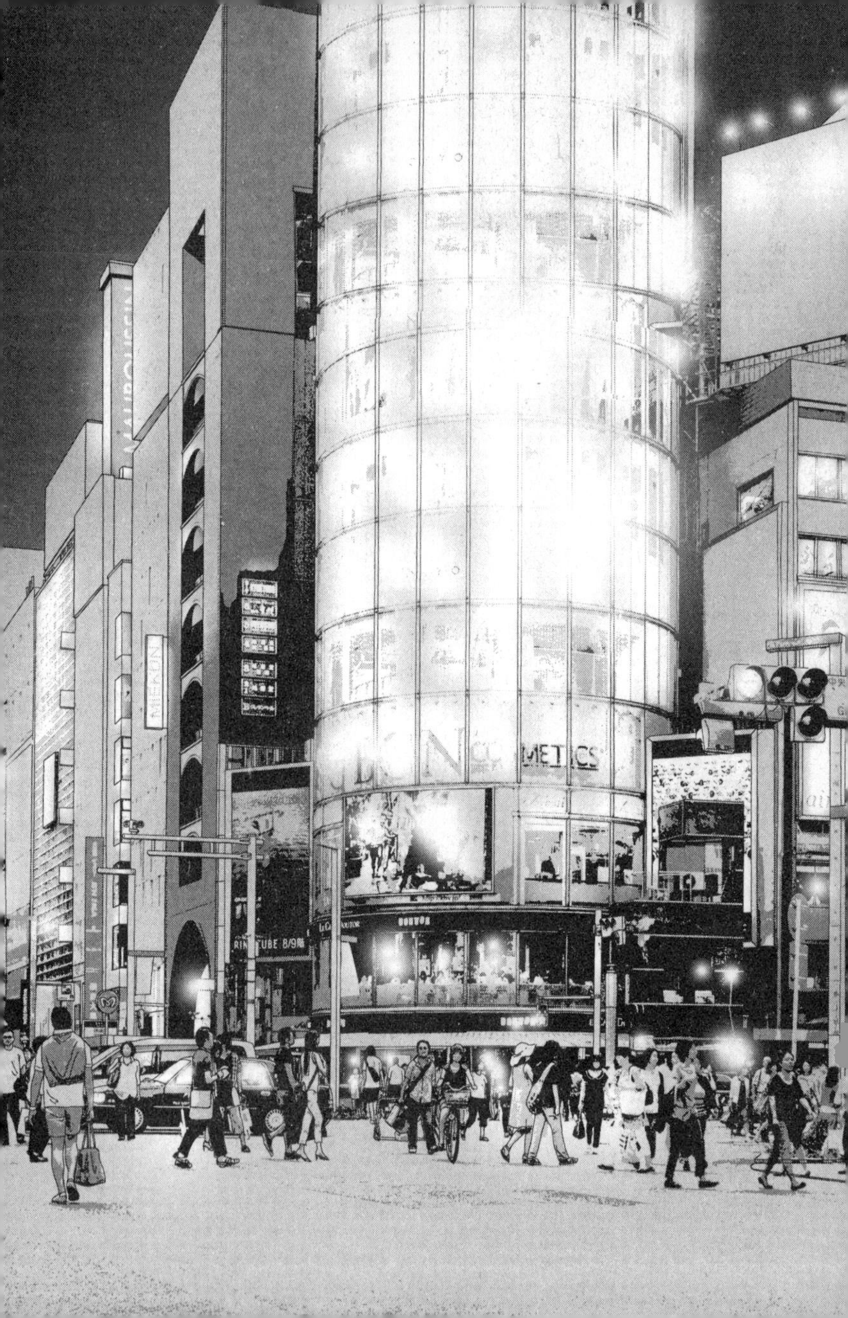
METICS
RIN TUBE B/9階

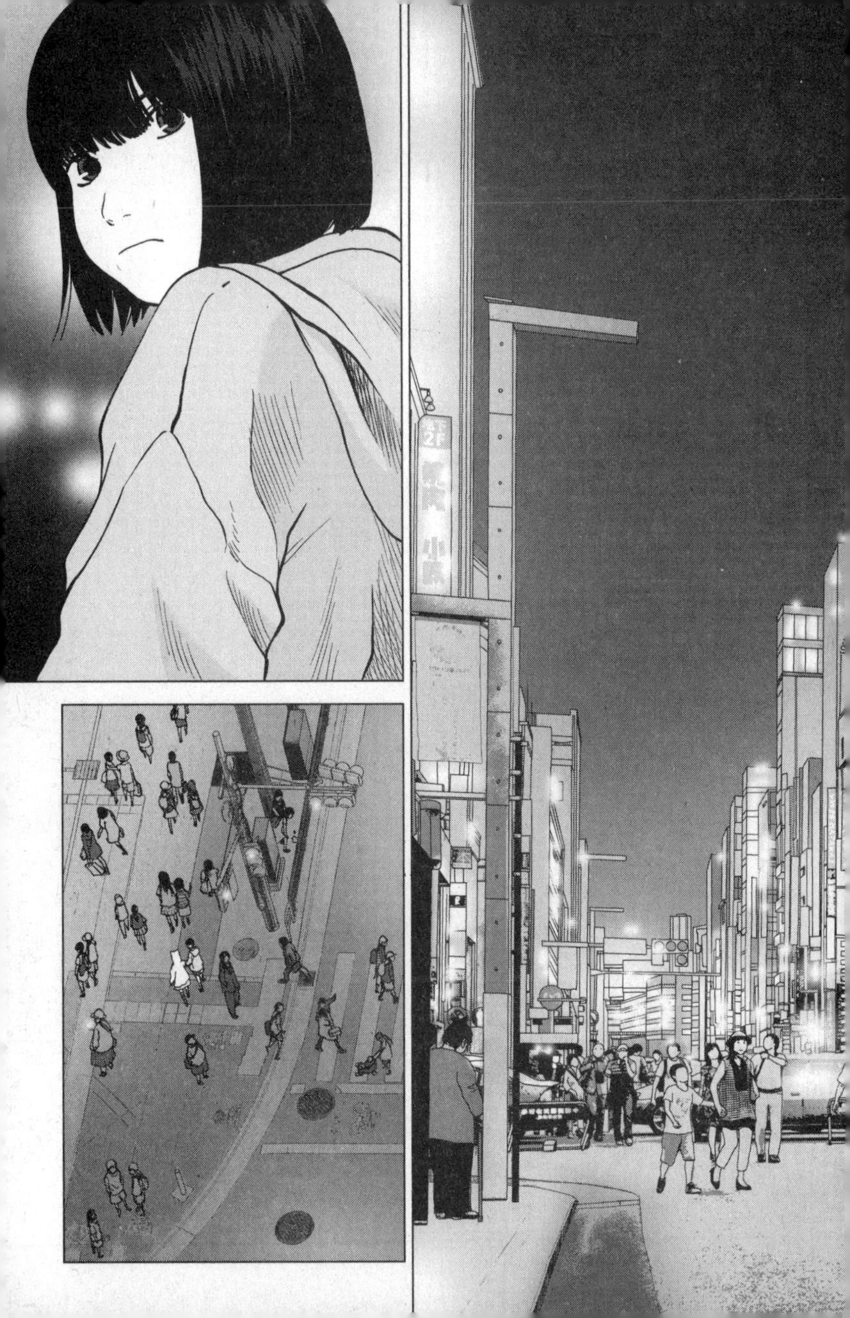

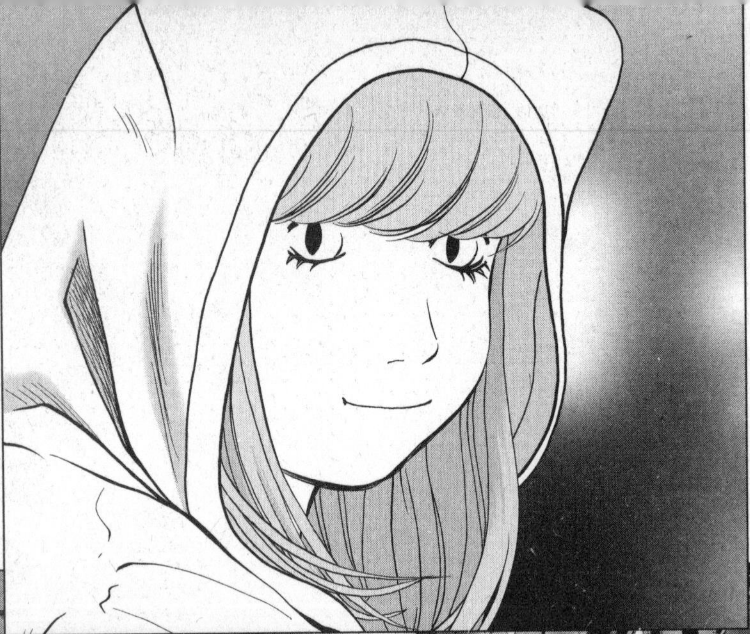

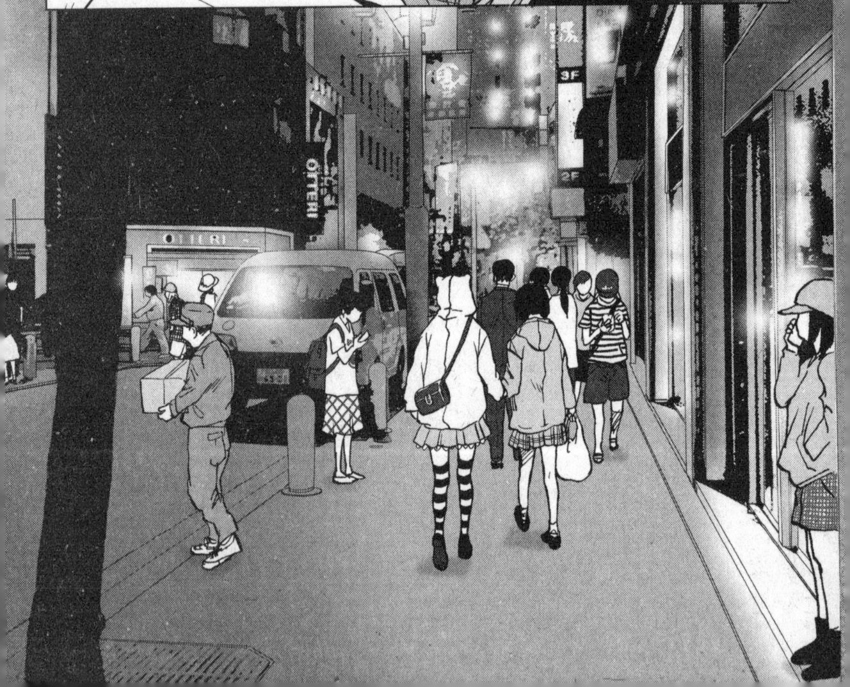
3F
2F

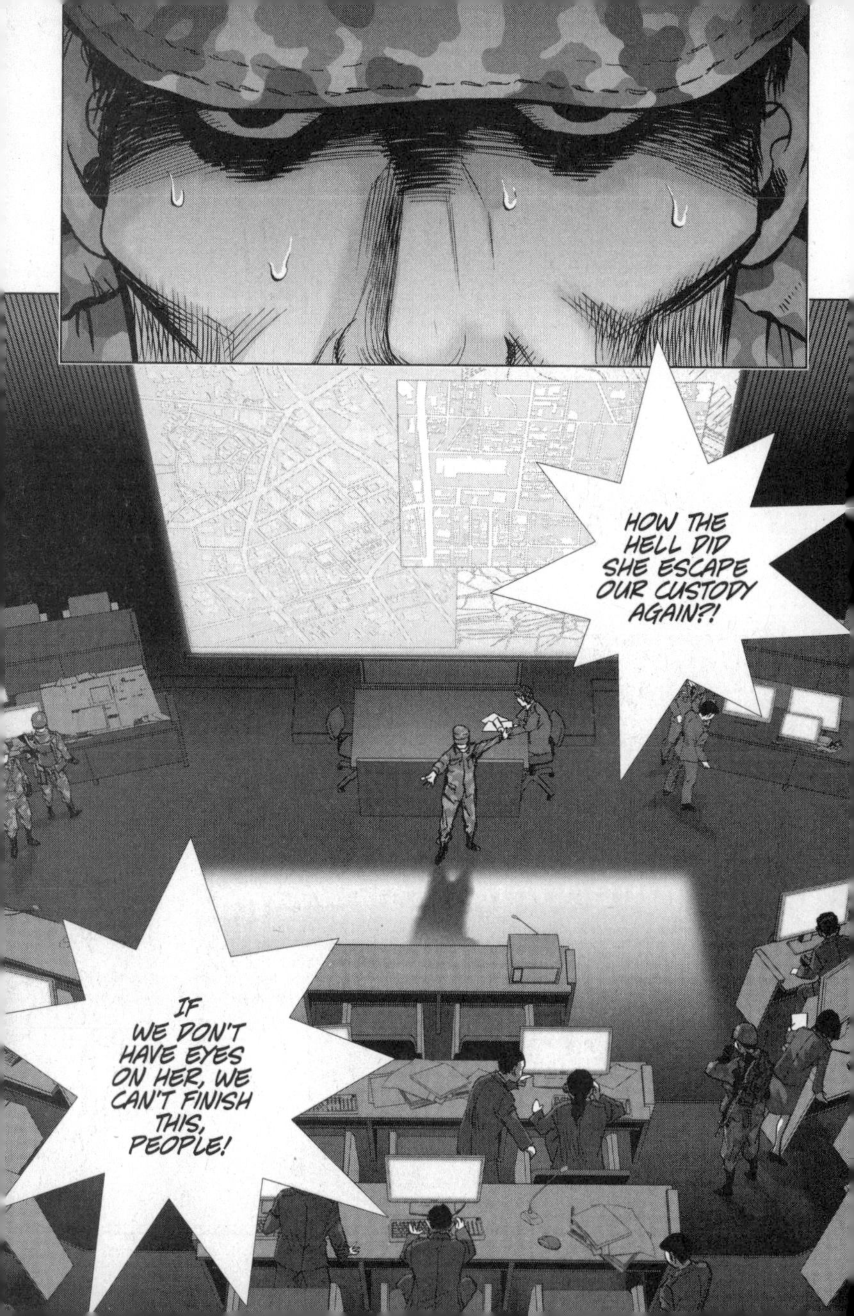
HOW THE HELL DID SHE ESCAPE OUR CUSTODY AGAIN?!
IF WE DON'T HAVE EYES ON HER, WE CAN'T FINISH THIS, PEOPLE!

CHIEF, IOSIF IS HEADED FOR THE CITY!

I'M CONCERNED WE MAY LOSE SIGHT OF HIM, TOO!

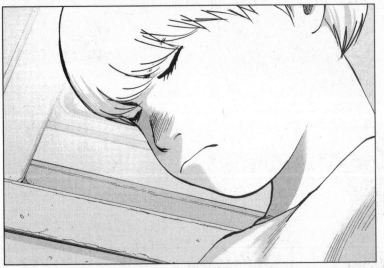

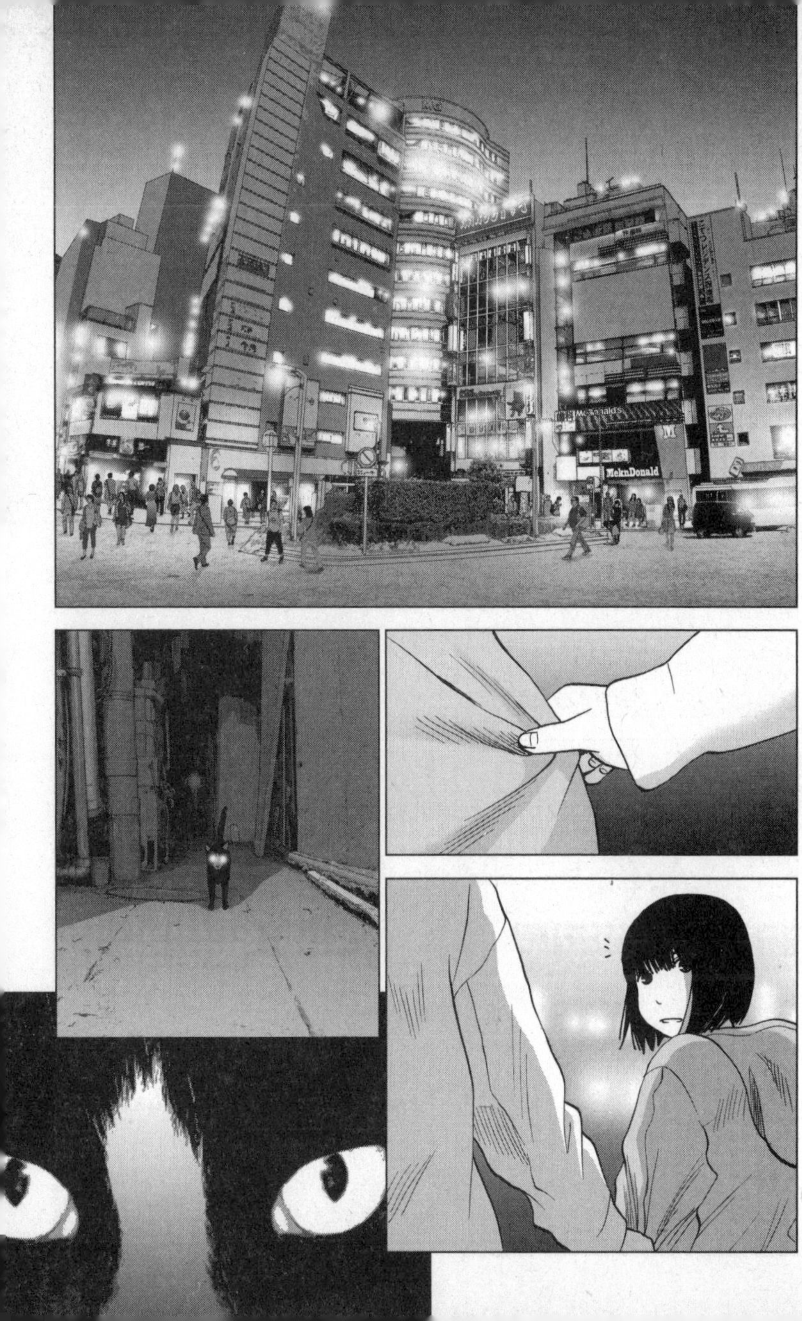
MeknDonald

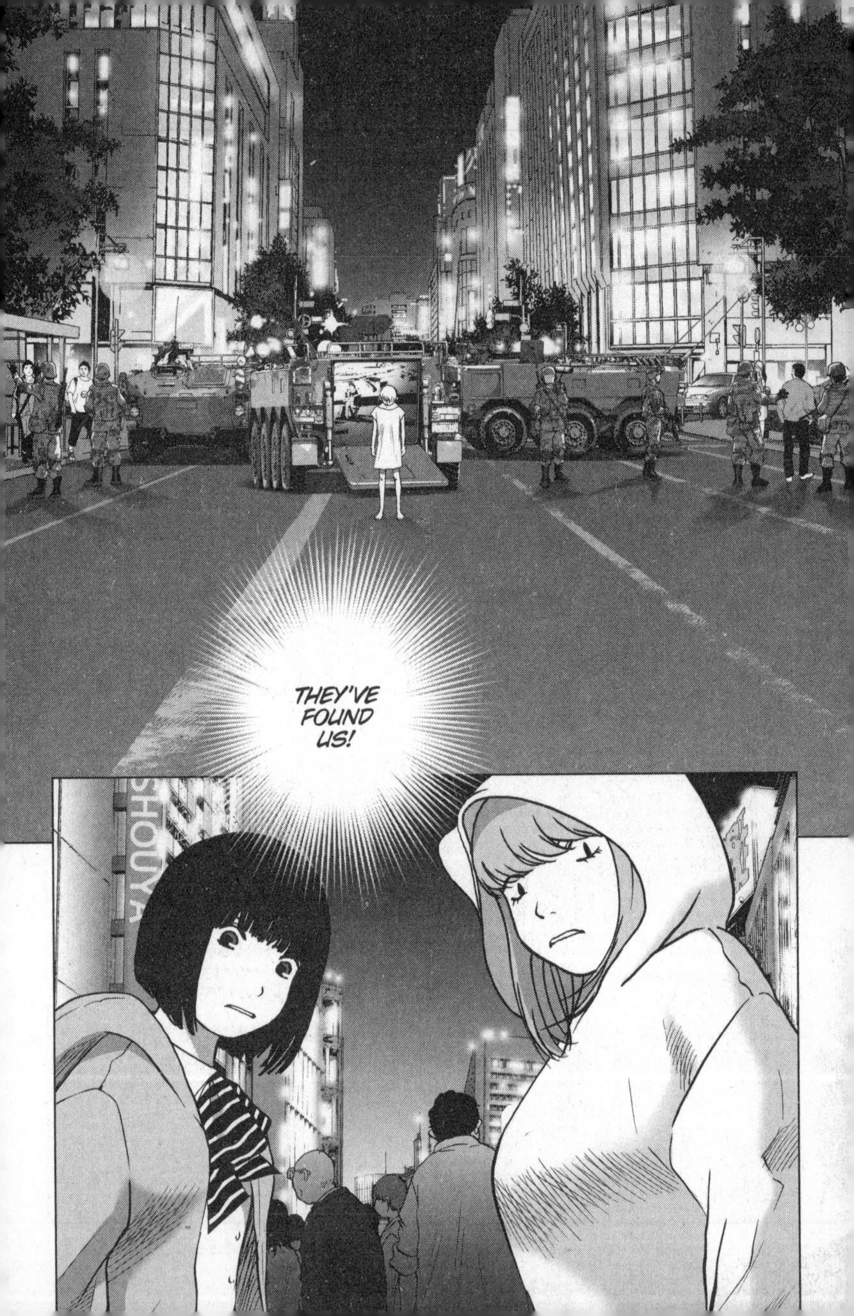
THEY'VE FOUND US!
SHOUYA

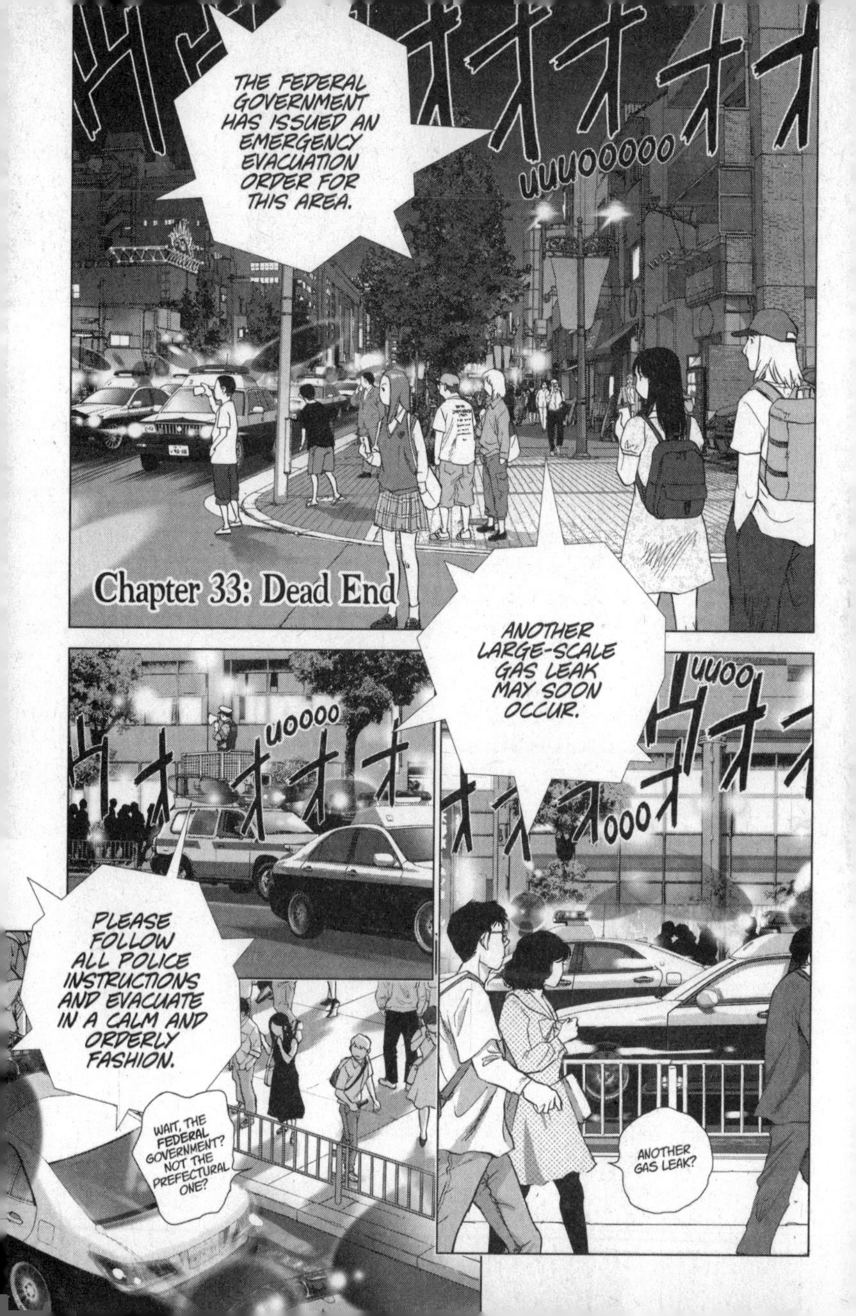
THE FEDERAL GOVERNMENT HAS ISSUED AN EMERGENCY EVACUATION ORDER FOR THIS AREA.
UUUOOOOO
Chapter 33: Dead End
ANOTHER LARGE-SCALE GAS LEAK MAY SOON OCCUR.
UUOO
OOO
ANOTHER GAS LEAK?
UOOOO
PLEASE FOLLOW ALL POLICE INSTRUCTIONS AND EVACUATE IN A CALM AND ORDERLY FASHION.
WAIT, THE FEDERAL GOVERNMENT? NOT THE PREFECTURAL ONE?

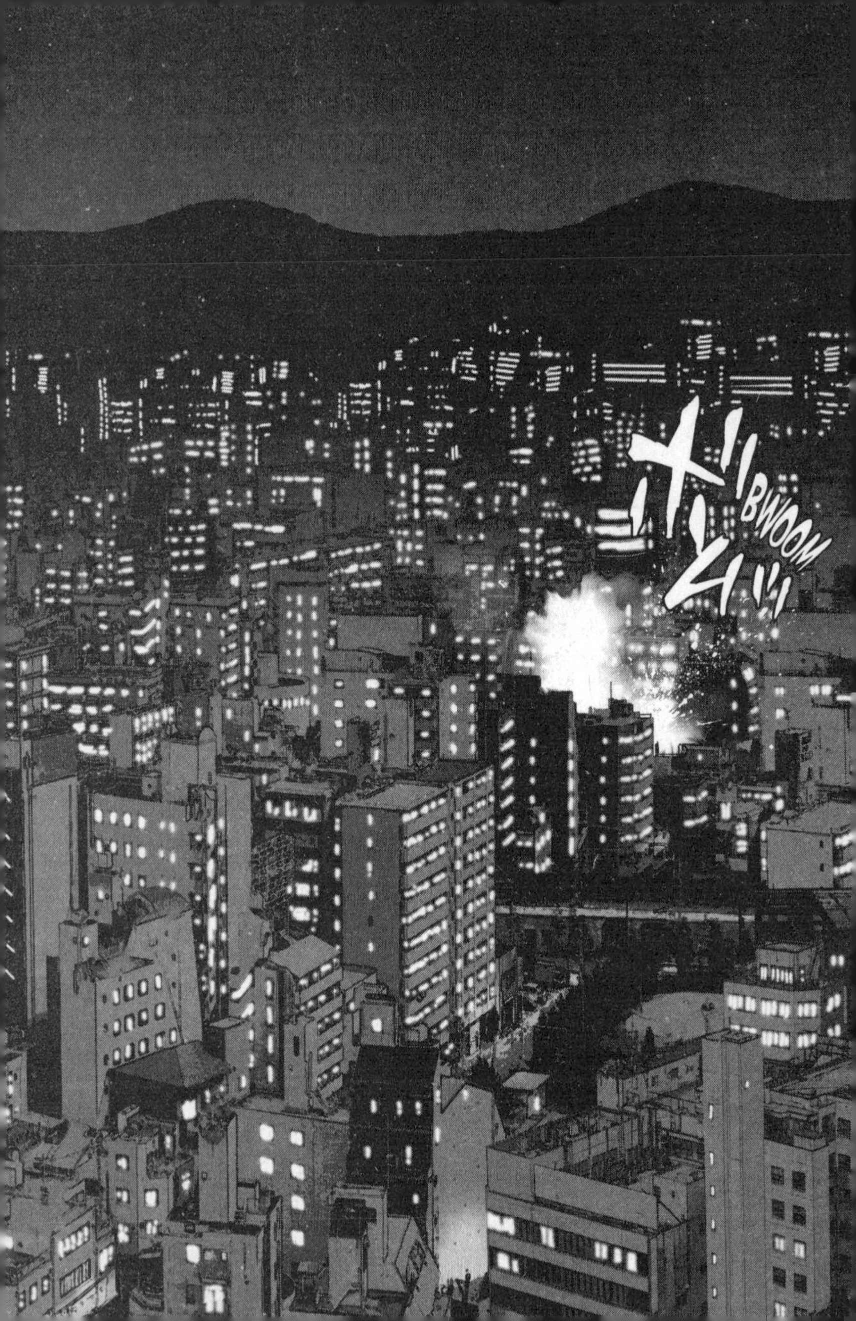
BWOOM

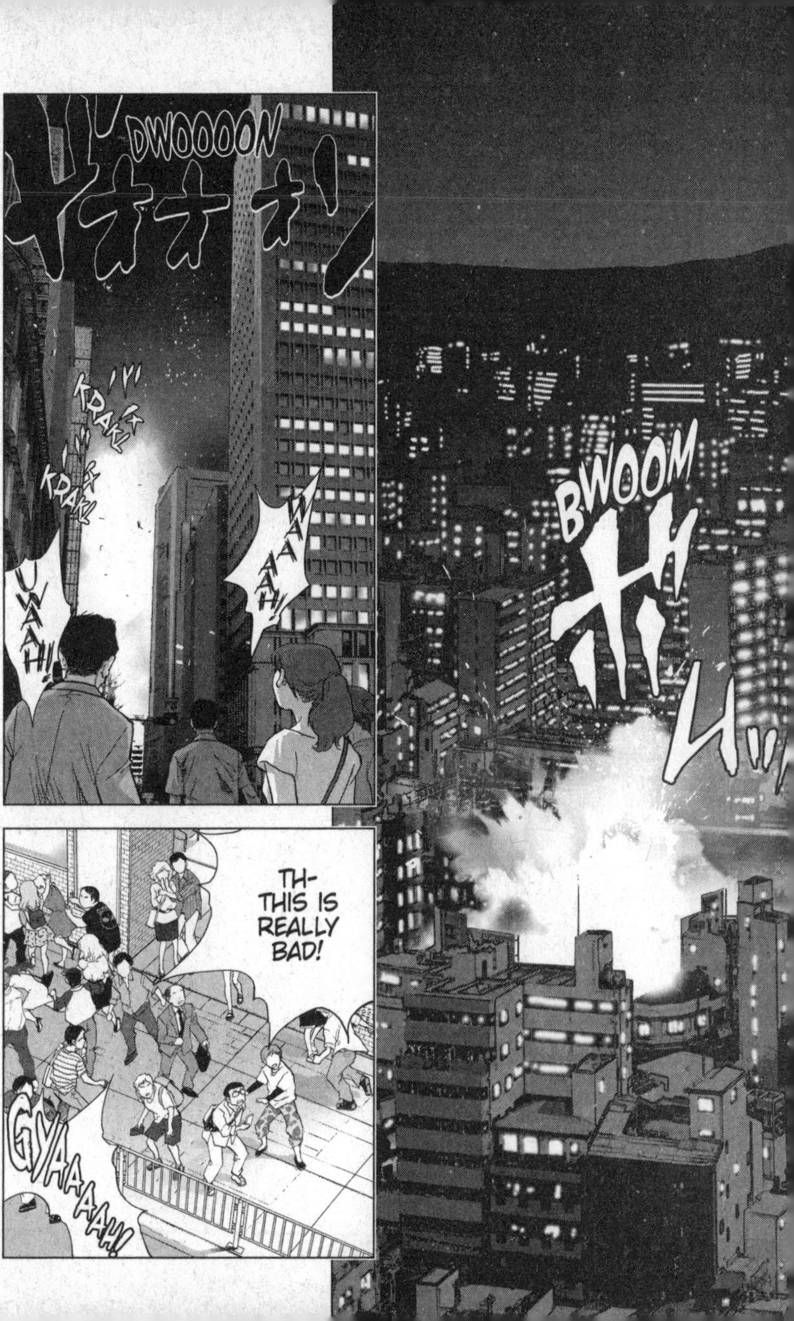
BWOOM
DWOOOON
KRAK!
KRAK!
WAAAAH!
UWAAAH!
TH-THIS IS REALLY BAD!
GYAAAAAH!

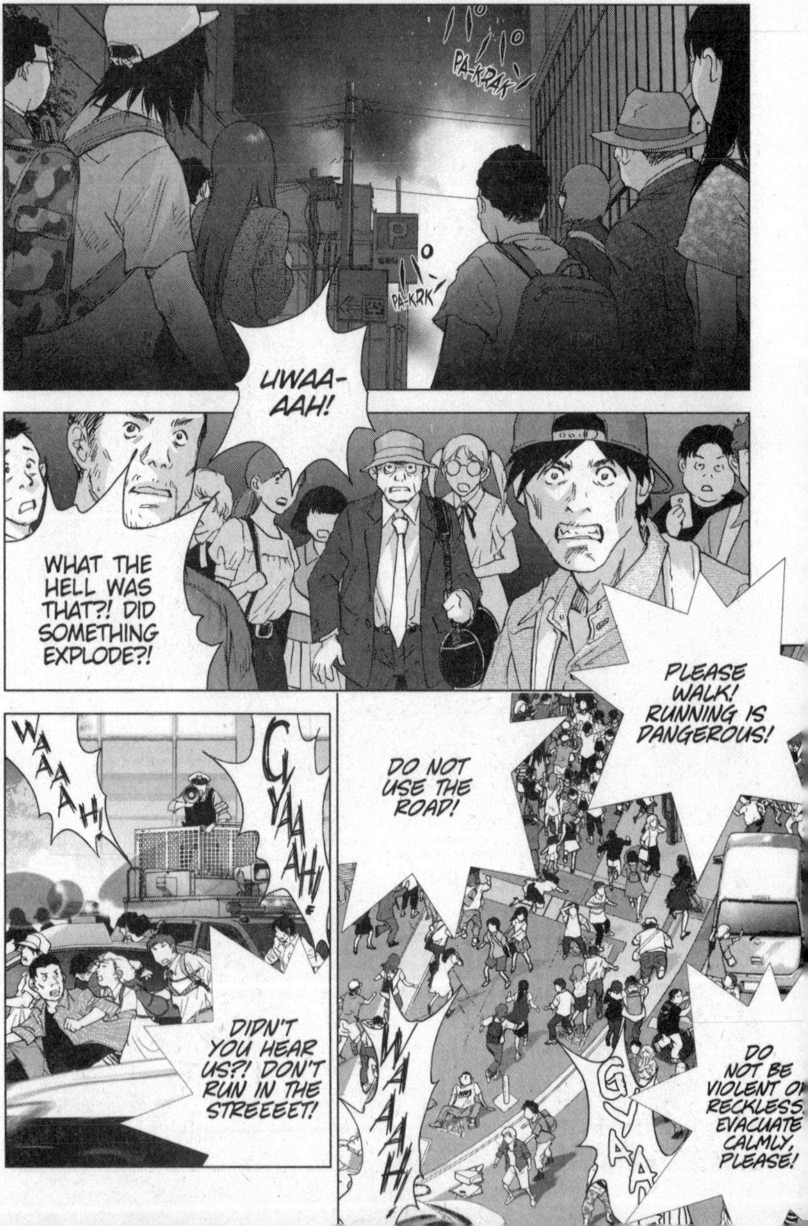
PA-KRAK
PA-KRK
UWAA-AAH!
WHAT THE HELL WAS THAT?! DID SOMETHING EXPLODE?!
PLEASE WALK! RUNNING IS DANGEROUS!
DO NOT USE THE ROAD!
DO NOT BE VIOLENT O RECKLESS. EVACUATE CALMLY, PLEASE!
GYAA
WAAAH!
GYAAAAH!
WAAAAH!
DIDN'T YOU HEAR US?! DON'T RUN IN THE STREEEET!

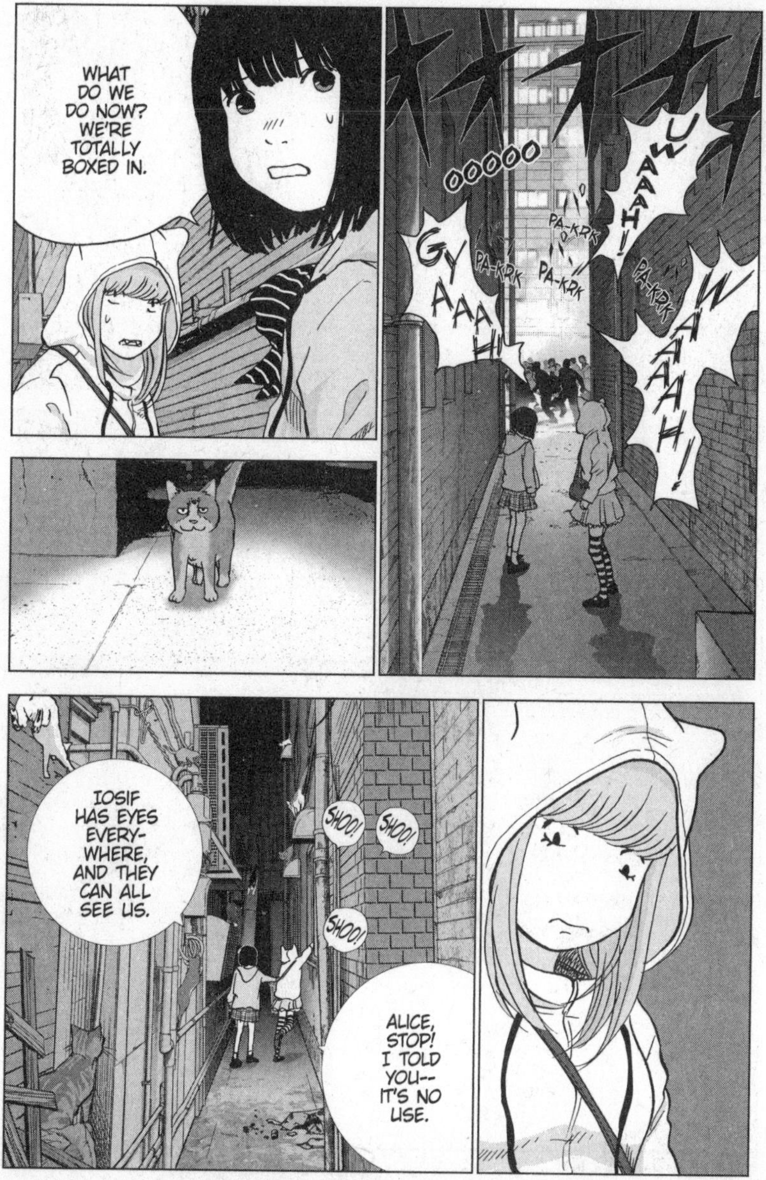
OOOOO
GYAAAAH!
PA-KRK
PA-KRK
PA-KRK
PA-KRK
UWAAAAH!
WAAAAAH!
WHAT DO WE DO NOW? WE'RE TOTALLY BOXED IN.
ALICE, STOP! I TOLD YOU-- IT'S NO USE.
IOSIF HAS EYES EVERY-WHERE, AND THEY CAN ALL SEE US.
SHOO!
SHOO!
SHOO!

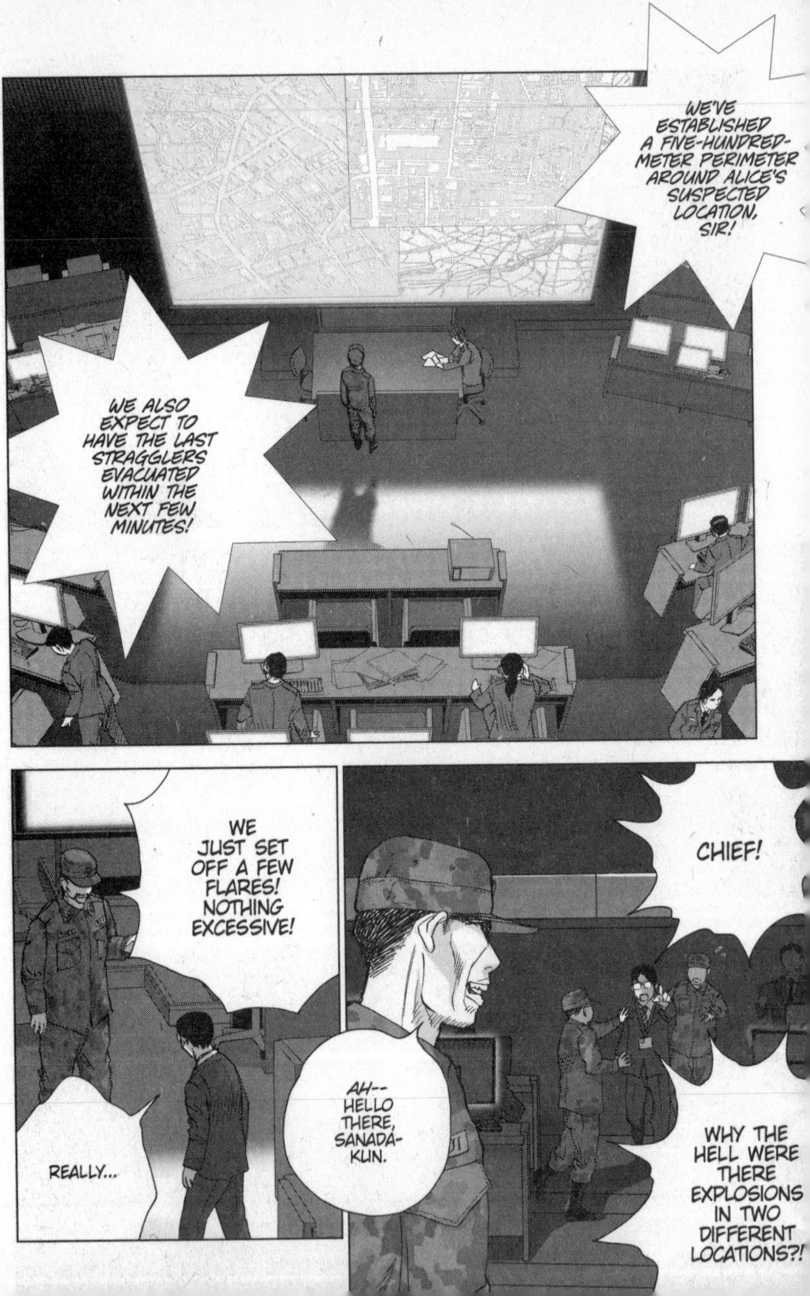
WE'VE ESTABLISHED A FIVE-HUNDRED-METER PERIMETER AROUND ALICE'S SUSPECTED LOCATION, SIR!
WE ALSO EXPECT TO HAVE THE LAST STRAGGLERS EVACUATED WITHIN THE NEXT FEW MINUTES!
CHIEF!
WHY THE HELL WERE THERE EXPLOSIONS IN TWO DIFFERENT LOCATIONS?!
AH-- HELLO THERE, SANADA-KUN.
WE JUST SET OFF A FEW FLARES! NOTHING EXCESSIVE!
REALLY...

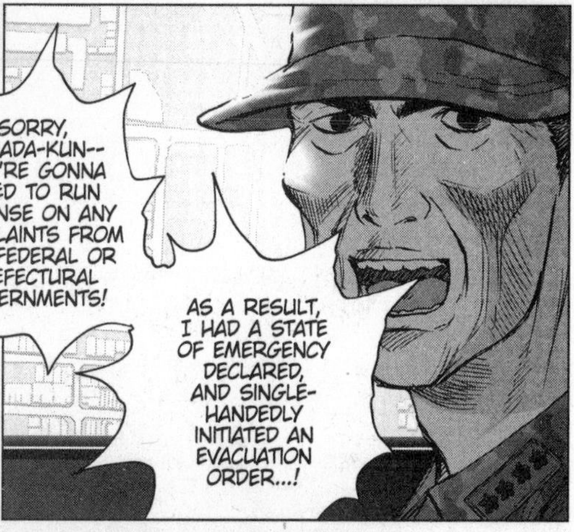
AS A RESULT, I HAD A STATE OF EMERGENCY DECLARED, AND SINGLE-HANDEDLY INITIATED AN EVACUATION ORDER...!
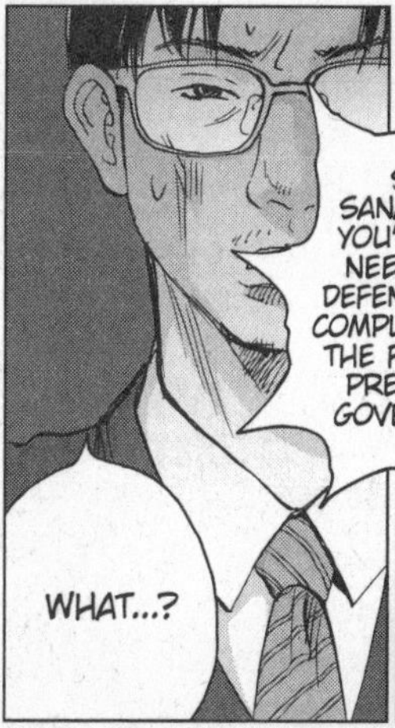
SORRY, SANADA-KUN-- YOU'RE GONNA NEED TO RUN DEFENSE ON ANY COMPLAINTS FROM THE FEDERAL OR PREFECTURAL GOVERNMENTS!
WHAT...?
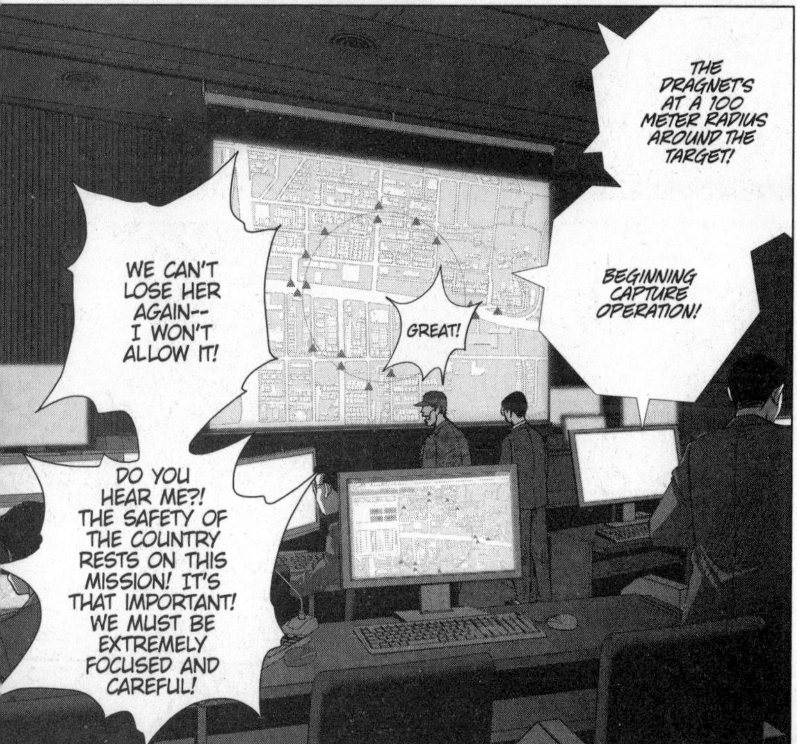
THE DRAGNET'S AT A 100 METER RADIUS AROUND THE TARGET!
BEGINNING CAPTURE OPERATION!
GREAT!
WE CAN'T LOSE HER AGAIN-- I WON'T ALLOW IT!
DO YOU HEAR ME?! THE SAFETY OF THE COUNTRY RESTS ON THIS MISSION! IT'S THAT IMPORTANT! WE MUST BE EXTREMELY FOCUSED AND CAREFUL!

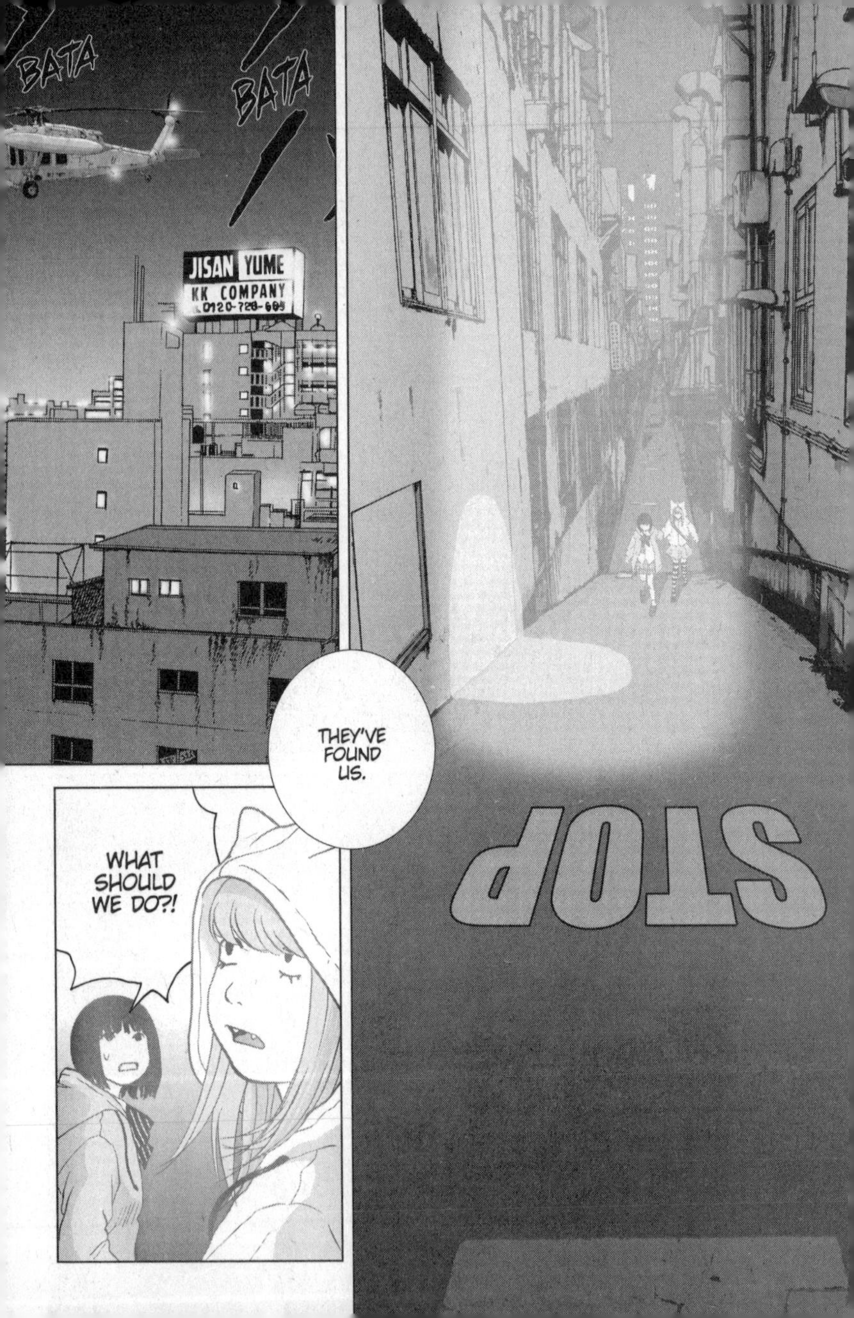
STOP
THEY'VE FOUND US.
BATA
BATA
JISAN YUME
KK COMPANY
WHAT SHOULD WE DO?!

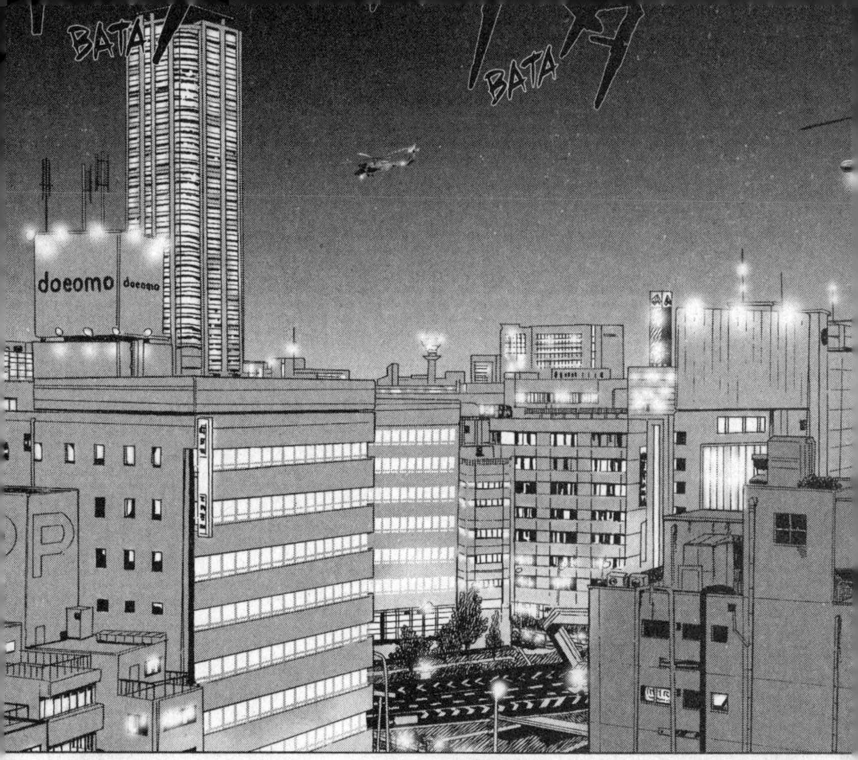
BATA
BATA
doeomo
docomo
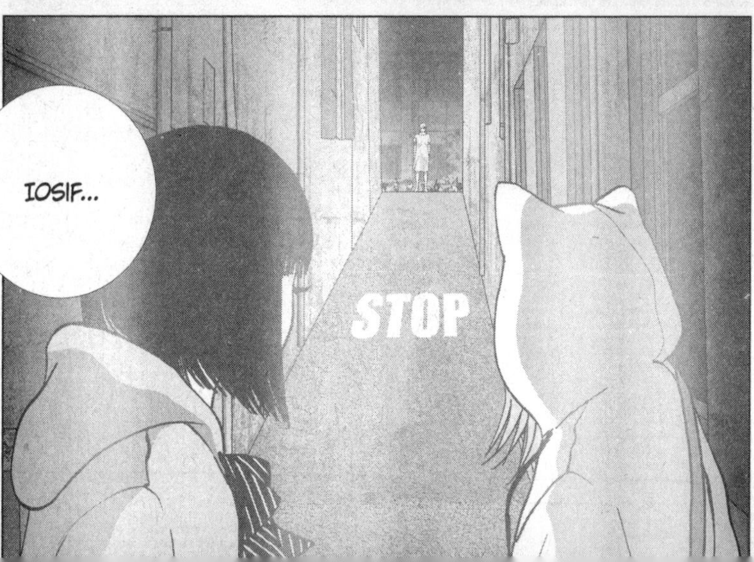
IOSIF...
STOP

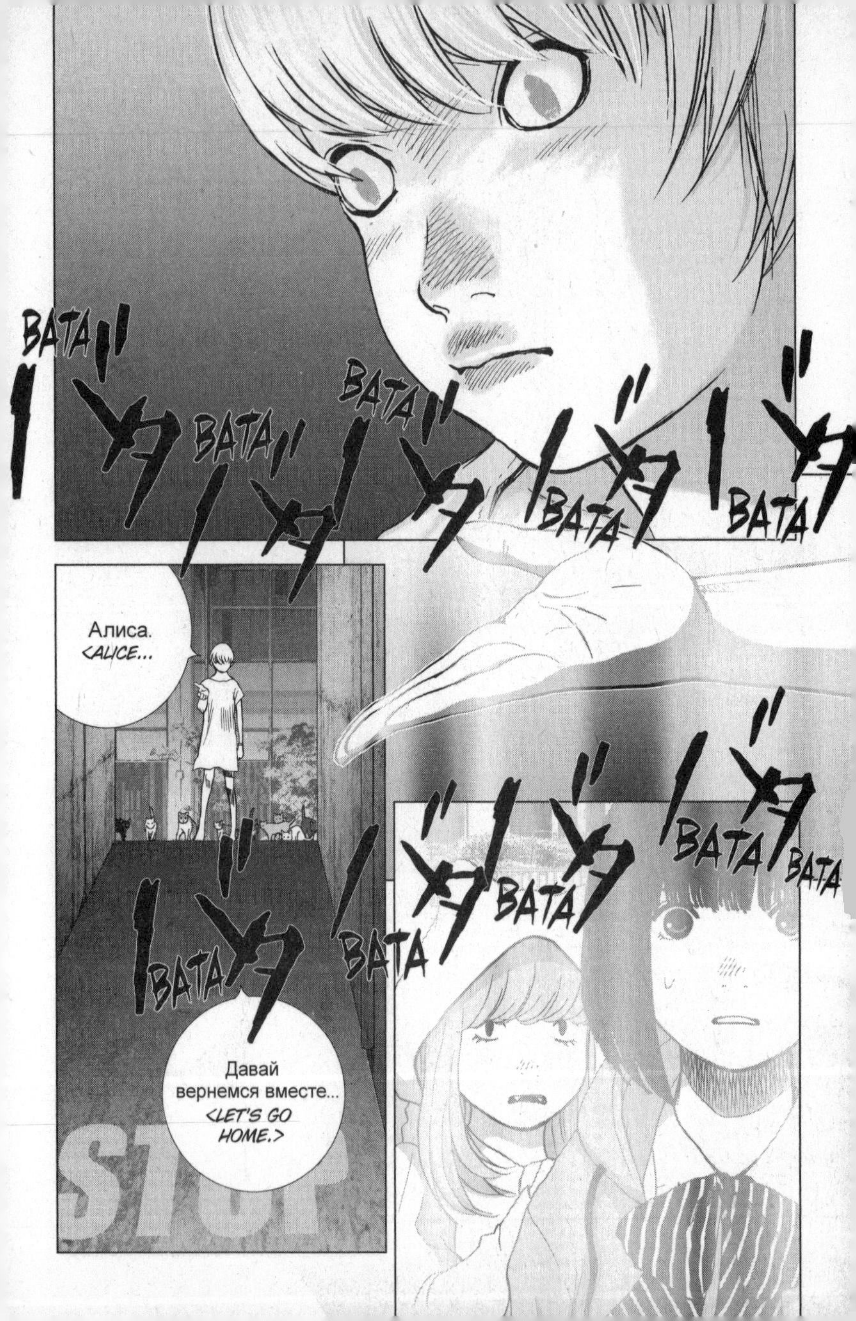

BATA
BATA
BATA
BATA
BATA
Алиса.
<ALICE...
BATA
BATA
BATA
BATA
BATA
Давай вернемся вместе...
<LET'S GO HOME.>

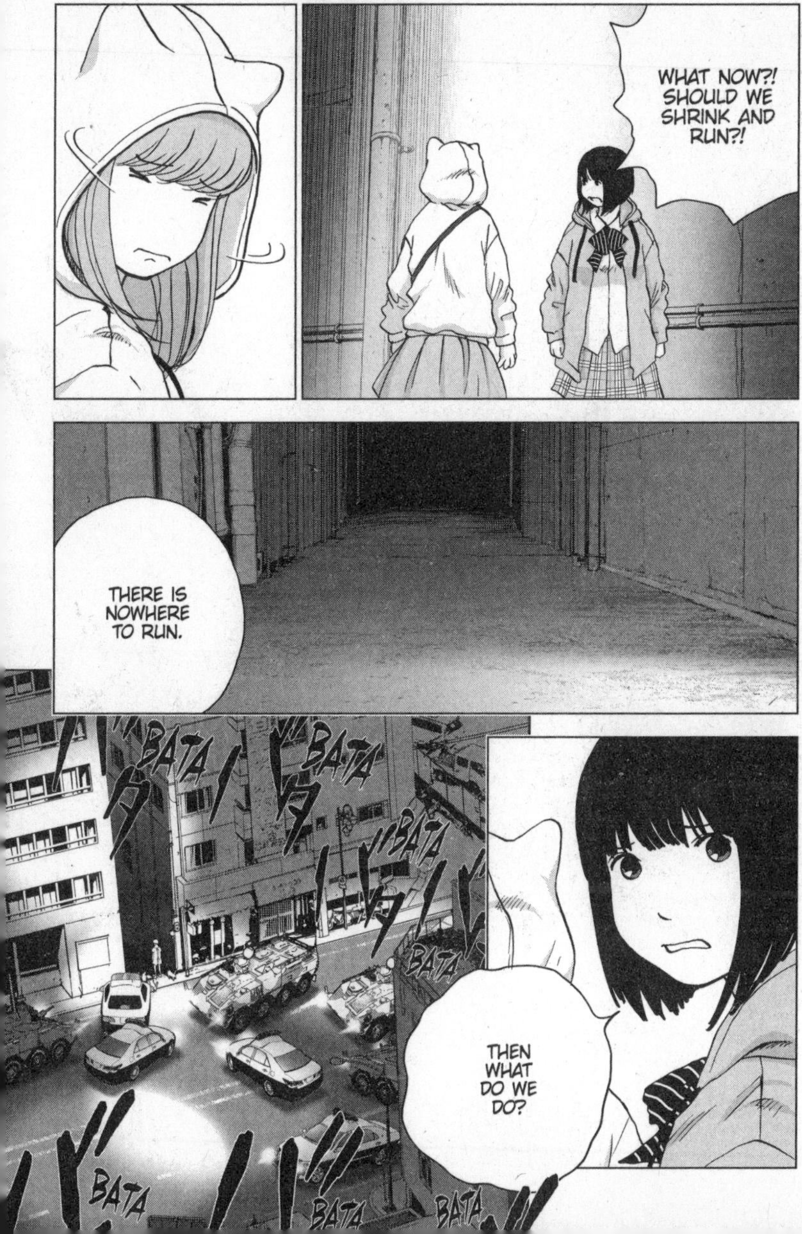
WHAT NOW?! SHOULD WE SHRINK AND RUN?!
THERE IS NOWHERE TO RUN.
THEN WHAT DO WE DO?
BATA
BATA
BATA
BATA
BATA
BATA
BATA

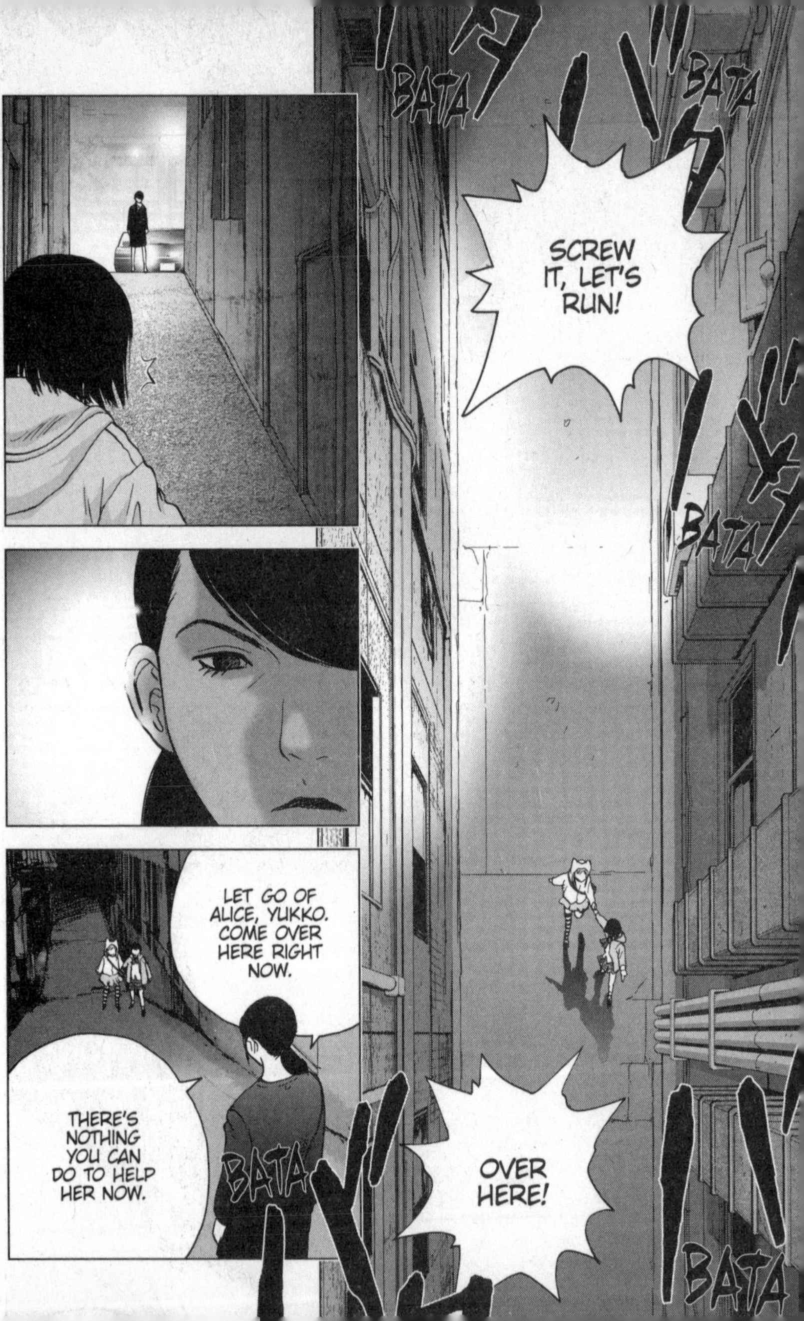
LET GO OF ALICE, YUKKO. COME OVER HERE RIGHT NOW.
THERE'S NOTHING YOU CAN DO TO HELP HER NOW.
BATA
BATA
SCREW IT, LET'S RUN!
BATA
OVER HERE!
BATA
BATA

WHY DO YOU HATE ALICE SO MUCH?!

AND WHY DO WE HAVE TO DO EVERYTHING YOUR WAY?!

SURE, SHE'S GOT SPECIAL POWERS...!

BUT WHY DOES THAT MEAN SHE CAN'T BE FREE?!

YUKKO-CHAN, I'M SORRY.

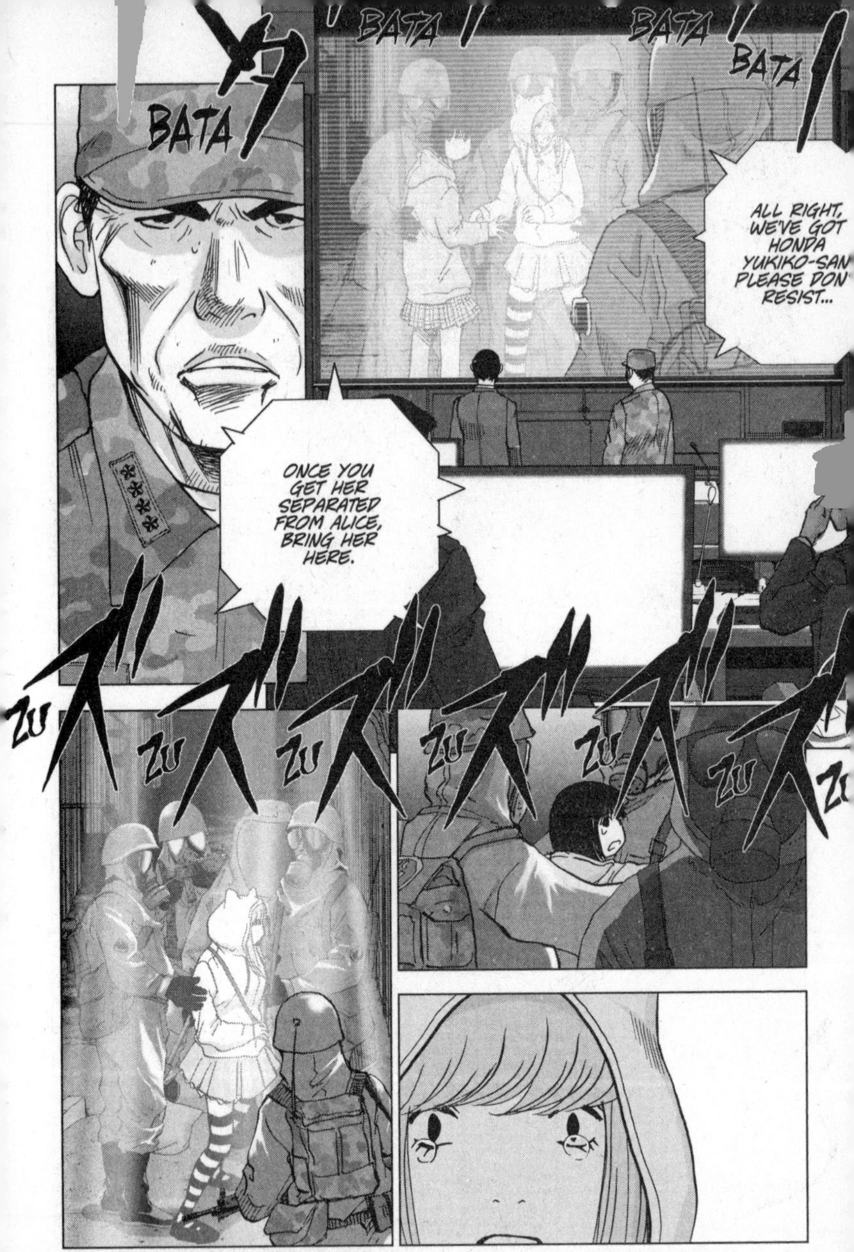
BATA BATA BATA
ALL RIGHT, WE'VE GOT HONDA YUKIKO-SAN PLEASE DON' RESIST...
BATA
ONCE YOU GET HER SEPARATED FROM ALICE, BRING HER HERE.
ZU ZU ZU ZU ZU ZU ZU

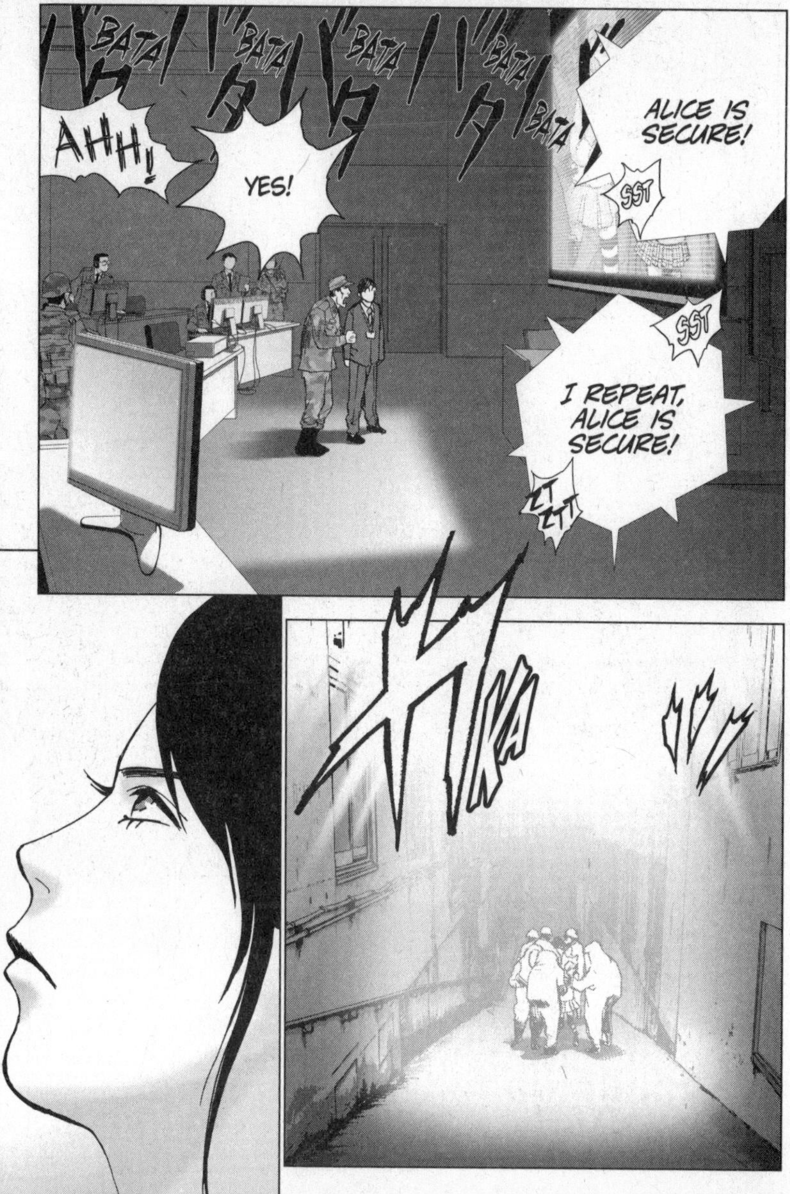
ALICE IS SECURE!
SST
SST
I REPEAT, ALICE IS SECURE!
BATA
BATA
BATA
BATA
BATA
YES!
AHH!
KA

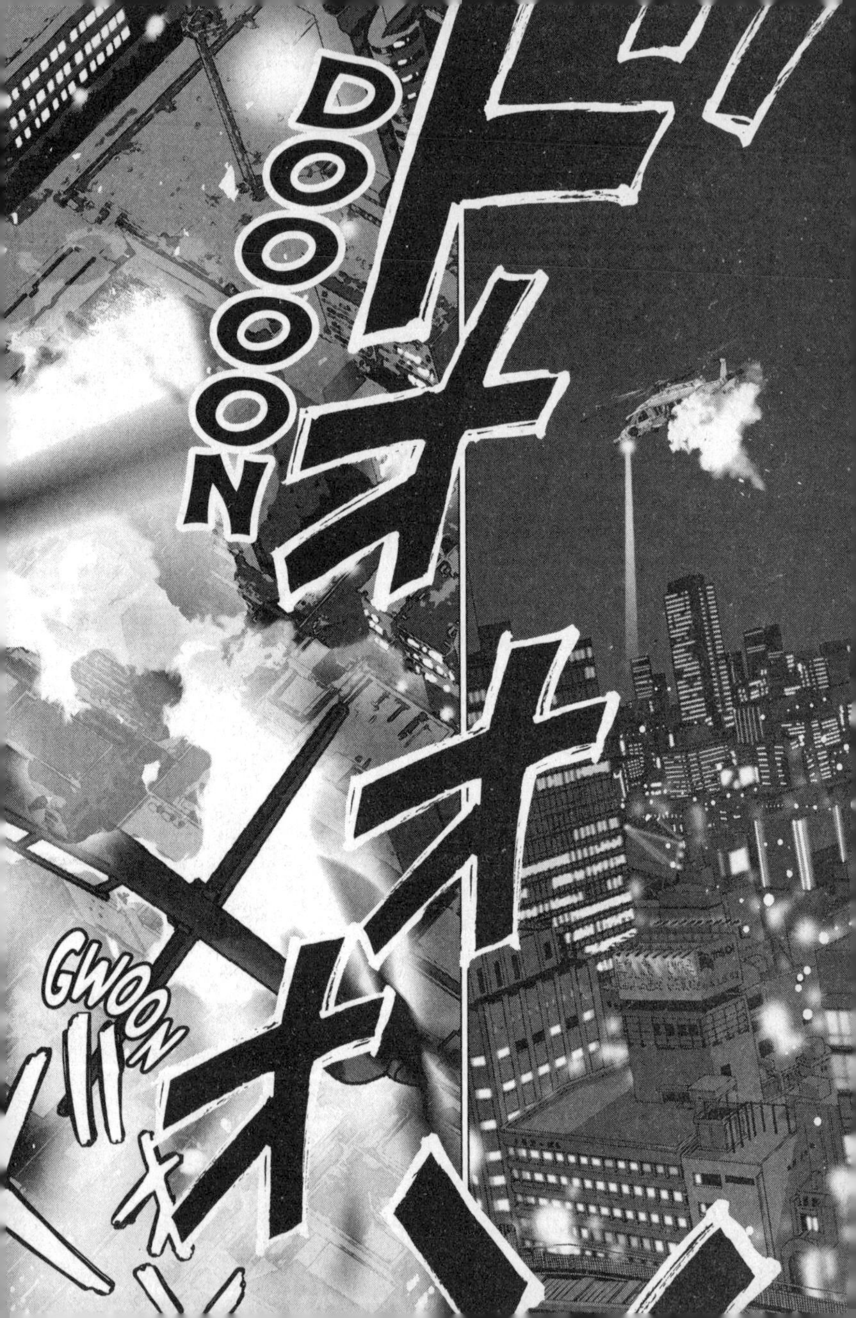
DOOOOON
GWOON

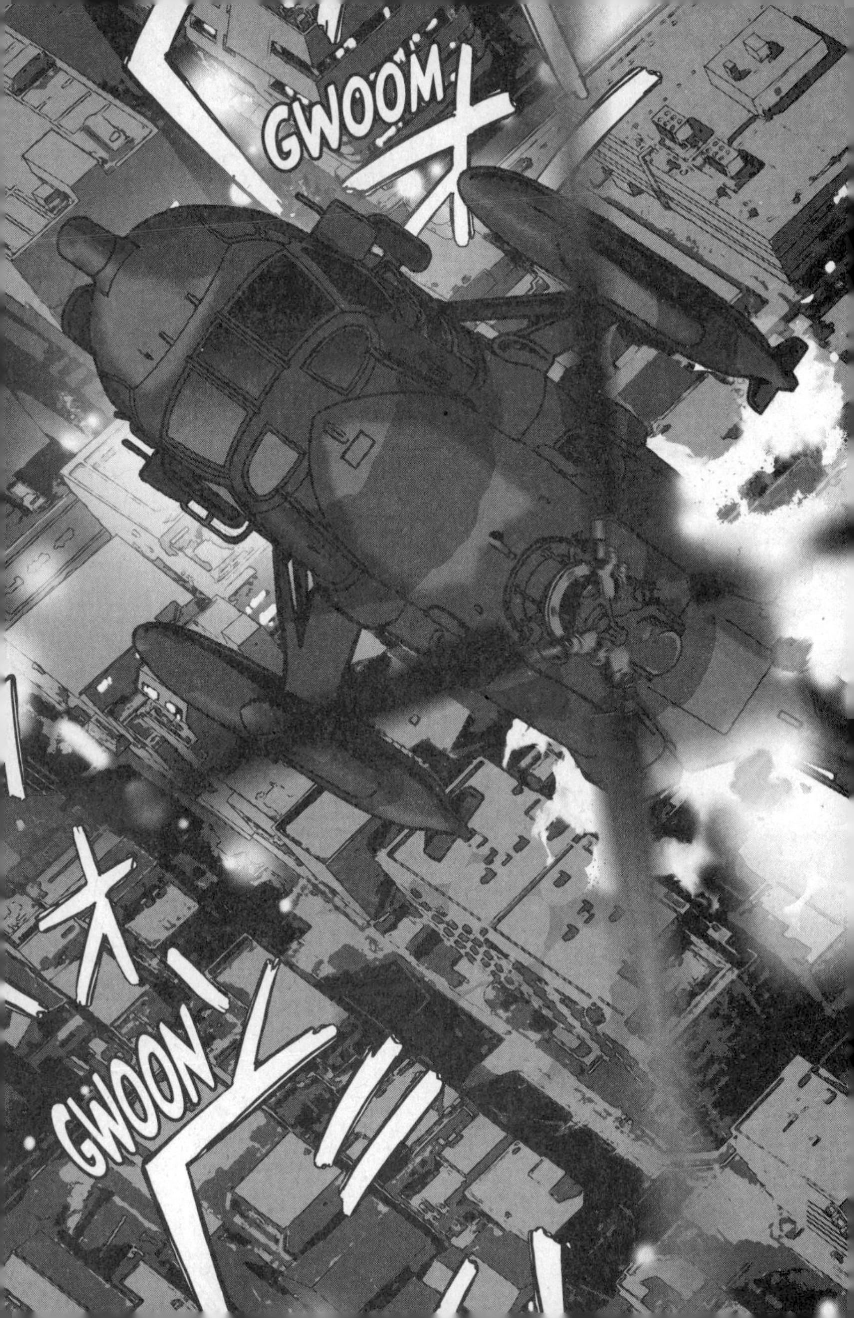
GWOOM
GWOON

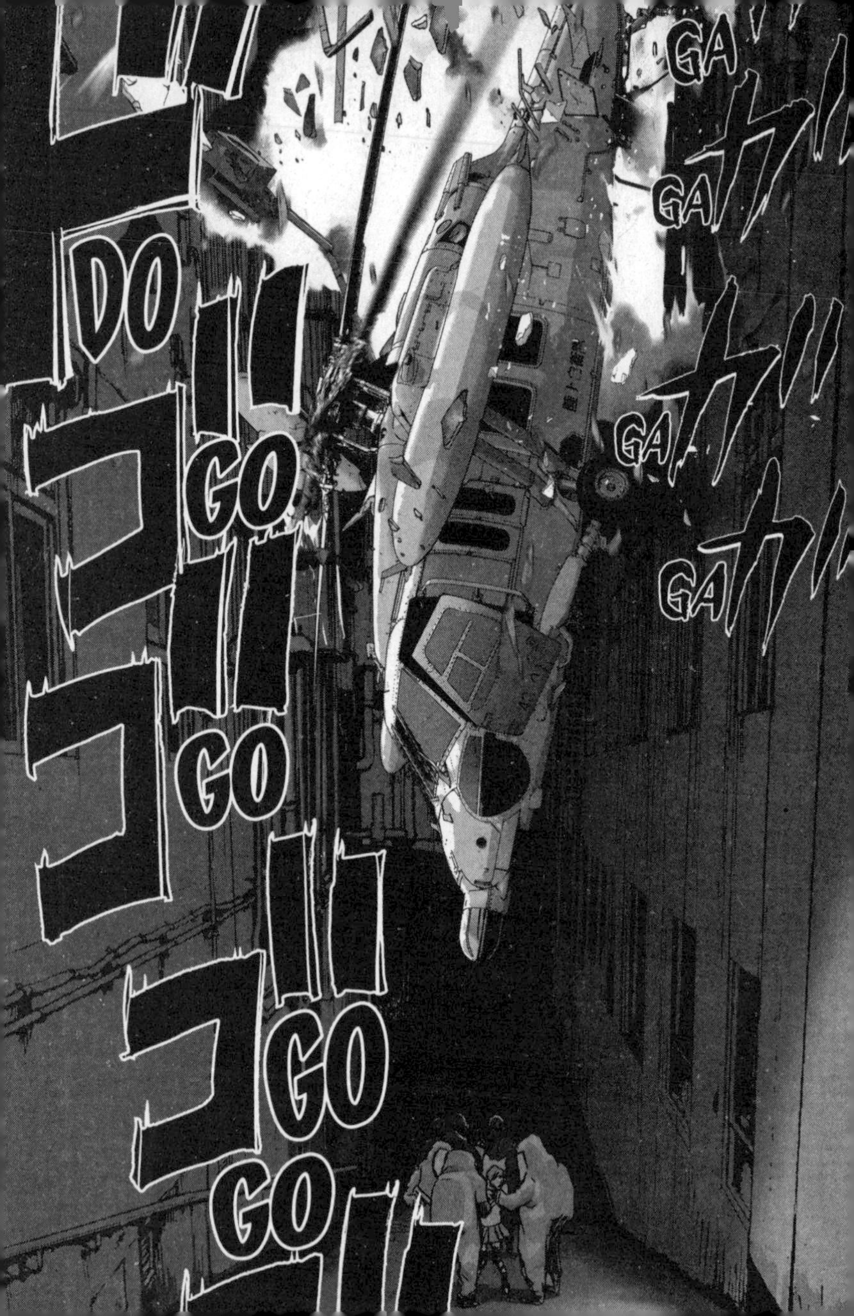
GA
GA
GA
GA
DO
GO
GO
GO
GO

Chapter 34: New Encounter

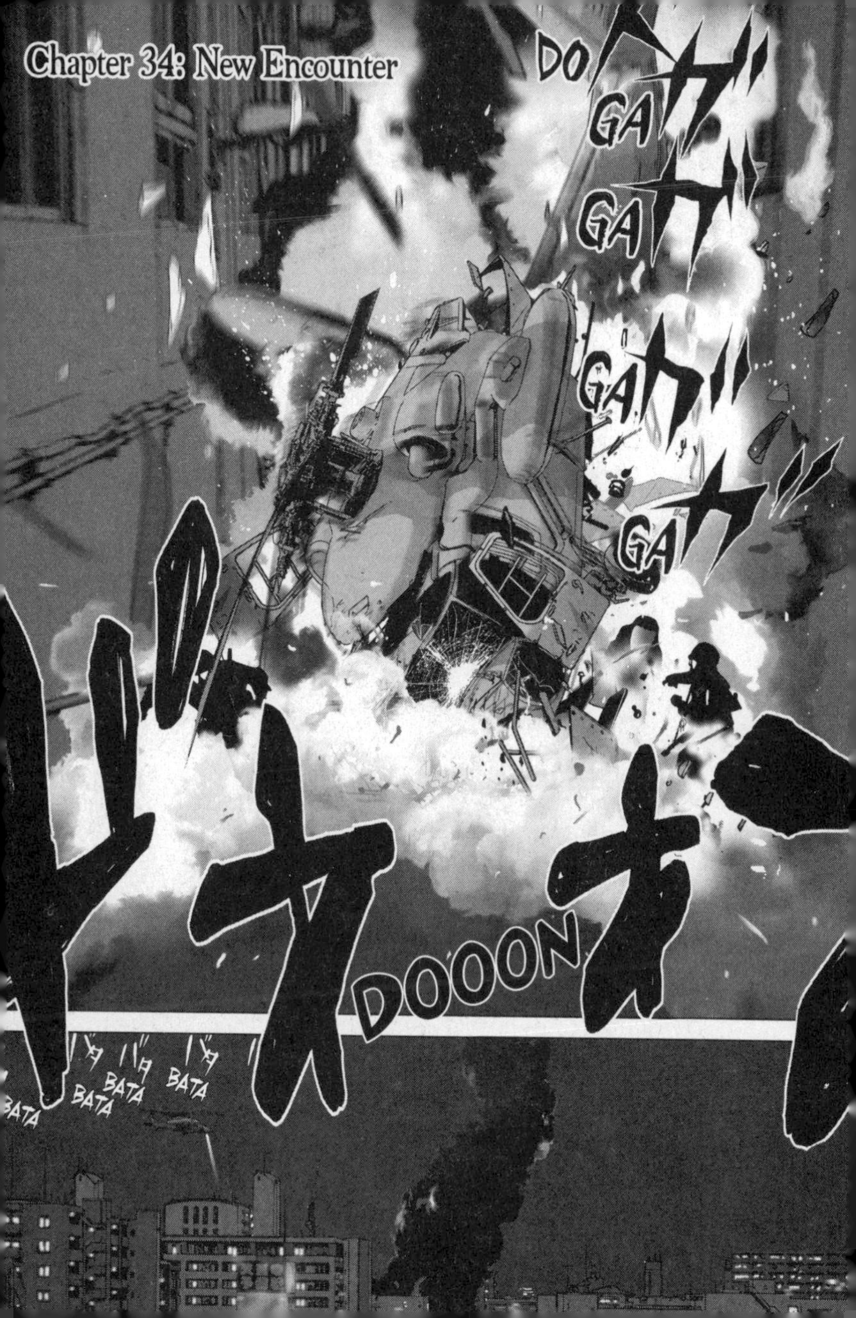
DO
GA
GA
GA
GA
DOOON
BATA
BATA
BATA
BATA

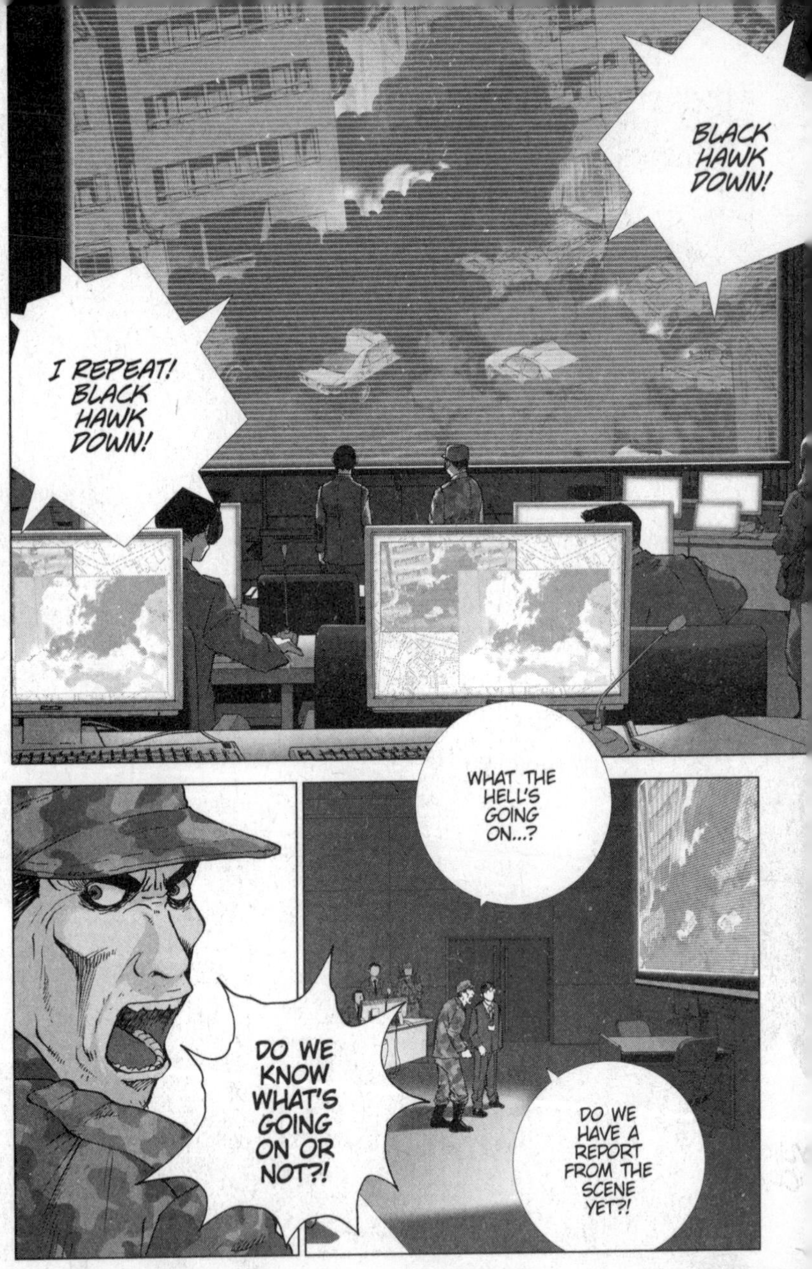
BLACK HAWK DOWN!
I REPEAT! BLACK HAWK DOWN!
WHAT THE HELL'S GOING ON...?
DO WE HAVE A REPORT FROM THE SCENE YET?!
DO WE KNOW WHAT'S GOING ON OR NOT?!

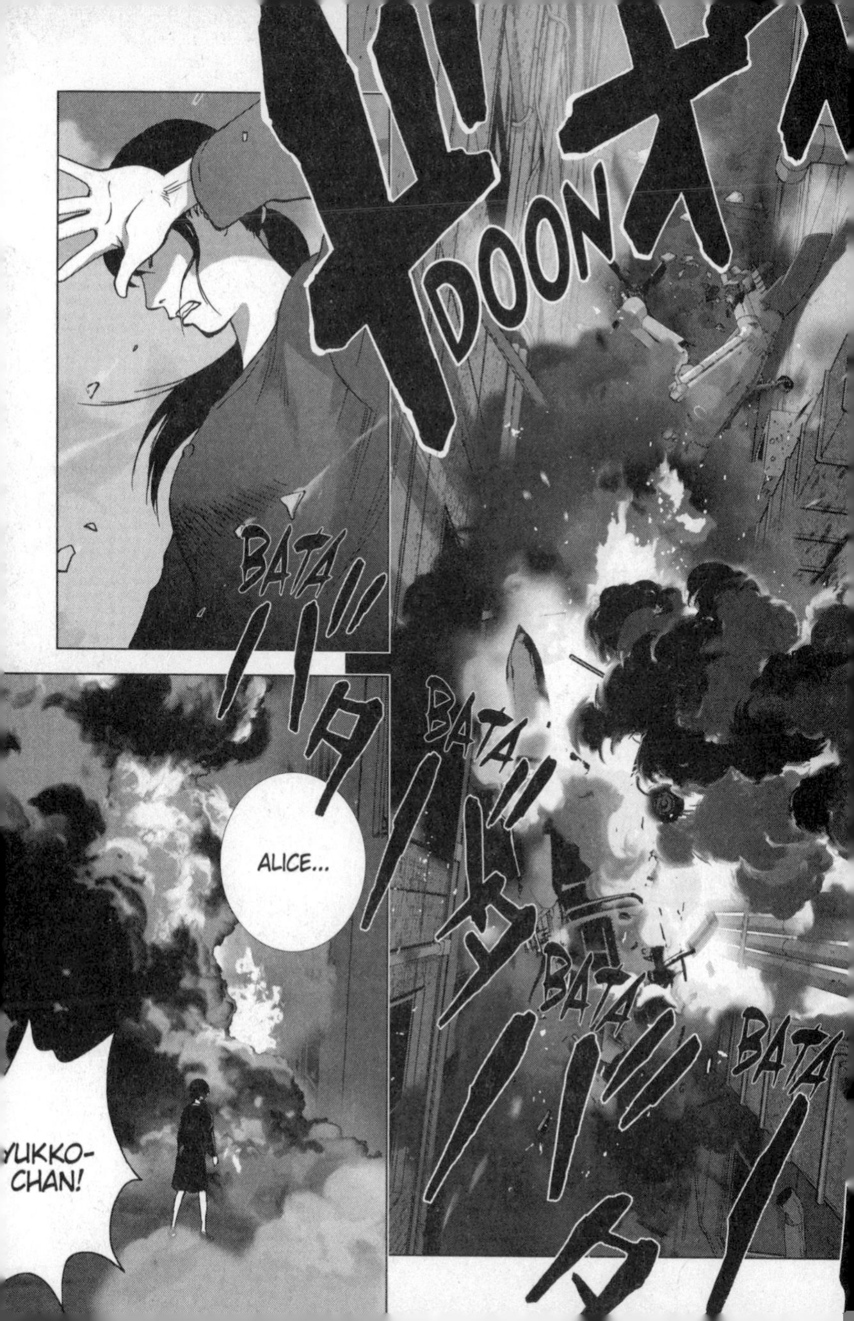
DOON
BATA
BATA
BATA
BATA
ALICE...
YUKKO-CHAN!

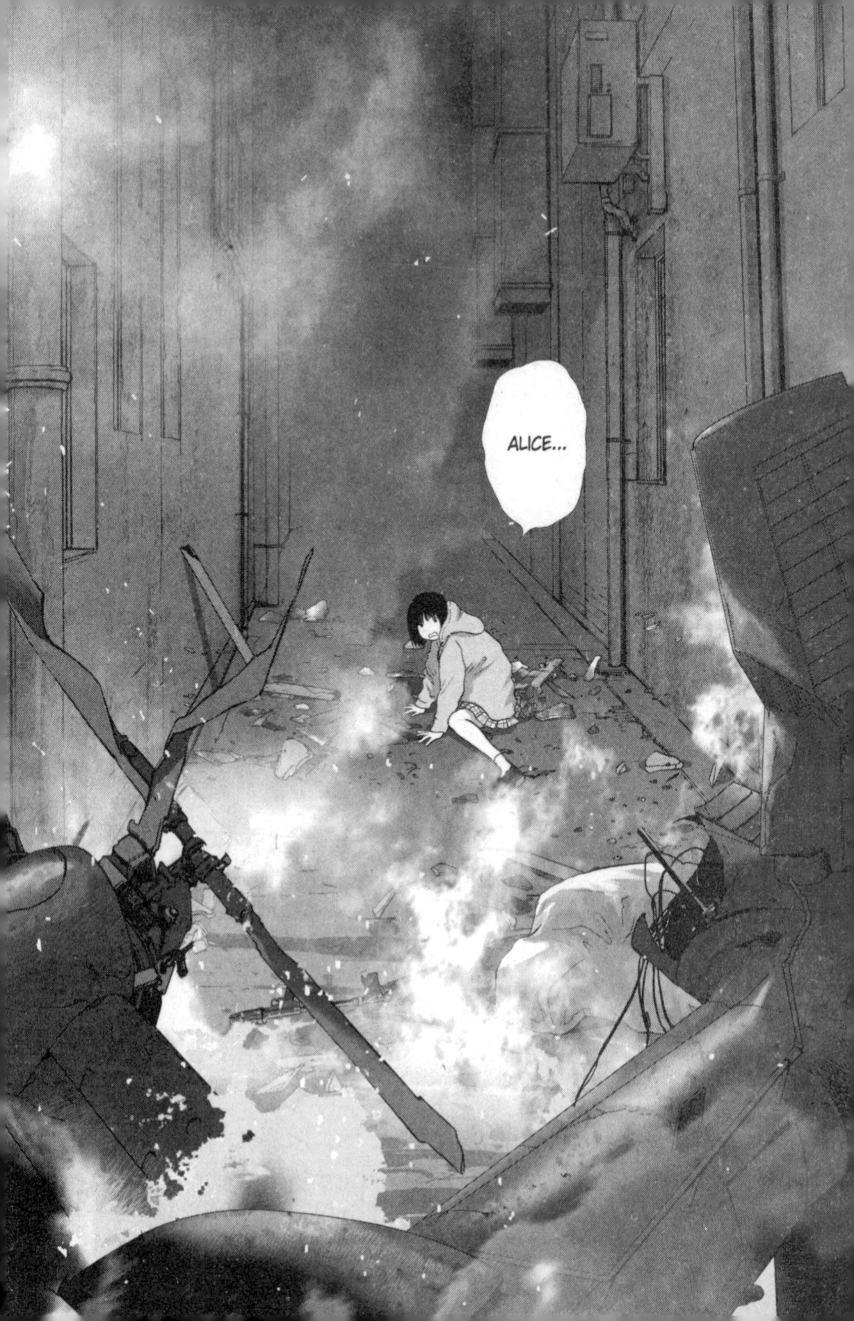
ALICE...

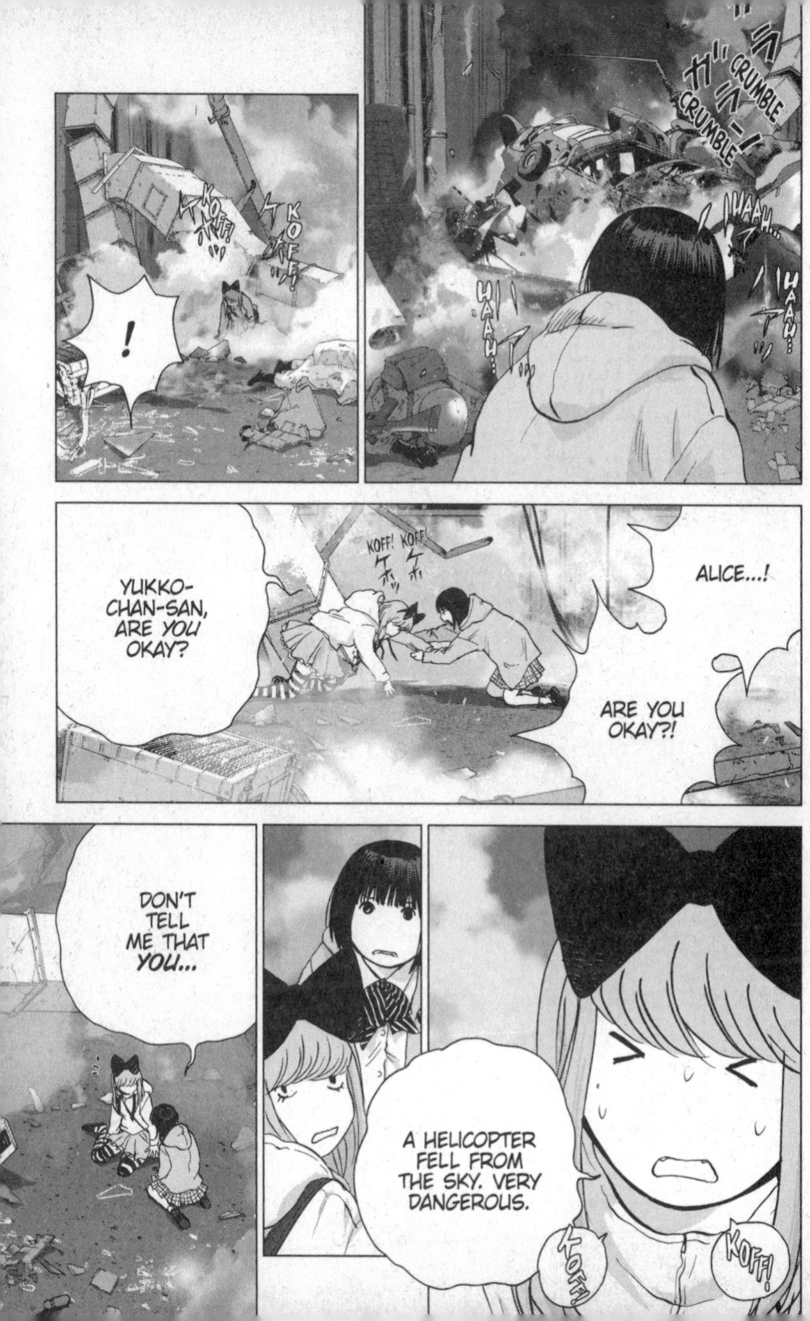
CRUMBLE
CRUMBLE
HAAAH...
HAAAH...
HAAAH...
KOFF!
KOFF!
!
ALICE...!
ARE YOU OKAY?!
KOFF! KOFF!
YUKKO-CHAN-SAN, ARE YOU OKAY?
DON'T TELL ME THAT YOU...
A HELICOPTER FELL FROM THE SKY. VERY DANGEROUS.
KOFF!
KOFF!

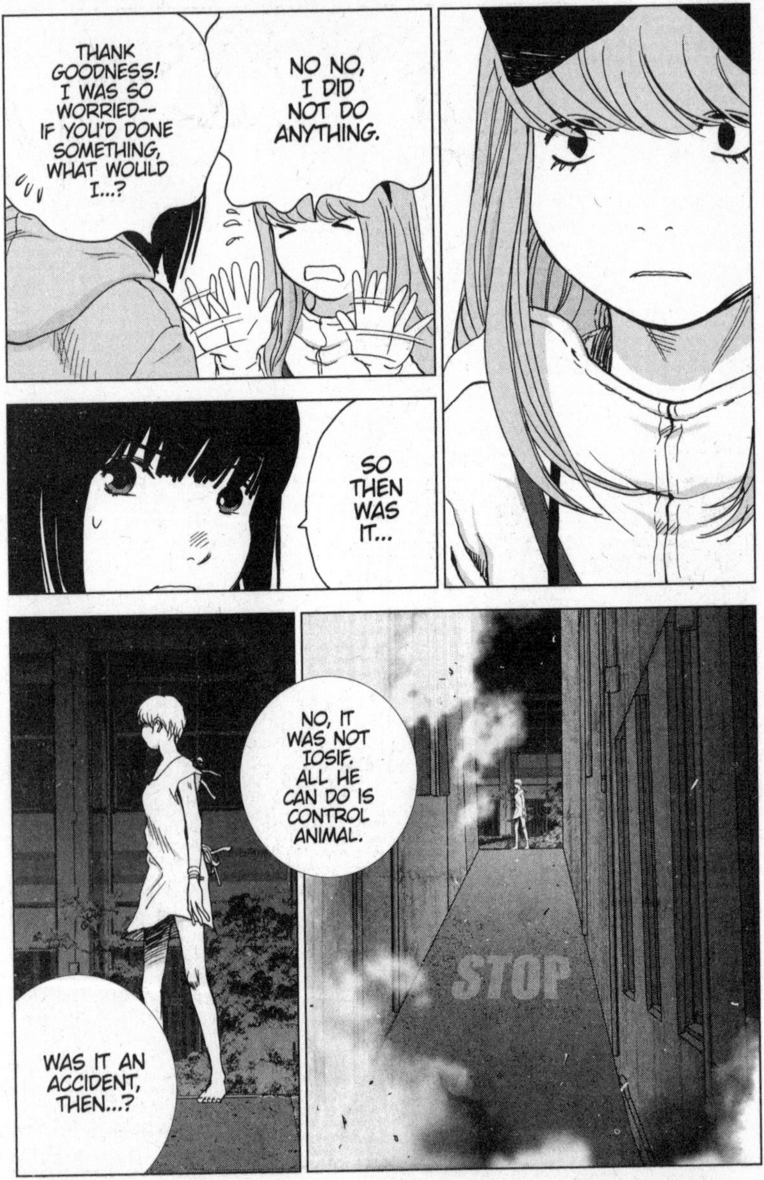
NO NO, I DID NOT DO ANYTHING.
THANK GOODNESS! I WAS SO WORRIED-- IF YOU'D DONE SOMETHING, WHAT WOULD I...?
SO THEN WAS IT...
NO, IT WAS NOT IOSIF. ALL HE CAN DO IS CONTROL ANIMAL.
STOP
WAS IT AN ACCIDENT, THEN...?

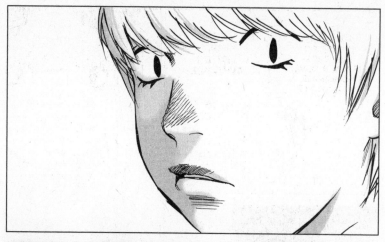

Алиса!!
<ALICE!!>

убегай!!
<RUN!!>

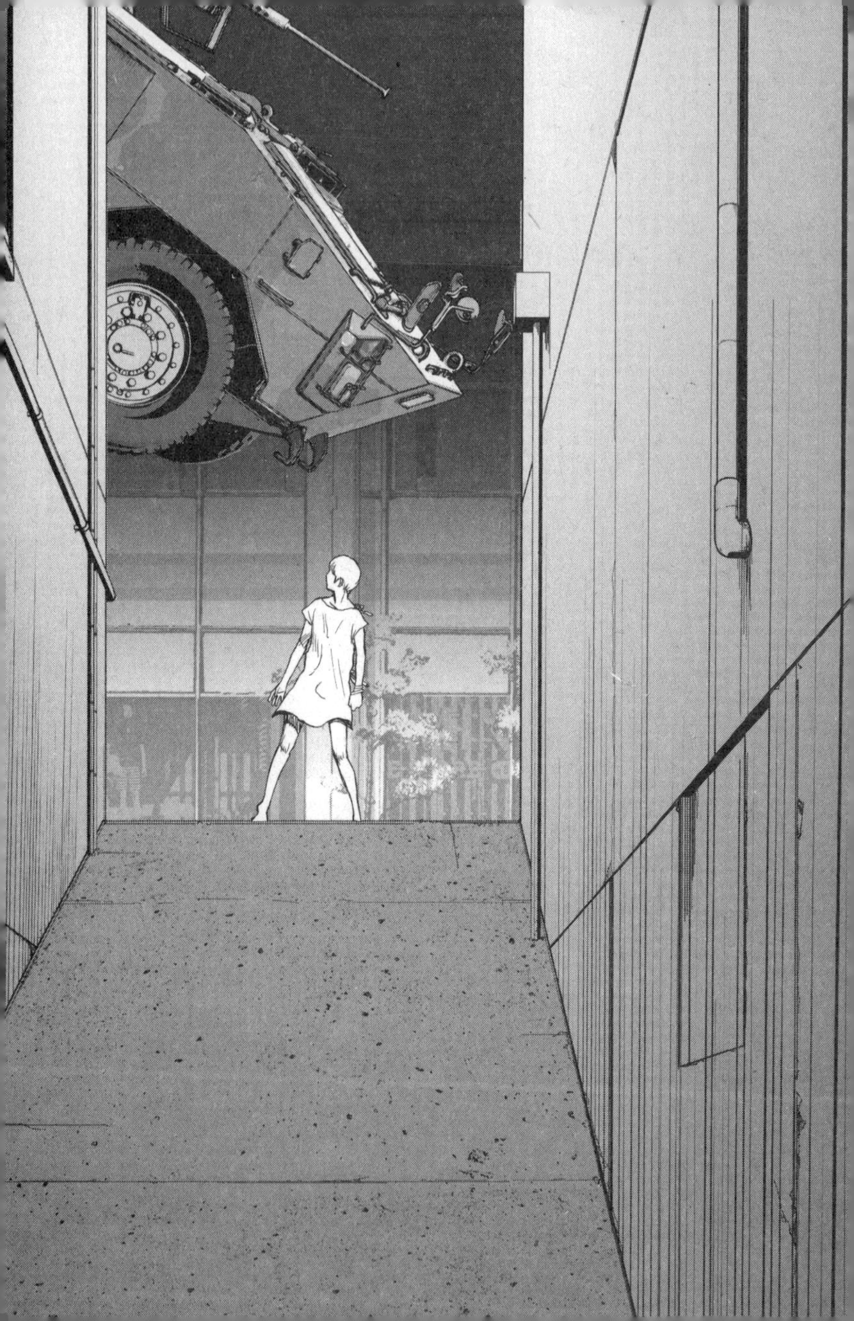

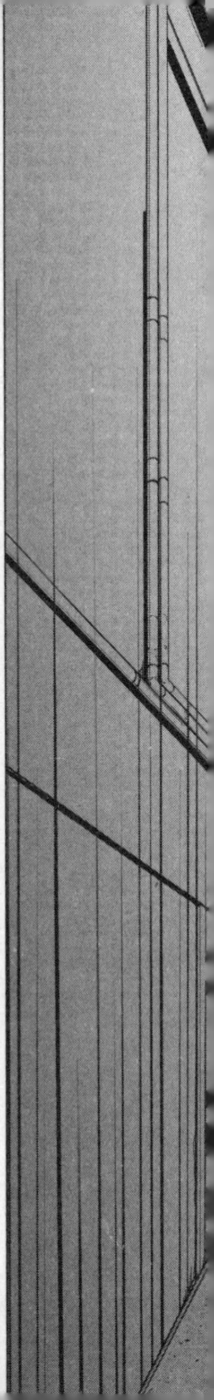

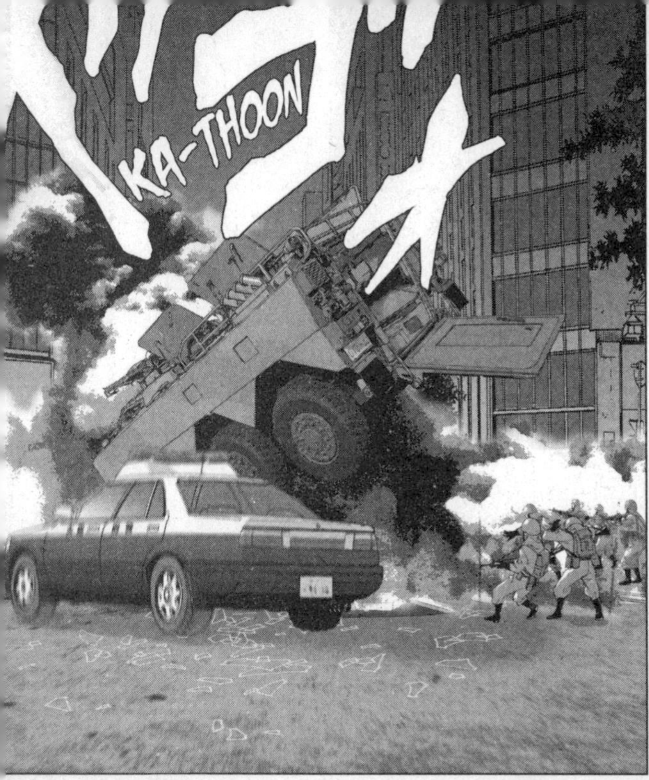
KA-THOON

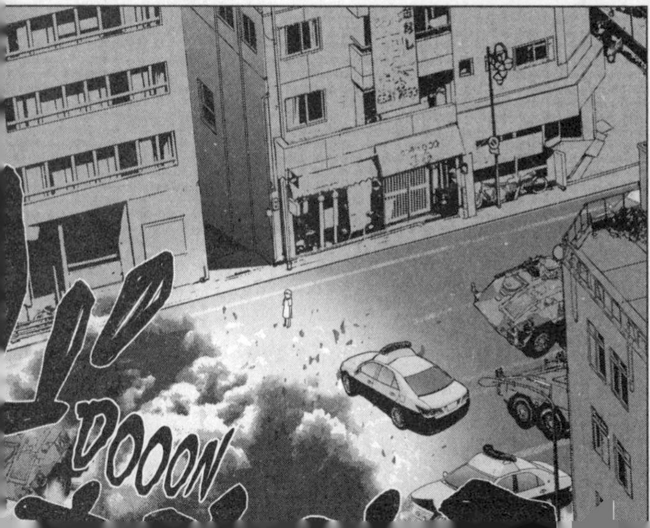
DOOON

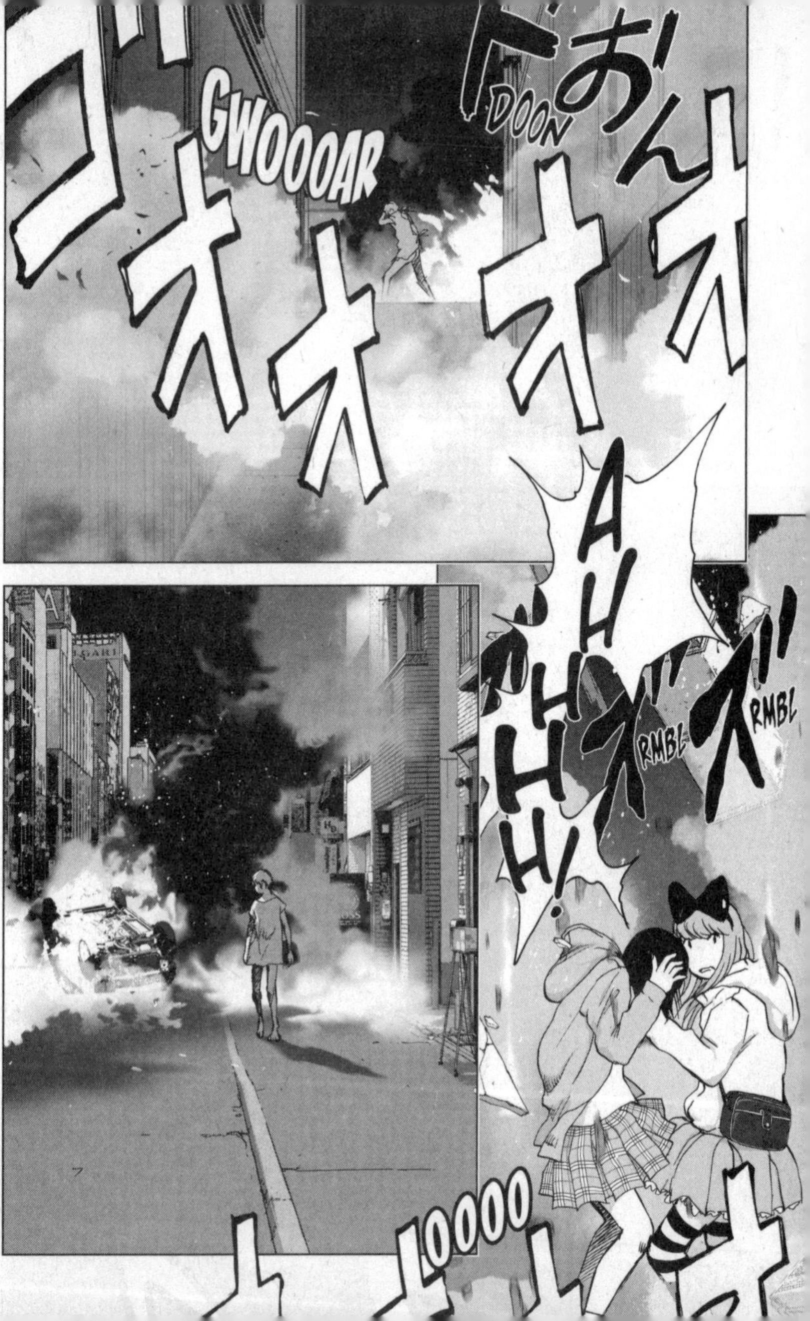
ドおん
DOON
ゴオオオオ
GWOOOAR
AHHHHH!
ズズ
RMBL
RMBL
LOOOO

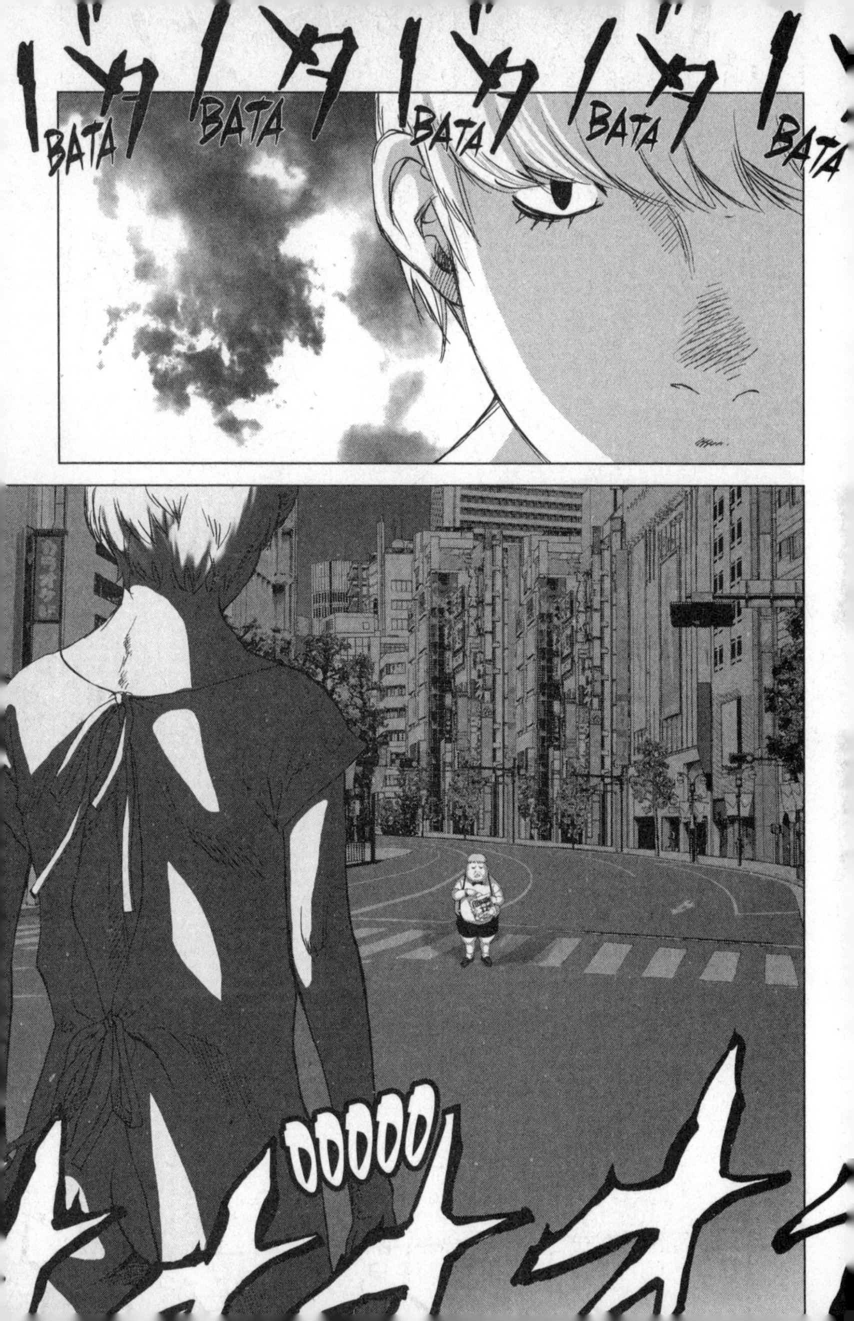
BATA
BATA
BATA
BATA
BATA
DDDDD

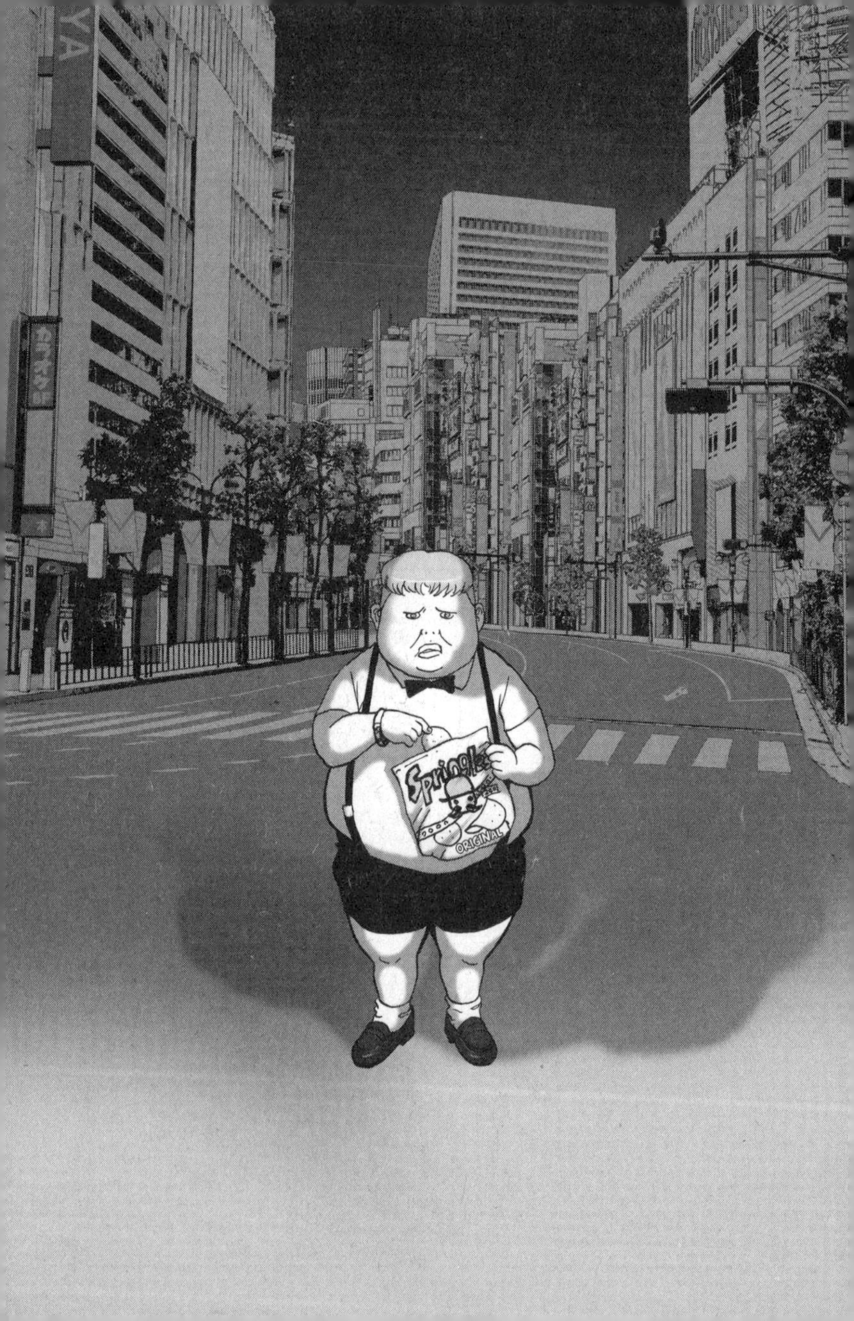
YA
ORIGINAL

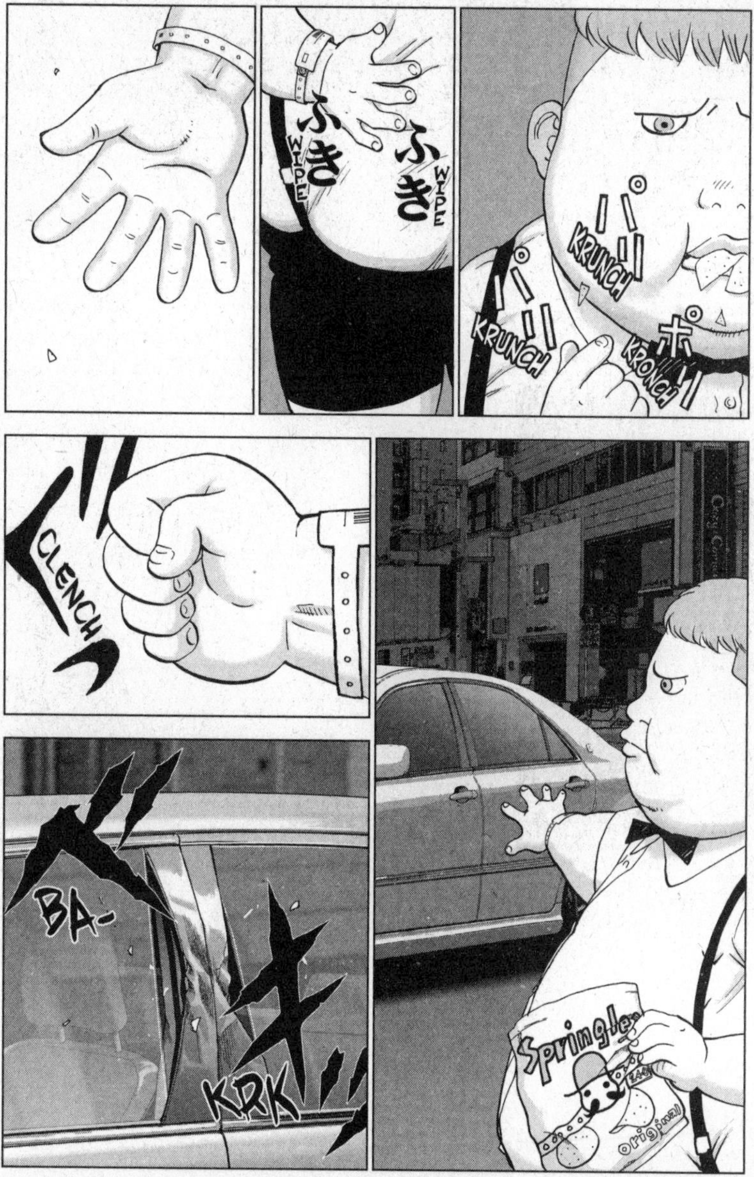

パ
KRUNCH
パ
KRUNCH
ポ
KRONCH
ふき
WIPE
ふき
WIPE
Springles
original
CLENCH
BA-
KRK

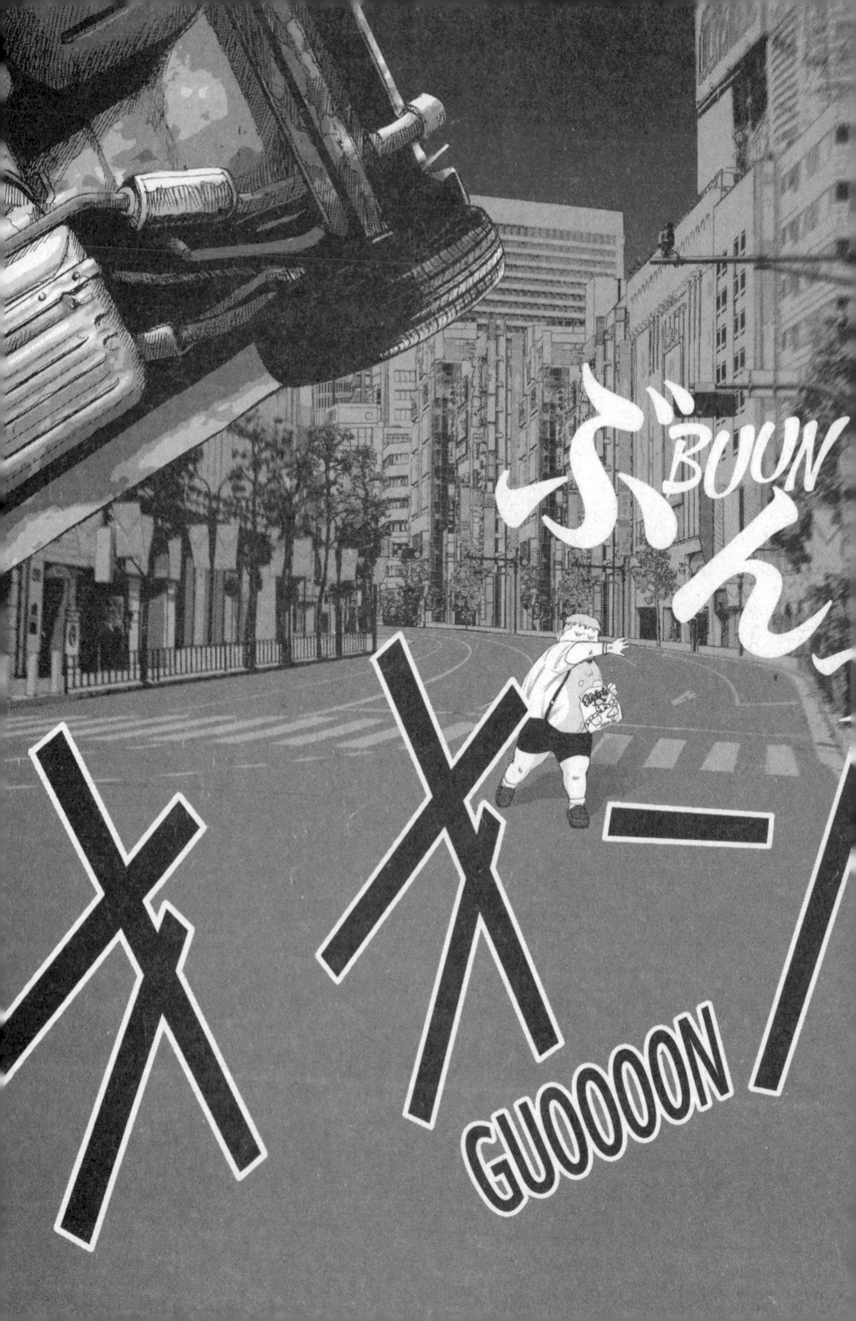
ぶん
BUUN
ズズーン
GUOOOON

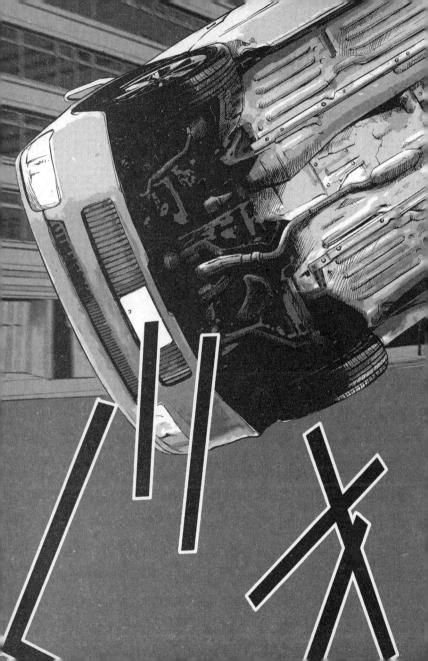

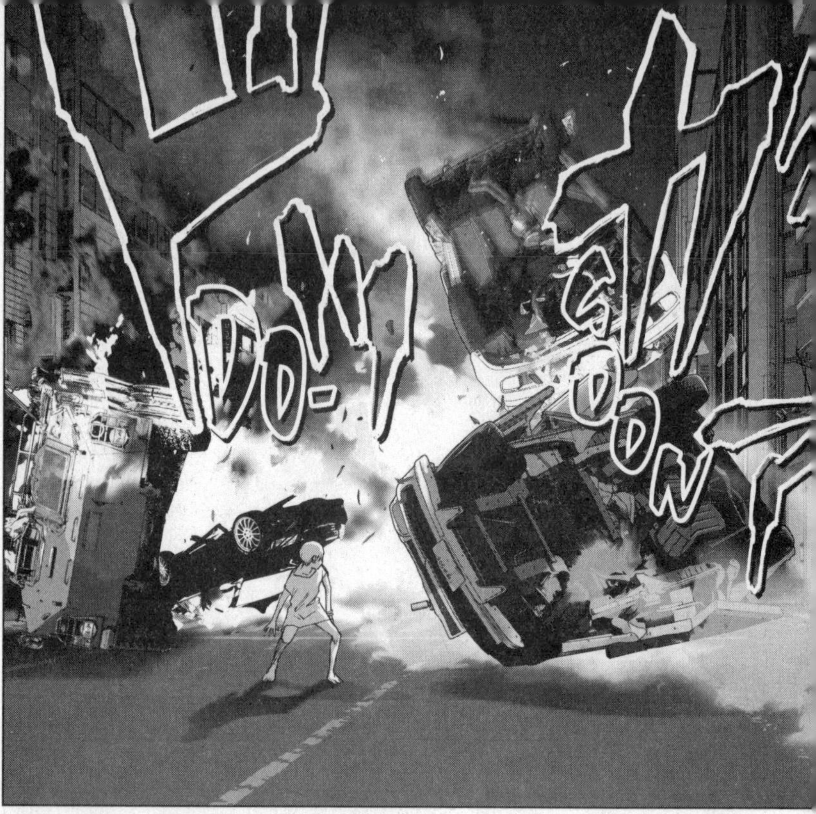
GADON
DO-
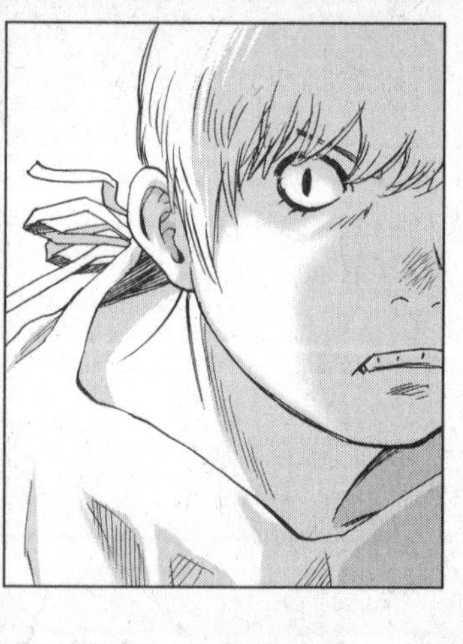
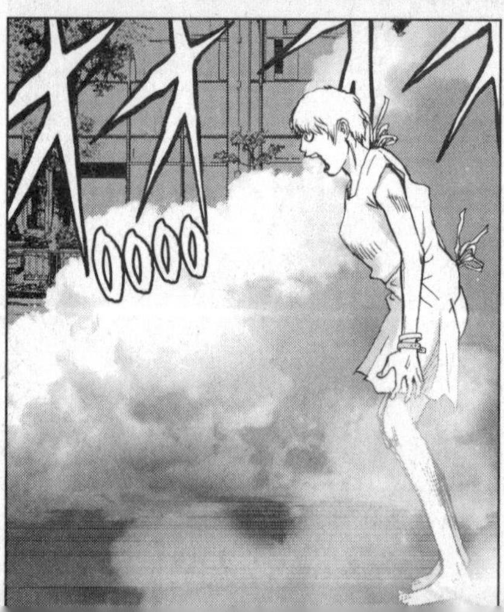
OOOO

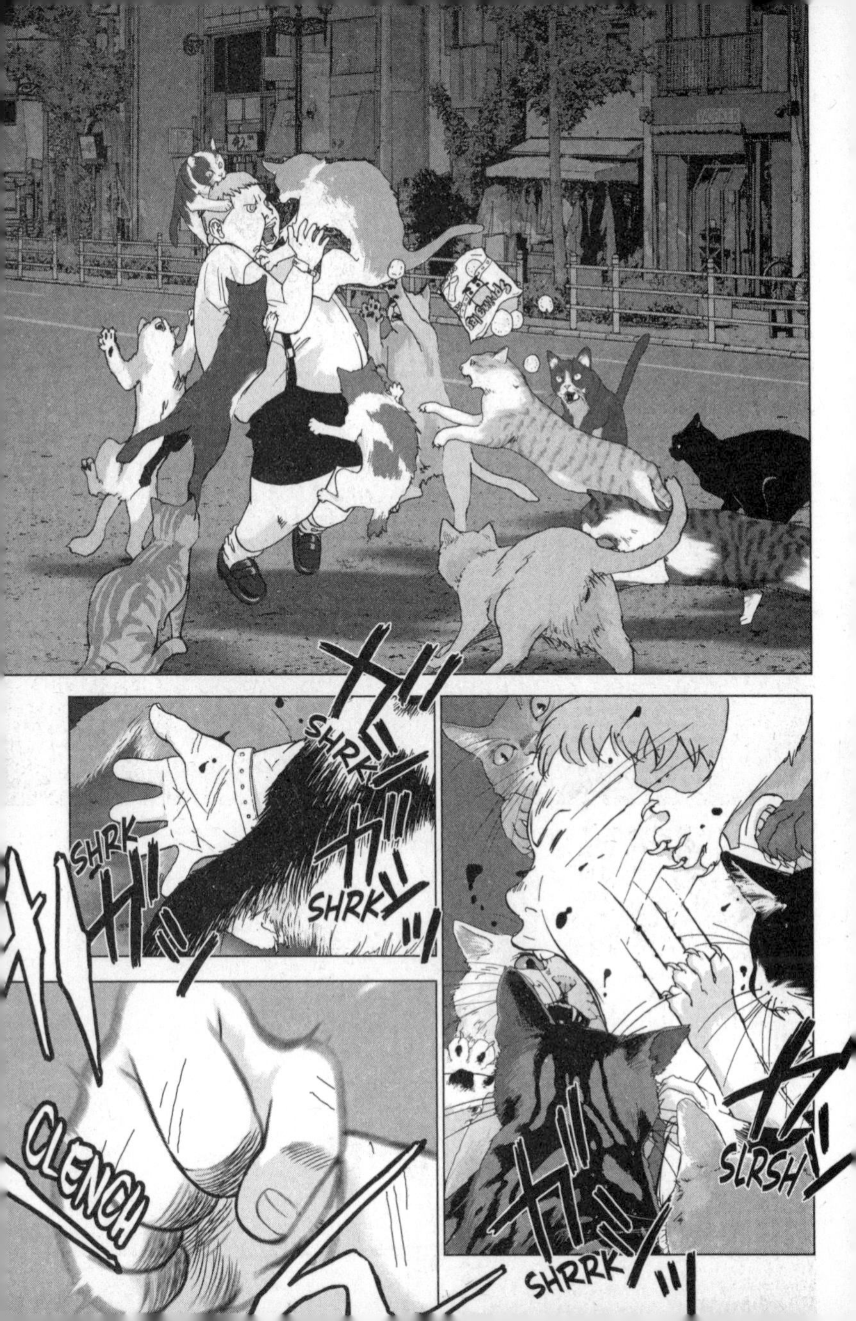
SLRSH
SHRRK
SHRK
SHRK
SHRK
CLENCH

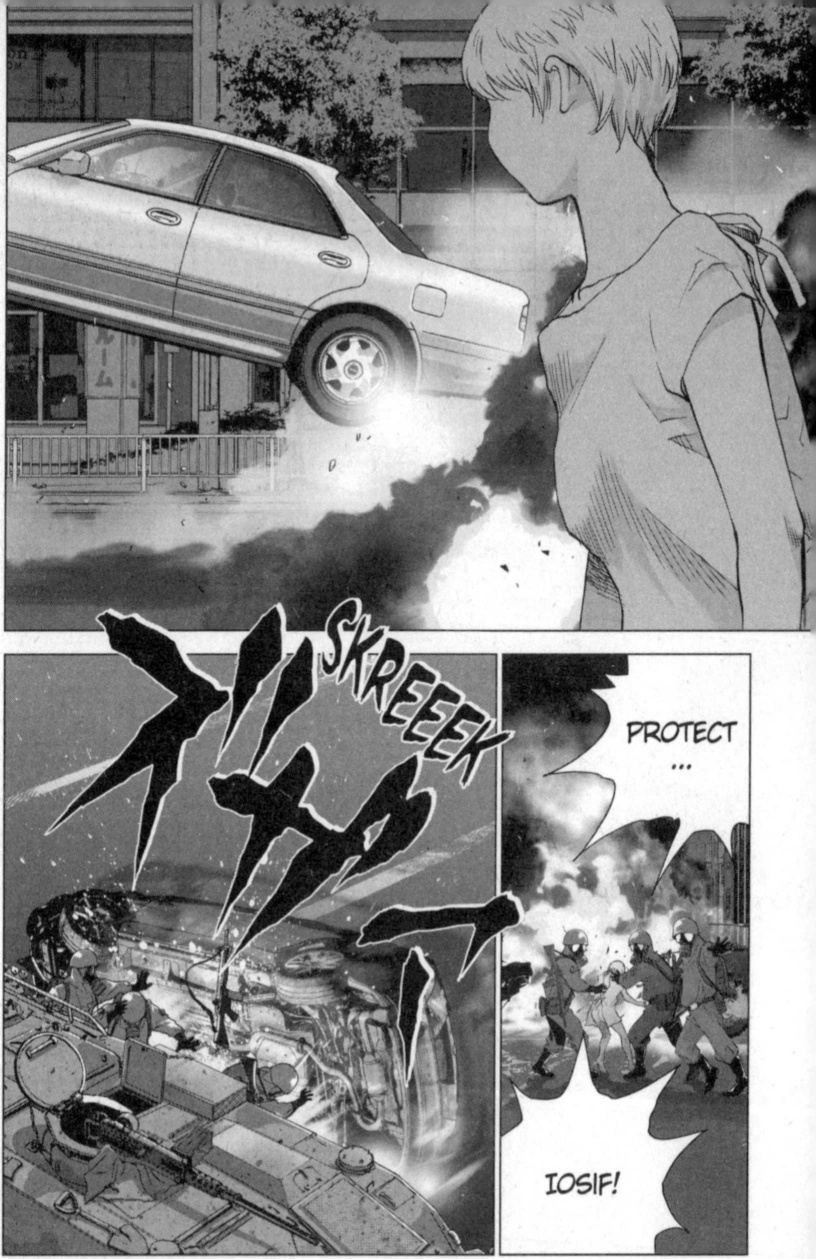
SKREEEK
PROTECT ...
IOSIF!

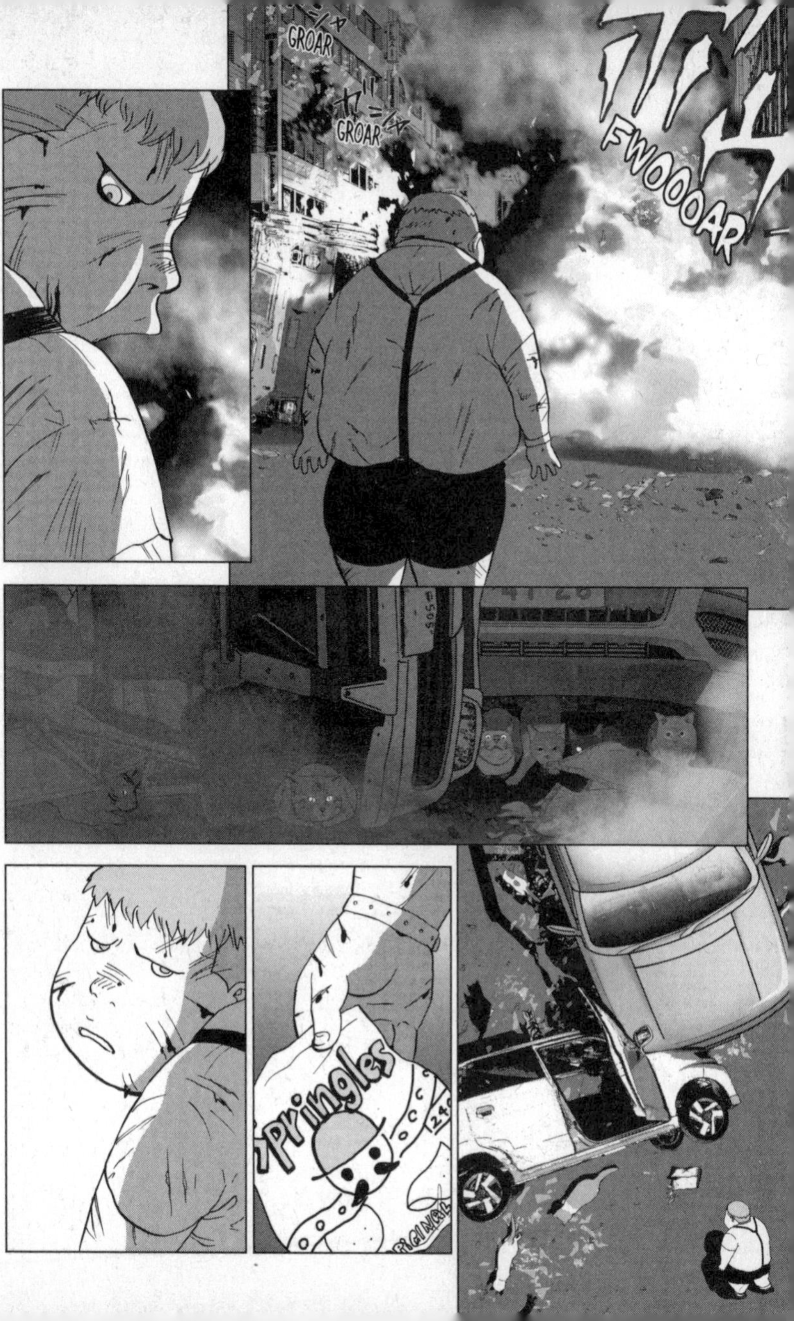
FWOOOAR
GROAR
GROAR
Pringles

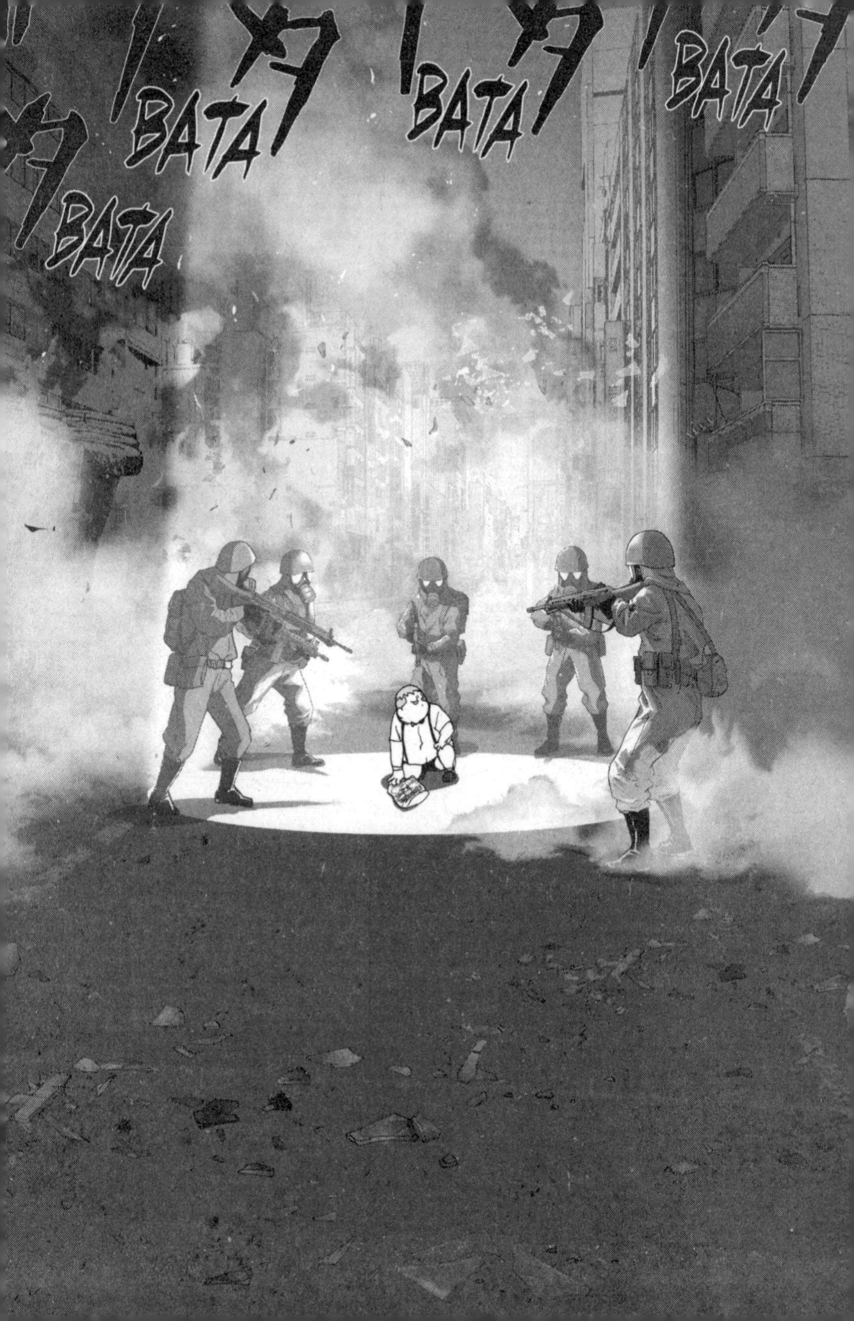

BATA
BATA
BATA
BATA

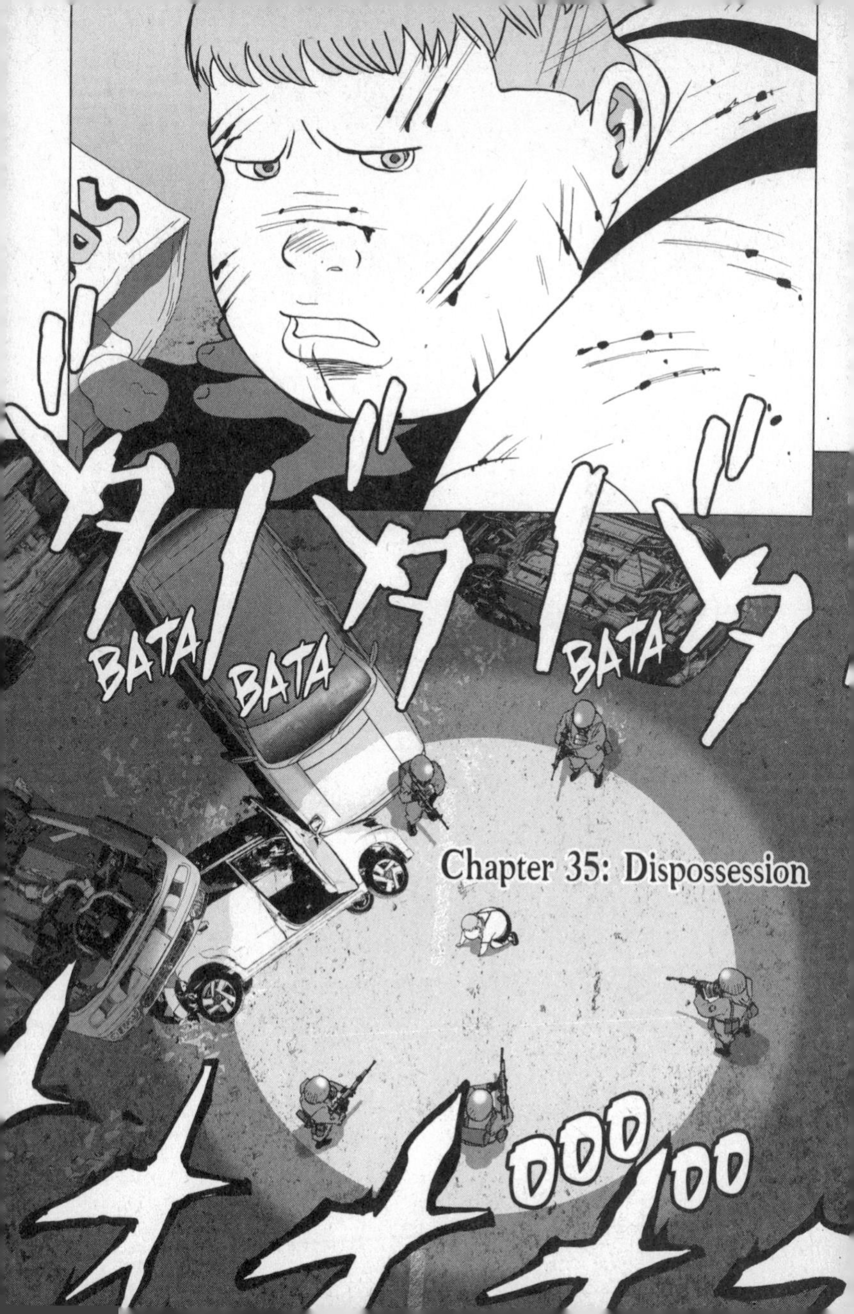
BATA
BATA
BATA
Chapter 35: Dispossession
DDD
DD

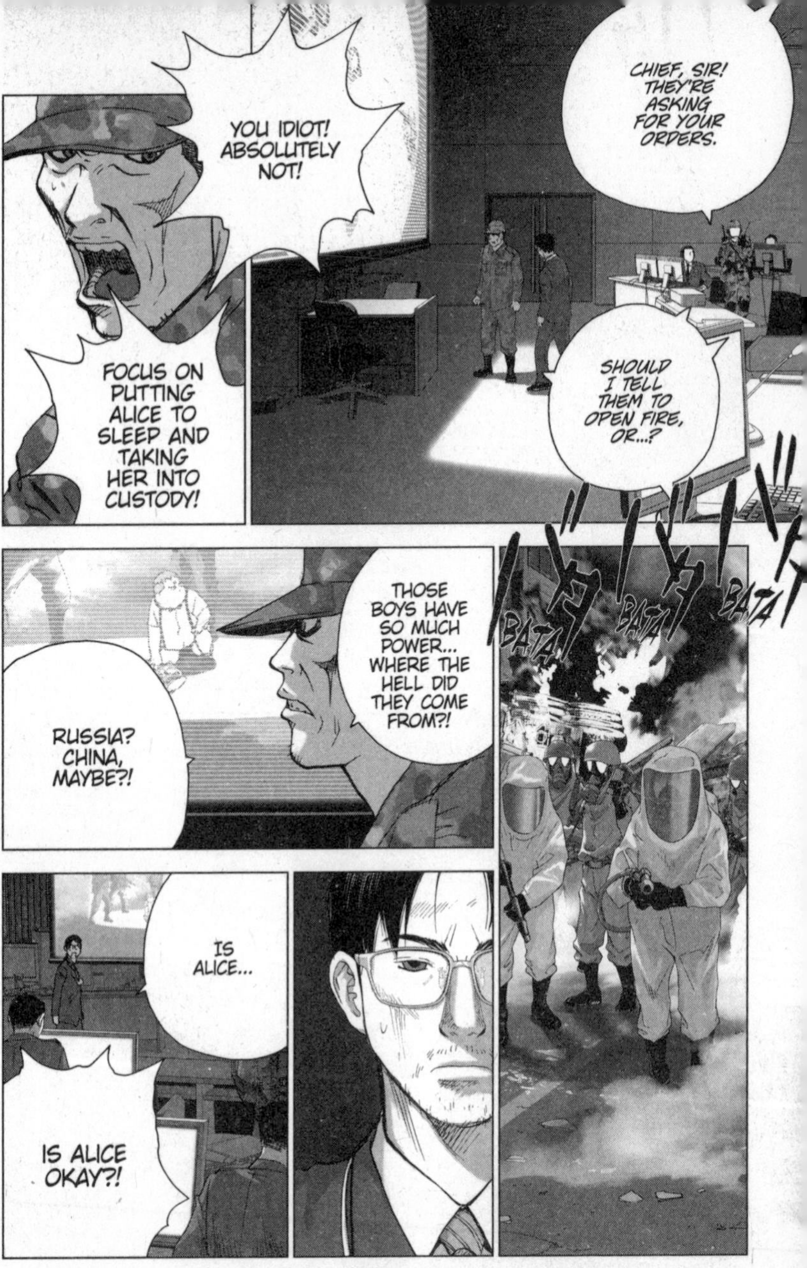
CHIEF, SIR! THEY'RE ASKING FOR YOUR ORDERS.
SHOULD I TELL THEM TO OPEN FIRE, OR...?
YOU IDIOT! ABSOLUTELY NOT!
FOCUS ON PUTTING ALICE TO SLEEP AND TAKING HER INTO CUSTODY!
BATA
BATA
BATA
BATA
THOSE BOYS HAVE SO MUCH POWER... WHERE THE HELL DID THEY COME FROM?!
RUSSIA? CHINA, MAYBE?!
IS ALICE...
IS ALICE OKAY?!

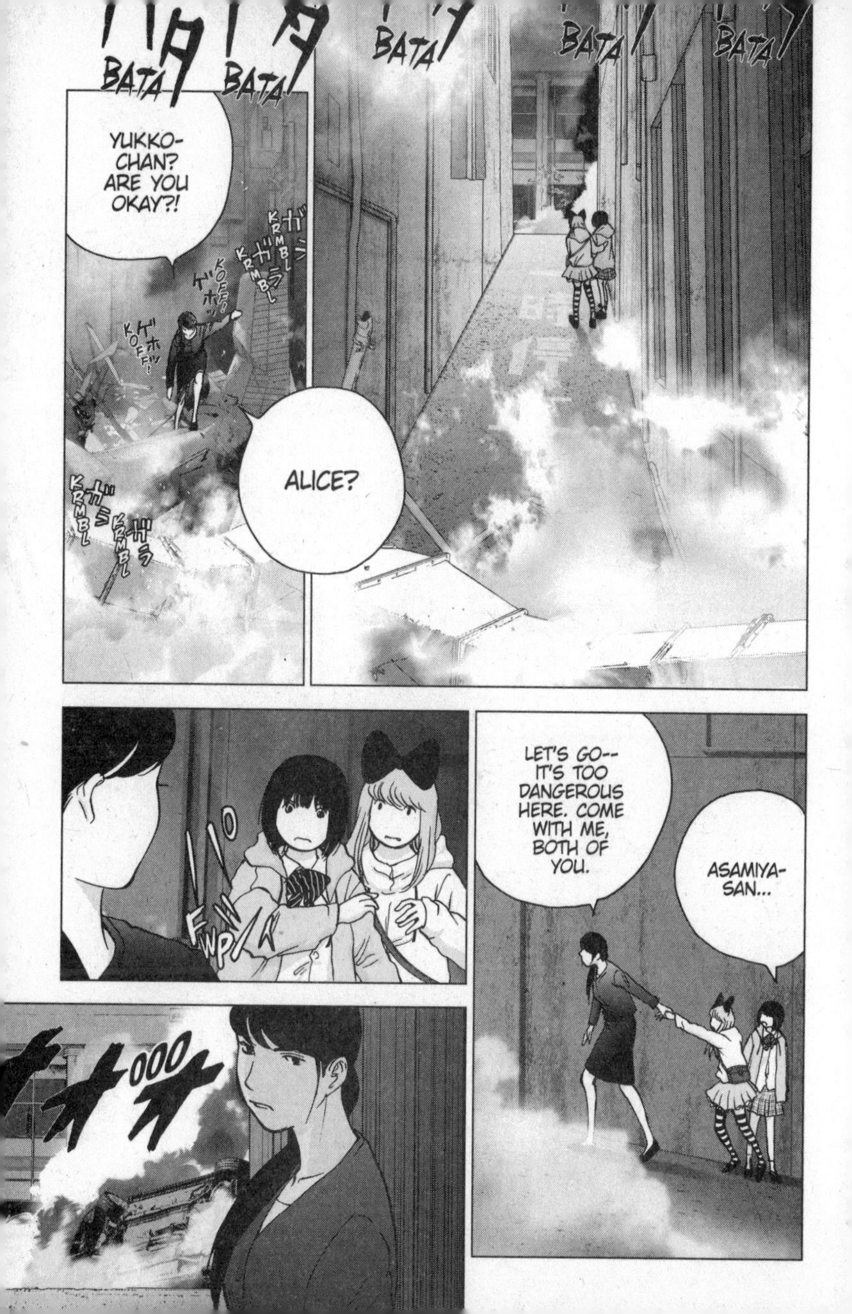
BATA BATA BATA BATA BATA
YUKKO-CHAN? ARE YOU OKAY?!
KRMBL KRMBL
KOFF! KOFF!
ALICE?
KRMBL KRMBL
ASAMIYA-SAN...
LET'S GO-- IT'S TOO DANGEROUS HERE. COME WITH ME, BOTH OF YOU.
FWP
FOOO

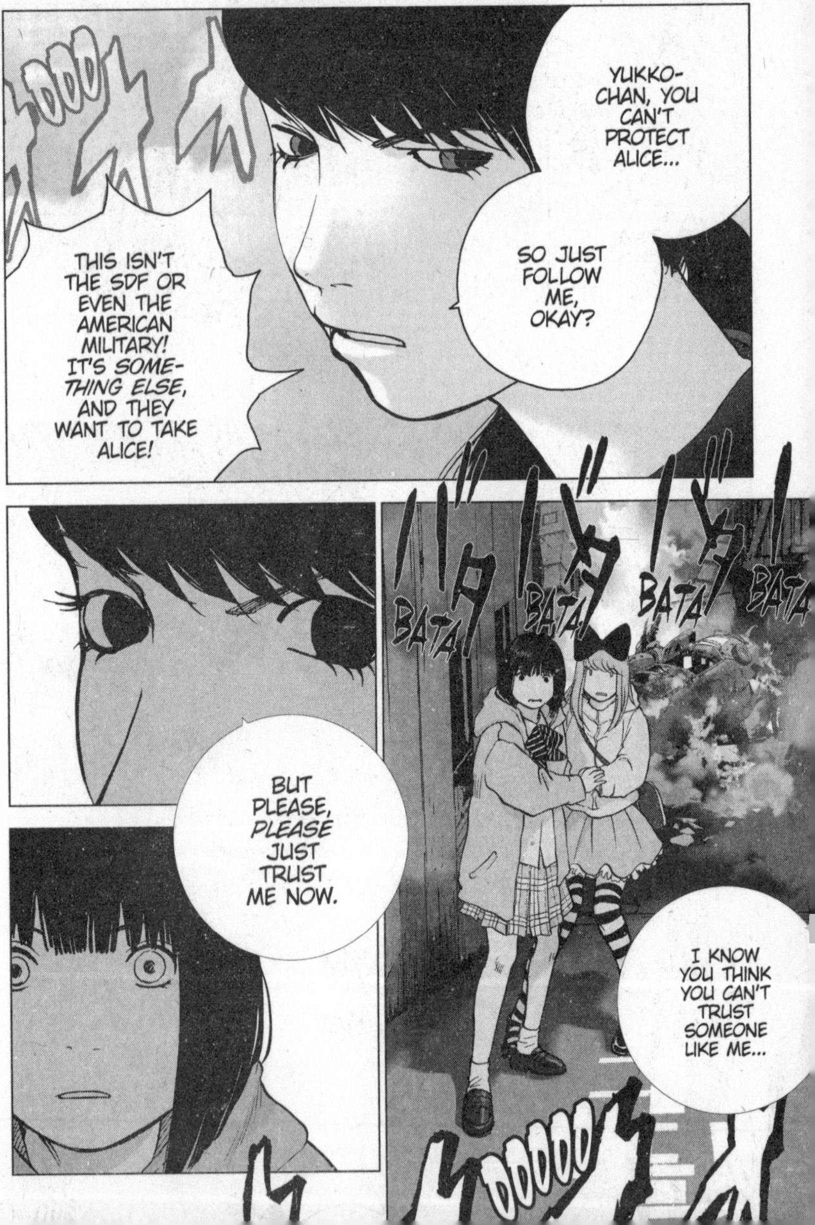
YUKKO-CHAN, YOU CAN'T PROTECT ALICE...
SO JUST FOLLOW ME, OKAY?
DOOO
THIS ISN'T THE SDF OR EVEN THE AMERICAN MILITARY! IT'S *SOME-THING ELSE*, AND THEY WANT TO TAKE ALICE!
BATA BATA BATA BATA
I KNOW YOU THINK YOU CAN'T TRUST SOMEONE LIKE ME...
BUT PLEASE, *PLEASE* JUST TRUST ME NOW.
DOOOOO

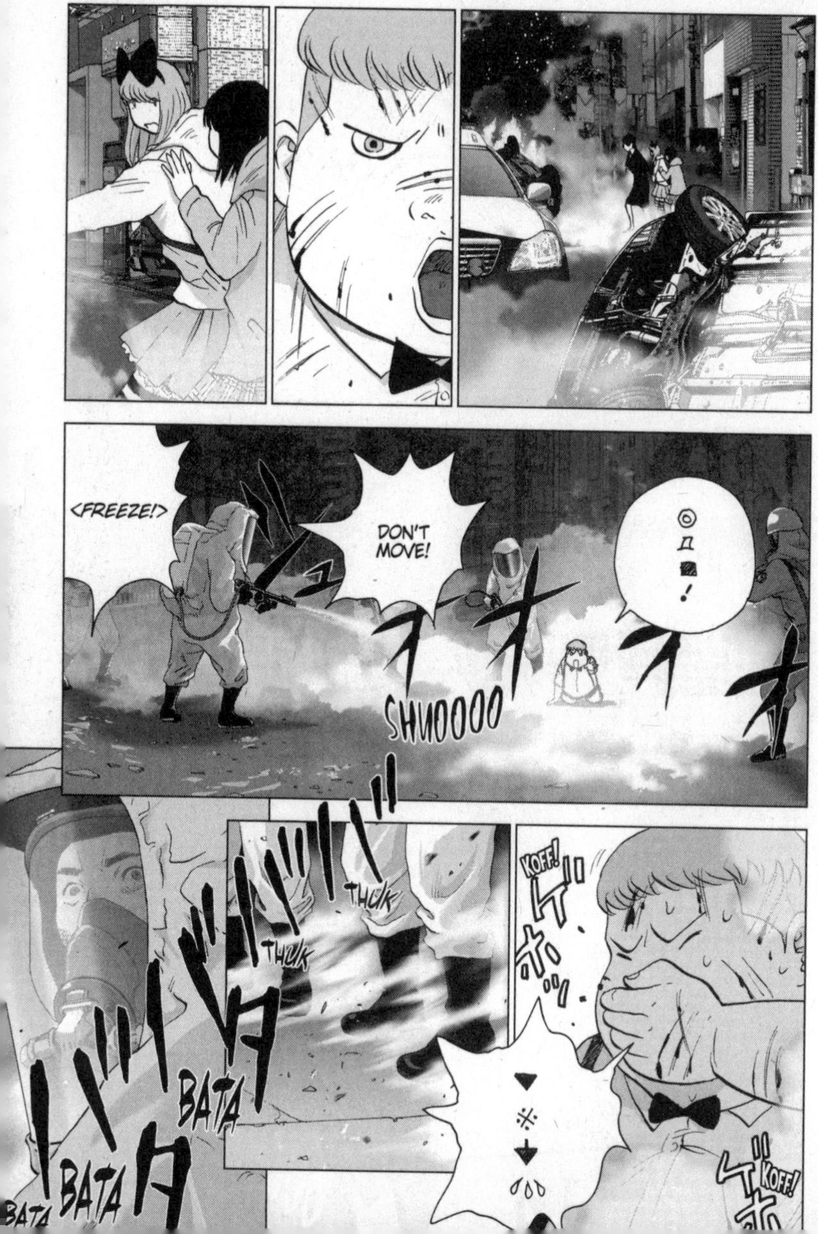
DON'T MOVE!
<FREEZE!>
SHUOOOO
KOFF!
KOFF!
THUK
THUK
BATA
BATA
BATA

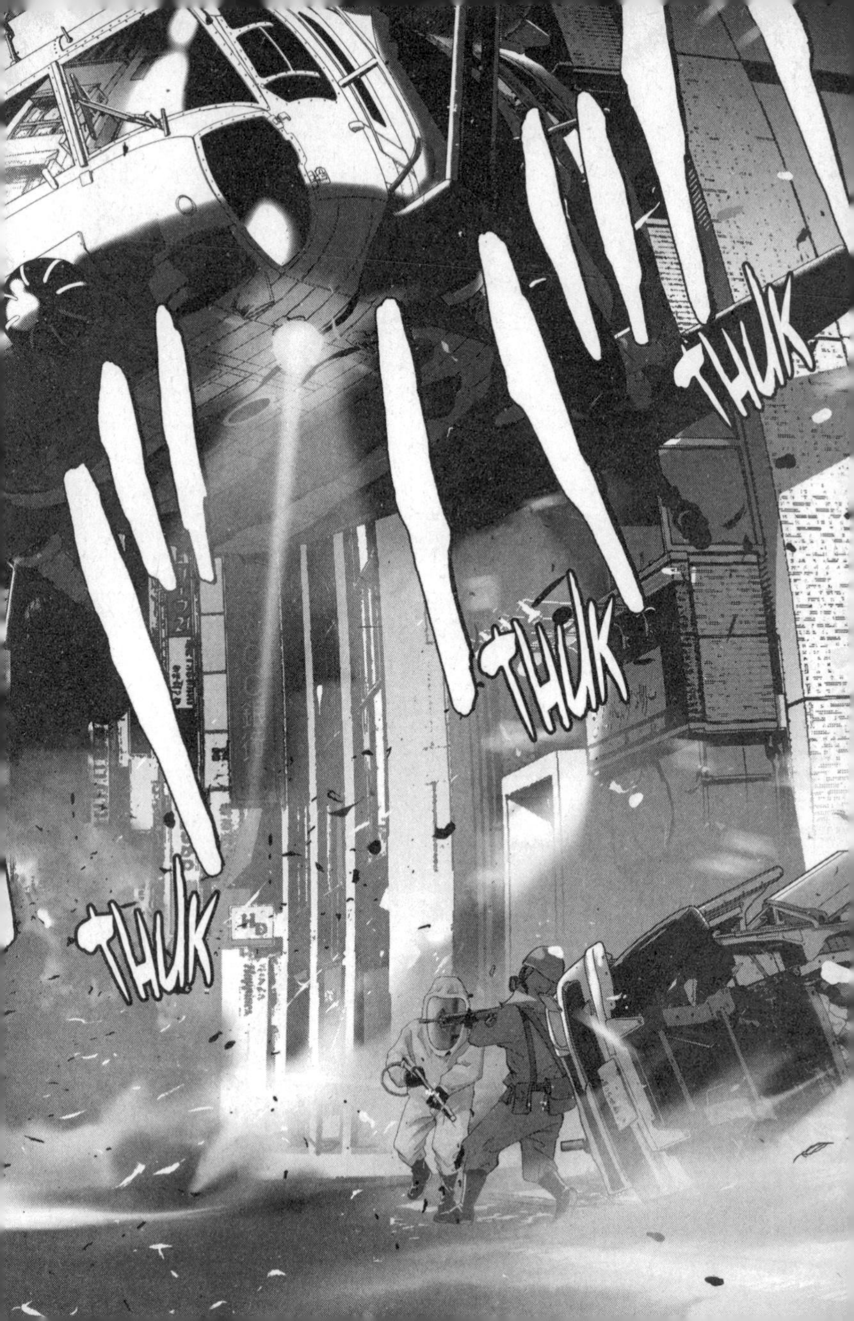
THUK
THUK
THUK

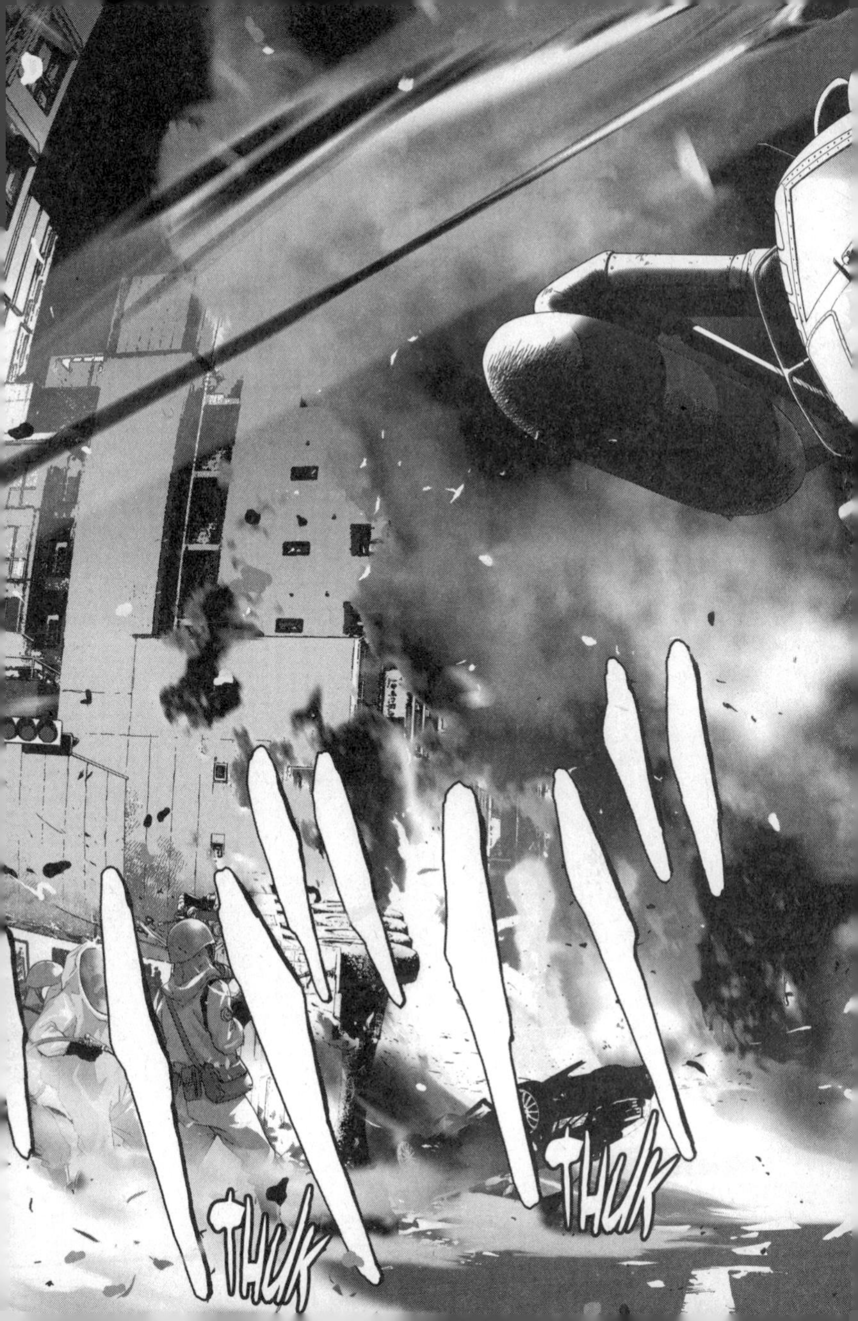
THUK
THUK

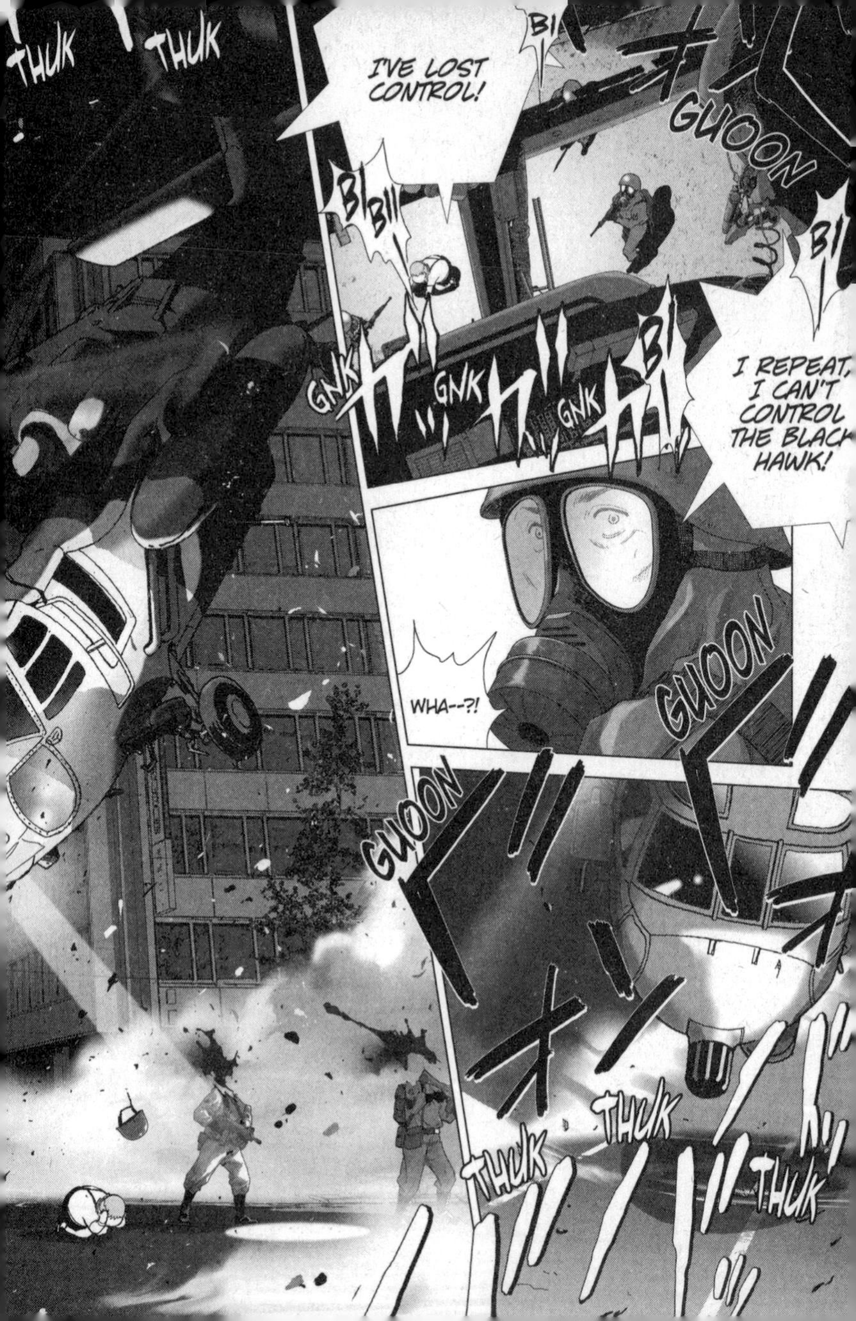
BI
I'VE LOST CONTROL!
GUOON
BI BII
BI
GNK GNK GNK BI
I REPEAT, I CAN'T CONTROL THE BLAC HAWK!
WHA--?!
GUOON
GUOON
THUK THUK THUK
THUK THUK

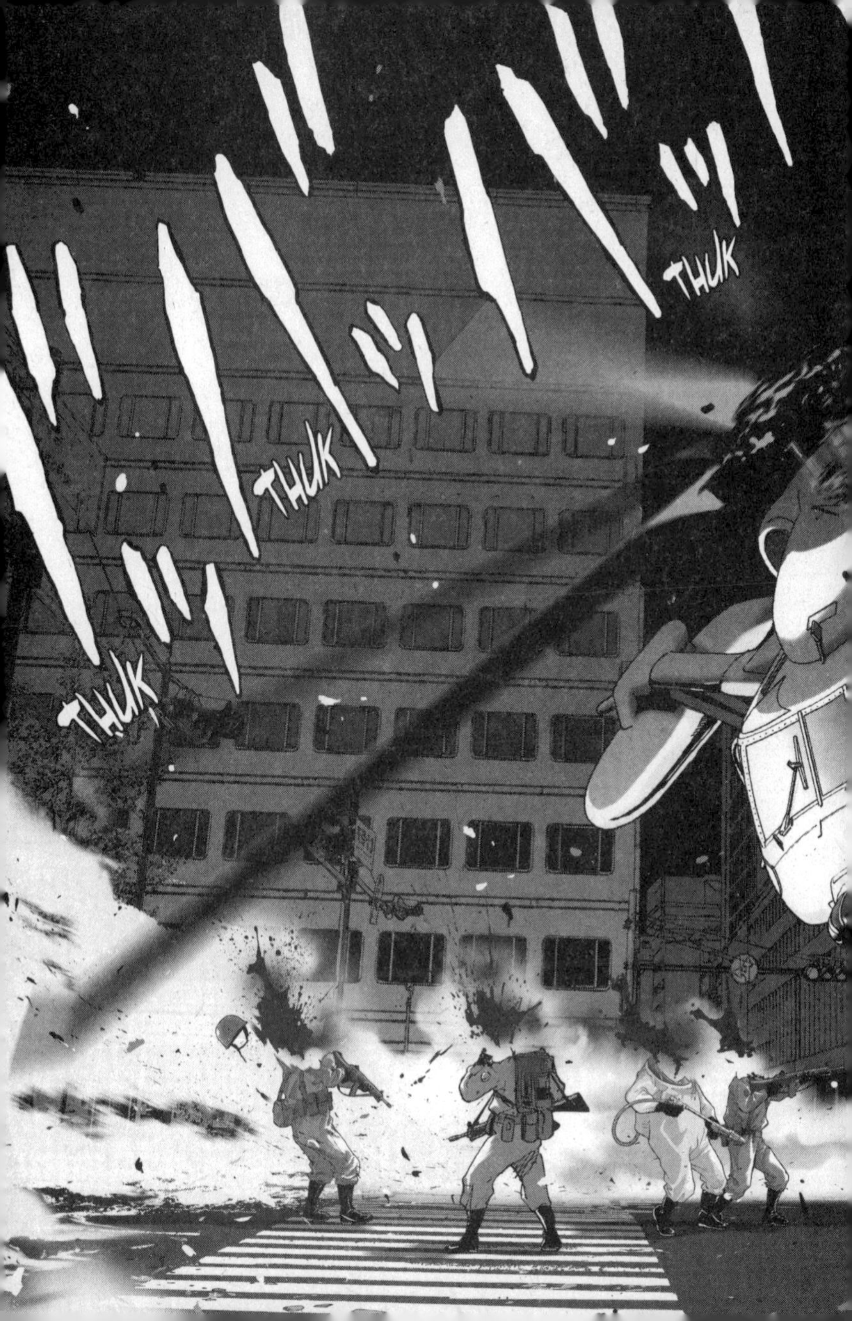
THUK
THUK
THUK

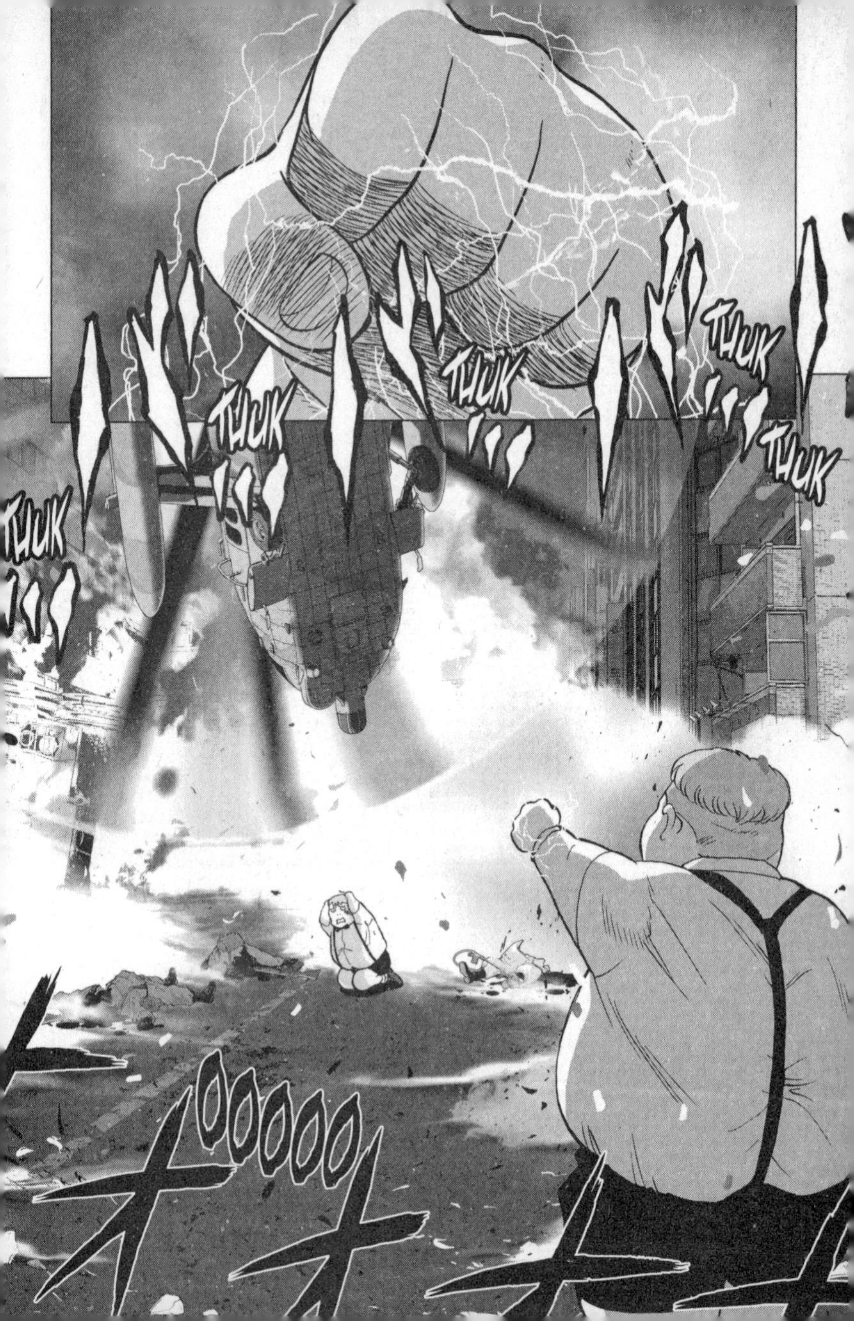
THUK
THUK
THUK
THUK
THUK
OOOOOO

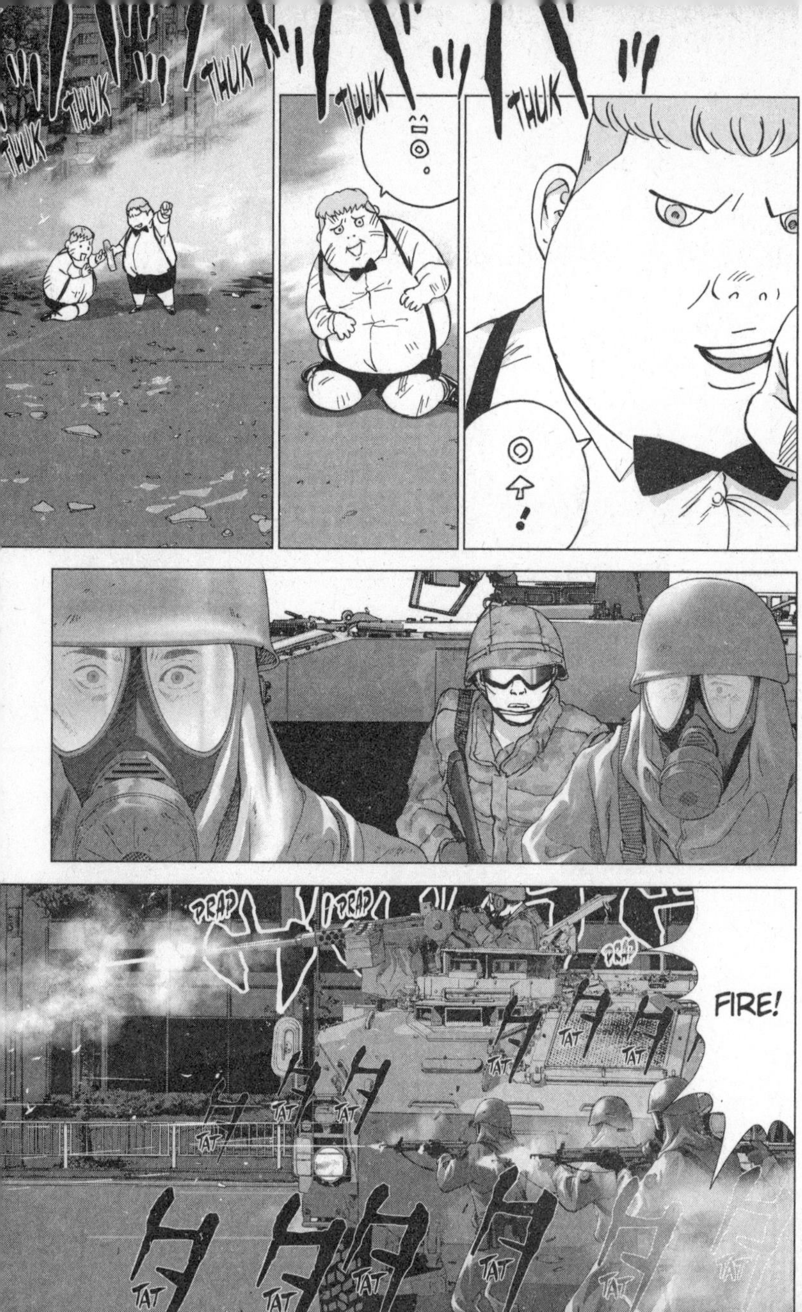
THUK
THUK
THUK
THUK
THUK
THUK
FIRE!
DRAP
DRAP
DRAP
TAT
TAT
TAT
TAT
TAT
TAT
TAT
TAT
TAT
TAT
TAT
TAT

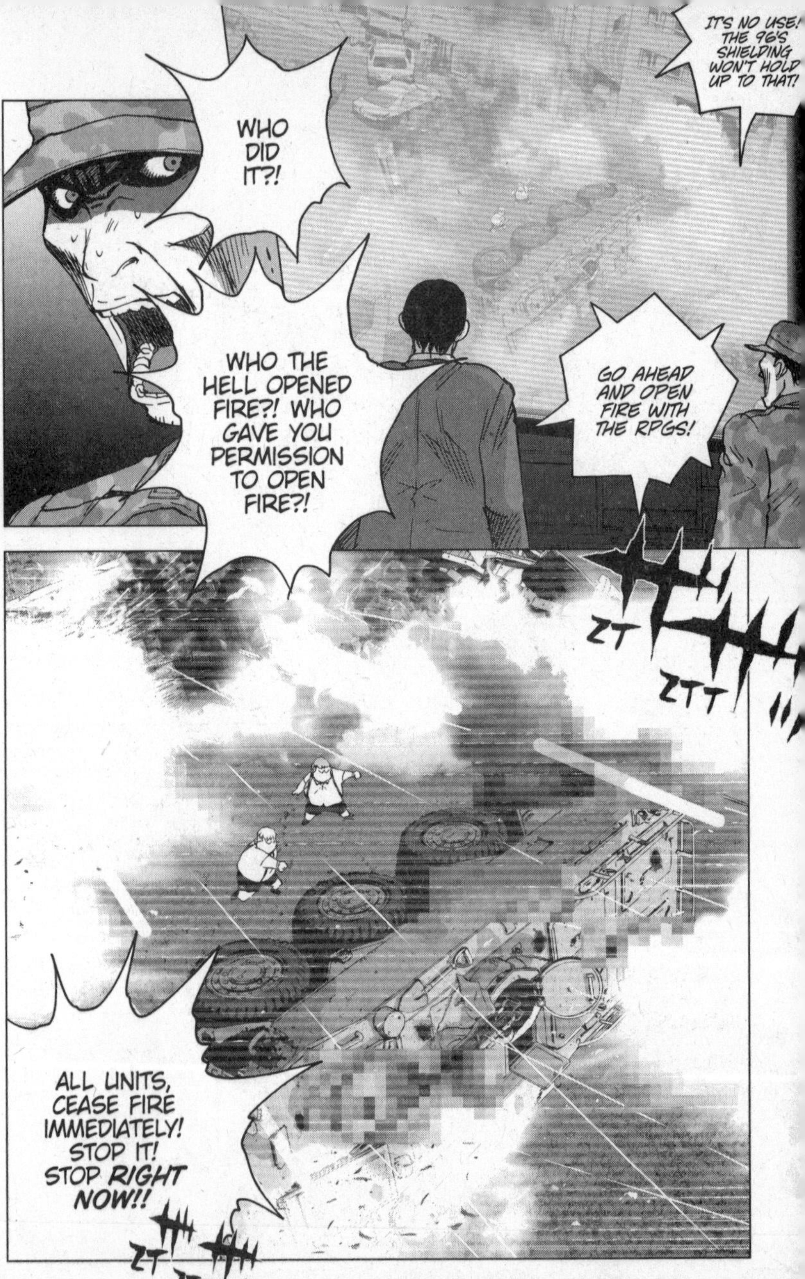
IT'S NO USE! THE 96'S SHIELDING WON'T HOLD UP TO THAT!
GO AHEAD AND OPEN FIRE WITH THE RPGS!
WHO DID IT?!
WHO THE HELL OPENED FIRE?! WHO GAVE YOU PERMISSION TO OPEN FIRE?!
ZT
ZTT
ALL UNITS, CEASE FIRE IMMEDIATELY! STOP IT! STOP RIGHT NOW!!
ZT
ZTT

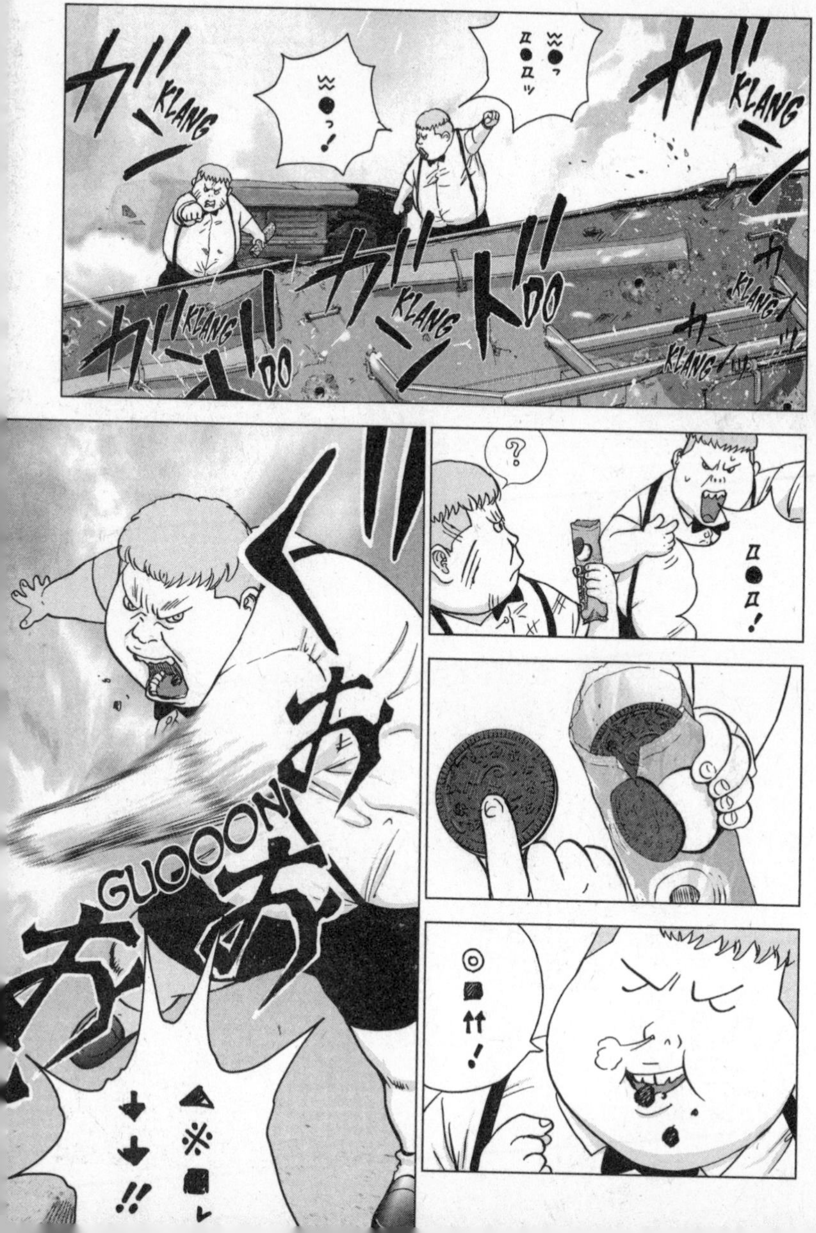
KLANG
KLANG
KLANG
KLANG
DO
KLANG
KLANG
DO
?
GUOOON

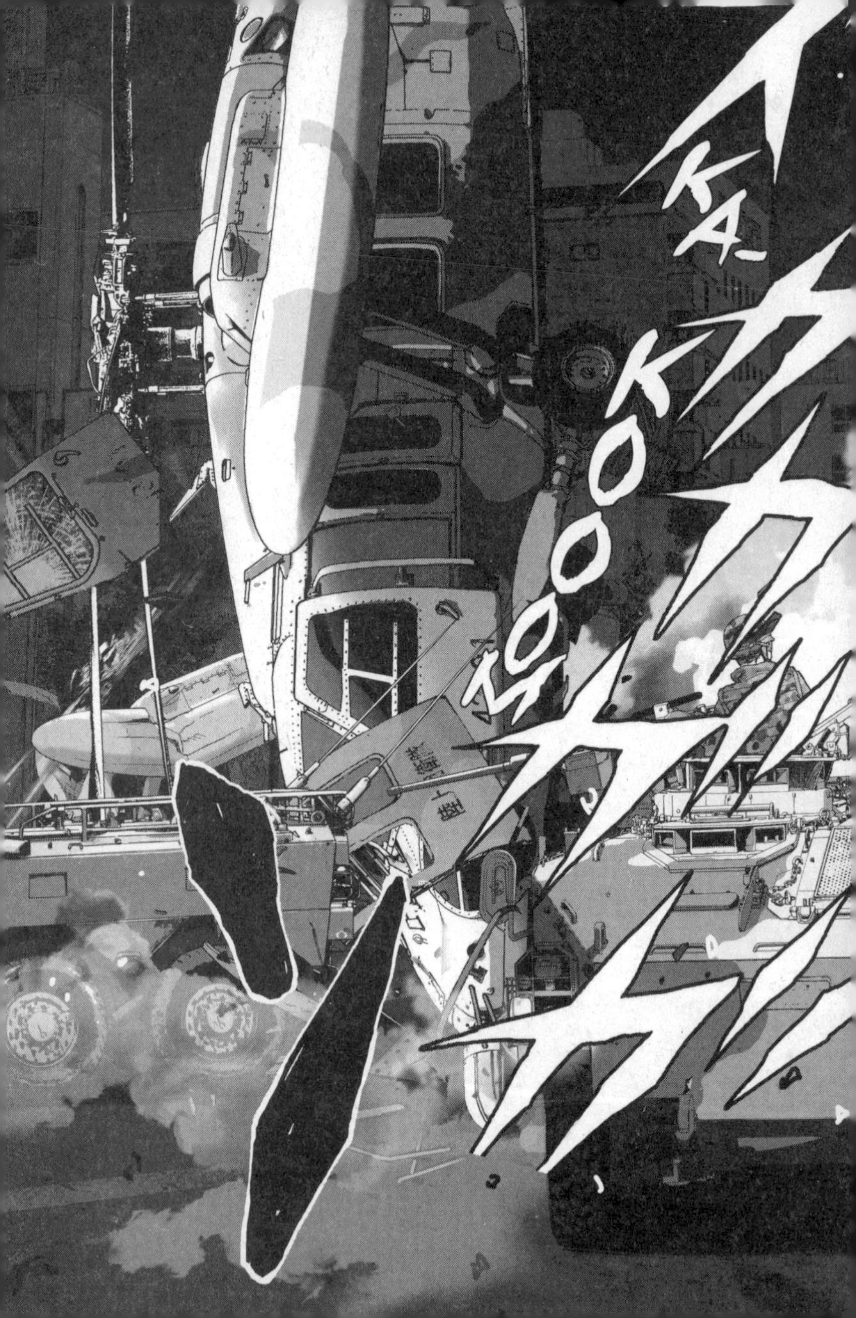
KA-KOOOOM

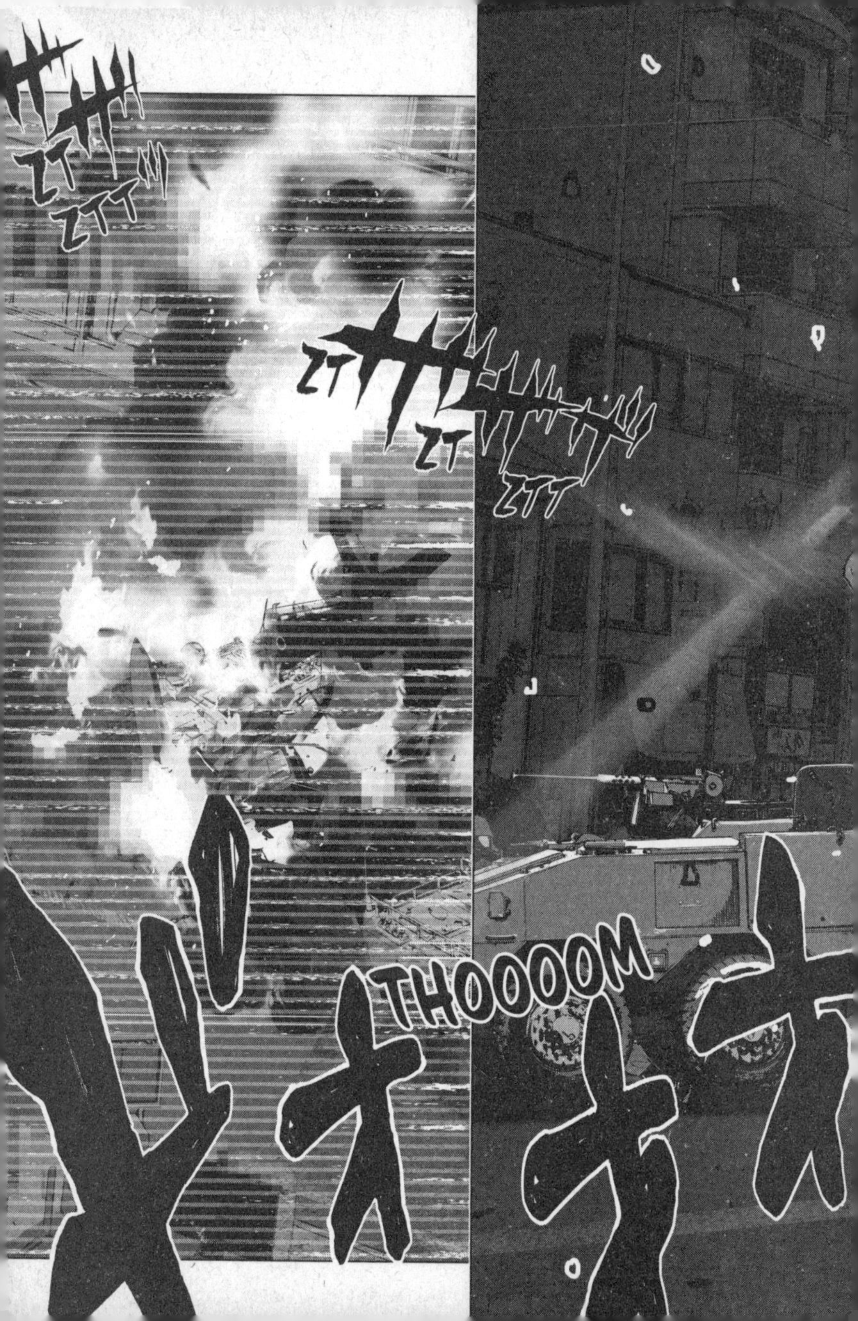
ZT
ZT
ZTT
ZT
ZTT
THOOOOM

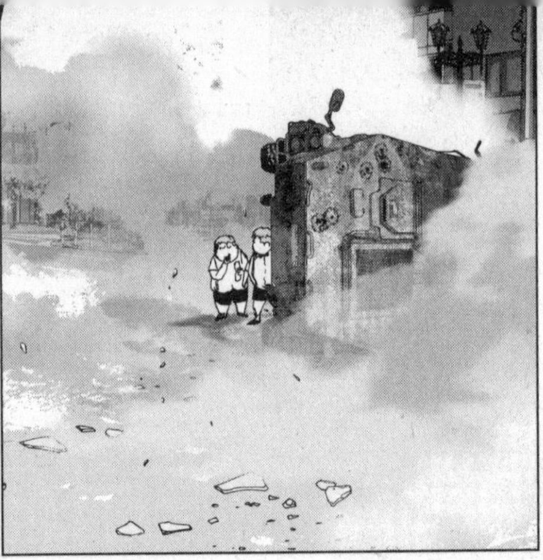
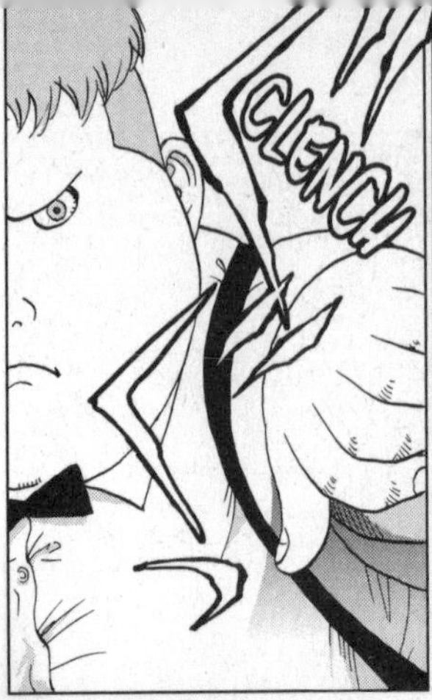
CLENCH
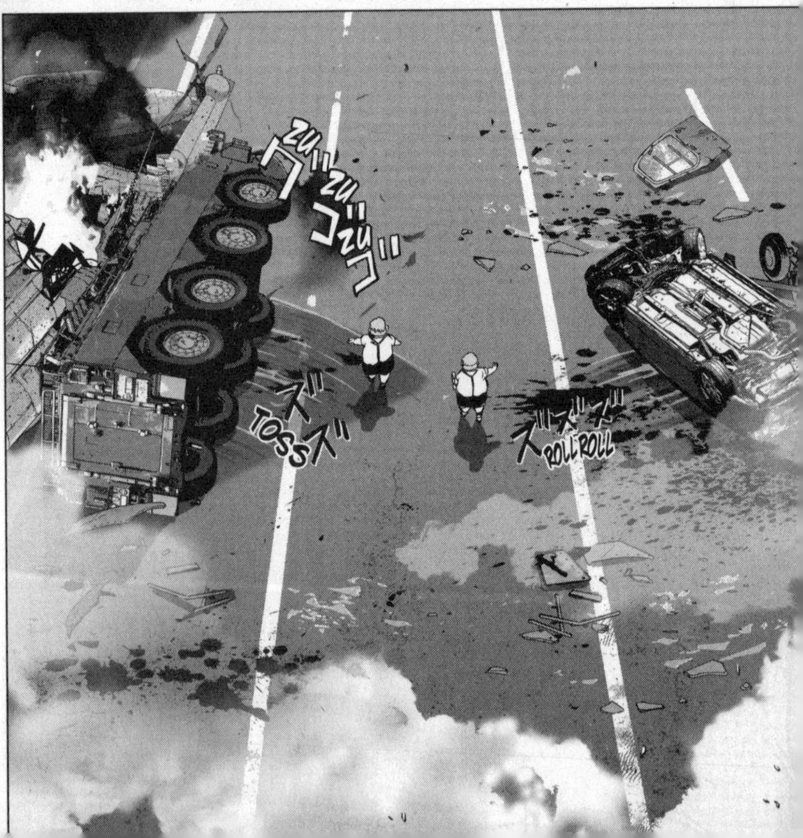
ZU ZU ZU
TOSS
ROLL ROLL

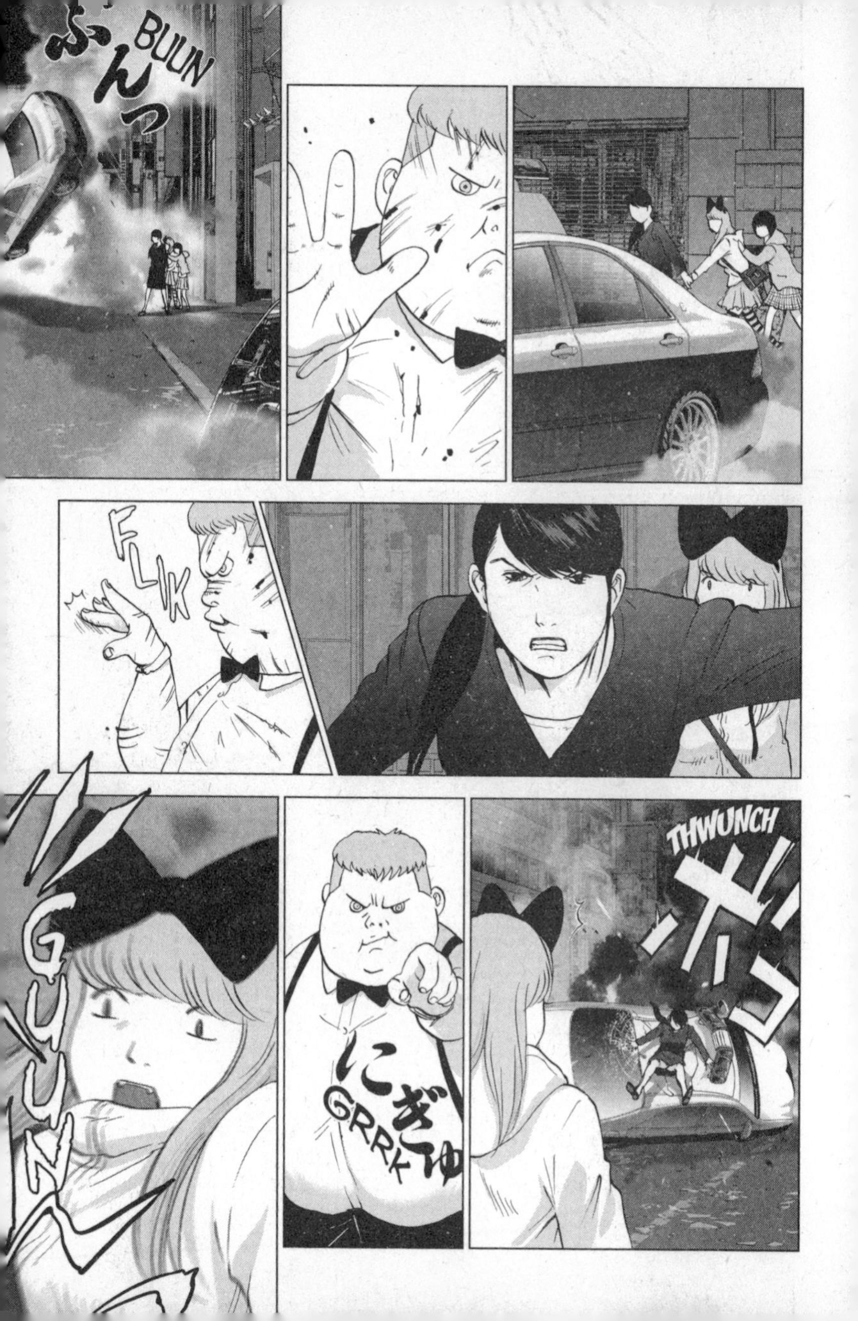

ぶんっ
BUUN
FLIK
THWUNCH
ガっ
にぎゅ
GRRK
GUUUN

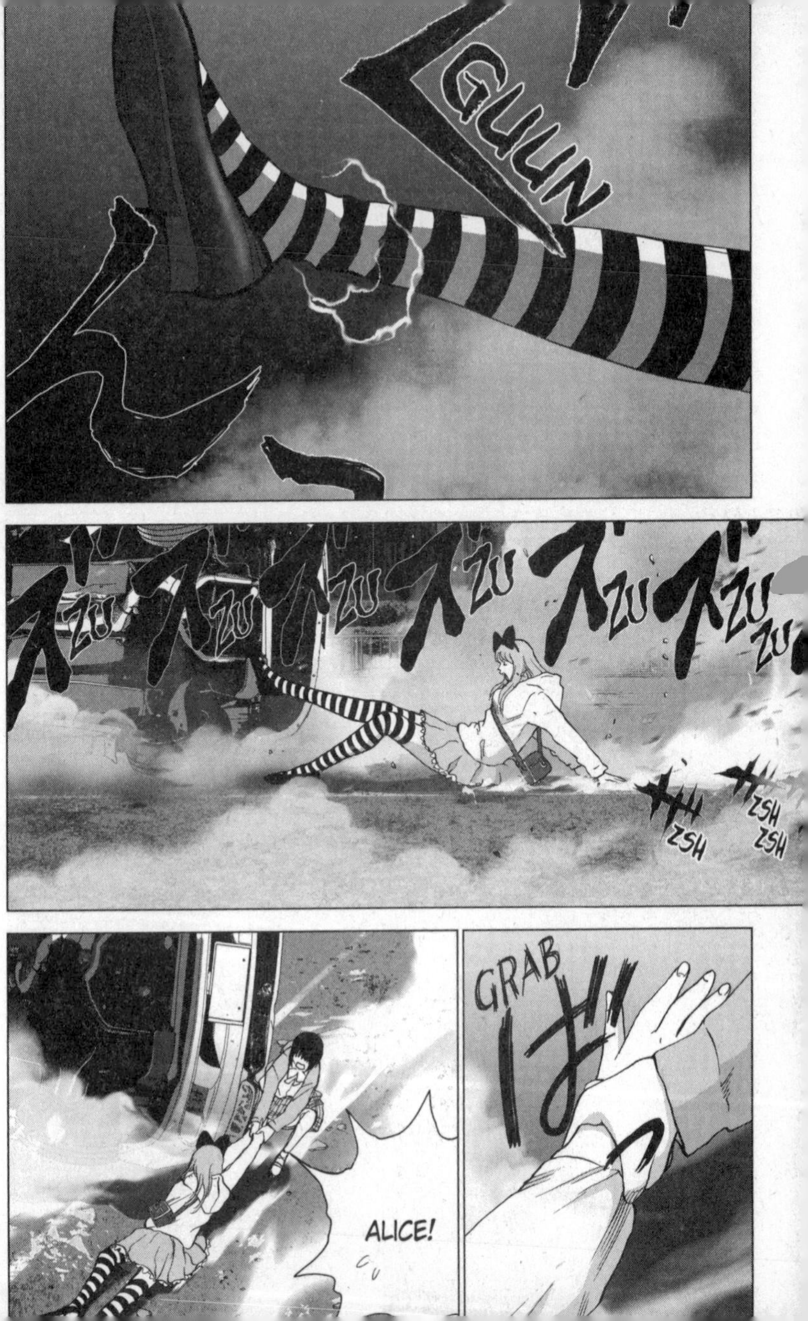
GUUN
ZU ZU ZU ZU ZU ZU ZU ZU
ZSH ZSH ZSH
GRAB
ALICE!

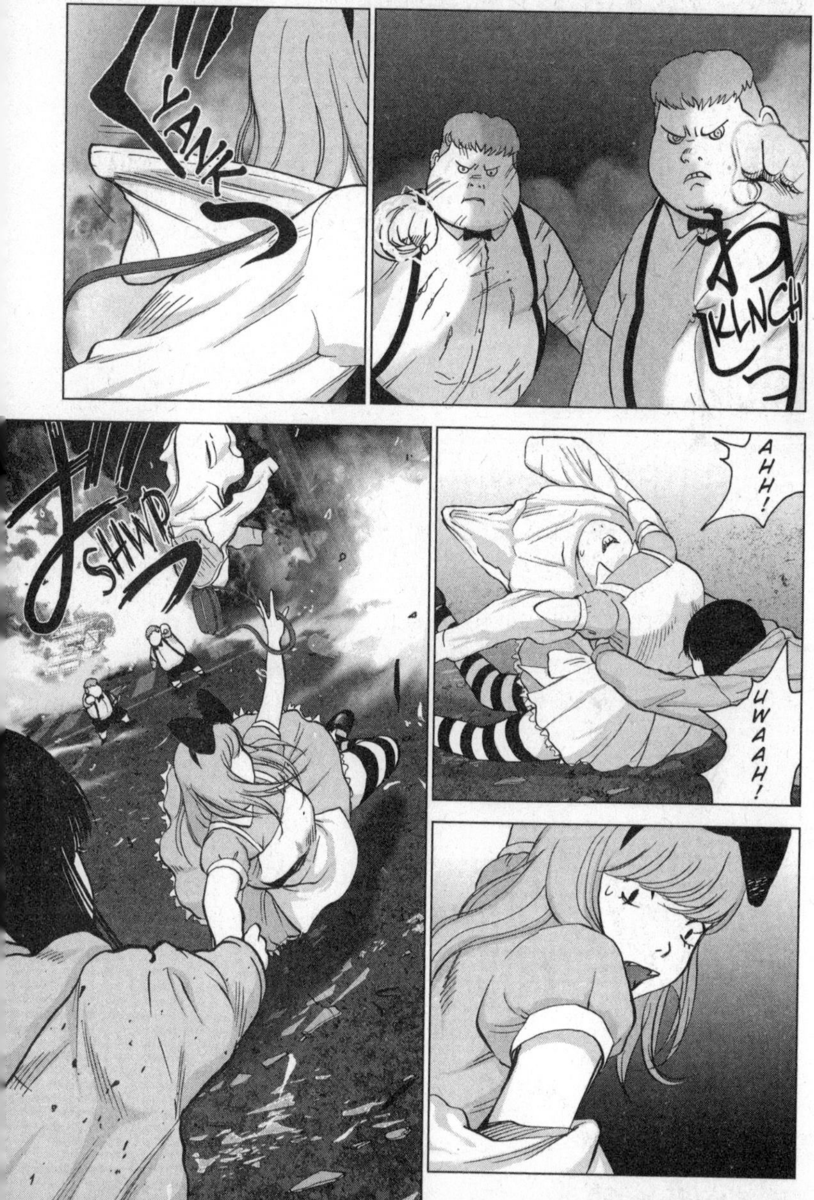
KLNCH
YANK
AHH!
UWAAH!
SHWP

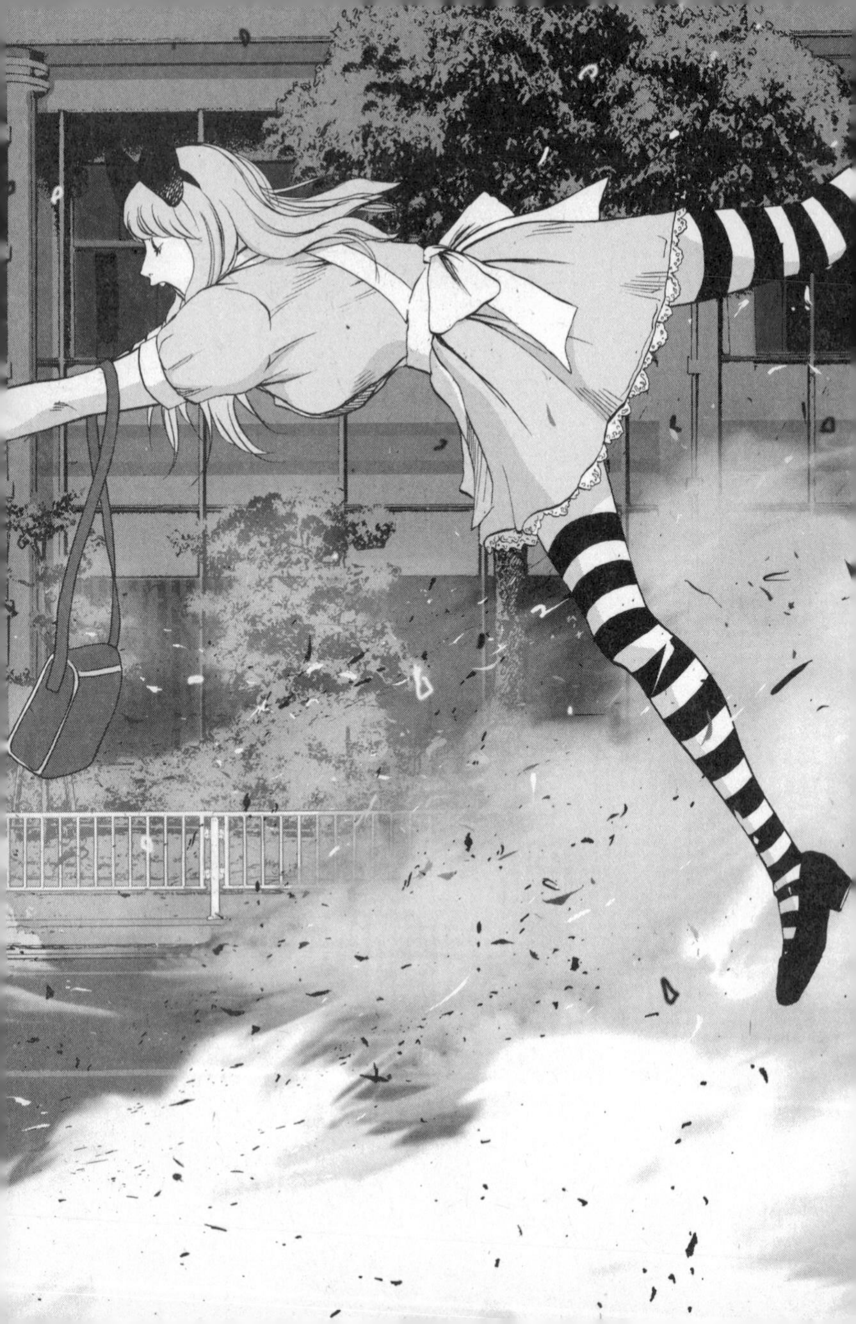

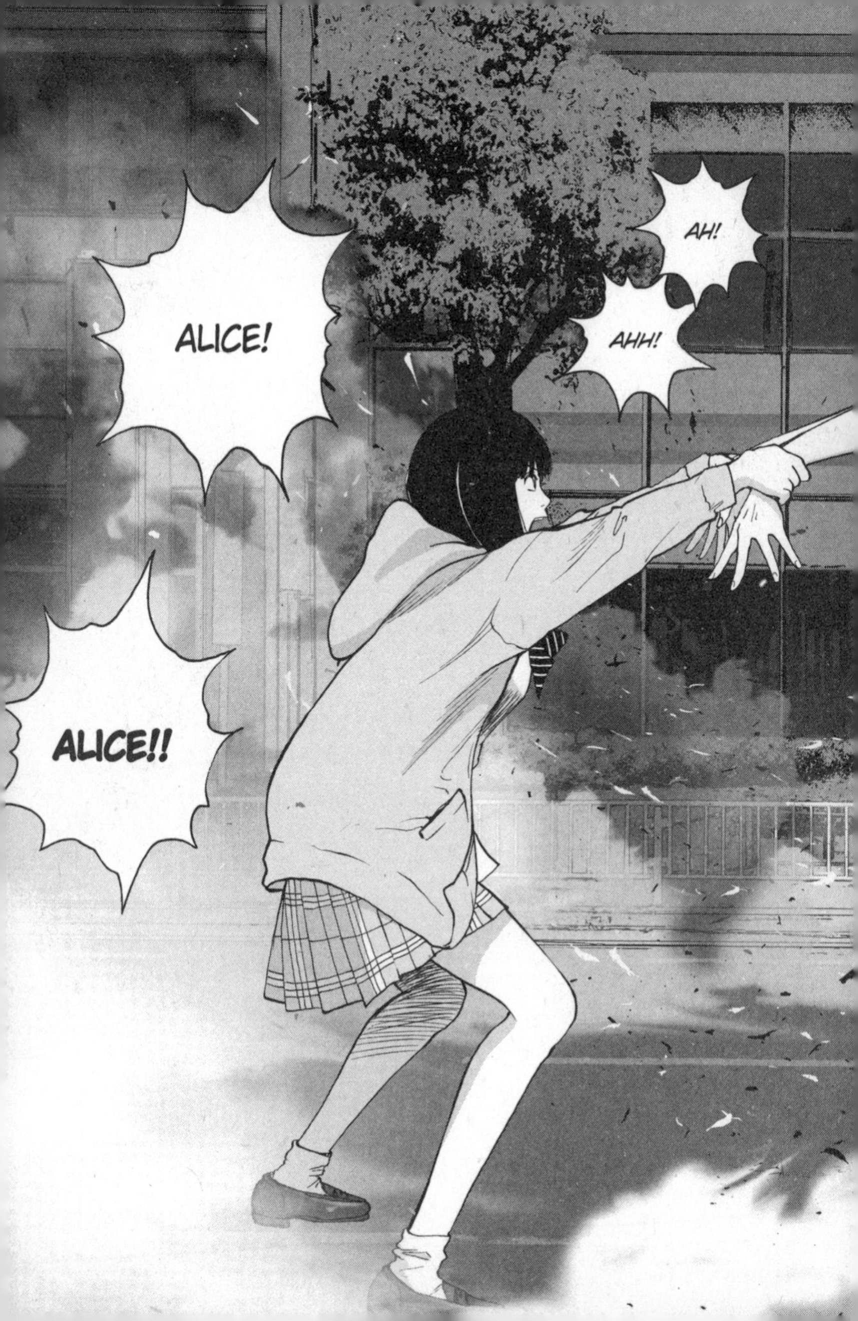
AH!
AHH!
ALICE!
ALICE!!

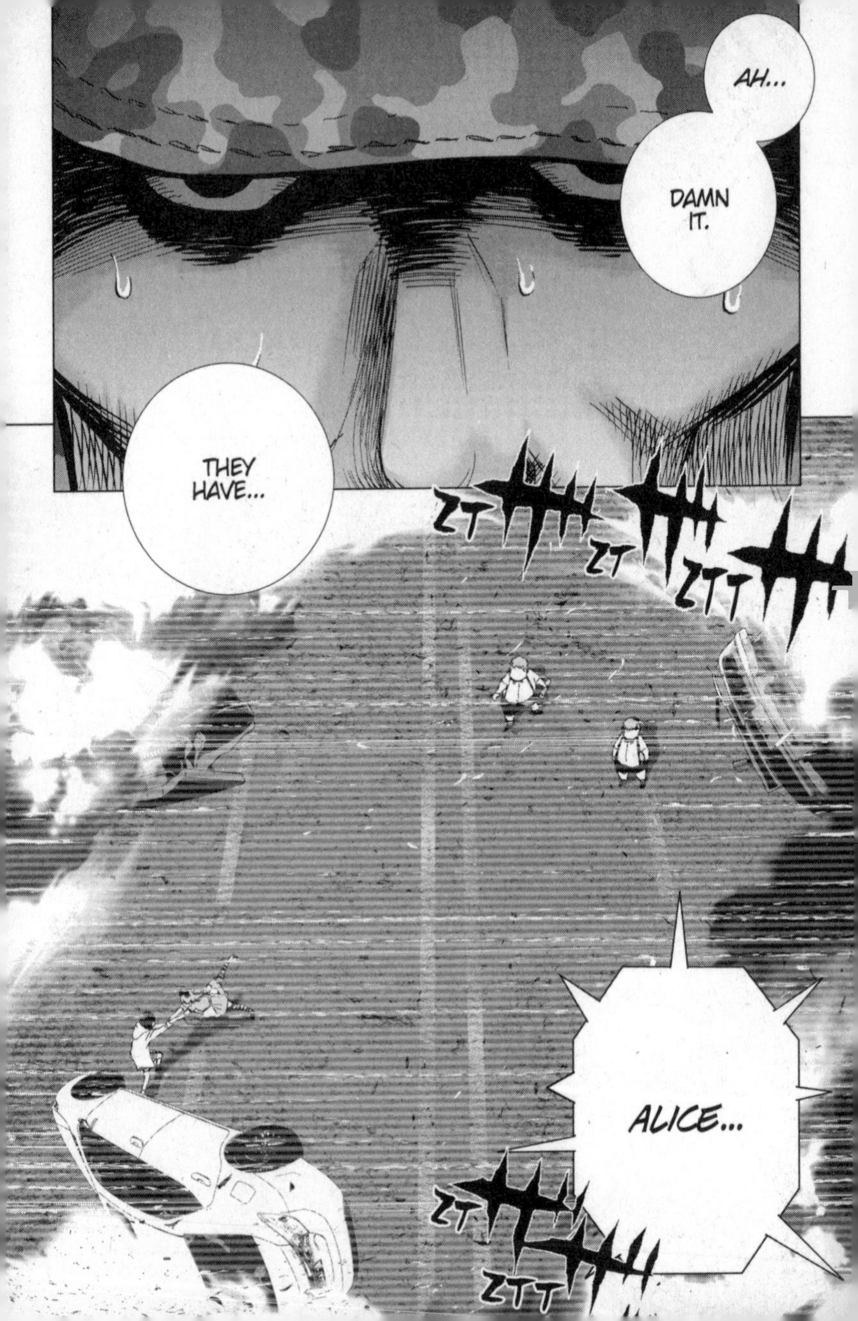
AH...
DAMN IT.
THEY HAVE...
ZT ZT ZTT
ALICE...
ZT ZTT

Chapter 36: Chance Meeting

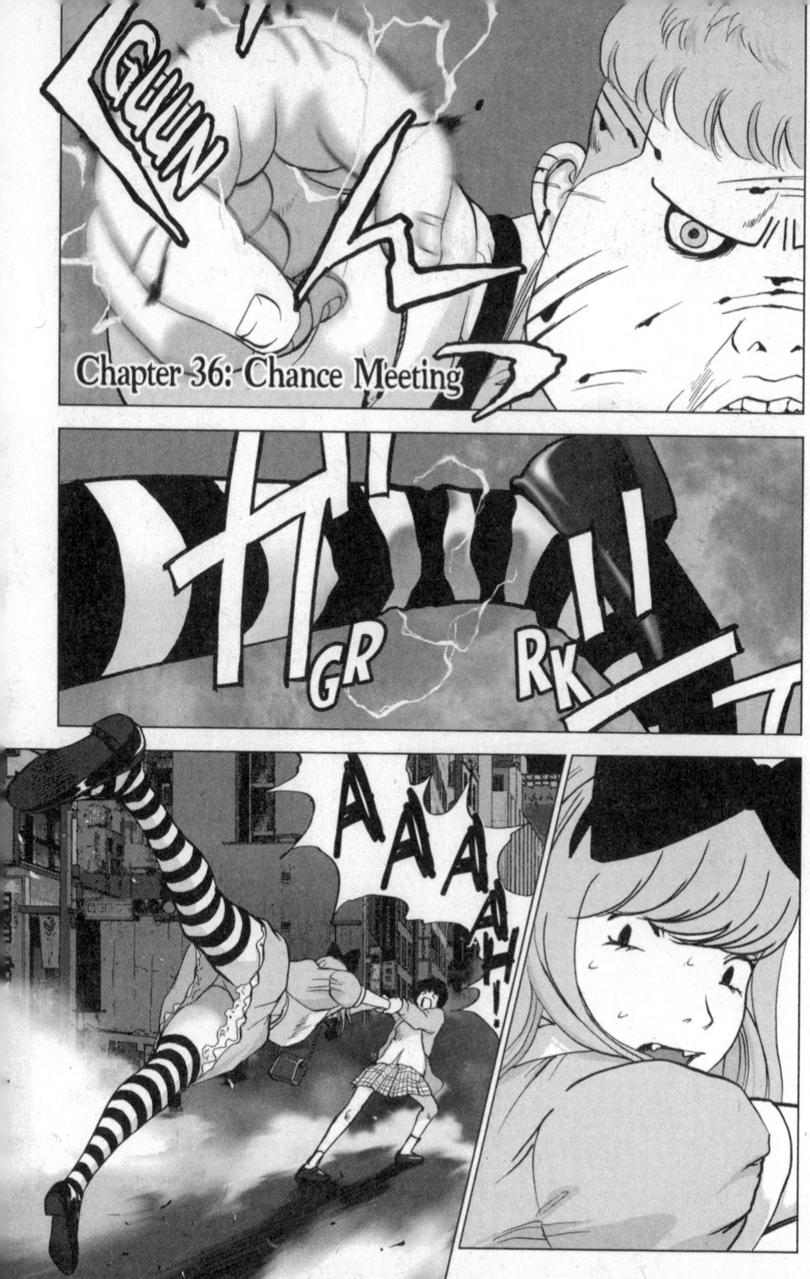
GUUN
GR
RK
AAAAAH!

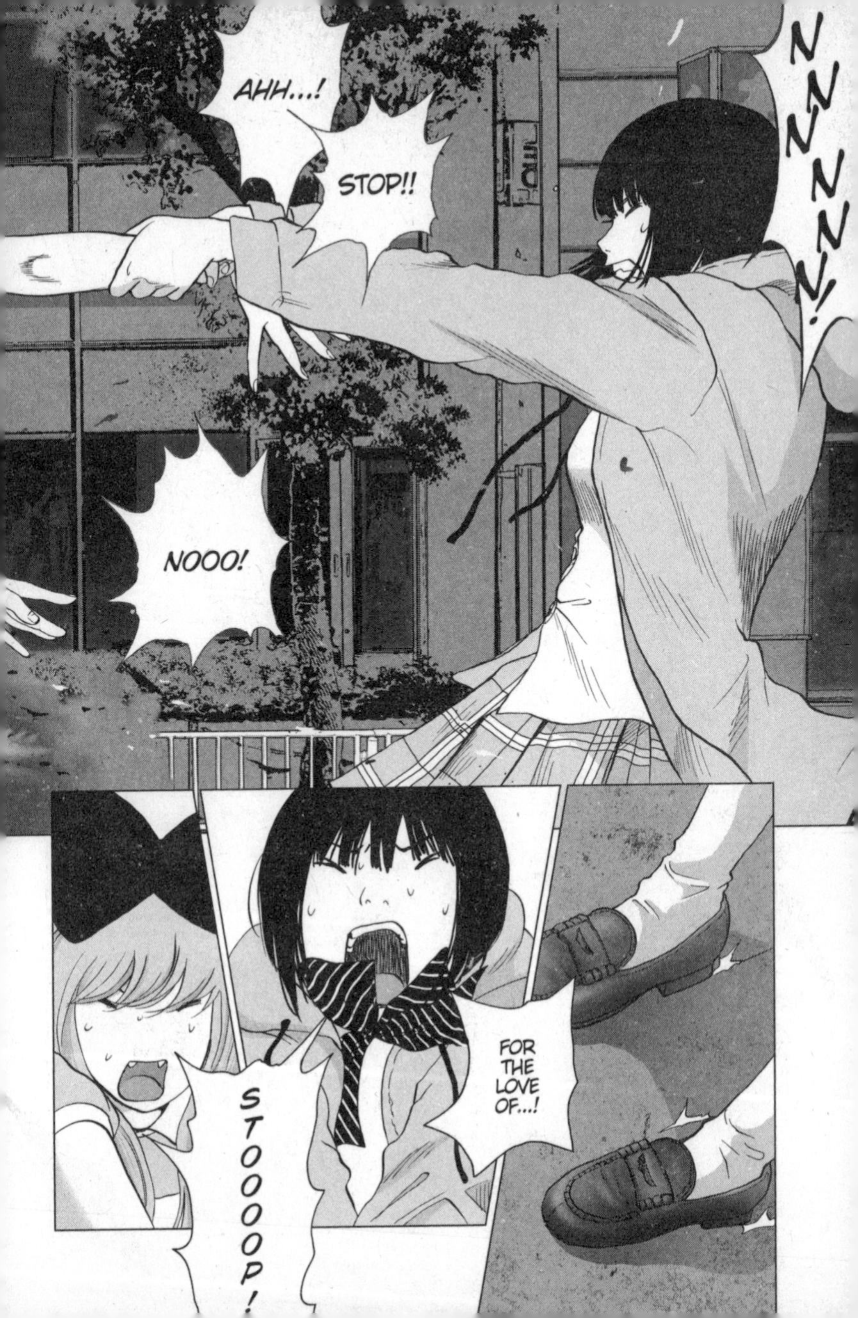
NNNNNNNN!
AHH...!
STOP!!
NOOO!
FOR THE LOVE OF...!
STOOOOOP!

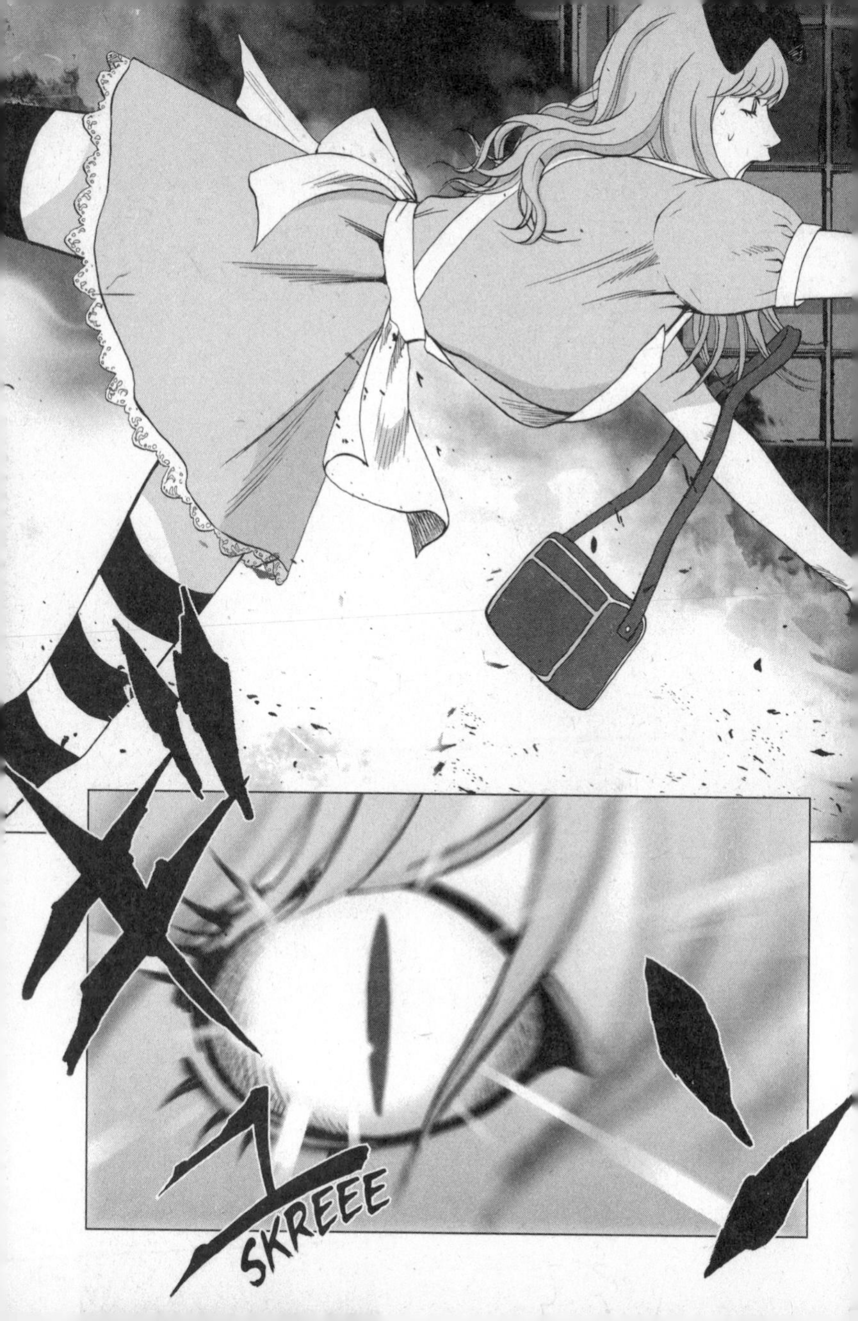
SKREEE

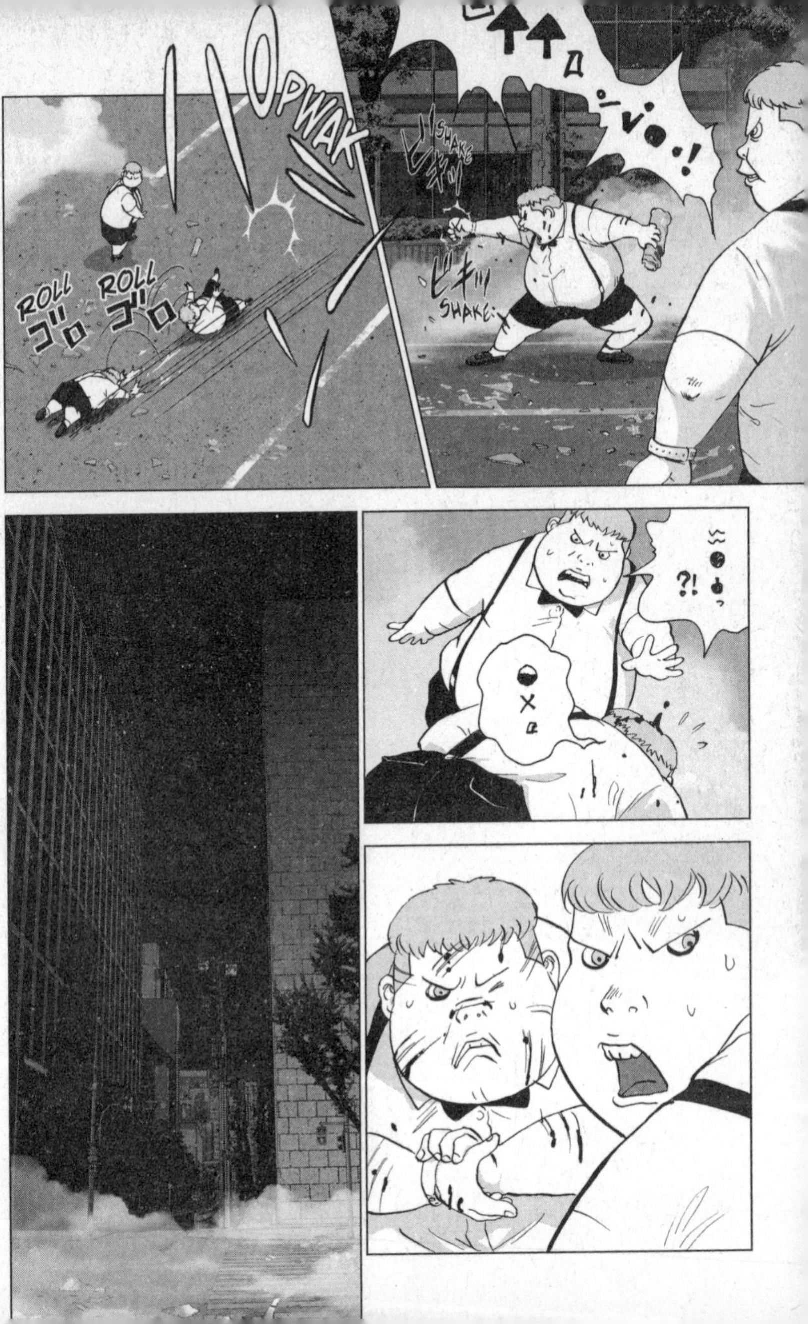
ビキッ
SHAKE
ビキッ
SHAKE
OPWAK
ROLL
ゴロ
ROLL
ゴロ
?!

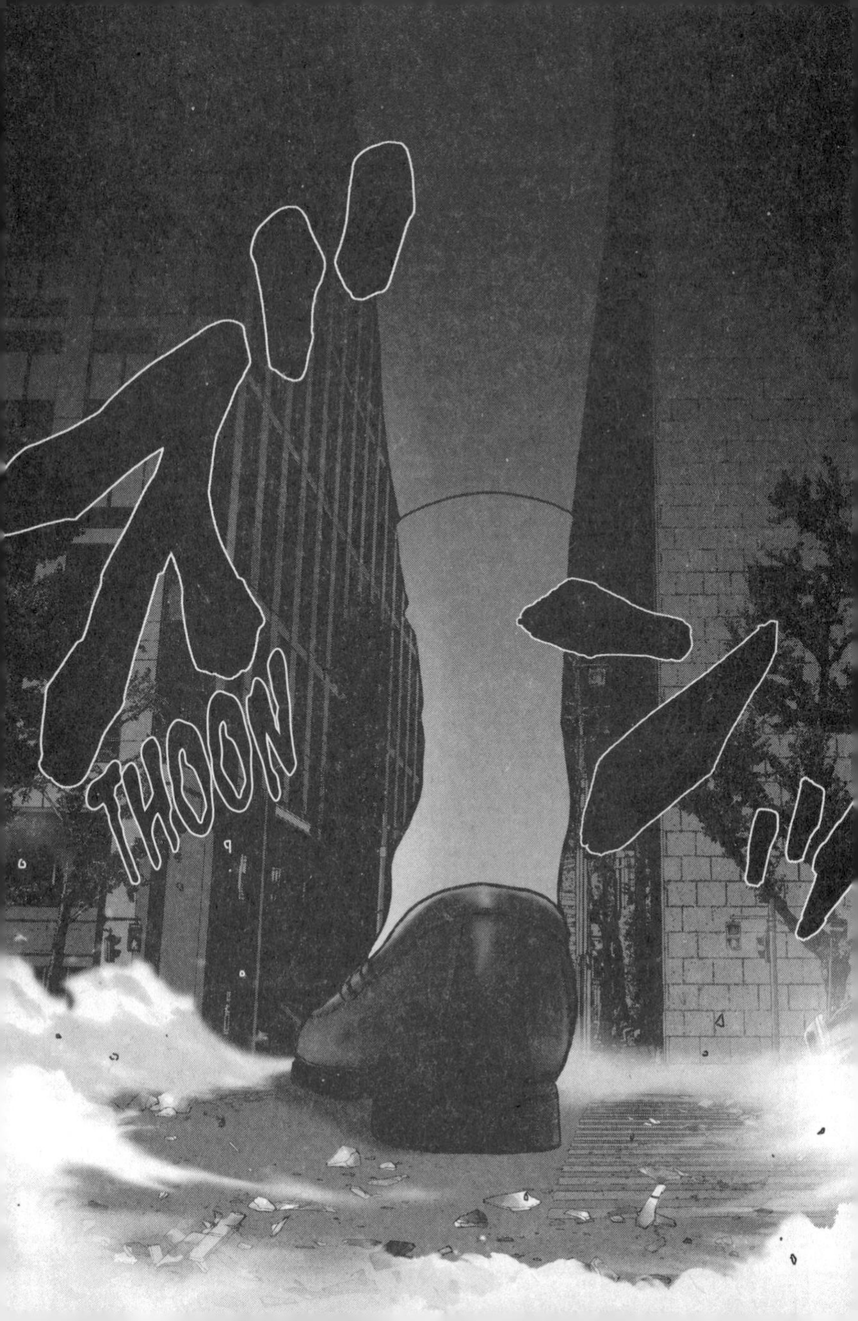
THOOM

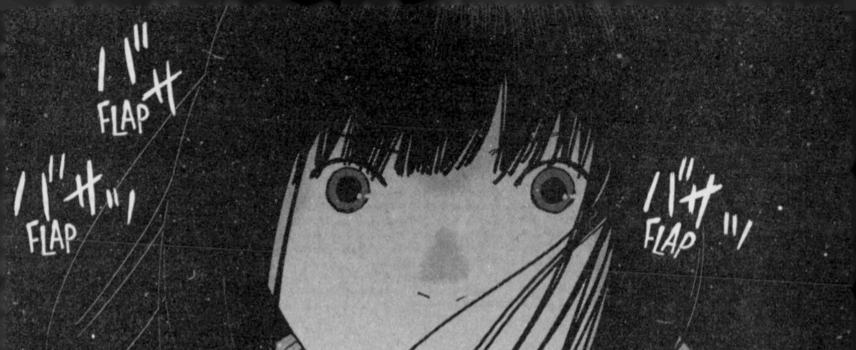
バサッ
FLAP
バサッ
FLAP
バサッ
FLAP
パタ
FLUTTER
パタ
FLUTTER

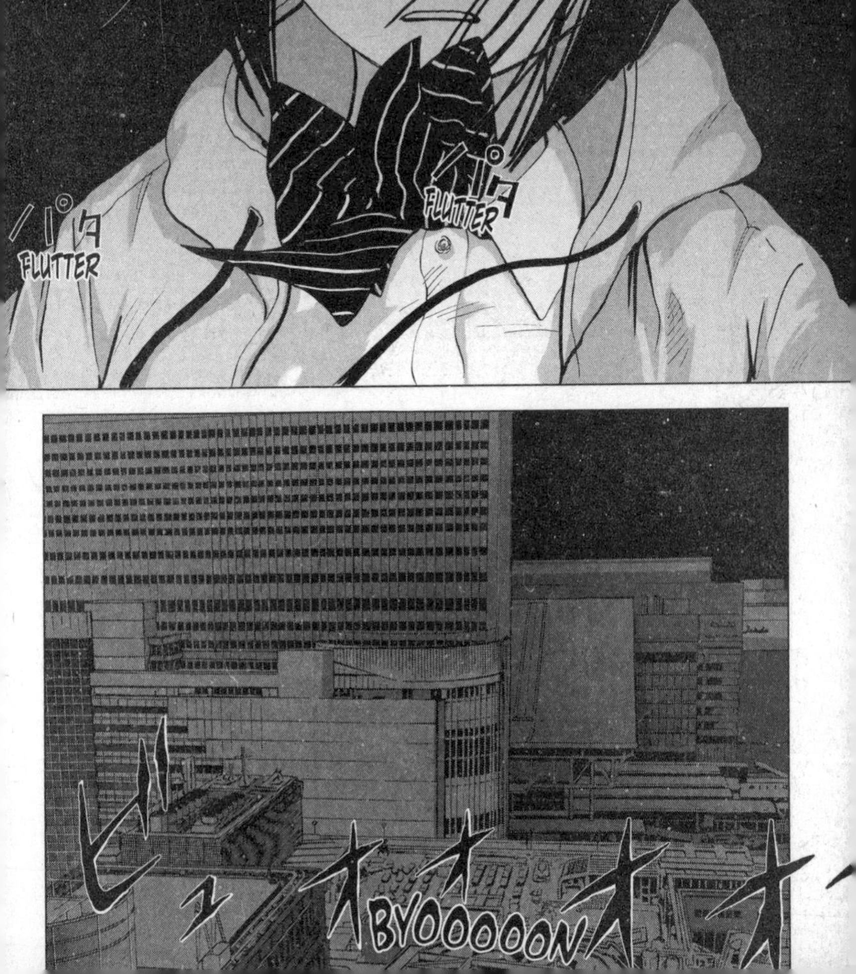
ビュオオオオ
BYOOOOON

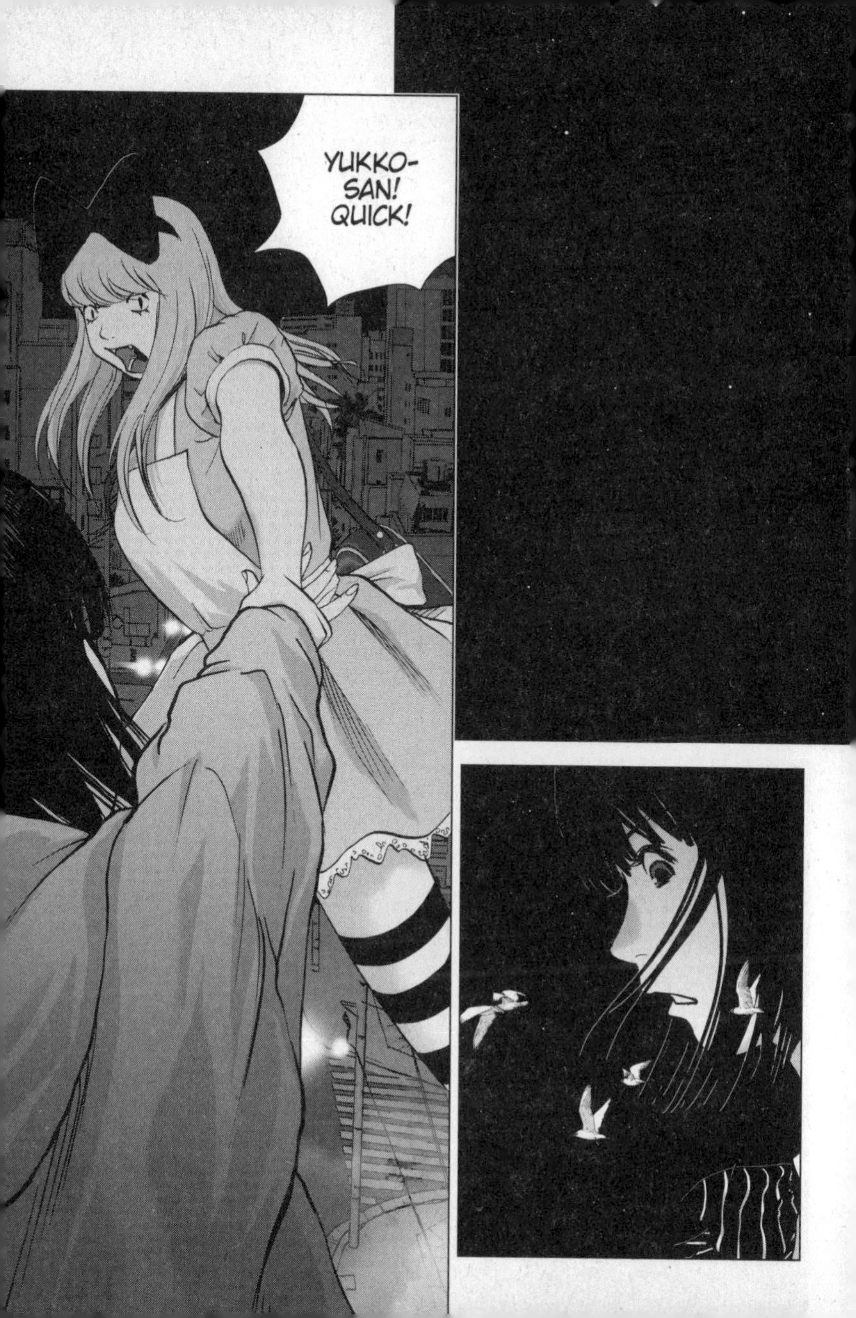
YUKKO-
SAN!
QUICK!

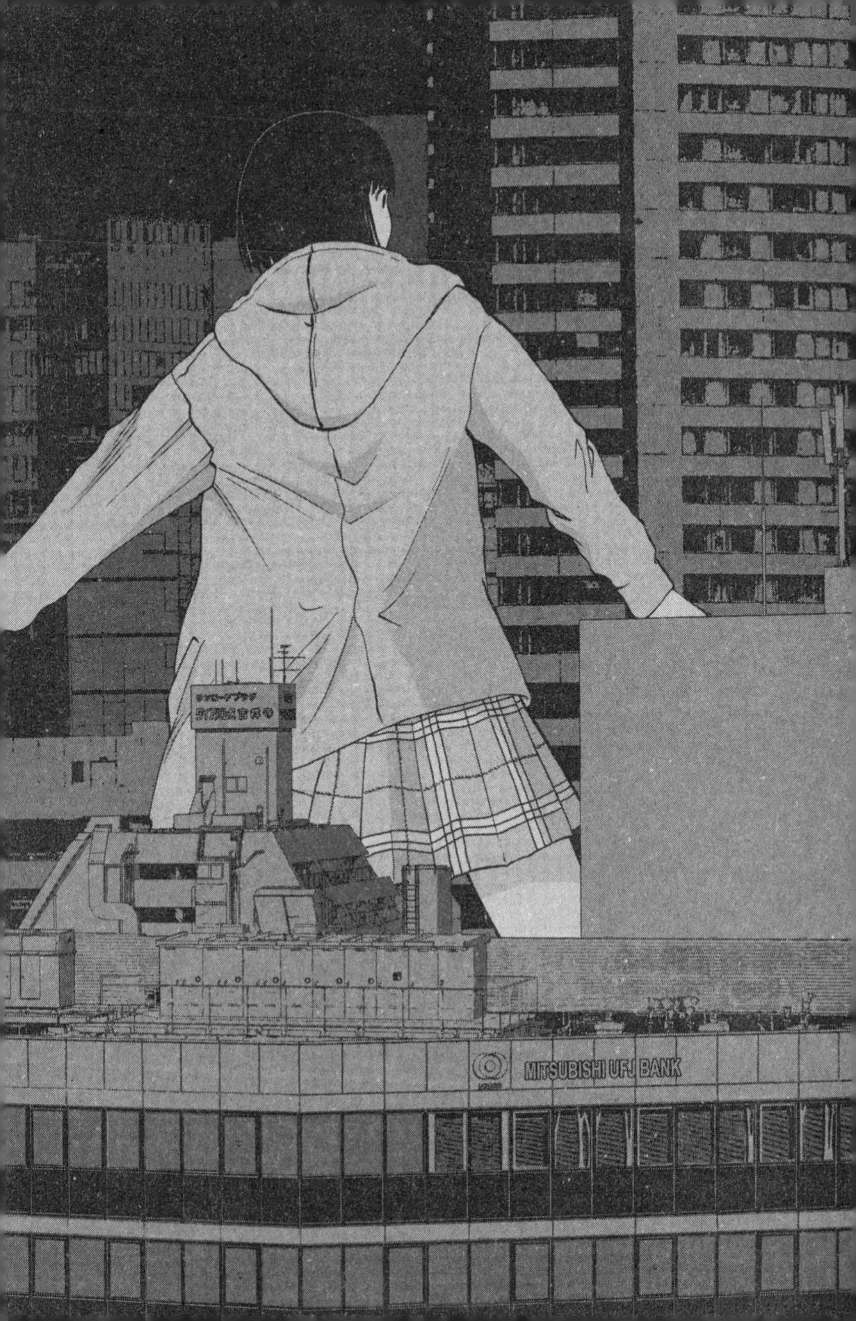
MITSUBISHI UFJ BANK

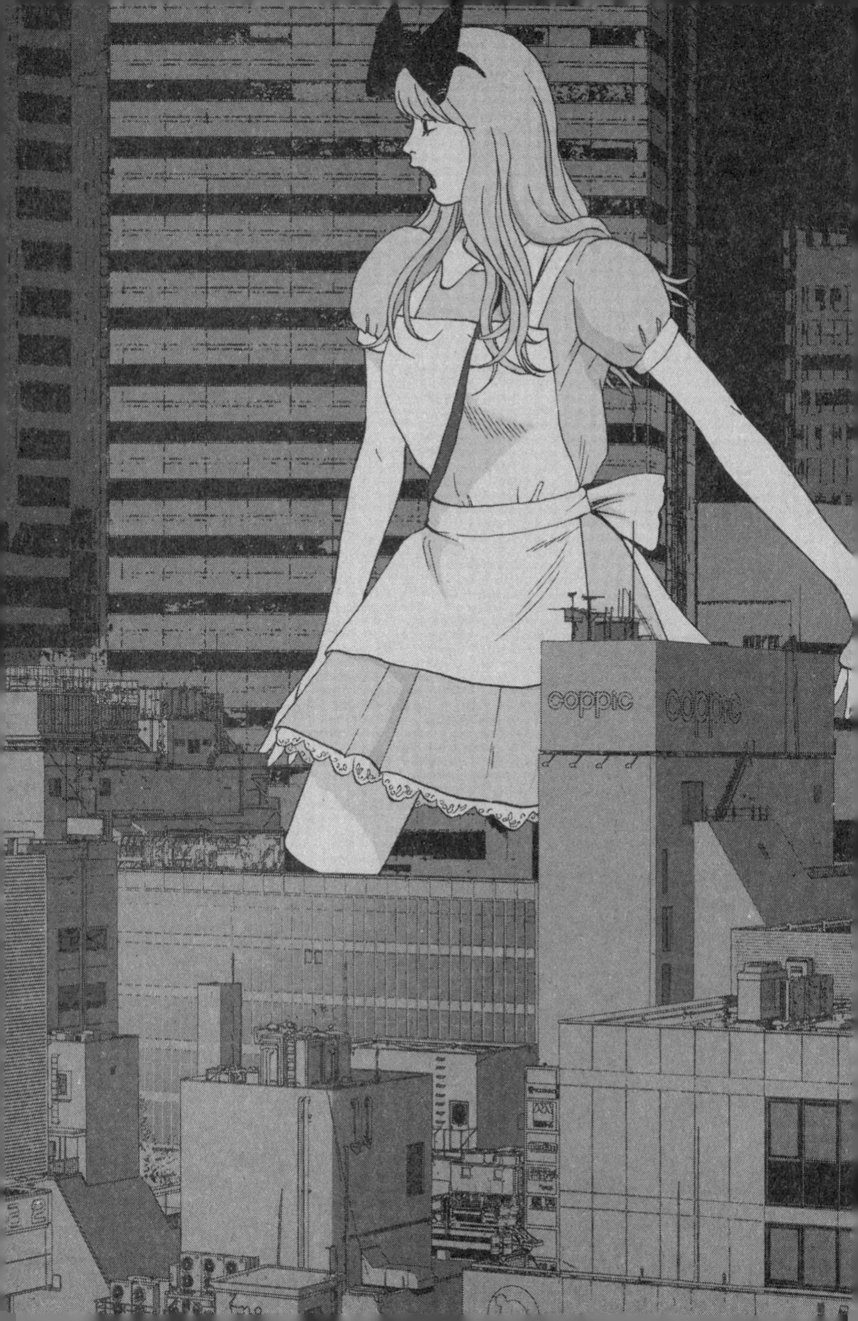
coppic
coppic

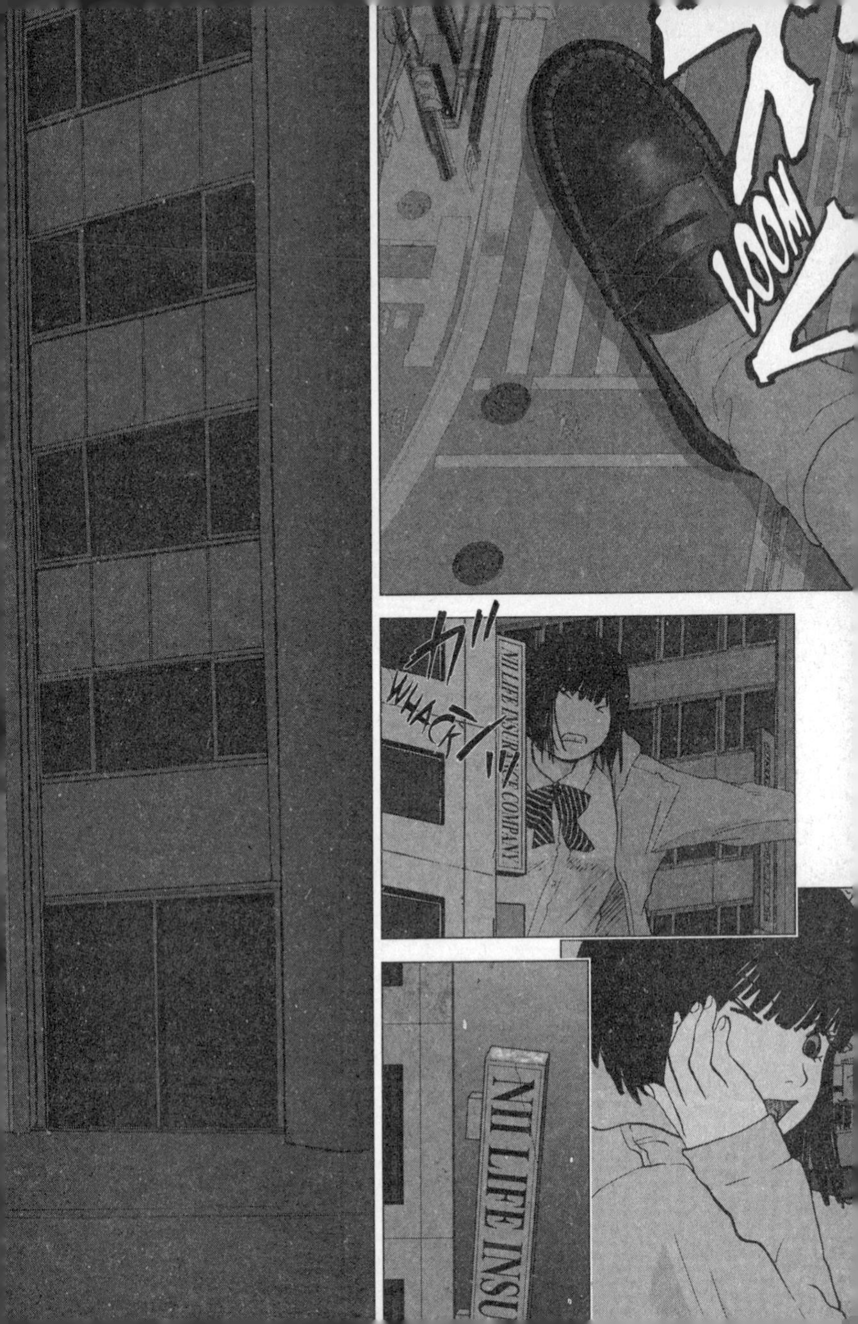
LOOM
ガ
WHACK
NII LIFE INSURANCE COMPANY
NII LIFE INSU

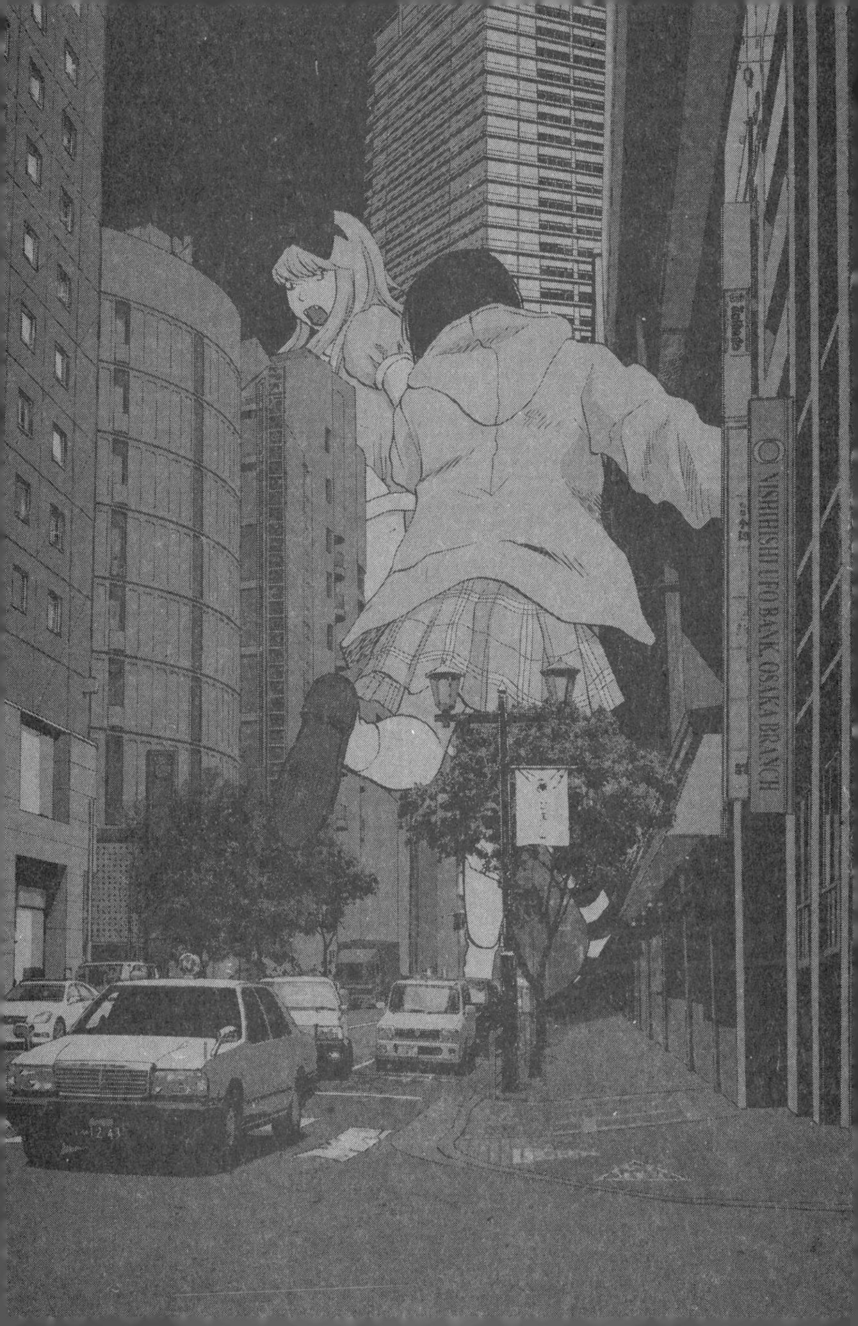
NISHIHISHI UFO BANK, OSAKA BRANCH

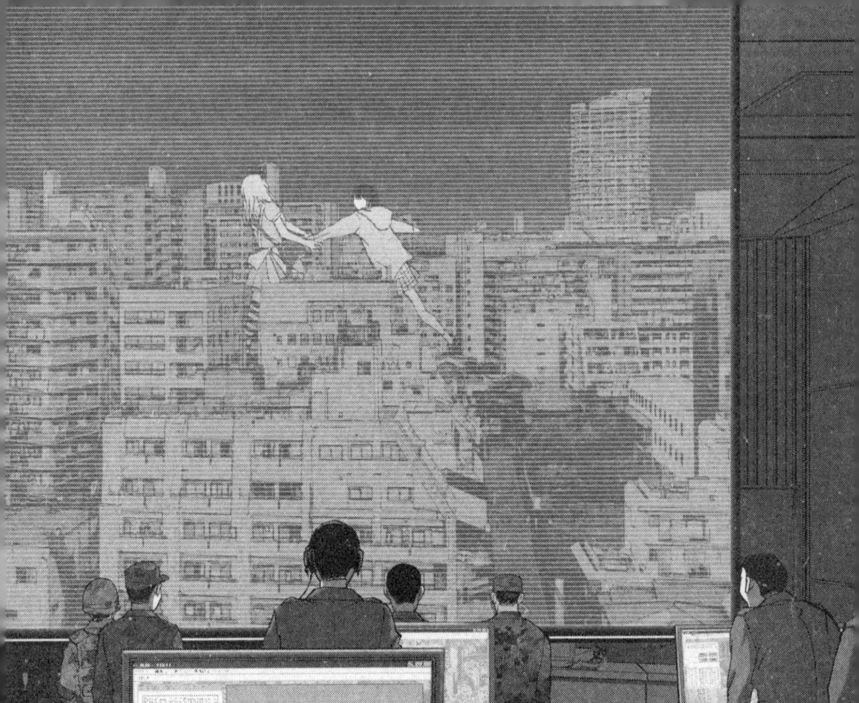
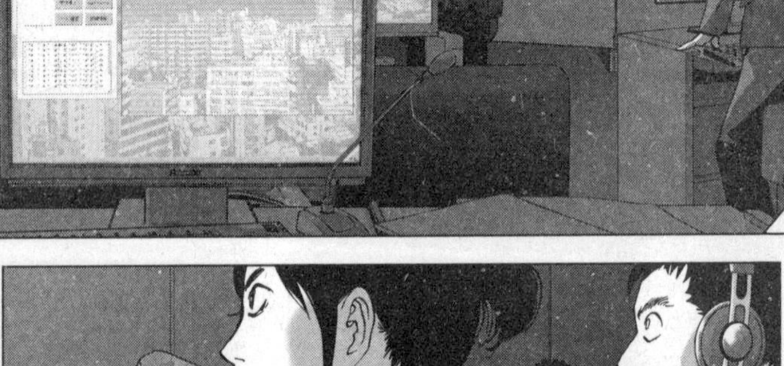
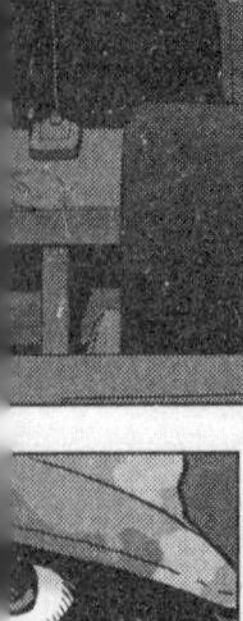

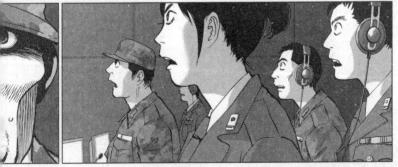

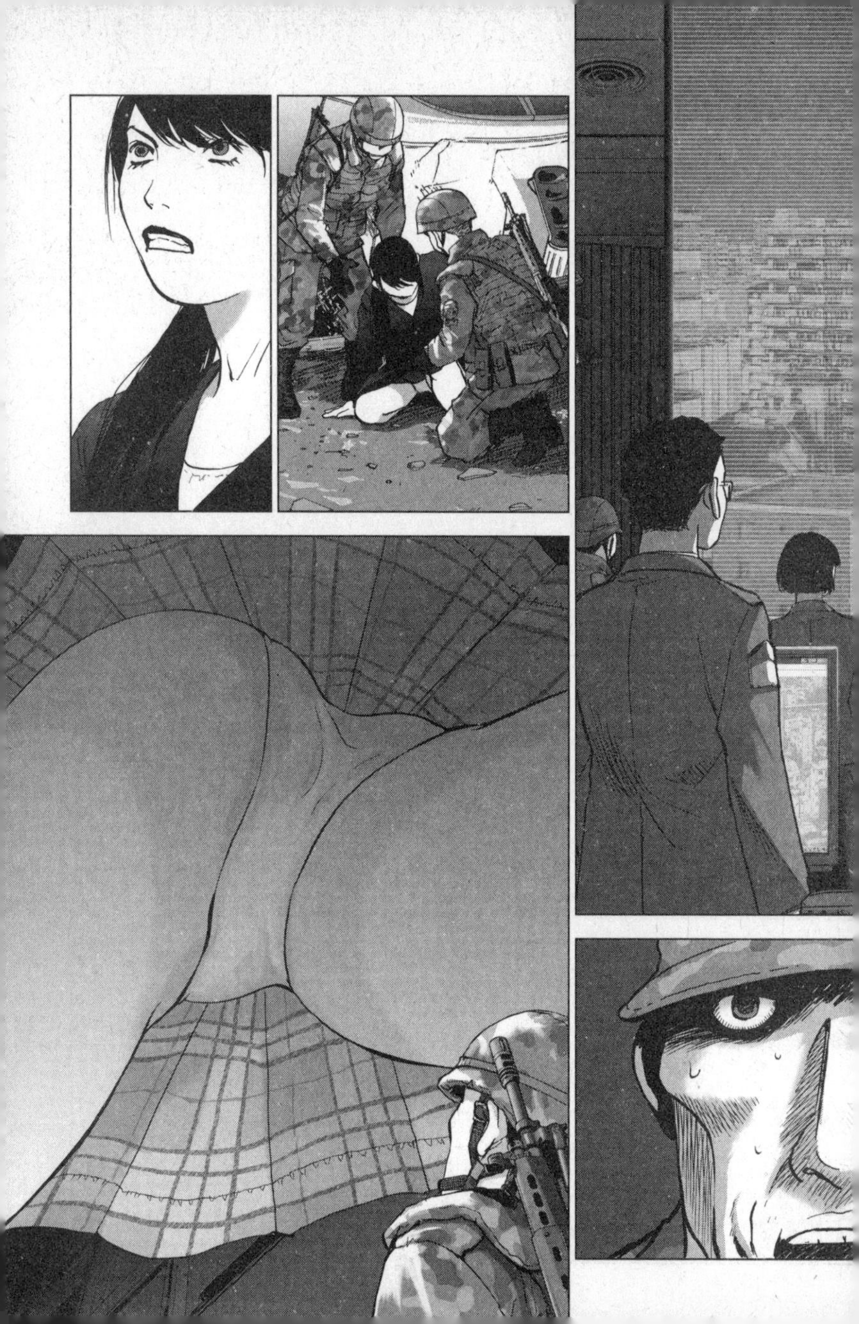

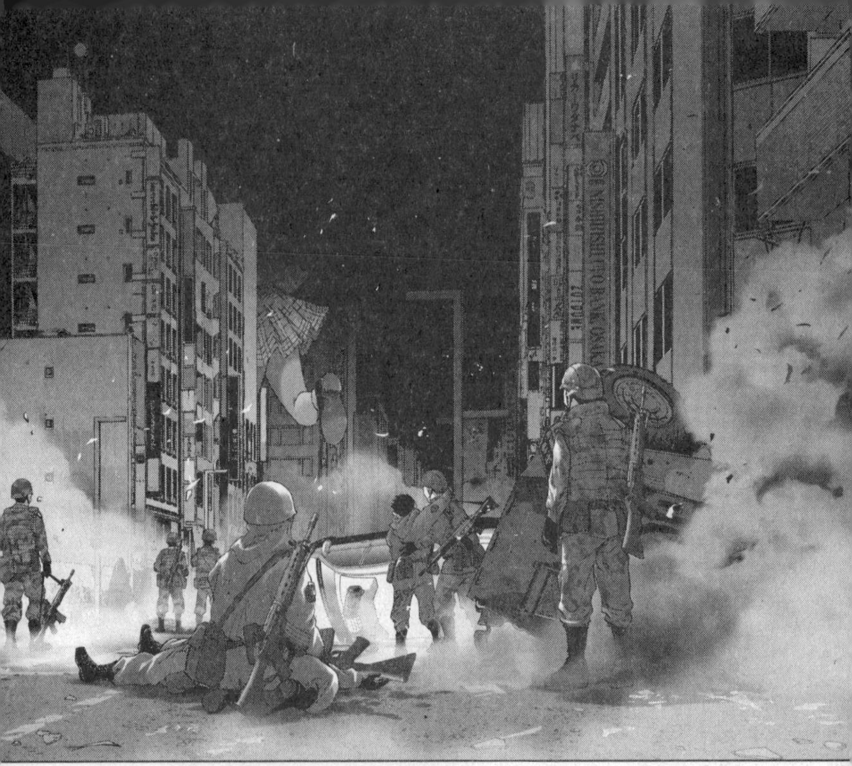
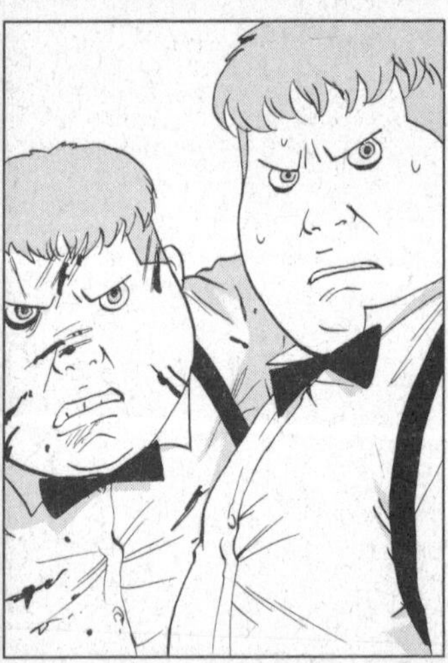
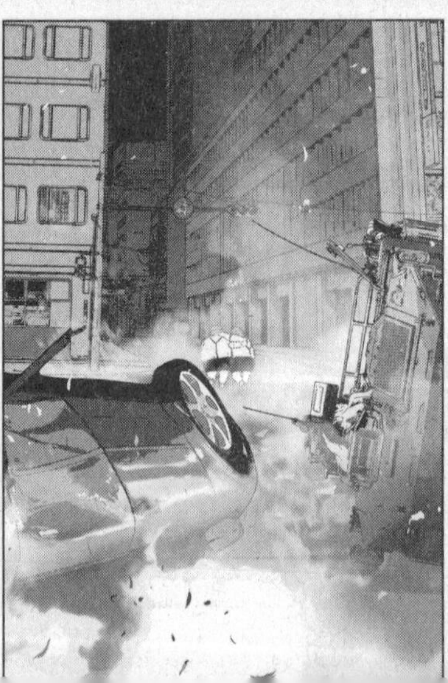
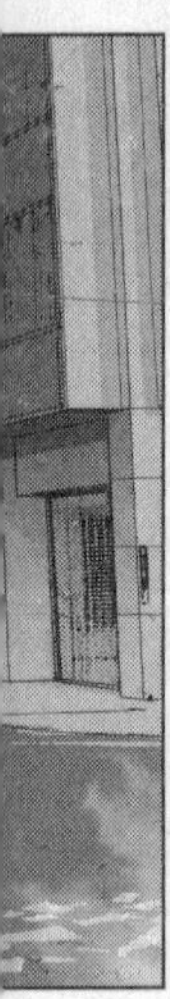

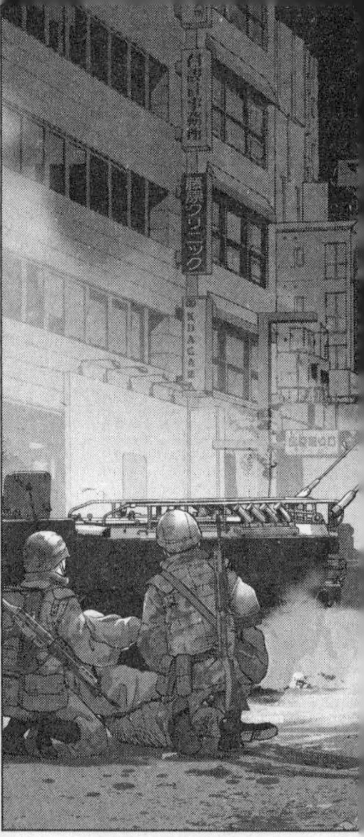
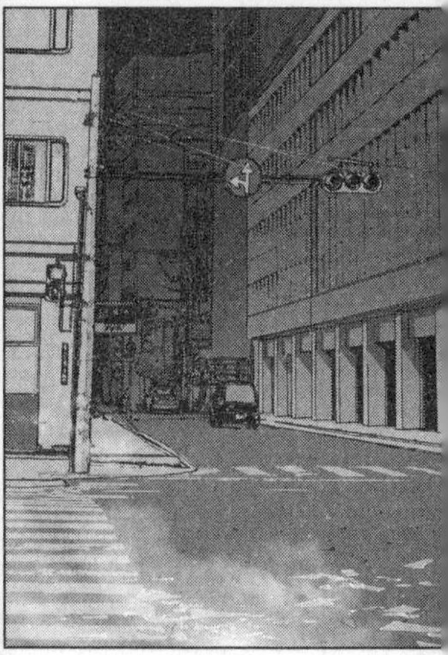
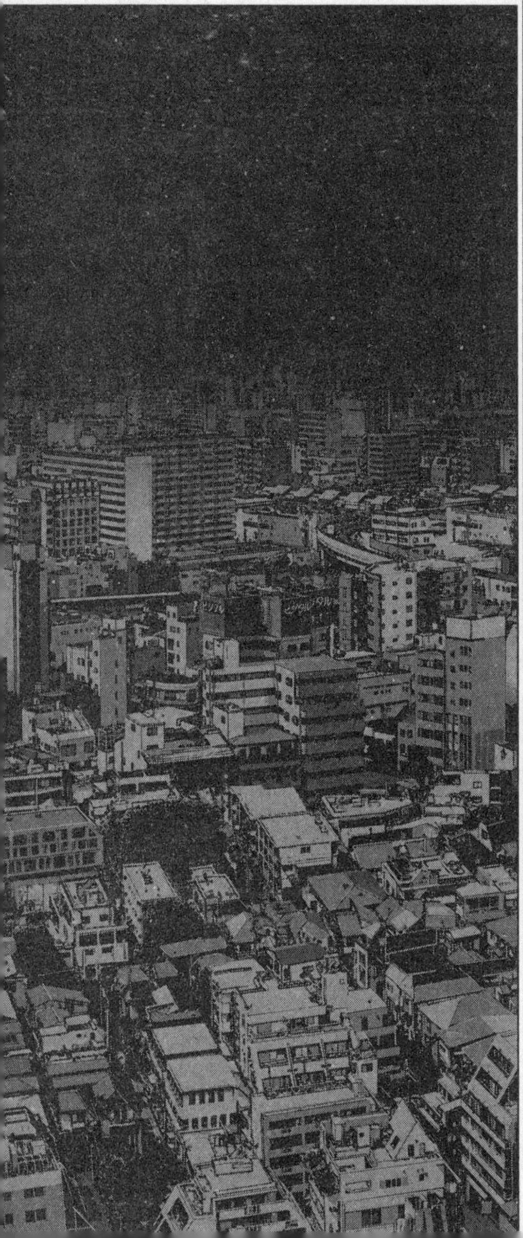

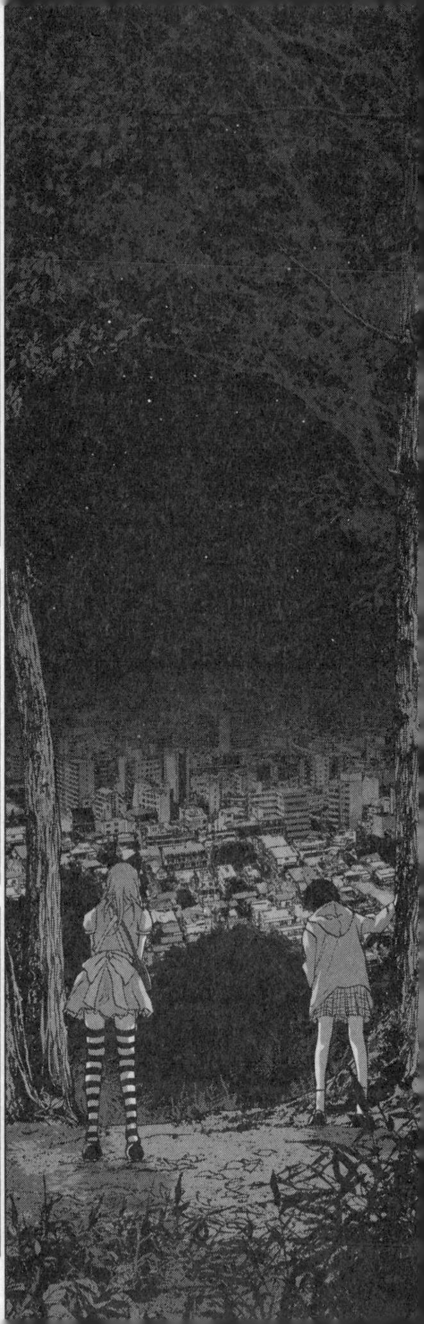

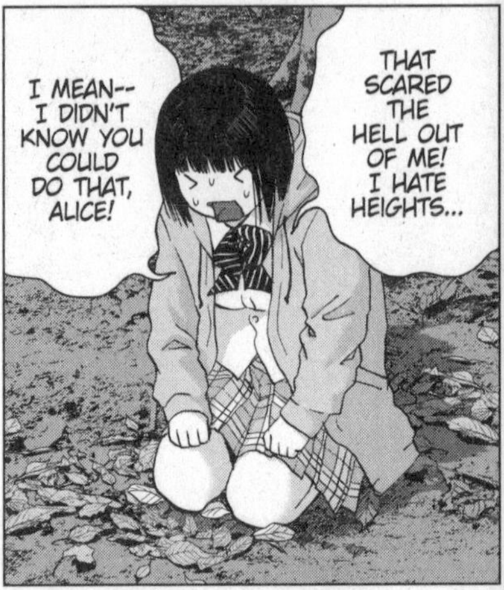
THAT SCARED THE HELL OUT OF ME! I HATE HEIGHTS...
I MEAN-- I DIDN'T KNOW YOU COULD DO THAT, ALICE!

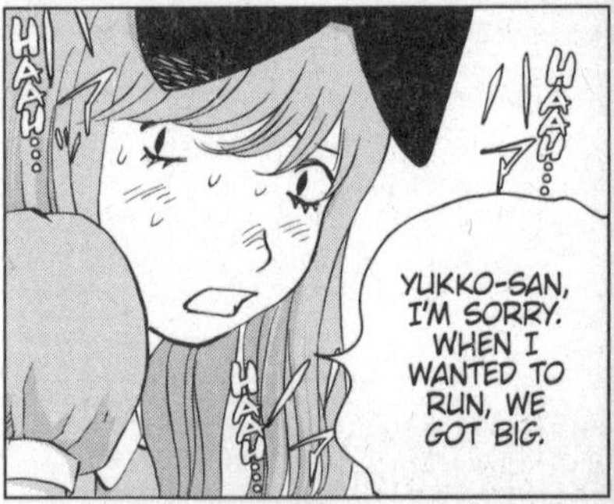
HAAAH...
YUKKO-SAN, I'M SORRY. WHEN I WANTED TO RUN, WE GOT BIG.
HAAAH...
HAAAH...

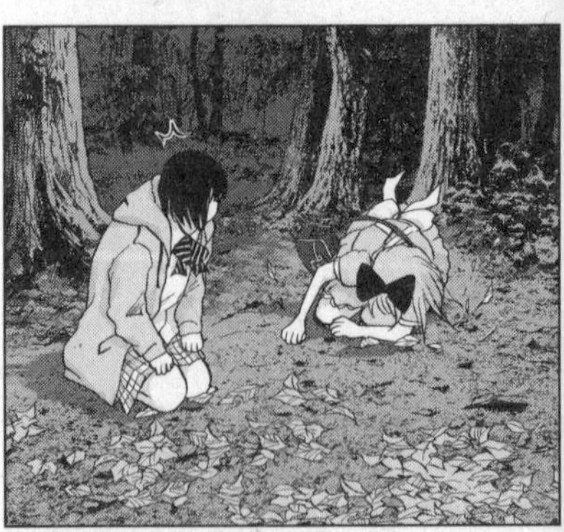

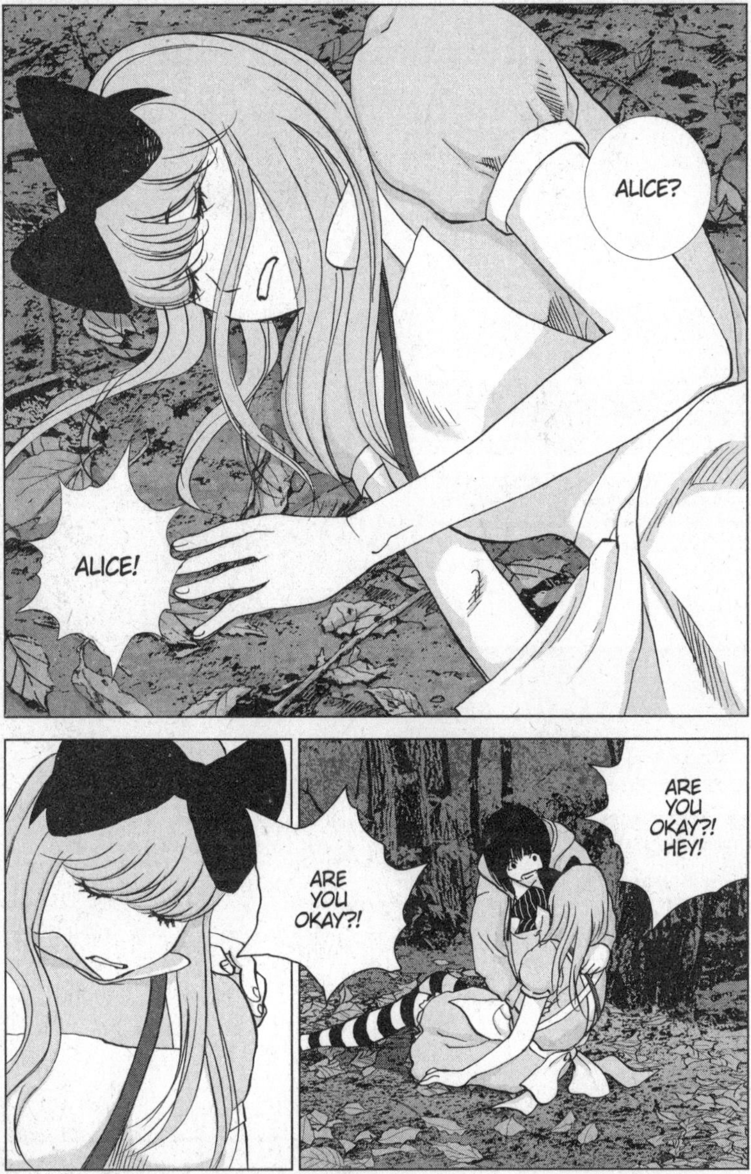
ALICE?
ALICE!
ARE YOU OKAY?! HEY!
ARE YOU OKAY?!

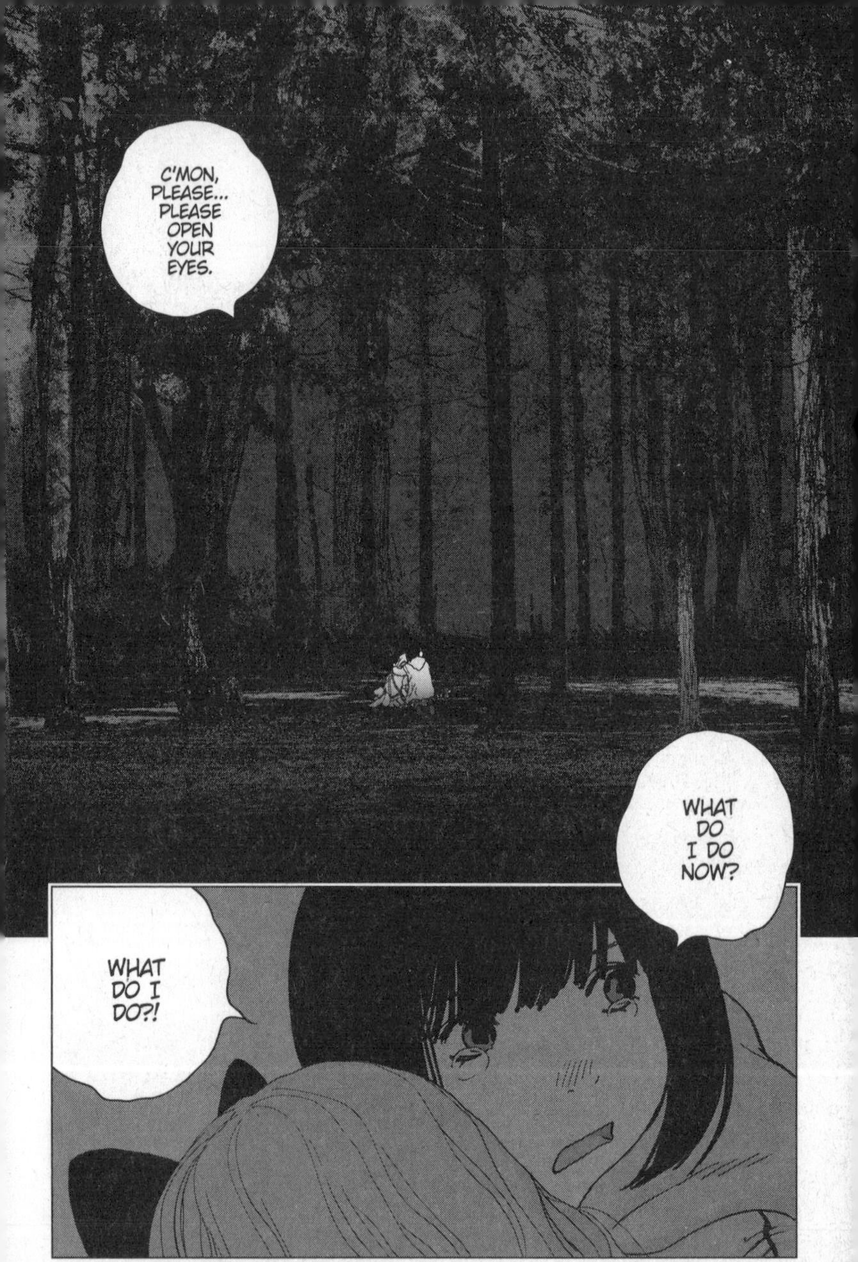
C'MON, PLEASE... PLEASE OPEN YOUR EYES.
WHAT DO I DO NOW?
WHAT DO I DO?!

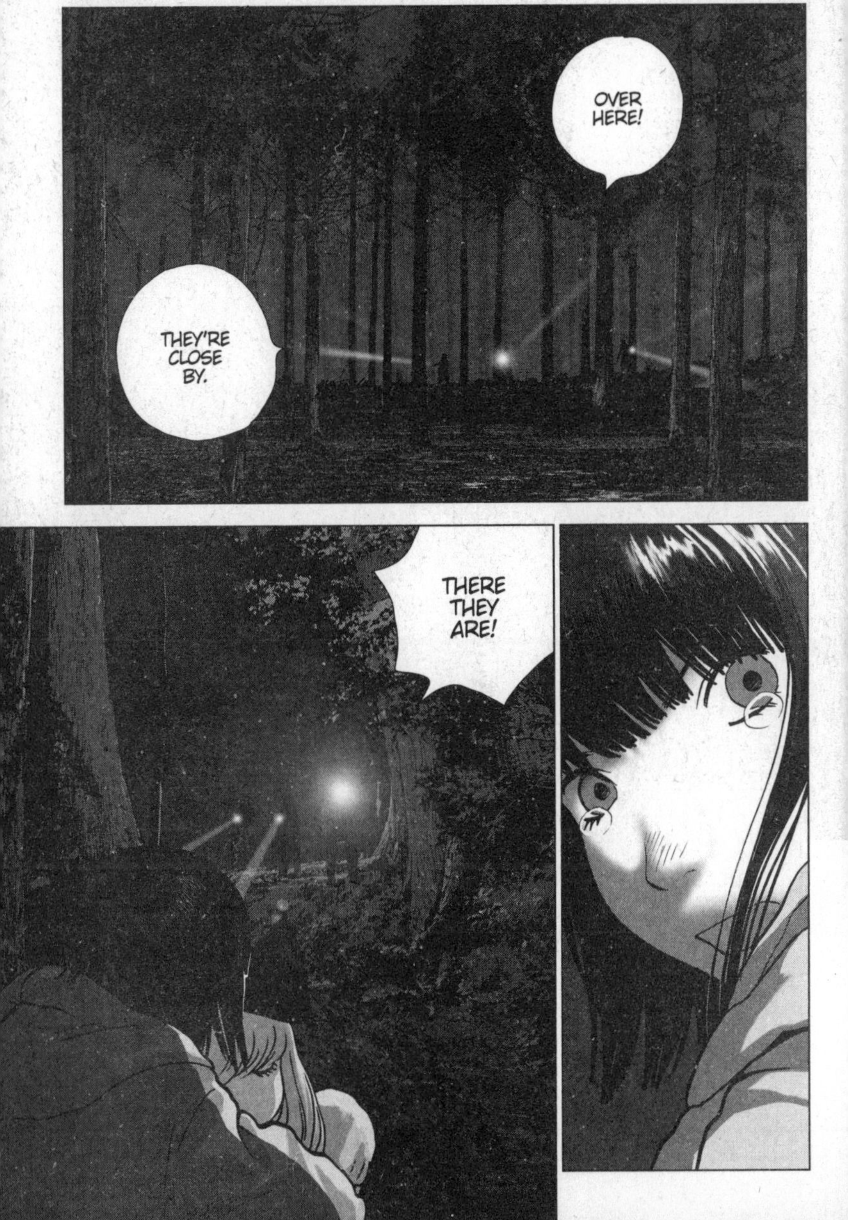
OVER HERE!
THEY'RE CLOSE BY.
THERE THEY ARE!

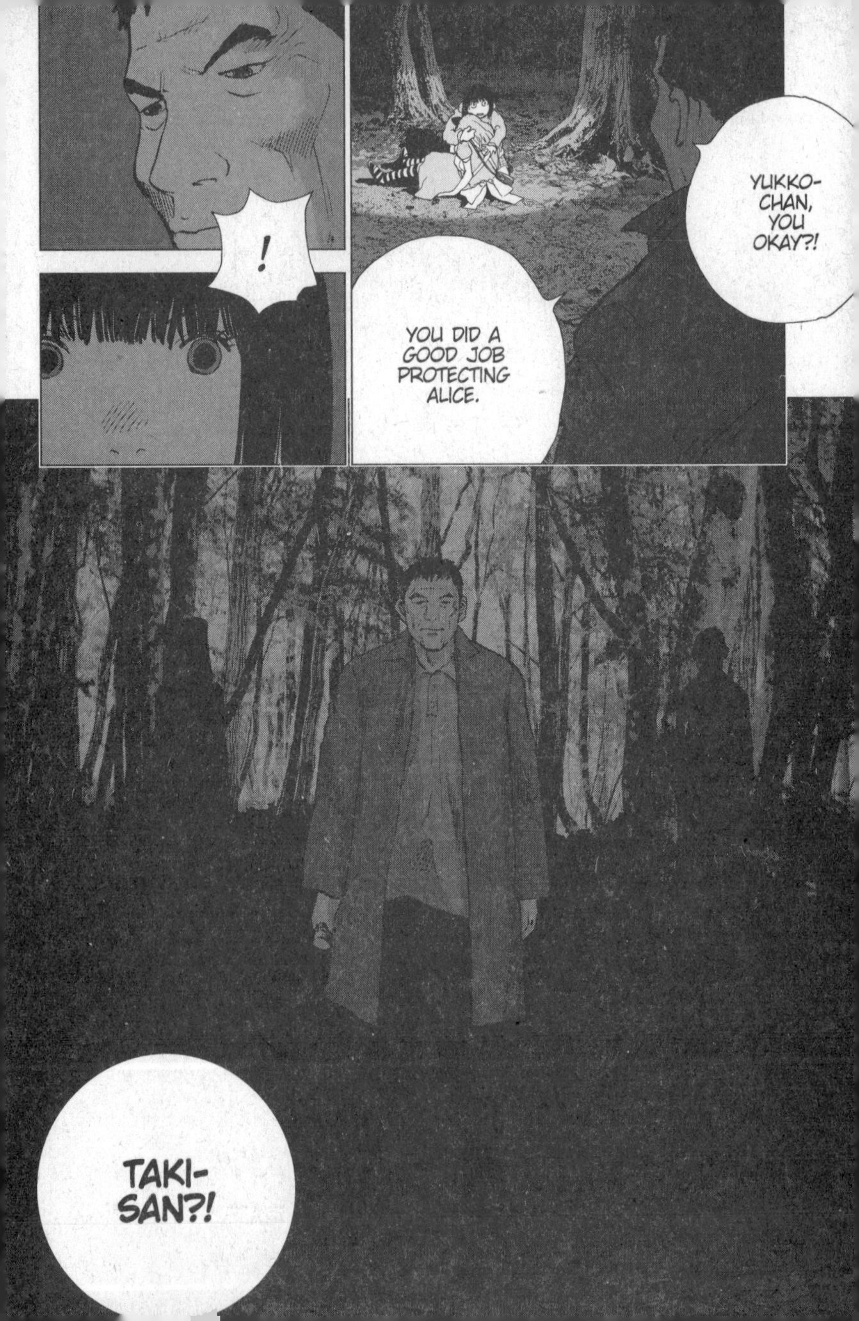
YUKKO-CHAN, YOU OKAY?!
YOU DID A GOOD JOB PROTECTING ALICE.
!
TAKI-SAN?!

Wonderland

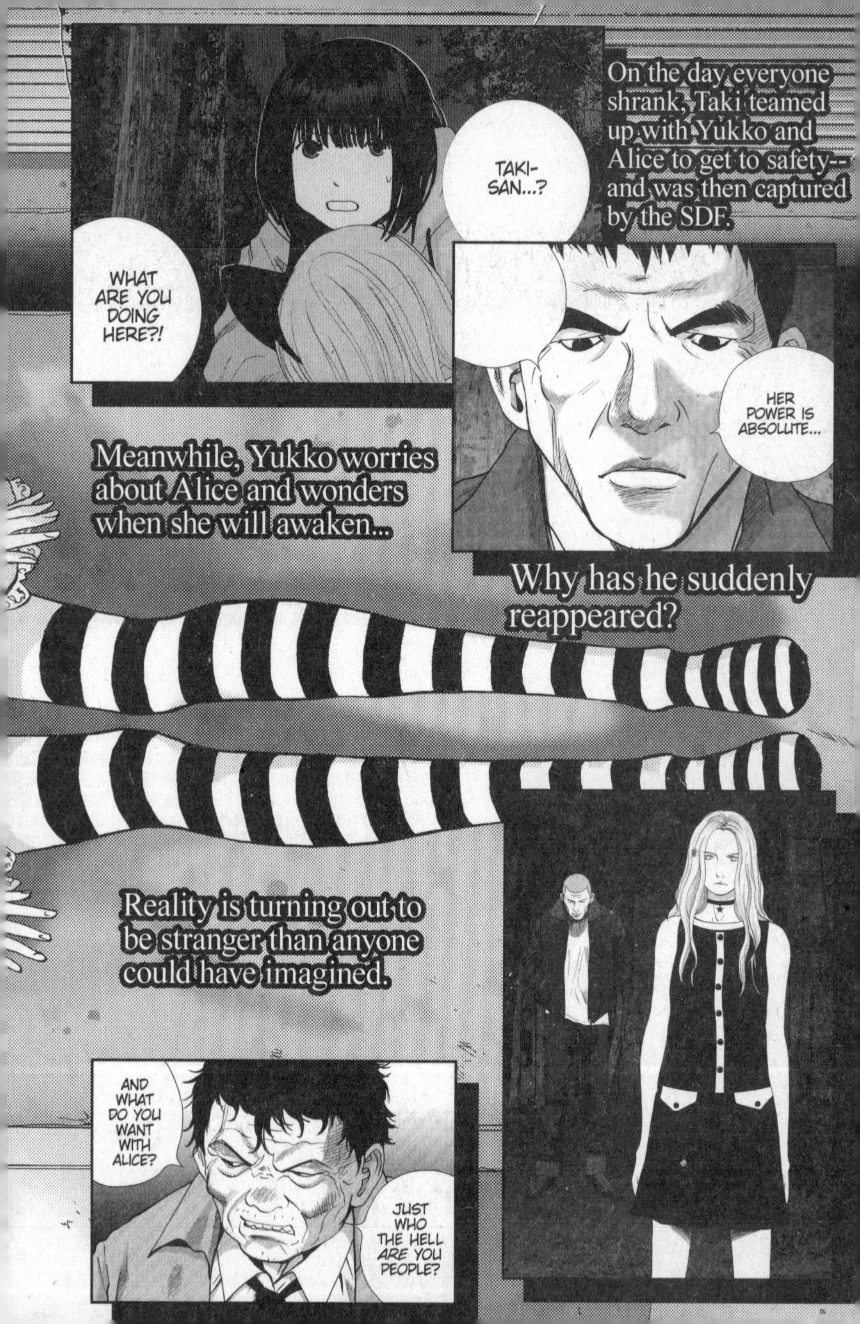
On the day everyone shrank, Taki teamed up with Yukko and Alice to get to safety--and was then captured by the SDF.
TAKI-SAN...?
WHAT ARE YOU DOING HERE?!
HER POWER IS ABSOLUTE...
Why has he suddenly reappeared?
Meanwhile, Yukko worries about Alice and wonders when she will awaken...
Reality is turning out to be stranger than anyone could have imagined.
AND WHAT DO YOU WANT WITH ALICE?
JUST WHO THE HELL ARE YOU PEOPLE?

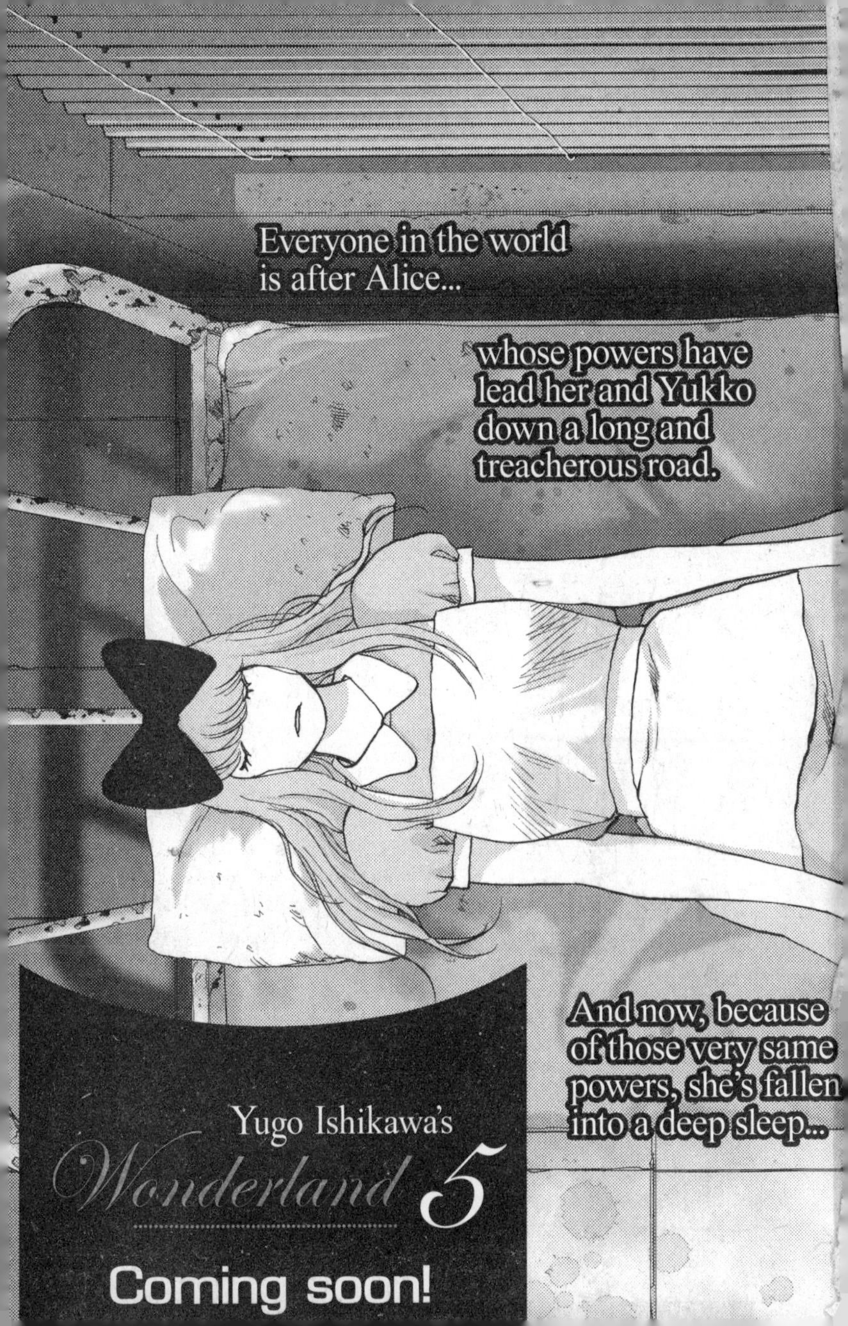
Everyone in the world is after Alice...
whose powers have lead her and Yukko down a long and treacherous road.
And now, because of those very same powers, she's fallen into a deep sleep...
Yugo Ishikawa's
Wonderland 5
Coming soon!

SEVEN SEAS ENTERTAINMENT PRESENTS

Wonderland Vol. 4

story and art by YUGO ISHIKAWA

TRANSLATION
Molly Rabbitt

ADAPTATION
Marykate Jasper

LETTERING AND RETOUCH
James Gaubatz

ORIGINAL COVER DESIGN
Mikiyo Kobayashi + Bay Bridge Studio

COVER DESIGN
KC Fabellon

PROOFREADER
Kurestin Armada
B. Lana Guggenheim

EDITOR
Jenn Grunigen

PRODUCTION MANAGER
Lissa Pattillo

EDITOR-IN-CHIEF
Adam Arnold

PUBLISHER
Jason DeAngelis

WONDERLAND VOL. 4 by Yugo ISHIKAWA

Original Japanese edition published by SHOGAKUKAN.
English translation rights in the United States of America, Canada, and the United Kingdom arranged with SHOGAKUKAN through Tuttle-Mori Agency, Inc.

Seven Seas press and purchase enquiries can be sent to Marketing Manager Lianne Sentar at press@gomanga.com. Information regarding the distribution and purchase of digital editions is available from Digital Manager CK Russell at digital@gomanga.com.

ISBN: 978-1-64275-732-3

Printed in Canada

First Printing: November 2019

2 1

FOLLOW ... asentertainment.com

REA...

This boo... e.
If this is ... rt
reading ... nd
take it fr... the
numbered diagram here. It may seem backwards at first, but you'll get the hang of it! Have fun!!

3
1
2
5
4
6
8
7
9

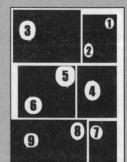